# NATIONS OF THE MODERN WORLD

---

**ARGENTINA**  H. S. Ferns
*Professor of Political Science,*
*University of Birmingham*

**AUSTRALIA**  O. H. K. Spate
*Director, Research School of Pacific Studies,*
*Australian National University, Canberra*

**AUSTRIA**  Karl R. Stadler
*Professor of Modern and Contemporary History,*
*University of Linz*

**BELGIUM**  Vernon Mallinson
*Professor of Comparative Education,*
*University of Reading*

**BURMA**  F. S. V. Donnison
*Formerly Chief Secretary to the Government of Burma*
*Historian, Cabinet Office, Historical Section 1949–66*

**CYPRUS**  H. D. Purcell
*Professor of English,*
*University of Libya, Benghazi*

**DENMARK**  W. Glyn Jones
*Reader in Danish, University College London*

**ENGLAND**  John Bowle
**A Portrait**  *Formerly Professor of Political Theory, Collège d'Europe,*
*Bruges 1950–67*

**MODERN EGYPT**  Tom Little
*Managing Director and General Manager of*
*Regional News Services (Middle East), Ltd, London*

**FINLAND**  W. R. Mead
*Professor of Geography, University College London*

**EAST**  David Childs
**GERMANY**  *Lecturer in Politics, University of Nottingham*

| | |
|---|---|
| NIGERIA | Sir Rex Niven<br>*Administrative Service of Nigeria, 1921–54*<br>*Member, President and Speaker of Northern House*<br>*of Assembly, 1947–59* |
| NORWAY | Ronald G. Popperwell<br>*Fellow of Clare Hall, and Lecturer in Norwegian, Cambridge* |
| PAKISTAN | Ian Stephens<br>*Formerly Editor of* The Statesman.<br>*Calcutta and Delhi, 1942–51*<br>*Fellow, King's College, Cambridge, 1952–58* |
| PERU | Sir Robert Marett<br>*H.M. Ambassador in Lima, 1963–67* |
| POLAND | Václav L. Beneš<br>*Professor of Political Science,*<br>*Indiana University* |
| | Norman J. G. Pounds<br>*Professor of History and Geography,*<br>*Indiana University* |
| SOUTH AFRICA | John Cope<br>*Formerly Editor-in-Chief of* The Forum *and South*<br>*Africa Correspondent of* The Guardian |
| THE SOVIET<br>UNION | Elisabeth Koutaissoff<br>*Professor of Russian,*<br>*Victoria University, Wellington* |
| SPAIN | George Hills<br>*Formerly Correspondent and Spanish Programme Organizer,*<br>*British Broadcasting Corporation* |
| TURKEY | Geoffrey Lewis<br>*Senior Lecturer in Islamic Studies, Oxford* |
| YUGOSLAVIA | Stevan K. Pavlowitch<br>*Lecturer in Balkan History, University of*<br>*Southampton* |

# NORWAY

# NORWAY

*By*

RONALD G. POPPERWELL

PRAEGER PUBLISHERS
New York · Washington

BOOKS THAT MATTER

Published in the United States of America in 1972 by Praeger Publishers, Inc., 111 Fourth Avenue, New York, N.Y. 10003

© 1972 by Ronald G. Popperwell

Library of Congress Catalog Card Number: 72–154357

Printed in Great Britain

# Preface

IN TERMS OF DATES Norway is a relative newcomer to the comity
of modern nations, having become an independent state as recently
as 1905. But though a young state, Norway is an old nation. Her
modern history starts quite clearly in 1814, a date which has an
almost mystical significance for the Norwegians as the year in which
the men of Eidsvoll promulgated the constitution and when, after
some 400 years of Danish rule, the national renaissance began. Then
it was that the work of reuniting the broken half-rings, as the poet
Henrik Wergeland put it, of medieval greatness and modern achievement began. Thus history has provided a firm *terminus a quo* for the
consideration of Norway as one of the nations of the modern world,
and the present volume has concentrated principally on Norwegian
history, life, and culture in the nineteenth and twentieth centuries. However, in the saga of modern Norway the past is as ineluctable as it is in
the dramas of Henrik Ibsen and due attention has been paid to it within
the general scope of the book. This has attempted, by taking a range
of sightings, to provide not only the basic data of Norwegian life and
culture but also to map interrelationships and, in particular, to highlight
those features of the terrain which are characteristically Norwegian.

Given the range of topics covered in this book, I have naturally
been very dependent on the available sources. I am especially indebted to Harald and Edvard Beyer's *Norsk litteraturhistorie* (1970),
Einar Haugen's *Riksspråk og folkemål: Norsk språkpolitikk i det 20.
århundre* (1968), Andreas Holmsen's and Magnus Jensen's *Norges
historie*, 4 vols. (1960–68), and to a lesser degree to the books listed in
the bibliography. I should also like to express my gratitude to Paul
Nielsen (Lektor in the Oslo Handelsgymnas), Knut Odner (Hambro
Visiting Fellow at Clare Hall during 1971), and Oddveig Røsegg
(Lecturer in Norwegian in the University of Glasgow), all of whom
read the typescript and saved me from many errors. The index has
been compiled by Mrs Anne Wilkins. Finally, I wish to thank
Øivind Johnsen (Cultural Counsellor at the Royal Norwegian
Embassy in London) for help in a number of connections.

*Cambridge*                                                           R.G.P.
*22 January 1972*

# Contents

# List of Illustrations

*(All are inserted between pages 176 and 177)*

# Maps

# Acknowledgements

ACKNOWLEDGEMENT for kind permission to reproduce illustrations is made to the following, to whom the copyright of the illustrations belongs:

Royal Norwegian Ministry of Foreign Affairs: 15, 21, 26, 30, 32
Royal Norwegian Embassy, London: 4, 6, 7, 8, 9, 10, 22
Fotograf Finne, Oslo: 23, 24
Norsk Telegrambyrå, Oslo: 12, 13, 14, 16, 17, 18, 19, 20, 27, 28
Norwegian National Tourist Office, London: 25
P. A. Røstad, Oslo: 29
Arne Svendsen, Oslo: 31
Universitetsbiblioteket, Oslo: 2, 3, 11
O. Væring, Oslo: 1 (painting in the Royal Palace, Oslo),
5 (painting in the National Gallery, Oslo)

# PART ONE

# Modern Norway Emerges:
# The Nineteenth Century

# Chapter 1

# The Growth of the Towns and the *Bonde*

PREVIOUS WRITERS ON NORWAY, both native and foreign, have tended to emphasize that Norway is different. Inevitably, this difference is seen primarily, and platitudinously for anyone who takes a glance at the map, as deriving from the geographical character and position of the country. Like the author of the companion volume in this series on Finland, one would not wish to preach geographical determinism, but it would be unreal not to take account from the outset of the moulding influence of geography on Norwegian history, life, and culture.

The bulk of Norway looks out over the North Sea and the Norwegian Sea. The country faces west rather than east and much of its important history derives from that fact. Its long and indented coastline, its fjords, and the mountain ruggedness of its central area, have made the Norwegians a nation of seafarers and valley dwellers *par excellence*.

By European standards Norwegian towns are still small, though they are growing the whole time. The concept of the village hardly exists and the sparsely populated countryside tends to cluster into small neighbourhoods or *bygder*. Only a fraction of the total land area of 125,000 square miles (somewhat larger than the British Isles) is habitable, and only a further fraction of this area is cultivable. Climatically, Norway is not as ill-favoured as one might at first suppose. Along the whole of the coastal region the climate is relatively mild, though in inland regions snow-cover may remain for up to several months of the year. The latitude of the country (between 58° and 71° N) means that even in the south summer days and winter nights are long, while north of the Arctic Circle, at a latitude of 70° N, in the town of Hammerfest, the sun does not rise above the horizon between 21 November and 23 January, nor sink below it between 17 May and 28 July. This then, 'Millom bakkar og berg utmed havet' ('Betwixt the hills and the mountains and out by the sea'), as the poet Ivar Aasen has said, is the habitat of the Norwegians, some 3,900,000 souls.

In the 1970s life in Norway has, naturally, many features in common with life in the other Scandinavian and West European countries. Especially in the capital Oslo (pop. 487,600) and the bigger towns (Trondheim (123,600),[1] Bergen (116,300), and Stavanger (80,800), Norway would appear to be just another consumer society in which, though a plurality of family cars and television sets is not exactly typical, a *hytte* (a cottage in the country) and a motorboat seem to be becoming increasingly indispensable to the middle-class townsman. Yet, even in this, one detects not simply the inevitable insatiability of a consumer society but also the continuance of the dictates of geography.

It may no longer be quite so true as it was formerly that every Norwegian town dweller has relatives in the country and thus a ready-made retreat, possibly to a family farm bearing his name, but certainly the comparatively recent urbanization of Norway has meant that Norwegians have a special attachment to their grass-roots and a passion for nature and the outdoor life. Of this the country cottage, the motor-boat, and the Norwegians' extraordinary devotion to skiing (not a sport but a way of life, as it has been described) are the visible signs.

Norway is not well endowed with natural resources, though recently the discovery of oil in the Norwegian area of the North Sea has brought an unexpected bonus. This, together with the handicaps of large, uncultivable areas and severe winter climate in many parts of the country, has meant that up to comparatively recently when, thanks to technological advance, many of them have been overcome, Norway has been a poor country. In fact the Norwegians' devotion in poetry, song, and sentiment to tyrannical Mother Nature seems in a sense strange, but the special dictates of Norwegian geography have on the other hand contributed to the homogeneity which has characterized and still characterizes Norwegian culture, life, and institutions; if not their language. According to the Norwegian sociologist Johan Galtung, Norway is an extremely anti-pluralistic country.

As in the United Kingdom, the population drift in Norway in recent times has been to the south-east. Since 1800 the population of the capital Oslo (then called Christiania) has increased by more than forty times. The consequences of this internal migration and the gradually increasing urbanization of the country have been manifold, and it will be convenient to start our consideration of the growth of modern Norway with an account of the growth of her principal towns in the nineteenth century.

## THE GROWTH OF THE TOWNS

### Christiania

At the beginning of the nineteenth century Christiania (Oslo)[2]

---

[1] Trondheim outstripped Bergen in population in 1967.
[2] Christiania was changed to Kristiania in 1897 and to Oslo in 1925.

must have lacked nearly all the distinguishing features of a capital city. According to the standard history it was at this time a 'stagnant, uninteresting small town with no traditions, which was only a capital in name', a description which may be slightly less than fair – the town could at least boast the medieval castle of Akershus (albeit in a ruinous condition); the seventeenth-century Vår Frelsers (Our Saviour's) Church; a few patrician houses of some magnificence; and just outside the town the estates of Bogstad and Frogner where members of the Anker family entertained with a lavishness that impressed foreign visitors. However, with a population of roughly 12,000, Christiania ranked second to Bergen, and the poet J. S. Welhaven, an unhappy exile from that town, described Christiania in his polemical poem *Norges Dæmring* (*The Dawn of Norway*; 1834) as a place where small-town prejudice did battle with metropolitan pretensions, making it neither one thing nor the other. But the national renaissance which followed the political events of 1814 (see below, p. 120) had particular consequences for Christiania. The town gradually became conscious of itself as a capital city and began to acquire the outward signs of its importance. It was here that the newly established Norwegian parliament (*Stortinget*) met; true enough, only once every three years to begin with and then only in the assembly hall of the town's grammar school. But in 1866 the Norwegian deputies could move into their new brick-built parliament building, situated in the town's new main thoroughfare, Carl Johans Gade (now Karl Johans gate).

In the nineteenth century the movement from country to capital involved especially two classes of persons. The so-called *Bondestudenter* (peasant students) began to make their appearance, frequently resorting to the celebrated crammer run by a pedagogue of genius, Henrik Anton Heltberg (1806–73), to acquire the modicum of Latin which the university entrance examination demanded. But the majority of the immigrants came from the most depressed class of rural dweller, the *husmenn*, or cotters, and for a less elevated purpose, to be recruited into the new industry which in the 1850s began to grow up along Akerselva (an unimposing stream running through Oslo) in the wake of the steam engine and the new railway from Christiania to Eidsvoll which was opened in 1854. In fact, the development of Christiania and its immediate environs during the nineteenth century was a vital element in the history of modern Norway.

Lying at the heart of this development though in an area then outside the confines of the old town was Karl Johans gate, so called from 1852 in memory of Jean-Baptiste Bernadotte, who was king of Norway and Sweden from 1818 to 1844 (see below, p. 122). Karl Johans gate, which was to be commemorated in verse by many

Norwegian poets and painted several times by Edvard Munch, soon became adorned by some of the principal institutions of government and of cultural and social life. At its western end it became dominated by its *raison d'être*, the new Royal Palace (*Slottet*) built on a site then in the open country by the Danish architect H. D. F. Linstow between the years 1825 and 1848, and at its eastern end (at least from the 1860s) it terminated in the East Railway Station (*Østbanestasjonen*). Roughly midway between these two extremities, at a point which also divided (and still divides) the street into a fashionable 'west end' and a rather ordinary 'east end', the Norwegian parliament buildings were erected during the years 1861–66 on an eminence called Bukkeberget, their main entrance looking straight over towards the Royal Palace, or as Henrik Ibsen put it in a poem: 'Like two neighbours looking each other freely in the eye.' Midway between Parliament and Palace the sciences and humanities had already got their home in the three fine buildings of the University of Christiania, built between 1841 and 1852. The founding of the university (then called the Royal Frederik University) had been one of the first fruits of the upsurge of Norwegian patriotism and national awareness during the years immediately preceding and following the turn of the nineteenth century. As an institution it had been founded as early as 1811 by a society of patriots calling themselves *Selskabet for Norges Vel* (The Society for the Good of Norway). Now, for the first time, it was possible for talented young Norwegians to obtain higher education within their own country–hitherto they had had to go abroad, usually to Copenhagen, and in general the establishment of the university gave a stimulus to the life of the capital which can hardly be overestimated. On its north side Karl Johans gate became a fashionable residential area, so much so that the residents bought up the land on the south side to keep others out and to preserve the view, an exclusive gesture which nevertheless promoted the public good when it passed to the state in 1855 and became the very pleasant park area of Eidsvolls plass and the so-called Studenterlunden (Students' Grove). The street also got its Grand Hotel in 1874, with a café, which especially in 1880s and '90s, became the resort of literary men and artists, and of which Henrik Ibsen became an *habitué* after his return to Norway in 1891, with a reserved and inscribed armchair of his own. On the other side of the street a military band played to entertain the strollers. Finally in 1899 the country got its National Theatre (*Nationaltheatret*), on a site on the west end of Studenterlunden opposite the university, but not until discreet opposition from that body, which believed that a theatre was not fitting company for the Palace, the *Storting*, and the university, had been overcome.

In the meantime Karl Johans gate had been developing as a business centre, as the venue for processions, demonstrations, and celebrations, especially of Constitution Day, 17 May, with colourful bands of schoolchildren making their way up to the Palace to be greeted by the sovereign.

Elsewhere, too, Christiania was gradually acquiring other organs of metropolitan life. The Bank of Norway had been founded in 1816 and, though for political reasons its head office had to begin with been placed away from the capital in Trondhjem, its Christiania office, built between 1827 and 1830, graced Bankpladsen, better known as the site of the *Christiania Theater*, the capital's principal theatre before the National Theatre was built. In 1837 the national gallery had been founded with a modest collection of pictures, among which were represented painters of the National Romantic school of painting (see below, p. 51). Statues also began to appear, notably those of King Carl Johan outside the Royal Palace (1875); Christian IV, the seventeenth-century founder of Christiania (1880); and of the poet Henrik Wergeland in Studenterlunden (1881).

All areas of public life expanded with explosive force. Christiania which, as we have seen, had a population of some 12,000 in 1800 had, within the same boundaries, expanded to 228,000 by 1900, including a doubling of the population in the last two decades of the century. Large new areas were developed for residential accommodation, including from the 1850s the area north of the Royal Palace known as Homansbyen; from the 1860s the area east of the Akers river known as Grünerløkka and other eastern areas; and towards the end of the century the areas of Frogner, Majorstua, and St Hanshaugen.

In the nineteenth century Christiania was an immigrant town *par excellence*. It is noteworthy that very few of the Norwegians who played a major role in its life and culture during the period were born there.

*Bergen*

In the early nineteenth century most Norwegian towns were very isolated and self-sufficient; indeed, there was an extraordinary lack of contact between them. The citizens of Christiania, Bergen, and Trondhjem would all, the historian Wilhelm Keilhau has stated, have claimed that their own town was the capital of Norway. At the same time they knew precious little about each other. This was particularly true of relations between Bergen and Christiania. There is no lack of evidence that, in Christiania, Bergen was hardly regarded as a part of Norway at all. The wealthy and much travelled Bernt Anker is reported as having referred to Bergen as 'the Dutchman's town', and it was uncommon for *Bergensere*, even prominent ones, to have set foot in Christiania. Poor communications due to the difficult terrain and lack of trade between towns were, in the main, responsible for this state of affairs, but in the early years of the century, at all events, there was little to encourage people to travel—even in the capital hotel accommodation was practically non-existent.

At the beginning of the nineteenth century Bergen was still the largest town and the most important trading centre in Norway with a population of just over 18,000. In character it was still very much marked by its medieval importance, its two centuries as a Hansa town from about 1350, and by the glories of its mercantile past and present—in the seventeenth century its trade exceeded that of Copenhagen—though, because of the fires to which Norwegian towns were formerly prone, the majority of its buildings went back to no earlier than the beginning of the eighteenth century.

Bergen's main source of wealth was fish, of which it was a principal centre not only for the area immediate to Bergen, but also for the important Lofoten fisheries in north Norway. Already by the beginning of the nineteenth century the long and hazardous trip south along the Norwegian coast from Lofoten to Bergen had become a tradition, although even then it was regarded as uneconomic to transport fish over such a long distance and as a needlessly dangerous undertaking. In 1810 the German traveller Leopold von Buch expressed the view that the facilities which had been established in Bodø in the province of Nordland in 1803 would soon put the fish merchants of Bergen out of business. But the Lofoten fishermen still seemed to be prepared to risk their necks on one of the worst journeys in the world, covering almost half the distance to Spain or Italy, the ultimate destination of most of their catch, rather than land it at Bodø practically on their doorstep. Their reasons were both commercial and sentimental: the credit facilities offered by the Bergen merchants had become a necessity when new gear was needed or when the catch failed; but more important, as Johan Bojer has shown in his novel *The Last Viking* (1921), the trip to Bergen from Lofoten was a glorious adventure, a test of manhood, a subsequent source of yarns and anecdotes, and a chance to experience the wonders of the town.

This was not surprising for, in the early nineteenth century, Bergen was undoubtedly the liveliest, most cosmopolitan town in Norway. Unlike Christiania, where the streets at this period usually had a deserted and desolate air, Bergen presented an appearance of great activity with many people out and about. The Bergen merchants, so it is recorded, sat in their doorways in high-backed leather chairs and shouted out their wares, whereas in Christiania a stranger to the town had to hire a guide to show him where the shops were.

The post-Napoleonic years in Bergen were ones of great difficulty, but the town nevertheless developed its public institutions, notably Bergens Museum (The Bergen Museum), founded in 1825, which in addition to its collections eventually provided the nucleus for the development of higher education in the town, culminating in the present University of Bergen founded in 1946. In 1850 *Det Norske Theater* (The Norwegian Theatre) opened its doors–the theatre at which both Henrik Ibsen and Bjørnstjerne Bjørnson served their theatrical apprenticeships–but in 1863 it had to cease operations because of economic difficulties. It was succeeded in 1876 by a new theatre called *Den Nationale Scene* (The National Stage), a title it has borne ever since, though the present theatre building dates from 1909. In 1874 private and public donations enabled the town to purchase the collection of Paul Botten-Hansen, noteworthy as a bibliophile (librarian of the university library in Christiania) and as an associate of Ibsen in his early days in Christiania, to provide the nucleus for the town's first public library.

However, though Bergen continued to develop as a trading centre and developed new industries, especially the textile industry, in the nineteenth century; and though it retained, and still retains, an individual character, a highly developed civic sense, and a characteristic dialect and style of speech, it did not have the same impact on the growth of Norwegian national consciousness and the national culture in the nineteenth century as did Christiania. An exception to this was the theatre. There is no doubt that during its thirteen years of life Bergen's *Det Norske Theater* was of fundamental importance to the development of a purely Norwegian theatre at a time when the stage in Norway was dominated by the Danes and plays by Norwegians were practically non-existent–the Norwegian book catalogue of 1848 records only twenty-five plays by Norwegians between 1814 and 1847, and many of these were only one-act trifles.

Individual *Bergensere* did, nevertheless, play a prominent part in the development of the new Norway. In politics, Wilhelm Christie (1778–1849), who was of Scottish descent, was a prominent member and secretary of the assembly of Notables which formulated and promulgated the Norwegian constitution at Eidsvoll in 1814 (see below, p. 120); later he was the first president of the *Storting* and the founder of Bergens Museum, outside which his statue now stands. In literature, the poet and polemicist Johan Sebastian Welhaven (1807–73) was one of the principal figures of the post-1814 generation, though he had to find a forum for his talents in Christiania. In painting, Johan Christian Dahl (1788–1857), often referred to as the 'Father of Norwegian painting', was the founder of the National Romantic (see below, p. 51) school of painting, but spent most of his life in Dresden. In music, in a town already noteworthy for *Harmonien* (the oldest musical society in the country, founded in 1765), Ole Bull (1810–80) became world famous in his day as a violin virtuoso, and Edvard Grieg (1843–1907) earned not only an honoured place in the history of nineteenth-century European music but also rendered enormous services to the music of his own country in his exploitation of Norwegian folk-melodies. In medicine, G. H. Armauer Hansen (1841–1912) isolated in 1873 the leprosy bacillus, a disease which was widespread in Norway during the nineteenth century. And in 1851 Michael Krohn (1793–1878), one of the town's most prominent businessmen, founded the Bergen Steamship Company (*Det Bergenske Dampskibsselskab*), destined to become one of the most important shipping companies in Norway.

## Trondhjem

Trondhjem (Trondheim),[1] the third principal town in Norway, had a population of nearly 9,000 in 1800. It was a small place, but it could boast of a past which, in some respects, was even grander than Bergen's. During the great part of the Middle Ages Trondhjem, or Nidaros as it was also called, had been the ecclesiastical and cultural centre of the country, and from 1031 until the thirteenth century the principal residence of the kings of Norway. At the beginning of the nineteenth century the town was still dominated by its most striking legacy from this period of greatness, the Cathedral of Nidaros, which though largely in a ruinous condition, was still sufficiently a symbol of Norwegian nationhood for the Notables assembled at Eidsvoll in 1814 to write into the constitution that it was here that future sovereigns of Norway were to be crowned.

In more recent times, too, Trondhjem had achievements to its credit which had excited the admiration of the nation. Chief amongst them had been the founding there in 1767 of the Royal Norwegian Scientific Society (*Det Kongelige Norske Videnskabers Selskab*). The Society's principal architect and driving force, Johan Ernst Gunnerus (1718–73), had paved the way for its establishment seven years earlier when, together with Gerhard Schøning (1722–80) and Peter Frederik Suhm (1728–98), he had founded the Trondhjem Society (*Det Trondhjemske Selskab*). All three men were prominent in the intellectual life of their day: Gunnerus had taught in Jena, had been a professor in Copenhagen, and had come to Trondhjem as bishop in 1758; Schøning was headmaster of the Trondhjem cathedral school, and later became a professor in Denmark and a noted historian; Suhm, also a historian, was Danish by birth but had married into the noted Trondhjem family of Angell and lived there from 1751 to 1765. Together, by their own contributions to the Society's publications

1 Trondheim has been the official spelling since 6 March 1931.

and by the high standards they maintained, they put Norway and Trondhjem intellectually on the map. Suhm also published a popular journal devoted to the arts and sciences called *Tronhiemske Samlinger* (*Papers from Trondhjem*), and when Schøning's learned dissertation on the Cathedral of Nidaros appeared in 1762, all eyes in the North were turned, as the Norwegian literary scholar Francis Bull has it, to 'the three wise men of Trondhjem.' In addition to the founding of the Royal Scientific Society, Trondhjem soon had other 'firsts' to its credit. In 1803 the first public theatre in Norway was established there. In 1816 the head office of the newly-founded *Norges Bank* (Bank of Norway) was situated there; and in 1818 Carl Johan was crowned the first king of the new Norway in the cathedral.

At the turn of the nineteenth century Trondhjem was a flourishing town, both economically and culturally. The timber trade was booming, copper prices at the Røros mines were rising, and in 1803 *Det Throndhjemske Handels- og Fiskerietablissement i Nordlandene* (The Trondhjem Centre for Commerce and Fisheries in the Northern Provinces) was established in an effort to wrest some of the Nordland fish trade from Bergen. The town's merchant families, many of whom were descendants of Danes, Germans, Dutch, and British who had come to Trondhjem in the seventeenth century, cultivated literary and artistic interests and led patrician existences. At his estate at Rotvoll, Count Schmettow's dramatic entertainments, with plays written especially for the occasion, were famous. And the new cathedral school, opened in January 1787, remained for generations the grandest school building in Norway.

However, all this was only relative. Although foreign travellers, after emerging from the wilds, might be impressed to find such a town, Trondhjem was still, in the early nineteenth century, with some notable exceptions like the so-called Stiftsgården, a town of low wooden houses, broad streets (a consequence of replanning after the many fires which had ravished the town), and narrow alleys. Shops were primitive and rustic in appearance and travellers were lucky if they could obtain quarters at Madame Holmberg's.

Like that of other Norwegian towns, the prosperity of Trondhjem was soon to be threatened. It was hard hit during the disastrous year of 1812 (*Det store uåret*) when the failure of crops and the fishing strained to breaking-point a situation already made precarious by the British blockade of the country during the Napoleonic Wars (see below, p. 117). As elsewhere in Norway, many bankruptcies occurred in Trondhjem between 1813 and 1816, reflecting the general economic difficulties of those years.

Nevertheless, Trondhjem and its citizens still managed to play an important part in the national life. When, after the provisions of the

Treaty of Kiel (see below, p. 118) had become known, the Danish crown prince, Christian Frederik, visited Trondhjem in February 1814 to sound opinion about proclaiming himself king of Norway, the citizens met him with an address. They asked him to call a representative gathering to decide Norway's future. This petition resulted in the calling of the meeting of Notables at Eidsvoll and the promulgation there of the Norwegian constitution of 17 May 1814 (see below, p. 120).

In business, the establishment of the Trondhjem Bourse in 1819 and the improvement of the harbour were important initial steps, and industry gradually developed along the banks of the river Nid, the so-called *Nidelvens Fabriker*. Especially important for the development of the town's economy was the opening in 1835 of the road from Sweden via Sul and Verdal to Levanger, which did much to promote trade between Trondhjem and the Swedish province of Jämtland. Shipping and shipbuilding also developed: in 1850 Trondhjem's first steamer was built; in 1857 the important steamship company *Det Nordenfjeldske Dampskibsselskab* was founded with a view to developing the route to north Norway; and in 1866 *Det Sønden-fjeldske Dampskibsselskab* inaugurated the coastal route Trondhjem–Christiania. In 1864 the first part of the railway-line to Røros (*Rørosbanen*) was opened, and by 1877 the line had been extended to Hamar; in 1882 the line into Sweden (*Meråkerbanen*) was brought into service.

These improved communications had a most stimulating effect on trade and they all conduced to make Trondhjem more and more of a trading and cultural centre for the whole of central Norway. In 1870 an important step was taken when the Trondhjem Technical College was founded (*Trondhjems Tekniske Læreanstalt*). The college became the most important centre of technical education in the country and paved the way for the founding in Trondhjem of the Technical University of Norway (*Norges Tekniske Høgskole*) in 1910.

In the literary, artistic, and cultural fields the achievements of Trondhjem in the nineteenth century were of a somewhat stop-go variety. In literature, the writers Mauritz Hansen (1794–1842) and Conrad Nicolai Schwach (1793–1860), though not natives of Trondhjem, were active in stimulating the literary patriotism which manifested itself early in the century, especially by encouraging the people of Trondhjem to celebrate 17 May as the Norwegian national day; but it was not until the end of the century, when the Trøndelag writers Peter Egge (1869–1959) and Johan Bojer (1872–1959) made their débuts, that the area was put on the Norwegian literary map. In 1860 a dramatic academy was established in Trondhjem and in the following year the Trondhjem Norwegian Theatre (*Det Norske*

*Theater i Trondhjem*) opened its doors and maintained a permanent repertory for a number of years. About the same period, too, musical life blossomed. The town had already produced a star of international repute in Thomas Tellefsen (1823–74), a pupil of Chopin and renowned in his day as a piano virtuoso and teacher; but in mid-century the most distinctive musical talent was the composer Martin Andreas Udbye (1820–89) who, though his achievements do not rank high in the annals of Norwegian music, was probably the most outstanding creative artist Trondhjem produced at this period. However, as with the theatre, the great expectations of the 1850s and '60s had evaporated by the 1870s, an ebbing of the National Romantic currents which had carried them forward.

The plans for restoring the cathedral really focused attention on Trondhjem in the second half of the century. Here was a national treasure which the nation was determined should be restored to its former glory. In the 1820s J. C. Dahl had already agitated for its restoration. In subsequent years private subscriptions and public funds enabled a start to be made in 1869. Since 1872 the Norwegian state has contributed regularly to the cost of the work which has attracted to its service some of the country's best architectural and artistic talents.

*Stavanger*

Norway's fourth city, Stavanger, also played a distinctive role in the country's development during the nineteenth century. In the Middle Ages it had been the seat of a bishop with a cathedral ranking only second to the Cathedral of Nidaros, and at the turn of the seventeenth century it was one of the most important towns. But decline set in, and at the beginning of the nineteenth century it had a population of barely 2,500. Stavanger's restored fortunes in the nineteenth century, and at times its severe setbacks, derived from the highly successful development of its herring fisheries and from its shipping, the importance of which moved the poet Bjørnson to compose his well-known *Norsk sjømannssang* (*Norwegian Seaman's Song*). Later on, from 1889, its prosperity depended very much on its canning industries which, under the leadership of Christian Bjelland (1858–1927), became the biggest in the North and among the world's most important. Stavanger society and commercial life until the 1870s and its economic crises of the 1880s are vividly reflected in the novels of Alexander Kielland (1849–1906), himself a scion of one of the most important merchant houses in Stavanger. His grandfather was reputed to be the richest man in Norway and the Kielland family residence, Ledaal (the Sandsgaard of his novels), now a museum and the official residence of the king when he is in Stavanger, gives one a very good idea of contemporary mercantile magnificence. The later development of the canning industry led inevitably to the jingle that Stavanger once Kielland's was now Bjelland's. Commercial growth was reflected in the amazing growth of the population: by 1850 it was 14,000, by 1890 24,000, and by 1910 37,000.

In the context of Norwegian social history, Stavanger has its importance as a centre of religious dissent and an often narrow Pietism, with teetotalism and skinflint politics as its concomitants; it also set in motion the ultimately large-scale Norwegian emigration to the United States when on 5 July 1825 the sloop *Restaurationen* set sail for New York with fifty-two Norwegian Quakers on board, all determined to settle in the New World. On arrival there they were greeted by Cleng Peerson from Tysvær (just north of Stavanger), one of the most enterprising pioneers in the history of Norwegian emigration to the United States. Their departure was also linked to an episode of interest in British–Norwegian relations. During the Napoleonic Wars, Norway, as part of the kingdom of Denmark, had been at war with Great Britain (see below, p. 116). Norwegian prisoners-of-war, interned in England, had come into contact with the Quakers and their writings, and on their return to Norway had founded their own Quaker groups. Their movement had, however, many similarities with the indigenous religious movement of Hans Nielsen Hauge (1771–1824). Both these religious movements fell foul of the Norwegian state Church and both were strong in Stavanger and its immediate area. Ingrid Semmingsen, in her book on Norwegian emigration to the United States, believes that adherents of the Hauge movement were also among those who emigrated on the *Restaurationen*. Stavanger was also the home of the Norwegian temperance movement. The first temperance society in the country was founded there by Asbjørn Kloster in 1859, making Stavanger the centre of the Norwegian temperance movement. This led in 1862 to the formation of a nationwide society, called from 1875 *Det Norske Totalavholdsselskab* (The Norwegian Total Abstinence Society). In the mission field, too, Stavanger led the way. A missionary society was founded there in 1826 and under the capable guidance of John Haugvaldstad (1770–1850), a factory-owner, who was a leading adherent of the Hauge movement and a lay preacher, *Det Norske Misjonsselskab* (The Norwegian Missionary Society) was founded in 1842.

Many of the tendencies of which Stavanger was the centre coalesced in the personalities of Lars Oftedal (1838–1900) and Ole Gabriel Ueland (1799–1870). Oftedal, who earlier in his career had been Norwegian seamen's pastor in Cardiff, held livings in the Norwegian state Church in Stavanger from 1874 to 1891; he also represented Stavanger in the *Storting* and was the editor and founder of the newspapers *Vestlandsposten* and *Stavanger Aftenblad*. Until he fell from power in 1891, after public confession of disgraceful conduct, he had exercised a powerful influence through an amalgam of political narrowness, Pietistic fervour, good works (he founded many charitable institutions), and journalistic skill, all of which made an especial appeal to the predilections and prejudices of the people of Stavanger and its hinterland, the area which the writer Arne Garborg (see below, p. 246) has called 'Det mørke Fastlandet' ('The Dark Continent'). The prayer-house empire which Oftedal had built up in Stavanger was mercilessly satirized by Alexander Kielland in his novel *Sankt Hans Fest* (*Midsummer Festival*; 1887). Oftedal had been one of those principally responsible for preventing Kielland from getting a writer's pension when his application came before the *Storting* in 1885–87. Oftedal's whole activity was also brilliantly though one-sidedly analysed by Knut Hamsun in a series of articles in the Norwegian newspaper *Dagbladet* in 1891.

Ueland, who became leader of the so-called Peasant Opposition (*Bondeopposisjonen*) and one of the most important politicians in nineteenth-century Norway, was born at Lund in Rogaland in the hinterland of Stavanger. He, too, was deeply rooted in the cultural and religious ethos of the region. He was strongly influenced by the Hauge movement and, though he was a clever parliamentarian who said that the Norwegian people had two jewels—religion and their constitution—and a deep patriot, he never completely shed a certain agrarian narrowness, of which the first article of his political programme, 'economy in affairs of state', was typical.

The role played by people like Oftedal and Ueland in the social and cultural history of Norway in the nineteenth century was, in many ways, linked with the role played by the country's peasant proprietors, the *Bonde*, both in fact and by the image which the *Bonde* had in the consciousness of Norwegians.

Christiania, Bergen, Trondhjem, Stavanger, and other smaller towns had an important moulding influence in the nineteenth century as centres of Norwegian life, trade, wealth, and culture, but the influence of the *Bonde* was a very pervasive and important one, of which due account must be taken for an understanding of the development of Norwegian life and culture of the period.

## THE BONDE

A specifically peasant culture (*Bondekultur*) began especially to flourish in the seventeenth and eighteenth centuries, and achieved its finest flowering around 1800. Though, like other folk-cultures, it was unsophisticated and in many respects derivative, it was undeniably Norwegian in character and was solidly anchored in Norwegian nature, history, and traditions. Even foreigners recognized that there was something special about the *Bonde* and his way of life and culture. Erik Pontoppidan in his *Norges Naturlige Historie* (*The Natural History of Norway*; 1752), which was translated into English in 1755, sees the *Bonde* as representing that which is characteristically Norwegian, and Samuel Laing in his *Journal of a Residence in Norway* (1836) states that: 'If there be a happy class of people in Europe, it is the Norwegian Bonder'. Basic to *Bondekultur* was the fact that it was in the country districts that the real Norwegian language was spoken, albeit in battered dialect forms. By contrast to the stiffness, and for the rural dweller the artificiality, of the official Dano–Norwegian of the day, the Norwegian dialects revealed the real temperament and character of the people as they were expressed in their speech and in their ballads, legends, folk-tales, rhymes, and riddles, all of which were kept alive by oral tradition. *Bondekultur* also flourished in other spheres. Jakob Bersvensen Klugstad (*c.* 1700–73) brought wood-carving to a very high degree of artistic perfection with his so-called *Døleskurd*, of which his carved pulpit in Skjåk church is a remarkable example. The achievements of peasant artists working in iron, silver, and gold were also noteworthy, as they were in weaving. Peasant dances with gay costumes, the music of the Hardanger fiddle, a dignified building style, and a punctilio and decorum in social life and occasions marked *Bondekultur* at its best. Nineteenth-century national sentiment, not to say sentimentality, about the *Bonde* derived very much from the ancient system of odal tenure of land which gave the *odelsbonde* a free and representative status in the country. It was a system to which Norwegians in all ages had clung tenaciously and it carried with it the conviction that Norwegians had nothing to envy in, or to adopt from, the social systems of other countries. The fact that Norway also had, especially at certain periods, a large class of underprivileged tenant cottars (*husmenn*) often tended to be overlooked as did the less laudable sides of Norwegian rural life and morality which the sociological investigations of Eilert Sundt (1817–75) brought to light in the mid-nineteenth century. As the poet Jens Zetlitz (1761–1821) put it, 'It is just our odal rights which make Norway up to this very day the blessed, the loved, the true land of liberty'. The importance of the *Bonde* and the country districts might also appear to be enshrined in the so-called *Bondeparagrafen* of the Norwegian constitution of 1814, which provided that the towns should elect one-third and the country districts two-thirds of the *Storting* deputies, but this was not so, for although it gave a majority of seats to the country districts, this majority did not measure up to the majority the country districts had in population. However, in the early years of the century, the peasantry showed little political awareness and still preferred to elect members of the official classes to represent them. It was not until John Neergaard (1795–1885) published his so-called *Olaboka* in 1830 and Peder Soelvold (1799–1847) started his periodical *Statsborgeren* in 1831, both of them critical of the official classes, in which the *Bonde* was urged to take affairs into his own hands, that the peasants began to develop political interests.

During the first half of the nineteenth century *Bondekultur* seemed to continue at its old level of excellence, but it was already less solidly rooted in the people and by mid-century a decline could be detected. Many of the old stave-churches (one of the most interesting survivals of the Middle Ages) were pulled down; peasant costume, arts, and crafts were neglected; the old folk-tales, legends, and melodies began to be forgotten or were treated with contempt. A major reason for this state of affairs appears to have been the power which Pietism had begun to have over the minds of country dwellers, making them believe that their old ways were far too much marked by the joys of this world and should thus be abandoned. We get a striking and at times horrific picture of the ravages which Pietism could work in the peasant community in Arne Garborg's novel *Fred* (*Peace*, 1892), when it coincided with economic difficulty and a disintegration of the old ways of life.

Fortunately, there were at hand at this very time a group of outstanding scholars and intellectuals who devoted themselves to the intense study of the language, oral literature, and culture of the *Bonde* and who were determined to rescue and record them before it was too late. Their efforts inaugurated the period in Norwegian cultural history called National Romanticism (see below, p. 225) which led to the collection of folk-tales, ballads, legends, and melodies, and research into the ancient arts and crafts, customs, beliefs, and mores, of the *Bonde*. This cult of the peasant had tremendous and pervasive consequences for Norwegian life right through the nineteenth century and beyond. Its precise manifestations are dealt with in more detail below under the headings of history, literature, and art. However, one further development, having consequences for rural culture around mid-century and later, must be mentioned here. Norwegian educationalists realized that if the Norwegian peasant was to be freed from the grip of Pietism so that he could develop both politically and culturally and play a proper part in the life of the country, more education was necessary. In 1851 *Selskabet for Folkeoplysningens Fremme* (The Society for Popular Enlightenment) was founded in Christiania by a number of leading educationalists and intellectuals with representatives in all parts of the country. The society's periodical *Folkevennen* (*People's Friend*), edited by Ole Vig (1824–57), performed a considerable educational task in the rural areas where it was read aloud and discussed in reading circles founded for this purpose. The movement he generated was one of the factors which led to the new School Law of 1860, which made provision for permanent schools in rural areas to replace the old system of peripatetic teachers who went from farm to farm. At the same time the school curriculum was broadened to include new subjects like history, geography, and natural science, as well as the traditional subjects of religious knowledge, reading, writing, and arithmetic. This educational process was carried a step further when, to cater for the needs of the young people in the rural districts whose appetites for knowledge had been whetted by what they had learnt at school, the first Folk High Schools (*Folkehøyskoler*) began to appear. Based on the model of the Danish Folk High School, founded by N. F. S. Grundtvig in Denmark, the first Norwegian Folk High School was founded by Herman Anker and Ole Arvesen in 1864 at Sagatun, near Hamar in eastern Norway. Its programme was to provide courses for rural youth during the winter months and to arouse their interest, especially in religion, history, and current issues through the use of the spoken word. They were to be popular (*folkelig*) in the best sense of the word. A few years later the next Folk High School, Vonheim, was founded in Gausdal in Gudbrandsdalen by a clergyman, Christopher Bruun (1839–1920), also noted as a model for the title figure in Ibsen's play *Brand* and for his book *Folkelige Grundtanker* (1878), an exposition of the national, democratic, and Christian idealism which lay behind the Folk High School movement. The movement soon spread to other parts of Norway and in combating the prevailing Pietism–the conflict between the new Grundtvigians and the Pietists is well brought out in Arne Garborg's novel *Bondestudentar* (*Peasant Students*; 1883) – played a great part in educating rural youth to greater religious, political, and cultural independence.

# Chapter 2

# Industrial and other Developments

THE DEVELOPMENTS AND ACHIEVEMENTS which have emerged from the foregoing outline had not been accomplished easily. In the early nineteenth century Norway was predominantly a primitive agricultural country with a largely self-supplying economy. There was little industry, unless one counts the large number of small distilleries, and little demand for goods within the country itself. In fact, after having lived in the shadow of Denmark for 400 years (see below, p. 100), the Norway of the time had many of the features which we today associate with underdeveloped countries.

However, even in the financially catastrophic conditions which prevailed during the years immediately after 1814, there were a number of potential economic growth-points in the sawmills, iron-works, copper-mines, shipbuilding yards, and glass-works, all of them on a limited scale, but some of long standing. The Norwegian constitution of 1814 had provided that no new restrictions should be placed on trade and industry, but the immediate difficulty for their development was the lack of capital, and abroad Norway was not regarded as a particularly creditworthy country. Thus in the 1830s Norway was still predominantly a farming and fishing community with some trade and shipping. It was not until the 1840s and '50s when Norwegian state finances were brought into balance, the Navigation Acts in England abolished, and with an increasing liberalization of trade including the abolition of the old guild system, that Norway was enabled to participate in the industrial expansion which had already become commonplace in other, larger European countries.

This expansion when it came was basically greatest in the sawmill industry, in the timber trade, and in shipping, but, more importantly, this expansion provided the basis for the import of the coal, the pig-iron, and the skilled labour which were essential for the development of a modern foundry and engineering industry. The textile industry also developed rapidly from the 1840s, five cotton-mills being founded in the year 1845. Thus while the foundries and the engineering-works provided the basis for an increase in the means of production, the textile industry provided for an increased consumers' market.

However, lack of development in other sectors of industry, limited purchasing power, a shortage of administrative talent and skilled workers, and limited credit and banking facilities made industrial development in Norway at this period uncertain and spasmodic. It was not until the last three decades of the century that all the inter-locking technical, financial, labour, and transport problems associa-ted with an industrial revolution were brought sufficiently into harmony for an explosive, though uneven, development to take place. In this respect the years 1871–75, 1886–89, and 1896–1900 are particularly noteworthy. During this period industry had advanced on a broad front and naturally it had involved change. The old Norwegian iron-works, with their quality product 'Norway Iron' which had earlier played such an important part in the Norwegian economy, and indeed in cultural life, had given way to the new foundries using English bar-iron, and the building of wooden ships, hitherto one of the biggest industries in Norway, had had to give way before the new iron steamships which were imported from abroad. By contrast, the timber products industry went ahead by leaps and bounds in the 1870s and '80s after the development of new processes for the production of cellulose. The Norwegian match industry also underwent a tremendous expansion in the 1870s and in 1879 the Stavanger Preserving Company began to tin smoked brisling in olive oil, thus laying the foundations of the Norwegian canning industry which was later to develop in a fantastic way. By 1900 the livelihoods of 27 per cent of the population of Norway depended on some form of industry or associated trades.

*Development of Communications*

An indispensable concomitant of nineteenth-century industrial–and national–development was the expansion of communications. In the early years of the century the major form of transport was by boat, along either the coast or the fjords. Inland, the nature of the country made easy communication difficult, though marked tracks had existed over large areas from time immemorial, some of which had been expanded to bridle-paths and even carriageways; but there had been little attempt to provide and maintain a road network on a national scale. In southern Norway winter was the best time for travel since it was then that snow and ice filled the holes in the roads. Thus it was in the winter months that markets were held and social life flourished. Nevertheless, in the years after 1814 many demands were heard for an improvement in communications, not least from those who had attended the meeting of Notables at Eidsvoll in early 1814 (see below, p. 120). In 1825 the government decided to pur-chase two steamers in England, the *Constitutionen* and the *Prinds Carl*, which were put into service between Christiania and Bergen, and Christiania and Copenhagen, respectively. Later the state purchased further steamers to cover the coastal routes of Norway from the Swedish border in the south to east Finnmark in the north, and abroad to Denmark, Germany, and England. A few steamers had also been put into service by private enterprise, but it was not until the 1850s when important steamship companies, which still exist, were formed in Bergen, Trondhjem, Stavanger, and Arendal, in the first place with an eye to overseas trade, that a modern shipping industry began to develop. Eventually, the state handed over its shipping interests to the private companies who, in return for subsidies and revenues from the conveyance of mail, agreed to maintain regular coastal services all the year round.

From mid-century greater speed and purpose began to be shown in the improvement of road communications. A Department of the Interior had been set up in 1845 with responsibilities for communications and, under the leadership of Frederik Stang, a later Prime Minister, the foundations were laid for the planned development of a Norwegian road network. In 1864 Christian Vilhelm Bergh was appointed to the newly established post of Director of Roads and under him and his successor, Hans Hagerup Krag (also co-founder of *Den Norske Turistforening*; The Norwegian Tourist Association), steady and solid progress was made, so that by the turn of the century the Norwegian roads amounted to some 29,000 kilometres, roughly double their length fifty years earlier.

The growing demand for up-to-date communications had led the *Storting* to agree as early as 1848 to obtain a loan to finance railway-building. The volume of traffic between Trondhjem and Christiania, and especially the transportation of timber between Eidsvoll and Christiania, made a solution imperative. In 1851 the *Storting* decided that it was between Christiania and Eidsvoll that the first railway should be built (see below, p. 127). In 1871 the line which had been built east from Lillestrøm to Kongsvinger was linked with the Swedish railway system, thus providing direct communication between Christiania and Stockholm; in 1877 the *Røros-banen* connecting Hamar and Trondhjem via Røros was completed which, when extended to Eidsvoll, enabled a through line from Christiania to Trondhjem to be opened in 1880. Other shorter lines were built and plans made for others, including the decision in 1894 to build a railway between Christiania and Bergen (*Bergensbanen*).

*The Growth of Tourism*

One of the consequences of the improvement of communications in Norway was the growth of a tourist industry. Norway had, of course, been visited and written about by celebrated travellers over the centuries, going back to the voyage to Thule of Pytheas in the fourth century B.C. In 1795 Norway was visited by Mary Wollstone-craft, who resided there for a short time and recorded her impressions in *Letters Written During a Short Residence in Sweden, Norway and Denmark* (1796), and in 1799 T. R. Malthus, accompanied by Dr E. D. Clarke of Cambridge, travelled through the country. Their accounts of the trip are recorded in Malthus's *Scandinavian Journal* and Clarke's *Travels*. They were followed by many other, mainly less notable, foreign travellers in the nineteenth century who also wrote books about their experiences, some of them both informative and lauda-tory, like Samuel Laing's *Journal of a Residence in Norway* (1836) and others which were simply anecdotal or even fantastic. The majority, however, were generally enthusiastic about the simple delights of life and travel in *Gamle Norge* (Old Norway). In fact the writing of travel books on Norway seems to have become something of a minor publishing industry in the nineteenth century. According to Erling Welle-Strand nearly two thousand foreign authors had written descriptions of Norway before the first official tourist brochure was published in Norway in 1904.

The Norwegians themselves were somewhat slower than foreigners to start travelling in their own country for pleasure, or indeed to understand what the country's tourist potential was. In 1820 the Norwegian geologist B. M. Keilhau (1797–1858) and the botanist Christian Boeck (1798–1877) undertook a scientific excursion into the Jotunheimen region, which later became celebrated, but they seem to have regarded its exciting natural attractions as unpleasant obstacles to be overcome. During the period of National Romantic-ism its chief proponents made their collections and pursued their studies in the field, and regarded Norwegian nature as the source of their inspiration. Ole Bull, when asked by the king of Denmark who had taught him to play, replied 'the Norwegian mountains, your majesty.' Some others wrote prose descriptions of Norwegian nature, like Bernhard Herre (1812–49) in his book *En Jægers Erindringer* (*A Hunter's Reminiscences*; 1849), but it was the writer Aa. O. Vinje (1818–70) who seems to have been the first Norwegian of note to have travelled in Norway as a foot tourist for the sheer pleasure of doing it, as we see from his book of travel reminiscences, *Ferdaminni* (*Travel Memories*; 1861).

Before the advent of the railway and, later, of motor transport, land travel in Norway was by cariole (*karjol*) and buggy (*stolkjerre*), and in the country districts accommodation of varying quality was provided by posting stations (*skysstasjoner*), which, as the guidebooks of the period show, were governed by precise regulations. If the traveller was important enough, he might find accommodation with the local parson or other official, but in any case a journey of any distance had to be planned and indeed provisioned as if it were an expedition. In the towns in the early years of the century the traveller had to find private quarters; hotels did not make their appearance in Christiania until the 1830s and in Bergen until about 1850. The opening of the railway-line from Christiania to Eidsvoll in 1854, the provision of regular passenger services from England to Norway, and the organizing talent of Thomas Bennett (1814–98), an Englishman who had settled in Christiania and had founded in 1849 the tourist bureau which still bears his name, made the 1850s the first important period for tourism in Norway. Top people now began to visit the country as tourists and when, in 1873, the king of Norway and Sweden, Oscar II, together with a distinguished company of guests, made a trip to North Cape after his crowning in Trondhjem, Norwegian tourism was really put on the map. Not only did the number of foreign tourists grow from over 13,000 in 1886 to over 20,000 in 1902, but so did the number of Norwegians who travelled in their own country for pleasure, something which Edmund Gosse commented on when he visited Norway in 1898: 'No feature surprised me more than to see what a very large number of Norwegians now travel for pleasure in their own country. This was quite rare a quarter of a century ago.' This was a development that had been going on for some time. In 1868 *Den Norske Turistforening* had been founded with the special objective of encouraging Norwegians to get to know their own country better by going on walking tours over the moors and in the mountains. To further these ends the society began to provide tourist huts in the mountains and to publish a yearbook. Later, in 1879, Yngvar Nielsen published the first edition of his guide to Norway for Norwegians, *Reisehaandbok over Norge*.

### Development of the Press

The growth of communications and especially the coming of the telegraph and the telephone had great consequences for the development of the Norwegian press. At the beginning of the nineteenth century newspapers were few and primitive, and their circulation and influence limited. The events of the war and the blockade of Norway during the years 1807–14 (see below, p. 116) provided a stimulus and a need for information. To meet this a more or less official newspaper, *Tiden* (*The Times*), was started, supported by the regent, Prince Christian Frederik, and with aims that were largely propagandistic on his behalf. Given the political power-structure of the day, the influence of the newspapers on the course of events was small, though the provision in the Norwegian constitution of 1814 which guaranteed the freedom of the press, provided one of the pre-conditions for its future power.

In the years after 1814 a number of new papers appeared, some of them critical of the crown prince and later king of Norway–Sweden, Carl Johan, especially *Det Norske Nationalblad* (*The Norwegian National Mail*) in which the Liberal politician and publicist Jonas Anton Hielm (1782–1848) played a prominent part. In 1819 Norway got its first daily newspaper when *Morgenbladet* (*The Morning Mail*) started publication. Its early years were undistinguished, but later, during 1831–57 under the editorship of A. B. Stabell (1807–65), it became (at least until the beginning of the 1850s) the principal organ of the Liberal opposition and thus prominent in the political and cultural battles of the period. Among its contributors was the poet Henrik Wergeland, who, nevertheless, found it necessary in his poem *Mig selv* (*Myself*) to complain of the treatment he had received in its columns. The apparent defection of Stabell to the Right in the 1850s aroused the wrath of Henrik Ibsen, then a young radical, prompting him to write his short satirical play *Norma* (1851) and engendering in him the dislike of compromising Liberal politicians which was to be reflected in his later work, notably *The League of Youth* (1869), *An Enemy of the People* (1882), and *Rosmersholm* (1886). The opposing party, the so-called 'Intelligence Party' of young conservative academics, led by J. S. Welhaven, also had its organ, *Den Constitutionelle* (*The Constitutional*), which appeared between 1836 and 1847. Its distinguished editorial committee, which included the jurist and politician Anton Martin Schweigaard (1808–70), and its talented contributors did much to raise the tone of public debate and the prestige of the press in general.

The 1830s and '40s were also noteworthy for the number of local newspapers which were founded and for the emergence of new periodicals of all kinds, many of which were short-lived, though the popular *Skilling-Magazin* (*Penny Paper*) continued to appear from 1835 until 1891. In the 1850s, with the increasing polarization of the political parties into Right (*Høire*) and Left (Liberal; *Venstre*), the dramatic improvement in communications, and a general upswing in the economic, social, and cultural condition of the country, the Norwegian press and periodical literature entered a period of continuing expansion and increasing sophistication. During the second half of the century *Morgenbladet*, now the organ of the Right, maintained its position as the leading Norwegian newspaper of the day. Under the editorship of Christian Frederik Gottfried Friele (1821–99) it became an institution in Norway, and Friele the archetype of the highly professional, all-powerful editor, hated and feared by his political opponents, a type which was often to figure in Norwegian literature.

Towards the end of the 1860s three other, ultimately highly important, newspapers, were founded: *Aftenposten* (*The Evening Post*; 1860), *Verdens Gang* (*The Globe*; 1868), and *Dagbladet* (*The Daily Mail*; 1869). Of these, during the last decades of the century, *Verdens Gang* had the most spectacular rise in popularity. Under the editorship of Olaus Anton Thommessen (1851–1942), one of the most outstanding journalists and editorial talents Norway has produced, and the somewhat distorted model for the title figure in Knut Hamsun's novel *Redaktør Lynge* (*Editor Lynge*; 1893), *Verdens Gang* developed into the liveliest and most modern Norwegian newspaper of the period, with a first-rate coverage of news and of political and cultural matters. When Thommessen left the paper in order to found *Tidens Tegn* (*Signs of the Times*) in 1910, *Verdens Gang* declined and ceased publication in 1923; it was reconstituted in 1945. By contrast to *Verdens Gang*, which after being politically uncommitted eventually developed into a right-wing paper, *Dagbladet* was from the start a supporter of the Left (*Venstre*) and valued by its relatively small number of subscribers for its well-written articles on political and cultural matters. It was not until the 1930s, when it developed a somewhat sensational reporting style, that its circulation began to grow until it eventually became the second largest newspaper in the country. *Aftenposten* set out from the start to be an advertising journal with a bourgeois appeal, concentrating on items which were newsworthy rather than of intrinsic importance, and on popular articles. Under the leadership of Amandus Schibsted (1849–1913), a son of the founder, and one of the great pioneers of the modern press in Norway, though not a great editor in the sense that Friele and Thommessen were, it overtook *Morgenbladet* in circulation around the turn of the century and soon became the country's biggest newspaper. Outside Christiania *Bergens Tidende* (*The Bergen Times*), founded in 1868, became one of the best and most influential newspapers in western Norway. The remaining decades of the century saw the founding in the provinces of other papers of high quality, some of which have continued publication to the present day, among them *Stavanger Aftenblad* (*Stavanger Evening Mail*), founded by Lars Oftedal. In 1884 Christian Holtermann Knudsen (1845–1929), himself a printer, began to publish *Vort Arbeide* (*Our Work*), which was to be the organ of the central committee of the newly-founded Norwegian trade union movement. In 1886 its name was changed to *Social-Demokraten* (*The Social Democrat*), and in 1894 it was taken over by the Norwegian Labour Party and began to appear daily. In 1924 its name was again changed, to *Arbeiderbladet* (*The Workers Mail*). Under the editorship from 1921 to 1949 (with the exception of the war years) of Martin Tranmæl (1879–1967), it played a great part in the rise of the Norwegian Labour Party in the 1920s and '30s, at the same time developing into a modern newspaper fully able to compete with its leading contemporaries.

During the second half of the nineteenth century Norwegian newspapers had become purveyors of news in the modern sense. Previously, long political and other articles had taken up most of the space, but with the advent of the press telegram (the first press telegram service was established in Christiania in 1867) and in particular the spur given by the events of the Franco-Prussian War (1870–71), a much greater urgency infused the collecting and publication of news. Gradually the old Gothic type was replaced, bigger and more eyecatching headlines were introduced, and in general style newspapers began to aim at a mass public.

The second half of the century also saw a continued expansion in the number of periodicals published in Norway, some of them again short-lived, but which between them covered a wide spectrum of interests. Periodicals written in *Landsmaal* (see below, pp. 195 and 229) were inaugurated with Aa. O. Vinje's *Dølen* (*The Dalesman*; 1858–70) and followed by *Fedraheimen* (*The Fatherland*; 1877–91), founded by Arne Garborg (see below, p. 246), and the newspaper *Den 17de Mai* (*The 17th May*; 1894–1935). The political aspirations of the *Bonde* were espoused in Søren Jaabæk's highly successful *Folketidende* (*People's Times*; 1865–79), while Olaus Fjørtoft's *Fram* (*Forward*; 1871–73), written in his own form of *Landsmaal*, is one of the curiosities of Norwegian periodical literature, with its combination of extreme linguistic and political radicalism. One of the most successful periodicals of the period was *Folkevennen* (*The People's Friend*; 1852–1900), devoted to popular enlightenment and numbering among its editors Ole Vig and the distinguished sociologist Eilert Sundt (1817–75). Paul Botten-Hansen's *Illustreret Nyhedsblad* (*Illustrated News*; 1851–66) was one of the most valuable periodicals of the half-century, popular in style, but with articles from a distinguished range of contributors, including the leading authors of the day, and with many book reviews from the editor who was probably the best-informed contemporary Norwegian littérateur. Towards the end of the century periodicals with a more academic or intellectual orientation began to appear, among them *Nyt Tidsskrift* (*The New Journal*; 1882–87) which, with its impressive array of contributors, provided a valuable conspectus of the cultural and political debates of the 1880s; *Samtiden* (*Contemporary Life*), a journal devoted to literature, politics, and matters of general cultural interest, founded in 1890 and still appearing; and *Ringeren* (1898–99), edited by Sigurd Ibsen, the son of Henrik Ibsen.

## EDUCATION

### Primary and Secondary Schools

The financial and other problems facing the new Norwegian state in the years immediately after 1814 meant that the enactment of new legislation on educational matters received very low priority. In fact, on the elementary level there was virtually no public education in Norway in 1814. The provisions of the law of 1739 which had required children to receive instruction in religious knowledge, reading, writing, and arithmetic had been rendered largely inoperative by local opposition on the grounds of expense, and it was left to each parish to make its own arrangements. Thus the provision or otherwise of primary education in these years had depended very much on private initiative, especially from the clergy, and there were many shining examples among them. But, in general, until the provisions of the new School Act of 1827 had been given effect, primary education in Norway was either non-existent or in a wretched state, with totally inadequate facilities and underpaid teachers who were frequently recruited from the dropouts of society.

At a higher, though still very elementary, level a number of *Realskoler* had been founded around the turn of the century with a view to meeting the more practical needs of the sons of the commercial bourgeoisie of the towns, but the really well-to-do merchants still continued to send their sons to Copenhagen or to England for their education. In fact, the only schools of the time with any real standards were the four so-called *Lærde Skoler* (Latin or cathedral schools), situated in Christiania, Bergen, Trondhjem, and Kristiansand, which together had less than 200 pupils, of which about twenty a year filled the requirements of the *Examen Artium*, or University Entrance Examination. In curriculum and character these schools were still half medieval, for in spite of the recommendations made in the last decade of the eighteenth century for a liberalization both of curriculum and pedagogical methods, and their embodiment in the Education Act of 1809, the study of the classics continued to dominate. It was a situation which led to the first *Kulturkamp* in Norway, and one in which A. M. Schweigaard was a powerful champion of liberalization. Progress towards reform was slow until the 1840s when (Ole) Hartvig Nissen (1815–74), probably the most noted Norwegian educationalist in the nineteenth century, founded his own combined *Latin- og Realskole* in 1843. Later, in 1849, he also founded a school for girls, *Nissens Pikeskole*. Nissen's ideas soon found acceptance, and during the period 1849–52 most of the grammar schools that had been established, with the exception of the Latin schools in Christiania, Bergen, and Trondhjem, adopted a curriculum which combined both Latin and science subjects. In the years that followed, the battle between classics and moderns continued to rage, but there was no doubt that the government was intent on reform. In 1865 Nissen became head of the education department in the ministry of church affairs (which also had responsibility for education) and there drafted the bill which formed the basis of the new Act of 1869, destined to be a milestone in the educational history of Norway. The battle for modern studies had been won, though the classics still retained some privileges. The most important feature of the new Act was the establishment of a so-called *Middelskole* course with a concluding examination, which was to provide both a general education and the basis for a three-year *Gymnasium* course leading to the university entrance examination. However, in spite of the advances which this reform represented, the *Gymnasium* was still in the eyes of the radical Left the *Latin* school and the preserve of the children of the official classes. With the accession of the Left (*Venstre*) Party to power in 1884, the influence of positivism, the battle for a more Norwegian language, and the ascendancy of the realist literature of the period, demands became more insistent that school curricula at all levels should be modern in kind and in keeping with national aspirations. In 1890 a royal commission was set up to consider further reform, and as a result of its recommendations a new Act was passed in 1896. This provided for a four-year *Middelskole* and a three-year *Gymnasium*. In both emphasis was to be laid on Norwegian language and literature, including *Landsmaal*, and in the teaching of foreign languages there was to be concentration on contemporary language and on oral and written proficiency in it. In other subjects, too, priority was to be given to those aspects which were immediately relevant to the pupil's own experience and future needs in Norwegian society. The commission actually recommended that Latin and Greek should disappear from the curriculum, but in the event machinery was devised for allowing individual *Gymnasia* to continue to teach Latin.

In the primary schools the new law of 1827, which was mainly relevant to schools in the country districts, did little more than promulgate afresh the ordinance of 1739, in that it made preparation for confirmation the chief aim of instruction, culminating in public catechization in church. However, the 1827 Act did establish an educational structure of some sort which included provision for permanent schools, some training for teachers and improved pay, and state aid to poor areas of the country. But the provision of new schools proceeded slowly and even at mid-century the vast majority of country children were still taught in so-called *Omgangsskoler*, an arrangement whereby the children were gathered together at one of the farms in their neighbourhood and taught by itinerant school-masters for a few weeks of the year, often in far from ideal conditions. In spite of their shortcomings, however, the *Omgangsskoler* had the merit of bringing parents, teachers, and pupils into close contact with each other and the gifted teacher often played a role in the life of the rural community which went far beyond the purely educational one, as we see exemplified in Baard, the schoolmaster in Bjørnson's short story *A Happy Boy*. In the towns the primary schools had been some-what improved by an Act of 1848 which had provided for a more organized educational structure than was the case in the country districts and by the possibility of adding additional subjects to the curriculum which, basically, was the same as that in the rural schools.

In the country districts the institution of local government in 1837 and the general climate of contemporary debate meant that opinion could not long remain satisfied with a system of primary education that only had confirmation as its aim. In 1860 a new Act was passed which, although not altering the fundamentally religious bias of the curriculum, did provide for an extension of the subjects taught and of the time spent at school, and for the appointment of directors of education to supervise the work and organization of the primary schools. Probably the most important educational innovation of the time, however, was the preparation of a new school reader for primary schools. Both Hartvig Nissen and Ole Vig had agitated for this, arguing that it was educationally indefensible for school reading material to be limited to religious and edifying texts. In 1863 P. A. Jensen's *Læsebog for Folkeskolen og Folkehjemmet* (*Reader for the Primary School and for the Home*), which had been commissioned by the government, appeared. It contained a wide selection of material, including passages on the history and geography of Norway, some fairy stories, and selections from Norwegian and Scandinavian writers. But in spite of its highly respectable provenance (its editor was a well-known ecclesiastic), it did not find easy acceptance. The Pietist faction was outraged by some of the 'worldly' passages and a great debate followed. The Reader, though slightly modified in later editions, emerged triumphant, to the great advantage of education and general cultural advance. It was later succeeded by Nordahl Rolfsen's *Læsebog for Folkeskolen* (1892–95), in three volumes, which probably became the most read book in the country and which, with its bias towards the national, the popular, and the democratic, has exercised a great moulding influence on Norwegian attitudes right up to the present day. New school laws passed in 1889 attempted to realize in organization, curriculum, facilities, and teacher-training the ideals implicit in the term *Folkeskole*, which was now used of the primary schools instead of the old *Almueskole* with all its lower-class implications. There can be no doubt that the popular-national character that educational reform took on in Norway in the nineteenth century owed much to other parallel movements for popular education and enlightenment which were going on at the same time, especially the Folk High School movement, the activities of the Society for the Promotion of Popular Enlightenment (*Selskabet for Folkeoplysningens Fremme*) founded in 1851, the extramural work of the university students, *Det Norske Studentersamfunds Friundervisning* founded in 1864, and the educational work of the Christiania Workers' Union (*Kristiania Arbeidersamfund*), also founded in 1864.

## The University

The original plans of the founding fathers of Norway's first university in 1811, then called the Royal Frederik University (*Kongelige Frederiks Universitet*), were broader in scope than a mere importation from Copenhagen of a university system for the training of the official classes, and included provision for subjects directly related to the economic life of the country. However, in the event, only mining studies, which had been transferred from Kongsberg where they had been established in 1757, were included. Because of this, mathematics and science played a part in the early years of the university, but in general it was dominated by the classics, especially Latin, which remained the official language of the university until 1845. In fact, its dominance was so absolute that in order to meet the need for lawyers and doctors a special examination with a reduced amount of Latin had to be instituted in 1816; students entering in this way were called *Præliminarister* and regarded as second-class academic citizens. In the years that followed, the primacy of Latin and classical studies was continually called into question, as also in the context of the battle for the liberalization of the curriculum of the *Middelskole* and the *Gymnasium*, and when in 1869 students were allowed to matriculate at the university on the basis of an examination primarily in scientific subjects (*Realartium*), the battle against Latin had been won. However, the university continued, very much in the tradition of German universities, as a centre for the training of the official classes. Thus it tended to become identified in the public mind with the outlook of those classes and was seen, generally speaking, to be out of sympathy with the radical, popular, and national movements of the time. In academic and organizational terms the achievements of the university during the nineteenth century were not inconsiderable. When it began operations in 1813 it had only eighteen students. There was an almost complete lack of facilities and until 1852 it had to make do with temporary accommodation of a very inferior kind. By 1900 student numbers had grown to 1,400, having practically doubled in the last twenty years of the century. In scientific research the university had produced such internationally known names as the mathematician Niels Henrik Abel (1802–29), the astronomer Christopher Hansteen (1784–1873), the zoologist Michael Sars (1805–69), the mathematician and physicist Carl Bjerknes (1825–1903), and Cato Maximilian Guldberg (1836–1902) who, together with Peter Waage (1833–1900), propounded in 1864 the so-called mass-effect law for chemical reaction. In a more purely Norwegian context the work of the historian Peter Andreas Munch (1810–63) and the philologist Sophus Bugge (1833–1907) laid the foundations both at home and abroad for the study of early Norse history, language, and culture.

However, the most famous name of the period was that of Fridtjof Nansen (1861–1930), whose exploits as an Arctic explorer in the 1880s and '90s, and his later humanitarian work (see below, p.287), tend to overshadow his very considerable contributions to scientific knowledge. Both before and after he had accomplished his first Arctic feat, the crossing of Greenland on skis in 1888, he held academic posts in Bergen and Christiania. After his return from the *Fram* expedition (1893–96), during which he and Hjalmar Johansen reached latitude 86° 14'–further north than any previous expedition –he became in 1897 professor of zoology at the University of Christiania and in 1908 professor of oceanography. Nansen's books on his polar expeditions and accounts of the scientific work carried out on them, especially his *The Norwegian North Polar Expedition 1893–96* (6 volumes, 1900–06), added scientific renown to the popular acclaim he had received, but it was in the field of oceanography that he became a leading authority, publishing the results of his many research expeditions in *The Norwegian Sea, Its Physical Oceanography Based Upon the Norwegian Researches 1900–04* (1906).

# Chapter 3

# The Theatre and the Arts

---

*The Theatre*

THE COURSE THAT HISTORY HAD TAKEN in Norway during tne Danish period (see below, pp. 96ff) meant that there had been no royal or other princely patrons to support the drama or to establish court or private theatres. The theatrical history of Norway before the nineteenth century is therefore practically non-existent. We know that in the mid-sixteenth century the pupils at the Latin School in Bergen, under the direction of the humanist Absalon Pederssøn Beyer (1528–75), performed plays including comedies by Terence, a practice which became part of the educational activities of the school. Later, in the mid-seventeenth century, travelling theatre companies from Germany began to visit Norway. In the eighteenth century the greatest contemporary dramatist of the North, the Norwegian-born Ludvig Holberg (1684–1754), was writing and having his plays performed in Copenhagen, but none of them was performed in Norway until 1771 and then by an indifferent travelling company.

The real beginnings of the theatre in Norway date from the 1780s when amateur dramatic societies (*Dramatiske Selskaber*) began to be founded in the towns, the first in Christiania on 24 October 1780, and soon after other towns followed suit. In character these societies were exclusive social clubs, their members being recruited from the merchant and official classes. Generally speaking, only members were permitted to take part in their activities. However, they took their theatricals seriously and made great efforts to achieve proper standards. Apart from their immediate merit of keeping the theatre alive in Norway, the economic strength of their members enabled them to acquire suitable premises and equip them for dramatic performances. In Bergen the so-called *Comoediehuset* was opened in 1800 and did service as a theatre until 1909, during which period it was also the locus of the great renaissance in professional theatrical activity in Bergen in the mid-nineteenth century when it housed *Det Norske Theater* from 1850 to 1863 and *Den Nationale Scene* from 1876. It was here that Henrik Ibsen and Bjørnstjerne Bjørnson served their theatrical apprenticeships. In Trondhjem the theatre of

the local society dates from 1816 and is still in use, and in Fredrikshald (Halden) there is a theatre dating from 1839.

These societies had their most flourishing period between 1800
and 1830. From then on enthusiasm seems to have declined. One
reason may have been the increase in the number of Danish travelling
companies which began to visit Norwegian towns from about the
mid-1820s and to whom the dramatic societies hired out their halls
and theatres. The members of the dramatic societies seem to have
decided that the role of spectator was less strenuous than that of
performer; at all events, their societies gradually disappeared or
changed character.

The next phase in Norwegian theatrical history was in its initial
stage coterminous with the activities of the dramatic societies. In
1824 Johan Peter Strömberg (1773-1834), a Swedish dancing-
teacher, actor, producer, and man of many parts, who had spent
some time in Trondhjem and Christiania earlier in the century and,
more recently, in Fredrikshald, where he had been associated with
the dramatic societies, returned to Christiania. There he tried hard
to realize a somewhat grandiose plan he had earlier failed to achieve,
that of founding a 'National Theatre' with Norwegian actors. On
this occasion he gained support, founded a dramatic academy, and
on 30 January 1827 opened his own theatre with Norwegian players
and an orchestra under the Norwegian composer Waldemar Thrane.
To start with, the critics were tolerant of the efforts of his company,
but after some months criticism of his Norwegian players led him to
import a Danish actor and actress to strengthen it. This turned out
to be a step which soon led to the Danicizing of the theatre in
Christiania, for when Strömberg was forced to resign, mainly
because he had offended the anti-Swedish susceptibilities of the time,
the practice was intensified and was continued when theatrical
activity was transferred to the new *Christiania Theater* in 1837 after
Strömberg's theatre had been destroyed by fire in 1835.

The Danicized nature of the *Christiania Theater* soon became a
bone of contention between the two opposing factions in the intellectual life of the capital–the so-called Norwegian Party (*Norskhets-
partiet*), led by Henrik Wergeland, and the Intelligence Party
(*Intelligenspartiet*), led by J. S. Welhaven (see below, p. 225), the one
urging an early Norwegianization of the theatre, the other a gradual
building-up of a Norwegian dramatic tradition based on Danish
expertise. In 1850 the founding of the Norwegian Theatre in Bergen
and in 1852 of the Norwegian Dramatic Academy's Theatre (*Den
Norske Dramatiske Skoles Theater*) in Christiania–called the Christiania
Norwegian Theatre (*Kristiania Norske Theater*) from 1854–with only
Norwegian players, gave a tremendous fillip to the cause of a purely

Norwegian theatre. In the 1850s, too, Bjørnson in his capacity as a theatre critic inaugurated a campaign against the *Christiania Theater* culminating in a demand that no further Danish actors should be engaged. When this demand was ignored, he organized in May 1856 a demonstration against the theatre, which developed into a regular 'battle of the theatre', the so-called *Theaterslaget*. Though Bjørnson was not in any way fanatically *norsk-norsk* in his views and valued the contribution the Danes had made to the theatre in Norway, his action had a decisive effect. No more Danish actors were engaged and in 1863 the Christiania Norwegian Theatre was absorbed into the *Christiania Theater*.

From now on a purely Norwegian theatre got underway, though only in Christiania. The theatres in Bergen and Trondhjem had to close down and the *Christiania Theater* remained not only the sole theatre in the capital but also, for many years to come, the only permanent theatre in the whole country. The position of the *Christiania Theater* was still precarious, but thanks to gifted directors (among them Bjørnstjerne Bjørnson and the Swede Ludvig Josephson, who staged the first performance of Ibsen's *Peer Gynt* in 1876), the growth of Norwegian drama, and the emergence of a generation of talented Norwegian actors and actresses, it achieved some notable artistic successes. A decisive turning-point in its history came when Bjørn Bjørnson (1859–1942), a son of Bjørnstjerne Bjørnson, joined the theatre in 1885 as a producer. He had trained in Vienna and at the court theatre in Meiningen, and on his return to Norway he was determined to modernize the Norwegian theatre in all its aspects. This was particularly important at a time when the realist drama of the day was beginning to make new demands on production and on acting style, and when electric lighting, which Bjørn Bjørnson introduced into the theatre in 1886, added another dimension to theatrical production both in the use that could be made of the stage and in the lighting effects that could be achieved. In the theatre at Bergen, *Den Nationale Scene*, which had been reconstituted in 1876, Bjørn Bjørnson's work was paralleled by that of the writer and dramatist Gunnar Heiberg (1857–1929) who was director of the theatre for four years from 1884. In Christiania Bjørn Bjørnson's greatest service to the theatre was his agitation for a new National Theatre to replace the *Christiania Theater* and this led ultimately to the building of the present National Theatre which opened its doors to the public on 1 September 1899.

## Painting

Painting in Norway in the early nineteenth century was intimately connected with the general cultural renaissance of the period.

During the 400 years of Danish domination folk-art had flourished, but as with other art forms Norwegian painting as such had hardly existed. Its revival in the 1820s and the character it took on were due principally to Johan Christian Dahl. After studies in Copenhagen, Dahl settled in Dresden where in 1824 he became professor at the Academy of Art. He was, however, regularly in Norway on study trips to select material for his work, and from sketches he made produced his monumental paintings of Norwegian landscape on which his fame mainly rests. His work owed something to impulses from the Danish painter C. W. Eckersberg and to the German painter Kaspar David Friedrich, but Dahl's romanticism was both realistic and spontaneous in kind, and free from the metaphysical overtones of his German contemporaries. In paintings like *Stalheim* (1842) and *Stugunøset paa Filefjeld* (1851) he combined monumental sweep with intimate detail, depicting Norwegian nature as never before or since, and at the same time he established the mountain (*Fjellet*) as a symbol which was constantly to recur in Norwegian art and literature. In a different though related vein is the vibrant and deeply felt quality of his notable canvas *Bjerk i storm* (*Birchtree in a Storm*; 1849). Dahl's most distinguished pupil, Thomas Fearnley (1802–42) – his grandfather was an immigrant Englishman – was also the only other Norwegian painter of the period whose work bears comparison with that of his master. Fearnley was, however, a more cosmopolitan artist than Dahl. As well as studying in Dresden, he spent periods in Munich, Italy, France, and England. His most specific contributions to the movement of National Romanticism in Norwegian art were his paintings *Labrofossen* (1837) and *Slindebirken* (1839). The former work, which must be regarded as his masterpiece, was painted in England, where Fearnley also completed some other notable paintings and came under the influence of Constable. Fearnley's early death deprived Norwegian painting of Dahl's only heir of real stature and was a factor in making the type of landscape-painting which he had inaugurated in Norway short-lived.

Another and more important reason for this was the influence of the Düsseldorf Academy of Art, to which the new generation of Norwegian painters turned in the 1840s, where a more literary, formalized, and even theatrical type of romanticism was cultivated. However, even in this context it was given a specifically Norwegian and National Romantic character by the two most prominent names of this generation: Adolf Tidemand (1814–76) and Hans Gude (1825–1903).

Tidemand originally came to Düsseldorf, where he settled in 1845, with the idea of becoming a painter of historical subjects, but under the influence of National Romanticism turned his attention to the Norwegian peasant as a subject. Indeed, he came to dedicate his life to depicting Norwegian rural life in all its historical, cultural, and emotional aspects. His work, of which *Haugianerne* (*The Haugians*; 1852) is the most celebrated, has perhaps its greatest interest as a quintessential expression of the idealizing peasant cult of the period. Artistically, his virtues lie more in a capacity for narrative suggestiveness, characterization, and harmonious composition than in original painting ability. At times he could penetrate deeply into Norwegian folk-character, as in his study of a Norwegian peasant for *The Haugians*, and even show a comic talent in his picture *Katekisation i en norsklandskirke* (*Catechization in a Norwegian Country Church*; 1847); but by and large he was a popular rather than a profound painter and as such his work did much to promote an interest in painting among the public at large.

Gude, who also became a professor at the Düsseldorf Academy, and later in Karlsruhe and Berlin, was intimately associated with Tidemand and their names are as often linked as they are mentioned separately. But whereas Tidemand painted Norwegian folk-life, Gude devoted himself to the depiction of Norwegian mountains and fjords. In his later work Gude made a determined effort to break away from the idealizing and literary tendencies of the Düsseldorf School—his well-known *Brudefærden i Hardanger* (*Bridal Procession in Hardanger*) is a good example of this aspect of his work—and acquire a deeper realism, though he found it difficult to renounce the idyllicism which always hangs over his work.

The many other Norwegian painters of talent who received their training in Düsseldorf included the highly gifted August Cappelen (1827–52), whose Romantic forest scenes show that his early death deprived Norwegian painting of a potential master; Lars Hertervig (1830–1902), whose intense feeling for nature often took on a dreamlike character which reflected his own isolated existence and disordered mind; Johan Fredrik Eckersberg (1822–1870), whose painting *Fra Jotunheimen* (1866) is a good example of his capacity as a painter of Norwegian landscapes; and Amaldus Nielsen (1838–1932), whose work contains a realistic aspect which points towards the changed direction of Norwegian art in the 1870s.

The departure of Gude in 1862 from Düsseldorf to Karlsruhe also meant that Düsseldorf ceased to be the Mecca of young Norwegian painters. The growing importance of Munich in the 1860s as an art centre also attracted many Norwegians. Later, towards the end of the 1870s, it was to Paris that they flocked. This transitional phase is well represented in the work of Eilif Peterssen (1852–1928) and Hans Heyerdahl (1857–1913).

Peterssen started as a painter of historical subjects and achieved early success, especially with his canvas of 1876 depicting Christian II of Denmark signing the death warrant of Torben Øxe. He left Munich not for Paris like his contemporaries but for Italy, where he turned to painting outdoor scenes and developed a greater realism. It was in Italy that he painted his celebrated altarpiece *Hyrdernes Tilbedelse* (*The Adoration of the Shepherds*). After he returned to settle in Norway in 1883 Peterssen played an important part in helping to get the new realism accepted and it was during this period that he painted his masterly portrait of the writer Arne Garborg.

Hans Heyerdahl also had early success, with his *Adam og Eva* which he exhibited in 1878 at the World Exhibition in Paris. Soon after, he left Munich for Paris and his subsequent work included the notable *Døende Barn* (*Dying Child*), which was purchased by the French government, and many portraits and landscapes. Though he was one of the most gifted painters Norway has produced, he did not always maintain his best standard, and the later influence of the Swiss painter Arnold Böcklin on him was foreign to the real nature of his talent.

The 1880s were in many respects a watershed in the history of Norwegian painting. As we have noted, German influence was replaced by impulses from France. Young Norwegian painters now went to Paris to learn and admire, especially the work of painters like Millet, Corot, Courbet, Manet, and Monet. However, unlike their predecessors, this generation of Norwegian painters returned home to practise their art and to develop an indigenous school of painting. Like the writers of the period, their aim was the realistic but vivid depiction of Norwegian daily life in all its contexts and aspects. They produced few pure landscapes, though open-air pictures are common; but these are dominated by figures, even figures of well-known contemporary personages; literary, historical, and foreign subjects have almost disappeared from their canvases. There was also less concern for the formal qualities of a painting and earlier principles of composition were made to give way to the effective exploitation of a given slice of life. Their paintings and the social ideas which were either explicit or implicit in them did not find easy acceptance at the time but, as with the literature of the period, the sheer talent of this generation of Norwegian artists soon silenced criticism.

Three names stand out in this 'generation of the 1880s': Frits Thaulow (1847–1906); Christian Krohg (1852–1925); and Erik Werenskiold (1855–1938). Thaulow is principally noteworthy as the champion of the new art and as the leader of the artists in their battle against the so-called 'Art Society', a wealthy but philistine institution which purchased works of art for its members, a battle which was eventually resolved by an artists' 'strike' which forced the Art

Society to have their purchases approved by a committee of artists. Thaulow also founded an open-air academy where, in accordance with current principles, artists were to learn and practise their art in the open air. However, though Thaulow painted some notable pictures of winter scenes during the 1880s, he was too internationally orientated and epicurean in his tastes to remain at home in Norway. From 1892 he lived abroad and his later work is remote from the naturalism which he did so much to promote in his own country.

Christian Krohg, on the other hand, was never in doubt that Norway was to be the locus of his work. In 1879 he returned from studies in Germany and threw himself into the depiction of the poor and oppressed of contemporary Christiania. Not only did he believe that pictorial art should have a social mission, but he also had literary talent which he used from time to time to reinforce the ideas he had expressed on canvas. In a series of pictures he depicted social discrepancies and injustices, sickness and the tribulations of family life. In 1885 Hans Jæger's confessional novel *Fra Kristiania-Bohêmen* (*From the Bohemia of Christiania*; 1885), describing the Bohemian and seamy side of life in the capital, had been confiscated as indecent and the author imprisoned (see below, p. 247). In this affair Krogh was one of Jæger's warmest champions and as a riposte to official action he wrote a short novel *Albertine* (1886) depicting the decline and fall of a young Christiania girl and the horrors of police supervision of prostitutes. Krohg's book was also confiscated and he himself fined, but the book had considerable influence in mobilizing opinion against official attitudes. In the following year Krohg gave pictorial expression to the same theme in his masterpiece *Albertine i Politilægens Venteværelse* (*Albertine in the Police Surgeon's Waiting Room*), a picture thought to be too shocking to be looked at in its day but which has lived on while the novel is not much more than a literary curiosity. Krohg's other major work of social protest, *Kampen for Tilværelsen* (*The Struggle for Existence*; 1890) is artistically less successful, though, unlike the Albertine picture, it was an effective contribution to the social debates of the day. In spite of the vividness and sincerity of Krohg's work and its artistic merits, there was, perhaps necessarily, something literary, even propagandist, and at times sentimental about it. From the purely artistic point of view he was probably most successful in his pictures of life at sea and in his portraits, especially *Svart-Anna* (*Black Anna*; 1887) and *Frøken Krohg* (*Miss Krohg*; 1893).

Erik Werenskiold was one of the Norwegian painters who moved from Munich to Paris and then returned to Norway in 1883 determined to place the new realism he admired in a specifically Norwegian context. He joined with Thaulow and Krohg in the artistic battles of the time and became in many respects the real leader of the movement opposed to the Art Society. During three summers among the peasants in Telemark in south-western Norway, Werenskiold found subjects which fitted perfectly into his artistic programme. His realistic and unsentimental *En Bondebegravelse* (*A Peasant Funeral*; 1885) stands in sharp contrast to the idealizing and literary quality of Tidemand's pictures of peasant life and is a first-rate example of Werenskiold's capacity to depict folk-life, something which he also turned to classic account in his illustrations to the folk-tales of Asbjørnsen and Moe. Werenskiold could also at times be a painter of enchanting landscapes and he was one of the best portrait painters Norway has produced. He painted a whole series of eminent Norwegians, among them the notable portrait of Henrik Ibsen (1895).

Other painters of this period include: Gerhard Munthe (1849–1929), notable for his paintings of landscapes and peasant life from eastern Norway, for his 'decorative' pictures based on Norwegian folk-tales and beliefs, and for his illustrations to Snorri Sturluson's *Heimskringla*; Christian Skredsvig (1854–1924), whose two principal paintings, *Ballade* (1884) and *Siljufløiten* (*The Willow Flute*; 1889), reflect his interest in the Norwegian ballad and folk-life; Theodor Kittelsen (1857–1914), who after a number of years in Munich returned home, first to become a severe critic of society in his painting *Streik* (*Strike*; 1879), but who is principally remembered for his illustrations to the folk-stories of Asbjørnsen and Moe; Harriet Backer (1845–1932), the most distinguished female painter Norway has produced, who devoted herself to the painting of interiors and, especially after her return to Norway in 1889, to the interiors of churches; and Kitty Kielland (1843–1914), a sister of the author Alexander Kielland, noteworthy for her paintings of the peat-bogs of Jæren in south-western Norway.

Edvard Munch (1863–1944), the greatest painter Norway has produced, had already begun his career at this period. His work had its roots in the realism of the 1880s and, as his earliest pictures show, had an affinity with that of Krogh and Heyerdahl, but his own special individuality and intuition are also there. His notable portrait of the writer Hans Jæger (1889) revealed his capacity both for characterization and for evoking atmosphere, and already in 1886 with his picture *Sykt Barn* (*Sick Child*) he had produced, as has since been recognized, a masterpiece which, shunning the demands of detailed realism, achieved its effect by sheer painting power and sensitivity. In 1892 he made his stormy international breakthrough at an exhibition in Berlin where he also met other exponents of the art of the 1890s, among them the writers August Strindberg and Sigbjørn Obstfelder and the sculptor Gustav Vigeland. From this

period date the frankly expressionist works, *Vaaraften paa Karl Johan*
(*Evening on Karl Johan*), *Pikerne paa broen* (*Girls on the Bridge*; 1893),
*Skrik* (*The Cry*; 1893); the mysterious summer night and moonlight
paintings; and the paintings with a pronounced erotic motif like
*Vampyr* (*Vampire*), *Madonna*, and *Jalousi* (*Jealousy*). In 1896 Munch
had an important exhibition in Paris and during the years spanning
the turn of the century he completed a number of important works
like *Mor og Datter* (*Mother and Daughter*; 1897), *Rød Vildvin* (*The Red
Vine*; 1898), and *Livets Dans* (*Dance of Life*; 1899–1900) in which he
further developed his earlier themes. Munch also painted many
portraits and produced his first etchings and lithographs, and in 1902
he exhibited in Berlin the series of twenty-two pictures to which he
gave the title *Livsfrisen* (*The Frieze of Life*). Most had been painted in
the years 1893–95 (some of which we have already mentioned),
bearing titles like *Fear*, *The Cry*, *Melancholy*, *Jealousy*, *The Death Room*,
*The Death Bed*, *The Hearse*, and *Calvary*, in which he aimed, rather like
Vigeland in his *Fountain* (see below, p. 292), at portraying a synthesis
of life, though of a deterministic and pessimistic kind.

The social interest which had been prominent among the realists
of the 1880s had already given way, as we have seen in the work of
Munch, to characteristics which are also associated with the literature of the 1890s, among them the evocation of atmosphere, mood,
dreams, and the subconscious life of the mind. Halfdan Egedius
(1877–99), with his fine evocations of rural landscape, scene, and
mood, and Harald Sohlberg (1869–1935), whose major work belongs
to the twentieth century, are particularly noteworthy in this context.

*Sculpture*

Unlike the other arts, sculpture in Norway did not benefit from
the impetus which the National Romantic movement provided. In
fact, because of the decline, if not the virtual cessation, of church
commissions, the nineteenth century offered fewer opportunities
than the eighteenth century had done when the demand for orna-
mental altarpieces and pulpits had provided much scope for sculptural talent. Historically, too, sculpture had begun to be an independent art and not merely an adjunct to architecture. But
Norway had no royal house, nobility, rich patrons, or public
corporations of her own, to provide commissions. The technical
difficulties sculptors faced, including those engendered by an unfavourable climate, were great. It is not surprising that the art of
sculpture languished in abysmal conditions. Another factor was the
lack of any real sculptural tradition. Earlier artists had been carvers,
mainly in wood, rather than sculptors. Moreover, any Norwegian
wishing to train in the art had to go abroad, usually to Copenhagen

where the New Classicism as practised by the Danish sculptor Bertel Thorvaldsen (1768–1844) was the dominating influence.

One form of sculptural art that had been carried over from the eighteenth century, though on a reduced scale, was the casting of relief figures, statues, and statuettes, usually of heroes from classical mythology, used for the ornamentation of the iron stoves (*jernovner*) commonplace in Norway at the time. This tradition and the connection of the iron-works with sculptural activity is shown by the fact that the first sculptured monument to be raised in Norway, the memorial to the politician Christian Krohg in 1833, was cast at the Nes Iron-works, one of the best-known centres for the casting of reliefs and statuettes. But, in general, both the art of sculpture and its few practitioners in Norway languished. During the early nineteenth century virtually the only name the country could boast of was the Thorvaldsen epigone Hans Michelsen (1789–1859). Later in the century Julius Middelthun (1820–86) combined the virtues of contemporary classicism with a new realism, qualities which are seen at their best in his bust of the poet Welhaven, and in his statue of Anton Martin Schweigaard which stands outside the University of Oslo in the centre of the city.

Certain sculptors had already used motifs from Norwegian folk-life, but National Romantic tendencies are given much more notable expression in the work of Brynjulf Bergslien (1830–98), whose major work was, however, the statue of Carl Johan outside the Royal Palace in Oslo. Both in this and in the realism of his statue of the folk-tale collector Asbjørnsen, Bergslien's work exemplified and promoted trends which were characteristic of the period. However, the real break with the older classicism came with the younger generation of Norwegian sculptors and under the impact of the new French sculpture; from the late 1870s it was to Paris that they made their way. One consequence of this was the choice of dramatic themes combining naturalism with a certain theatricality. A good example of this tendency is *Volven* (*The Prophetess*; 1886) by Søren Lexow Hansen, virtually the only work we have from him. Much the same can be said of the so-called *Barbargruppe* (*Barbarian Group*; 1883) by a much more important sculptor, Stephan Sinding (1846–1922), and of other of his works. However, in his statue of an embracing couple, *To Mennesker* (*Two Human Beings*; 1889), he employs softer lines in a subject which was to recur in his work, where naturalism tends to be subordinated to compositional interest. Sinding's work also tended to be somewhat literary in character, but whatever criticisms one may make of it, especially of his statues of Ibsen and Bjørnson outside the National Theatre in Oslo, among his poorest pieces, he made an important contribution to Norwegian sculpture. The popularity he enjoyed in his own day did much to awaken an interest in sculpture and thus pave the way for the easier acceptance of the work of his successors. A number of other, more purely naturalistic, sculptors were contemporary with Sinding, like the portrait sculptor Jo Visdal (1861–1923); but with the 1890s came, as in the other arts, a development towards a more personal, inward, and spontaneous type of sculpture concerned with the depiction of the inner life, a tendency which in its transitional stage was often expressed in traditional or historical themes, as in *Helfærden* (*Journey to the Realm of the Dead*; 1897–1900) by Gunnar Utsond (1864–1950) and in Gustav Vigeland's *Helvede* (*Hell*). A principal influence in this development was Rodin, whom Vigeland knew and of whom Utsond was a pupil.

## Music

The development of nineteenth-century Norwegian music, like the development of other arts, owed a great deal to the impetus given by the National Romantic movement. Like the ballads and the fairy stories, folk-music had been preserved by oral tradition in the country districts and handed down by untutored vocalists and instrumentalists. Some of their instruments, like the *lur* (a birch-bark or bronze horn), the goat-horn (*bukkehorn*), the jew's harp (*munnharpe*), and the willow-flute (*seljefløyte*), were of great antiquity. The long-harp (*langeleik*) and the Hardanger fiddle (*Hardingfele*), a distant relative of the viola d'amore, were instruments of greater sophistication, the latter, then as now, being the national instrument *par excellence* and often played with virtuosity.

The task of writing down Norwegian folk-music, embarked upon in mid-century, presented problems of notation analogous to the orthographical problems which faced Asbjørnsen and Moe when they started to record the Norwegian fairy stories (see below, p. 226). The fact is that both the tonality and the intervals employed in Norwegian folk-music differed from those of the diatonic system. Quarter tones, modal tonality, and insistent dance rhythms all contributed to giving Norwegian folk-music its special and easily recognizable character.

The great collector of Norway's heritage of folk-music was the composer, organist, and musicologist Ludvig Mathias Lindeman (1812–87), who from the 1840s onwards published some 600 melodies and collected many more. However, Lindeman was not a particularly imaginative or subtle arranger of the material he had collected, rendering much of it in the form of four-part songs. It fell to other composers, principally Grieg, to incorporate satisfactorily Norwegian folk-music into art music.

Already in the 1820s Waldemar Thrane (1790–1828) had provided music with a 'folksy' colouring for H. A. Bjerregaard's play *Fjeldeventyret* (*The Mountain Adventure*; 1824). Later Ole Bull championed the cause of Norwegian folk-music, including the sponsorship of Myllarguten (The Miller Boy), a famous performer on the Hardanger fiddle, and himself composed the well-known, quintessentially Norwegian, melody *Sæterjentens Søndag* (*The Milkmaid's Sunday*).

The influence of folk-music entered more subtly into the songs, choral and piano pieces of Halfdan Kjerulf (1815–68), whose compositions are still performed in Norway and who must be regarded as the most important figure in Norwegian art music before Grieg. The life of his younger contemporary Rikard Nordraak (1842–66) was too short for him to add much to the corpus of Norwegian music, though he enriched it particularly with his songs, and achieved immortality in his native country by his setting of Bjørnson's poem, *Ja, vi elsker dette landet* (*Yes, We Love This Land*), which became the national anthem. Nordraak's enthusiasm for Norwegian folk-music and his belief that it could form the basis of an individual Norwegian art music inspired Edvard Grieg in his own highly effective efforts to bring it into the concert room.

Grieg's international breakthrough dates from a series of concerts he gave in London in 1888, by which time he had published most of the music which has made his name famous all over the world, including the piano concerto, the *Ballade* for piano, and the orchestral suites arranged from his incidental music to *Peer Gynt*. As a young man Grieg had determined to put the folk-music of his country, and, by implication, Norwegian nature and national culture on the world map. His melodious, harmonically exciting, and individual music fell on ears already made receptive to nationalism in music through the work of composers like Mussorgsky, Smetana, Dvořák, and others. But in the development of music during the nineteenth century Grieg was not simply a purveyor of piquant musical delights, but a composer who made serious contributions to the development of the art of musical composition and to whom many later composers, like Ravel and Delius (who set the poems of a number of Norwegian writers to music), admitted their indebtedness. Among his most interesting and typically Norwegian compositions are the lesser-known *Haugtussa* songs, set to poems from the verse cycle by Arne Garborg, and the highly original piano pieces called *Slåtter*. Grieg's influence on other Norwegian composers was, as one might expect, destined to be enormous and, as we shall see, the 'national' element in Norwegian music was its predominant feature, a feature continued in the twentieth century.

Johan Svendsen (1840–1911), who after Grieg was the most important figure in Norwegian musical life – together they dominated the musical scene in much the same way that Ibsen and Bjørnson dominated in the literary sphere – shared Grieg's ideal of giving Norwegian folk-music an art form which would bring it into the world's concert halls; his *Romance* for violin and orchestra is a good example of this. However, while Grieg, apart from the piano concerto, did so mainly in vocal and chamber music, and other smaller-scale forms, Svendsen attempted to show in his two symphonies, and more particularly in his four *Norwegian Rhapsodies*, that Norwegian folk-music provided suitable material for incorporation into larger works. Svendsen was much influenced by his three years of study in Leipzig and his work was also very much in the tradition of the German Romantic symphony as represented by Schumann and Mendelssohn.

Conditions for music-making in Norway in the early nineteenth century were, generally speaking, abysmal. During the period of the union with Denmark the only official support for music came through the Church and the office of *Stadsmusikant* (town musician), who had a monopoly within his district for the provision of music for weddings, funerals, festivities, and the like; the choirs of the Latin schools were also able to contribute to such music-making as there was. The real musical life of Norway at this period, as we have already noted, was to be found in the folk-music of the country districts.

In the late eighteenth century public and private music-making entered a more flourishing period. In 1765 the musical society *Harmonien* was founded in Bergen, in 1786 a musical society was founded in Trondhjem, and in 1810 the so-called *Det Musicalske Lyceum* was founded in Christiania for the purpose of promoting the cause of music. The well-to-do merchant and official families of the time also had their own private music-making and musical *soirées*, and the amateur dramatic societies which were founded around the turn of the century (see above, p. 48) made a contribution to musical life when they put on plays requiring music.

However, standards were, in general, low and the activities of the so-called Philharmonic Society (*Det Philharmoniske Selskab*), formed in the capital in 1846, did nothing to raise them. Attempts were made to get subscription concerts going in the 1850s, but they foundered after a couple of seasons, as did other concerts which the Philharmonic Society organized in the 1860s. It was not until 1871, with the founding of the Musical Society (*Musikforeningen*) in Christiania, and with Grieg and Svendsen as its musical directors, that an adequate orchestra was got together and serious orchestral concerts became possible. From 1899 the orchestra of the new National Theatre under Johan Halvorsen also added to the musical life of the capital. During this period, too, opera was heard more frequently in Christiania, especially during Ludvig Josephson's directorship of the *Christiania Theater* from 1873. Altogether, the decades spanning the turn of the century were ones in which Norwegian musical life came into its own. Naturally, this owed a very great deal to the prestige of Grieg, but the renaissance would have been impossible without the emergence of composers like Svendsen, Johan Halvorsen, and Christian Sinding (see below, p. 295), and of executants of international standing like the pianist Agathe Backer Grøndahl (1847–1907) and Erika Nissen (1845–1903). The Swedish-born opera-singer Ellen Gulbranson (1863–1947), well-known at Bayreuth before World War I, was domiciled in Norway from 1890.

# PART TWO

---

# The Span of History

# Chapter 4

# The Viking Age to the Period of Greatness

---

*Beginnings*

THE EARLIEST SIGNS of human habitation in Norway derive from the so-called Komsa and Fosna cultures. Both show the same general adaptation to the environment. The Komsa culture from the Alta area in Finnmark in north Norway tells of a people living on the coast and existing from seal-fishing at a time some 11–12,000 years ago when the ice of the last Ice Age began to melt. The Fosna culture which, it is now thought, is probably the older, takes its name from Fosna near Kristiansund and also included reindeer-hunters who operated in the mountainous interior in their area of the country. These cultures were essentially static in character, probably relying chiefly on bone for implements, and it was not until the early Stone Age, some thousands of years later, that a new culture developed. This occurred during the period of the so-called *Nøstvet-økser* (a kind of stone axe), named from the area at the south end of Bunnefjorden, an arm of the Oslo fjord, about 5000 B.C. However, the most remarkable archaeological evidence from this period is the sites which have been uncovered at Træna off the coast of Helgeland in the province of Nordland.

The development of agriculture in the later Stone Age (*c.* 2700–1500 B.C.) and of animal husbandry were linked with the arrival of immigrant peoples from the East who entered Norway at different points: firstly by people belonging to the Funnel-Beaker culture (*Trakb ger-kulturen*) and then by the Battle-Axe people (*Stridsøks-folkene*), noted for their elegant battle-axes, and the Boat-Axe people (*Båtøks-folket*), whose invasions had far-reaching consequences for Norwegian culture of the late Stone Age. At this period Norway had, in fact, two peoples and two cultures: the hunters and fishers, and the farmers. Intercourse between the two groups, often leading to a way of life combining both, led to changes and clashes in culture which gave Norwegian life many enduring characteristics.

The Stone Age in Norway was still in full flower when other, more southerly, countries had long since taken metals into use. The Bronze Age in Norway (*c.* 1500–500 B.C.) depended almost entirely on the import of bronze objects, mainly brooches and other ornaments, from

Denmark or Skåne in Sweden, areas which, by contrast to Norway, were rich in amber, a commodity they were able to trade for copper and tin from the bronze-producing countries. Bronze was expensive and Norway was a poor country. It is therefore of interest to note that most of the bronze finds in Norway come from areas known to have been settled principally by the Battle-Axe people, and we have in these evidence that their culture was essentially an aristocratic one. The most important feature of the Bronze Age in Norway was, in fact, not bronze but the further development of agriculture and animal husbandry, and the practice of the arts and crafts of settled life. Artistically, the period marks a development from the naturalistic rock-carvings, depicting people, animals, ships, life in its practical, warlike, and festive aspects, and the advent of non-figurative designs, all of which had a symbolic or religious value. The religious beliefs of Norwegians in the Bronze Age can also be deduced from their burial practices. While the people of the hunting and fishing cultures buried their dead in kitchen middens and the Battle-Axe people dug simple earth graves, the people of the early Bronze Age built burial mounds over carefully constructed grave vaults and placed food, drink, and other equipment in the coffin, a clear indication of a belief in life after death. In terms of social organization these practices indicate the existence of powerful chieftains; the work involved in building these burial mounds meant that only the elect in Bronze Age society could receive this treatment, people who after their death were worshipped as gods. The Bronze Age chieftain may have been both chieftain and priest; he must also have been rich; his riches were, no doubt, connected with the development of agriculture and husbandry.

Around 500 B.C. three factors had far-reaching consequences for development in Norway: the movement of Celtic tribes on the continent of Europe which caused Norway to be isolated from earlier cultural impulses; the climate which took a decided change for the worse; and the fact that iron came gradually into use.

The climatic changes meant that the standard of life sank to a very low level; many people must have perished in this cold period. Those who survived did so because they were able to adapt themselves to the changed conditions. This involved a radical change in methods of agriculture and husbandry. Real farms had to be created to secure the provision of fodder, winter storage, and shelter for animals, which hitherto had grazed outside all the year round. Such farms tended to be concentrated in areas where good grazing and feeding stuffs were most easily obtainable and the new situation also demanded larger groups of people and more co-operation between them. The grouping of the population into farmers and hunters and fishermen also tended to disappear, all of which led to a levelling of society.

In the early Iron Age in Norway little iron was in fact used; Norwegians still tended to use weapons and implements of stone in the last centuries B.C. and there was probably less metal in use then than in the Bronze Age. It was the extension of Roman influence that led to iron being brought into wider use. This shows itself in the number of finds, principally in graves, in the first and second centuries A.D., and gradually the Norwegians themselves learned the use of iron. From the fifth to the eighth centuries A.D. there are very many finds of iron, a rapid expansion which was mainly due to the large amount of bog-iron available in the country which anyone could learn to gather and smelt. As the study of farm names shows, the use of iron made a real agricultural revolution possible and this led gradually to the emergence of a class of well-to-do farmers. In fact these new farm units, and the increased social cohesion they brought, created nothing less than a revolution in Norwegian ways of life.

Farm names from this period seem to indicate that Norwegian farming families made up a society where each patriarchal head was as highly esteemed as his neighbour. Farm buildings were very large and each household included several families. However, from the fifth and sixth centuries A.D. there is evidence, in farm names and from sites which have been excavated, that social differences had crept in between farming families, particularly in the coastal areas where new land was in short supply. Trade was also an important factor in the development of a Norwegian upper class, especially through the trade connections with Denmark. Runic inscriptions in Norway which date from about A.D. 200 are also evidence of a development towards an aristocratic society. Cutting runes was a difficult art; their usage was subject to secret rules; and their supposedly magical power made them the preserve of a privileged minority. From A.D. 600 new influence of a more purely European type penetrated to the North and also to Norway. This was the Merovingian period, when the influence of Frankish culture made itself felt especially in western Norway. During the seventh and eighth centuries eastern Norway came under other influences which reached the country from south and central Europe via Sweden. This was the so-called Vendel culture, named after finds which have been made at Vendel near Uppsala in Sweden. The Vendel culture also seems to have been connected with historically known princely families of the North–at Uppsala in Sweden with the Swedish royal house and in Norway, through the mounds at Borre in Vestfold, with the Norwegian Ynglinger, the forbears of Harald[1] Hårfagre (Harald Fairhair).

---

[1] The Norwegian names of the early kings, etc., of Norway are given in their modern Norwegian equivalents.

The next step in the development of Norwegian farming society was one away from the large communal settlements towards the establishment of more individual farmsteads. The increasing use of iron was a factor which caused the number of farms to multiply rapidly, a development which soon had consequences for the organization of society. The *bygd*, or rural district, evolved and with it came the emergence of social institutions: first in the shape of central places of worship. Again, it is place names, either referring to the Norse gods or to heathen ritual, which provide evidence of this development. At the same time there was a development towards a more formalized legal system to replace the ancient practices of blood-revenge (*blod-hevn*) and compensation (*bot*); indeed the practices of law and religion were connected, in that to violate the proceedings of the *Ting*, or assembly, was a religious offence.

Further evidence of the development of social institutions is to be found in the so-called *bygdeborger* from the same period. Placed in a concealed position on the tops of mountain ridges, they were places of refuge and protection for the whole community; indeed, these *bygdeborger* may have served more than one *bygd*. Often they were associated with look-out positions from which a lighted beacon gave warning of impending danger to the neighbouring communities. Such co-operative measures inevitably led to the formation of larger social units which eventually covered whole areas of the country. These emerge fully in the next period–the Viking Age.

## The Viking Age

This period, stretching from a little before 800 to a little after A.D. 1000, is the most famous and turbulent period in Norwegian medieval history. It saw, among other things, Norse expansion overseas, the beginnings of Christianity, and the emergence of historically known personages. In many respects the Viking period was a continuation, at a greatly accelerated pace, of developments which had begun earlier. It owed much to the increased use of iron, the development of agriculture, and the emergence of legal, religious, and military organization over large areas of the country.

Viking expeditions set out principally from the coastal areas of Norway, particularly from the west, *Vestlandet*, and the south, *Sørlandet*, where the lack of good land for further cultivation had been a problem for some time. However, this fact only partly explains the Viking period. It was also a consequence of the rapid growth, in the country as a whole, both of population and of material prosperity. Norwegians had now acquired the means and the skills to exploit their natural resources more effectively, especially the use of bog-iron, a development to which improved climatic conditions may have contributed. Higher standards of living divided families into smaller groups with looser social ties, and at the same time they provided more scope for personal initiative. The Viking Age was, in fact, very much the age of the individual. Another factor of great importance was the vast improvement in boat-building techniques without which the Viking expeditions would have been impossible.

Land-hungry Norwegians living on the western and southern coasts of their country had a number of possibilities open to them: they could move eastwards, sail north, westwards, or to the south. But it was the route to the West, in the first place to Orkney and Shetland, that proved most attractive to them. In fact the Viking raids on the British Isles which followed were really a continuation of earlier Norwegian colonization of Orkney and Shetland.

According to the Anglo-Saxon Chronicle, it was in the year A.D. 787 that three ships of the Northmen came to England for the first time. Their occupants, it is recorded, responded to the sheriff who came to meet them by cutting him down. Later Viking raids on the east coast of England are described in more detail. For 793, the Chronicler records: 'on the sixth day before the ides of January in the same year, the harrowing inroads of heathen men made lamentable havoc in the church of God in Holy-island, by rapine and slaughter.'

Later, when they met with resistance, the Vikings turned their attention to churches in the Hebrides, in Ireland, and on the coast of Wales; and in 802 and 805 they plundered St Columba's monastery on the island of Iona.

However, it was not only plunder that appealed to the Vikings but also the prospect of new land for settlement. In the Hebrides and other islands off the west coast of Scotland, on the coast of Ireland, and in the north of Scotland, colonization followed rapidly and by mid-century most of the Celtic area was under Norse control.

Elsewhere the Norsemen carried their raids, often together with the Danes, to the continent, up the rivers of France, round Spain, into the Mediterranean, and as far as Constantinople, where they met with Swedes who had penetrated through Russia to the Black Sea. Towards the end of the ninth century the Scandinavian Vikings had encircled Europe, and in the North Sea and in the Baltic their mastery was complete. To the north and west they had colonized the Faroes, discovered and colonized Iceland and Greenland, and they had discovered America. At home, the whole of the Norwegian coast northwards round to the White Sea had been explored.

To Norway the foreign invasions of the Vikings brought wealth, material gain of all kinds, and the experience of older, richer, and more civilized cultures. By their victims the Vikings were regarded as a scourge, but historically their significance lies in their success as colonizers and in the organizational talent they brought to their newly-won territories.

In a sense, they were least successful in Ireland, though it was here their attempts at colonization cost them most dear. According to Irish annals and chronicles, Viking attacks on Ireland developed from A.D. 795 and by the second decade of the ninth century their summer raids on Ireland had become a regular occurrence. Gradually they established themselves there and in the year 841 Dublin castle was built by Torgisl, the overlord of the Norsemen in Ireland. Torgisl was succeeded in 853 by Olav the White who consolidated the Norse kingdom based on Dublin, and from here he harried the west coast of England where settlements were also made. Later members of Olav's family extended Norse sway to Northumberland with head-quarters in York. However, in spite of their position of power in Ireland, the Norsemen never really managed to settle the country and remained there as overlords in the areas around the towns of Dublin, Wexford, Waterford, Cork, and Limerick. Eventually they intermarried with the Irish and adopted Christianity, though they retained their special position within the ruling classes in Ireland.

On the Isle of Man, however, the role of the Norseman was different. Here, as placenames show, they stayed as settlers, especially in the northern part of the island. In fact the kingdom they founded on Man persisted, though at times under Scottish or English overlordship, until 1405 when the island submitted voluntarily to Henry IV of England. But even after that the Isle of Man retained its old form of government and its legal code. The Manx House of Keys, which goes back to Old Norse models, provides striking evidence of the capacity of the Norse immigrants to impose their own institutions on the island. The stone crosses found on the Isle of Man also speak of a mingling of Celtic and Norse cultures, for although these crosses were originally Celtic, they also came to include Norse motifs in their ornamentation and even runic inscriptions.

Orkney, on the other hand, was purely Norse – the island's original population having been completely eliminated – and from about 900 it was an independent Norse earldom. Later the Orkney earldom also included Caithness and at the period of its greatest influence, the Hebrides as well. The Norse community in Orkney was distinctly aristocratic in character, no doubt because of the proximity of the islands to Scotland and the military importance this gave them. Shetland and the Faroes, by contrast, were of much less importance both militarily and economically.

It was the Norse colonization of Iceland and their adventures beyond to Greenland and the eastern coast of America which provide the big story of this period. Traditionally, the settlement of Iceland dates from the year 874, though the island had been discovered some-what earlier and Irish monks had been there since before the year 800. Once it started, the colonization of Iceland proceeded rapidly and by the year 930 the whole island had been occupied. Fortunately, we have a very full account of the settlement in *The Book of the Icelanders* (*Íslendingabók*) by Ari Þorgilsson, about 1130, and in the *Book of Settlements* (*Landnámabók*), from about a century later. According to the latter there were some 400 settlers, but as this does not include the subordinate retainers of chieftains, the number of farm-steads must have run to several thousands. It is reckoned that some 15 to 20,000 people emigrated to Iceland during the period of the settlement. These included whole families, among them some thirty-eight chieftains with their families, tenants, retainers, and thralls. By acquiring large tracts of land and directing the settlement of others, the chieftains set their stamp on the settlement and its subsequent character. Many of them came from central *Vestlandet*, in Norway, but also from the Norwegian settlements in the Scottish islands and from Ireland. They controlled, in fact, small kingdoms in Iceland, later called *goðorð*, and they functioned both as chieftains and priests (*goðar*).

By the second half of the tenth century there were thirty-nine *goðorð* in Iceland, almost the same number as the original number of chieftains. The settlers soon found it necessary, however, to establish a common code of law and a central parliament to govern the affairs of the island. The Norwegian Gulating Law (see below, p. 74) was adopted and about the year 930 the *Althing* or parliament was established in Iceland. It was to meet every summer on the broad plain north of the Tingvellir Lake in the south-western part of the island. At it the *goðar* (nominally thirty-nine but actually thirty-six) were to constitute a court with powers to pass judgement and to legislate. They also appointed a Law-speaker to guide the court and whose duty it was to recite the whole of the law during the course of three meetings of the *Ting*. In spite of these arrangements, however, the real power continued to lie with the individual chieftains, and it is for this reason that the Icelanders attached such importance to the genealogies of their families.

The colonization of Greenland which followed Erik the Red's voyage of discovery along the coast about the year 980 was a much more modest affair. Here, the settlers, probably some two to three thousand altogether, were not powerful chieftains but modest farm-ers, who led the marginal existence which the more favourable climatic conditions of the time made possible. The Greenland settle-ment was principally noteworthy for the fact that it was from here that Leiv Eirikson and his men reached Vinland (i.e. North America), but the population resources they left behind them in Greenland were insufficient to carry colonization further.

## The Kingdom of Norway

The vigour and enterprise of the Viking Age had brought both wealth and new cultural impulses to the country and in so doing they had also set the scene for the emergence of a powerful leader capable of subduing the chieftains and the petty kings, and welding the country into one.

As the excavations made in Vestfold in southern Norway in 1904, when the Oseberg ship was dug out of its burial mound, showed, it was in this area that the seat of the greatest power lay. The material wealth and the high artistic achievement which the find revealed were evidence not only of the special position of Vestfold and its links with abroad, but also of the power of the Ynglinger family; it is generally supposed that the Oseberg ship was the burial ship of Queen Åse, wife of the Yngling king, Gudrød Storlatnes, and mother of Halvdan the Black (ninth century). It was from this family and from this background that the man of destiny, Harald Fairhair (Harald I), emerged.

According to tradition, the Ynglinger belonged to the same family as the Swedish Ynglinger in Uppsala, and had come to Norway through eastern Sweden and the upland districts of eastern Norway about a century before the Viking period began. In addition to their position in Vestfold they had also tried to retain power in the upland districts. One reason for this was the possibility of attack from Denmark, especially when, in the ninth century, Jutland had been formed into a kingdom and the Danes had secured a foothold in the areas at the entrance to, and at the eastern end of, the Oslo fjord. Such a situation may have set Harald to think of creating a kingdom for himself in Norway. Another factor was that the idea of Norway as an entity existed in the ninth century in the concept of *Norðvegr*, the North Way, that is the coastal stretch from Vestfold in the south to Hålogaland in the north. At all events, Harald moved northwards from Vestfold to win his kingdom, but the first certain evidence we have of this is in a meeting he had in the province of Trøndelag with Earl Håkon, one of the earls of Hålogaland, who was himself out on a similar conquering expedition southwards.

Conditions in north Norway at the time and the background which led to Håkon's southward march emerge from an account of north Norway given by Ottar, a Norwegian from Hålogaland, to King Alfred of England in the 880s, and included by Alfred in his Anglo-Saxon version of world history, based on the Latin work of Orosius. From this we see that the chieftains of north Norway had important trading interests in the south and that they also transported their goods to the south themselves. A safe passage along the Norwegian coast, which at the time was infested by Vikings, was therefore an absolute necessity. Thus the north Norwegians under the forbears of Earl Håkon found conquest southwards imperative. Håkon's family had come from the most northern part of Hålogaland (in the neighbourhood of present-day Tromsø), but his father had already penetrated far to the south and had established himself near Agdanes at the mouth of the Trondhjem fjord. Håkon's meeting with Harald did not, as one might have expected, lead to war but to a compact between them. No clear picture of Harald's later battles to consolidate his kingdom in the strife-ridden Norway of the time emerges until his greatest and most decisive battle at Hafrsfjord, in south-western Norway, about 900. Here he finally crushed the Viking chieftains and the petty kings, and established himself, says the scald, as the king of the Norwegians. Later, as if to emphasize his royal position, he married Ragnhild, the daughter of King Erik of Jutland.

Harald succeeded in maintaining his conquests, though he had to contend with rebellions both in Trøndelag and in Møre. He also attempted to establish his authority over Vikings outside Norway, and in 930 he concluded a pact with King Athelstan of England which was directed against the Vikings, both Danish and Norwegian. As a pledge of his friendship Harald sent a son, Håkon, to be fostered at Athelstan's Court.

Harald's success as a conqueror and, subsequently, in keeping the country under his control must have been aided by the Viking riches he had acquired during his campaigns. These enabled him to attract the best men to his service. Yet, although there is no authentic account of him, there seems no doubt that in that violent age his personal qualities were crucial to his success as a leader.

Before he died (c. 940) Harald had named Erik Bloodaxe (Erik I), his only son by Ragnhild, as his successor. However, once Harald's personal authority had gone, the kingdom he had created soon divided into petty kingdoms ruled over by his other (bastard) sons and by local chieftains. Erik Bloodaxe's reign was one of continual battle. Only in *Vestlandet* did he prevail and then not for long. Eventually, on the arrival from England of Håkon Adalsteinsfostre (the son Harald had sent to Athelstan), Erik fled to England. We hear of him in the winter of 947–48 established in York as king of Northumberland, where he was later killed in 954.

Håkon Adalsteinsfostre (Håkon I) or Håkon the Good, as he later became known, had better luck. He had been well received in Trøndelag and became king not only of that region but also of those to the south and west. At the time of his death he was acknowledged king over the whole coastal area, from Oslo in the south to Hålogaland in the north. Håkon tried to introduce into Norway the Christian faith he had learnt in England, but eventually had to give up the attempt. As a reformer in the fields of law and defence, however, he was much more successful.

The first steps towards creating an administrative and legal entity in Norway of more than purely local scope had been taken at a meeting in Gulen (then in the province of Hordaland) about the year 900, when representatives from Hordaland and neighbouring Sogn and Fjordane agreed that they wished to establish a common *Ting* and a common legal code. From their discussions the so-called Gulating Law was evolved, though it can scarcely have taken effect until Harald Fairhair had subdued the warring chieftains of the region, and it is likely that the final organization of the Gulating did not occur until Håkon Adalsteinsfostre's time. Håkon also extended the area covered by the Gulating, which later came to embrace the whole of *Vestlandet*. In Trøndelag, too, steps were taken to create a similar administrative and judicial scheme to replace earlier arrangements. These led to the establishment of the Frostating Law, named from Frosta in the heart of the Trondhjem fjord area. It is likely that the setting-up of this *Ting* also took place during Håkon's reign.

National defence was a factor of prime importance both in generating a sense of nationhood and in the formulation of legal codes covering large parts of the country. Earlier, petty kings and chieftains had had the right to call out men in defence of their territories, but with the consolidation of the kingdom, the situation had changed radically. Especially crucial was the question of the defence of the extended Norwegian coastline. This led to the setting-up of the system of *leidang*, i.e., the division of the coastal districts into areas, each responsible for the manning and equipment of a ship of war. Both the Gulating and the Frostating codes made provision for this, and, again, there can be no doubt that the credit for these new arrangements belongs to Håkon. He had good reasons for them. Although secure at home, he was threatened from without by the sons of Erik Bloodaxe who came over from Northumberland. Håkon defeated them, but they then turned to their uncle, the Danish king, Harald Bluetooth, for help. Harald Bluetooth had, in any case, designs on the old Danish territories in the Viken area of Norway at the mouth of the Oslo fjord. Håkon's first encounter with the forces of Harald was successful, but the decisive battle came about 960 when a large Danish fleet met him off Fitjar in western Norway. Håkon's forces were defeated and he himself was killed. His fall inspired the celebrated lay *Hákonarmál* by the scald Eyvindr Skáldaspillir.

Håkon was succeeded by Harald Eriksson (Harald II), called Greyfell, one of Erik Bloodaxe's sons. His reign had been inaugurated by military power and was sustained by it. He extended his sway to include the whole of north Norway as far as the White Sea and appropriated the revenues from these areas. He also did battle with old Norse paganism and plundered the temples of their treasures. Harald was not a popular man with the saga-writer who preferred his predecessor Håkon. Nevertheless, Harald's achievements were not inconsiderable. His qualities as a leader ensured that he remained sole ruler of Norway, though in the context of the times one might have expected that he would have been obliged to share the kingdom with his brothers. In the event relations with Denmark led to his fall. He had come to power with the help of Harald Bluetooth, but he had shown himself far too independent for the liking of the Danish king, especially by retaining control of the Viken area. Their differences did not lead to battle, but Bluetooth connived at his death, causing him to be killed in an ambush in Danish waters about 970.

Harald was succeeded by Håkon Sigurdsson, one of the so-called Lade earls of Trondhjem (a family originally from Hålogaland in north Norway). He began his reign practically as a vassal of Harald Bluetooth, with his authority limited to the western coastal area. Unlike his predecessor, Håkon strongly supported the heathen gods, This earned him the praise of the scald, but displeased Harald Bluetooth. Håkon may also in other ways have attempted to free himself from Danish overlordship. At all events, hostility developed between them and eventually Harald Bluetooth despatched a Danish fleet to deal with Håkon. The battle which followed at Hjørungavåg (now Livåg) in Sunnmøre resulted in a resounding victory for Håkon. He afterwards developed despotic ways which in 995 led to open revolt against him. He was forced into hiding and murdered by his thrall.

About the time of Håkon's death there landed a new pretender to the Norwegian throne. This was Olav Tryggvason (Olav I), the son of a former petty king, who claimed to be a descendant of Harald Fairhair. Olav Tryggvason had already acquired a great reputation abroad as a Viking chieftain and from about 980 had played a leading part in Viking attacks on England. During this time he had also enriched himself by sharing in the Danegeld which the English king paid in an attempt to buy off the Vikings. It may even be that the people of Trøndelag, dissatisfied with Håkon, had sent for him. In any case, they lost no time in hailing Olav as king in 995, and he was also soon accepted in *Vestlandet*, in Viken, and in Hålogaland; his influence also extended to the Norse colonies in the West. Olav had been baptized and confirmed in England, and he soon proceeded to Christianize Norway with a ferocious proselytizing zeal. In the south and west things went smoothly for him, but in Trøndelag and to the north, where pagan beliefs were deeply embedded, he had to resort to savage force. His preoccupation with Christianizing these areas caused him to lose his grip on other parts of the country, and this was to prove fatal when Denmark once more proved a menace. Svein Forkbeard, Harald Bluetooth's son and successor, regarded Norway as part of his own kingdom and allied himself with Erik Håkonsson, Earl Håkon's son, to win back Norway from Olav Tryggvason. They also succeeded in persuading the Swedish king, Olav the Tax Gatherer, to join the alliance. Olav Tryggvason, on his side, allied himself with King Boleslav of Poland who had recently subdued Wendland, the area south of the Baltic, and was thus at odds with the king of Denmark. The two opposing forces met probably in Øresund in September 1000, not at the island of Svold as the saga says, in a famous battle which resulted in a victory for Olav's enemies. The victors divided Norway among them and the kingdom which Harald Fairhair had created seemed to have been dissolved.

## Saint Olav and his Successors

It happened, however, that once again a man of destiny was at hand. He was Olav Haraldsson (Olav II), the son of Harald Grenske, a petty king under the Danes in Vestfold, through whom Olav could trace his descent back to Harald Fairhair.

Olav had been brought up in the eastern uplands of Norway on the estate of his mother's second husband, Sigurd Syr, a petty king in the area. He had gone off on Viking expeditions at an early age and had spent several years in England. He had also been in Spain and France. Future prospects abroad did not seem very enticing and Olav decided to try his luck at home. With the small company of men and the Viking riches he had acquired, he set off for Norway, making landfall at Selja in Nordfjord in the autumn of 1015. A lucky chance gave him some initial success on the west coast, but in Trøndelag opposition was too strong, so he made his way to the eastern uplands where he received support both from members of his own family and from other powerful men which soon gave him control of the area.

In Trøndelag Earl Svein (brother of Earl Erik Håkonsson), together with the powerful chieftain Einar Tambarskjelve, gathered forces to deal with Olav. The opposing sides met on Palm Sunday 1016 off Nesjar in southern Norway where, after a hard battle, the victory went to Olav. Later Olav extended his sway to cover *Vestlandet*, Trøndelag, and Hålogaland, principally by persuading powerful men in these areas, especially the well-to-do farmers, to become his henchmen.

A factor of importance in Olav's success was that the Viking period was now at an end; the emergence of powerful states meant that the Viking freebooter could no longer play the same role. Moreover, trade between Scandinavia and southern Europe had declined. All this meant that power in Norway came more and more to depend on the ownership of land at home, especially land of agricultural value. Thus Trøndelag became more important than *Vestlandet*, and the upland districts, formerly the back-of-beyond and hardly a part of Norway at all, now became, on account of their agricultural potential, an important part of Olav's kingdom. In this way the power of the farming aristocracy rose and that of the old warrior aristocracy declined. In the context of the administrative and judicial structure of the *Ting*, too, the farming class had a much more influential and central position than the old chieftain class. Thus Olav showed a keen sense of the political realities of his time when he chose prominent farmers and the younger sons of the old chieftains as his nearest henchmen. His own close connection with the farming aristocracy was also of great importance for the consolidation of his power, and the fact that he could reward his farmer supporters with grants of the land he had acquired in his campaigns completely matched their own aspirations.

On the other hand, Olav's efforts to Christianize the country were not kindly received everywhere. When he returned from England he was clearly determined to put an end, once and for all, to old Norse paganism, and with his bishop, Grimkel, and other ecclesiastics, who had probably come with him from England, he set about laying the foundations of church organization in Norway. To begin with, his plans went quite well, even, it seems, in Trøndelag; but in the upland districts which had been little exposed to missionary activity in the past, his attempts at conversion were resented and jeopardized the political support he received from the farmers of the area. In general, too, Olav's position was not as secure as it might have seemed. His age was one of change, a fact he had been quick to turn to his advantage, but the situation was still fluid and his kingdom had not been acquired without his making enemies, many of whom still held powerful positions.

Events abroad, however, were to prove fateful to him. King Canute the Great of Denmark, now feeling that his English kingdom was secured, turned his attention to Sweden and Norway. Canute was determined to gain possession of Norway, both because he regarded it as part of the inheritance he had received from his father and also because he wanted to consolidate his Norse empire. Morale in Norway was low at the time. Hardly anybody believed that Olav could prevail against the forces which Canute could muster; moreover, there were powerful factions which believed that they would have more freedom under Canute than under Olav. The killing of the powerful chieftain Erling Skjalgsson in an encounter with Olav in 1027 was also a decisive factor in reducing Olav's potential support when Canute appeared off Norway in the spring of 1028. His forces outnumbered Olav's by ten to one. In the face of such odds Olav gave up the struggle and fled with a small band of followers to his kinsman Jaroslav, prince of Kiev. In Norway Canute was hailed as king and he installed the Lade earl Håkon Eriksson to govern the country for him.

Earl Håkon died in the following year, the last of his line. On hearing the news Olav returned post-haste from Russia to recover his kingdom. But the support he was able to enlist on the way and in Norway was small. By 29 July 1030 he and his forces had reached Stiklestad in Verdalen in Trøndelag where they were met by a force of local farmers and others who had most to fear from Olav. This army outnumbered Olav's by two to one, and this was the decisive factor in the hotly contested battle. Olav was slain with most of his men.

However, an extraordinary change in the victor's attitude to Olav occurred almost immediately after the battle which, given the political situation of the time, had been an unnatural one. After the death of Earl Håkon, Canute had sent his own young son, Svein, and his concubine English mother to rule Norway. This the Norwegian chieftains found unacceptable, and after his death Olav's virtues were now seen. People also began to recall how signs and wonders had been seen at Stiklestad during his last battle and after his death. This feeling grew and on 3 August 1031 Olav was declared to be a saint, though he was never canonized, and his body placed in a casket on the high altar of the church of St Clement in Nidaros. After his death he became a symbol, *perpetuus rex Norvegiae*, and his memory kept alive the conception of Norway as one united kingdom for centuries to come.

Soon those who had fought against Olav at Stiklestad were openly opposing Canute's son Svein, and in 1034 the chieftain Einar Tambarskjelve and others journeyed to Russia to bring back Olav's eleven-year-old son Magnus. On their return in the following year, Svein and his mother fled and Magnus Olavsson (Magnus I), called the Good, was hailed as king of Norway.

Magnus's reign was to inaugurate a new and more peaceful era. When Olav's half-brother, Harald Sigurdsson (Harald III) called Harald Hardråde, returned to Norway in 1046, after having enriched himself in the service of the Byzantine emperor, Magnus agreed to share the kingdom with him in return for Harald agreeing to share his wealth, and after Magnus's death in 1047, Harald became sole king.

In the years following Saint Olav's death Christianity made its way imperceptibly and without further opposition as the religion of the country. Relations with Denmark also entered a new and peaceful phase, principally thanks to the death of Canute in 1035, and in 1038 the two countries sealed a non-aggression pact, an agreement which also provided that whichever of the two kings, Magnus of Norway and Harde-Knut of Denmark, survived the other should take over the government of the other's kingdom. This agreement was also the first occasion on which Norway had been recognized in Denmark or anywhere abroad as an independent kingdom. Magnus became, in fact, king of Denmark when Harde-Knut died in 1042, and he played a considerable part in defeating a Slav people, the Wends, who had invaded Denmark. But Magnus's right to Denmark was contested by a cousin of Harde-Knut, Svein Estridsson, and although Harald Hardråde continued the battle against Svein after Magnus's death, he eventually gave up the struggle. Harald also tried to establish by force the right to the English throne which Magnus had acquired as Harde-Knut's successor, but his attempt ended in his defeat and death at Stamford Bridge in 1066 in battle with Harold II of England.

The boundaries of Norway as they had been fixed in Saint Olav's time seemed to be definitely established. During his reign Harald had consolidated his grip on the eastern uplands and had extended his influence to the Orkneys. He had also asserted himself *vis-à-vis* the leading magnates and had had Einar Tambarskjelve killed to remove him from the powerful position he had enjoyed while Magnus was alive. Harald is also remembered as the founder of Oslo, which he intended should provide a counterbalance to Nidaros in Trøndelag. He even provided the town with a patron saint, Hallvard, a distant kinsman of his, who was murdered while protecting a pregnant woman and his body thrown into a fjord with a stone round his neck. The body refused to sink and this, it seems, was Hallvard's main claim to sainthood. Harald also increased the power of the monarchy by demanding that only he should maintain a *hird* (an armed body of retainers). He also developed the apparatus of government by appointing representatives throughout the country: *årmenn*, who ran the royal estates, and *lendmenn*, who themselves were usually landowners in their districts. Like other Norwegian kings of the period, Harald himself had to lead a peripatetic existence travelling from one royal estate to another, both to acquire the means of support for his Court and to dispense his royal functions.

Harald was succeeded by his sons, Magnus (1066–69) and Olav (Olav III; 1066–93), called the Peaceful, whose reigns were marked by peace, economic development, and progress in church organization, including the building of Christ Church in Nidaros, to which Saint Olav's body was removed, and which later became incorporated in the Cathedral of Nidaros. Olav also founded the towns of Bergen and Stavanger.

Olav's son, Magnus (Magnus II; 1093–1103), called Bareleg, succeeded to the throne on his father's death, but he had to share it with his cousin Håkon, until the latter died the next year. Magnus devoted his reign principally to bringing the Norse islands off the coast of Scotland and the Norse colony in Ireland completely under his sway. He succeeded in subjugating the Orkneys, the Hebrides, the Isle of Man, and Dublin, but he met his death fighting against the Irish in Ulster in 1103. His campaigns resulted in the Orkney earls becoming nothing more than the vassals of the Norwegian king, and the Church, both in Orkney and in the Hebrides, was brought within the orbit of the Church in Norway.

### Kings, Pretenders, and the Church

After Magnus's death, the law of succession that prevailed in Norway meant that the country now had three kings; his sons, Olav, Øystein (Øystein I), and Sigurd (Sigurd I), all of them minors. Olav died young and Sigurd went on a crusade to the Holy Land in 1107, during which he fought the Moors in Spain and took part in the conquest of Sidon. On his return to Norway he was dubbed Jorsalfarer (the Crusader). At home, Øystein had devoted himself to the development of the kingdom. He had improved its fisheries, its harbours, and its roads. He had founded churches and monasteries, including the Munkeliv monastery at Nordnes in Bergen, and had even erected hospices over the Dovre mountains for the benefit of pilgrims on their way to Nidaros. Relations with his brother after he had returned from the crusade were not always good, but peace between them was maintained. When Øystein died in 1123, Sigurd ruled the kingdom alone until he died in 1130. Some time before his death, Sigurd had received a visit from a man from the British Isles who called himself Harald Gillekrist, saying he was the son of King Magnus Bareleg and a Celtic woman. After he had sworn not to assert a claim to the kingdom while Sigurd and his son Magnus were alive, his claim was put to the test by his being led barefoot by two bishops over nine red-hot ploughshares. Three days later it was seen that Harald's feet showed no signs of burns and he was declared to be of royal birth. But, in spite of his oath, Harald (Harald IV), or Harald Gille as he was called in Norway, allowed himself to be hailed as king of Norway in competition with Sigurd's son Magnus. Magnus (Magnus III), later called the Blind, was obliged to accept the situation and for a time they ruled the kingdom jointly, but eventually strife broke out between them. After their first encounter in 1134, Harald had fled to Denmark, but later he returned, gathered forces, and fell upon Magnus in Bergen and captured him almost without a fight. Magnus was then blinded, mutilated, and castrated, and placed in the monastery of Nidarholm at Nidaros.

Harald Gille did not, however, enjoy the fruits of this savage act for long. In 1136 he was confronted in Bergen by a new pretender to the throne, Sigurd Slembe, who also claimed that he was a son of Magnus Bareleg. Harald gave Sigurd short shrift and, had he not succeeded in escaping, would probably have had him killed. Later in the year Sigurd returned secretly to Bergen and murdered Harald. He then succeeded in getting himself hailed as king in part of western Norway, but Harald's *lendmenn* had also arranged for his infant sons, Sigurd (Sigurd II) and Inge (Inge I), to be hailed as joint kings. When support for Sigurd Slembe dwindled, he released Magnus the Blind from Nidarholm, believing this would help his cause; but though Magnus received support, Sigurd was shunned and the two parted company. Magnus the Blind and his men were later defeated in an encounter with the supporters of Sigurd and Inge in 1137, after which Magnus was taken by his friends to Denmark. In Denmark Magnus's presence once again turned the thoughts of the Danes to the possibility of reconquering Viken, for which they had contested so many times before. But the attempt, made later in 1137, failed. Sigurd Slembe, who in the meantime had been in Orkney, now returned to Denmark and with the support of Magnus the Blind engaged in Viking-style raids on Norway. In 1139 they felt strong enough for a frontal attack, but after a bitter struggle Magnus was killed and Sigurd captured and done brutally to death.

After Sigurd Slembe's death, power devolved on the supporters of the child kings Sigurd and Inge, who were concentrated in the Viken area in the south, but in 1142 the people of Trøndelag made Øystein (Øystein II), another son of Harald Gille, king. As time went on, it became clear that many of the *lendmenn* in Norway wanted Inge to be sole king. In this they were supported by leading churchmen, partly because of the Church's views on marriage – Inge was the only one of the three kings who was of legitimate birth – but also because of the Church's general support of legitimacy, a policy which derived from her ambition to be a powerful institution independent of the will of the temporal power.

In the context of subsequent events, these ambitions were of considerable importance. A prime objective of Norwegian churchmen

was the establishment of an archbishopric in Nidaros. About the year
1150 this project was ready to be launched, and soon after, Reidar,
bishop of Nidaros, was consecrated archbishop by Pope Eugenius III,
but he died on the way home. Two years later the Pope sent the
English-born cardinal Nicholas Breakspear to Norway. As a result
Jon Birgersson was consecrated archbishop of Nidaros with ten bishops
under him, their dioceses to include the Hebrides and the Isle of Man,
Orkney and Shetland, the Faroes, Iceland, and Greenland. Church
organization was to be strengthened and the new arrangements also
defined the legal position of the Church *vis-à-vis* the state. Other provisions had as their object the making of the Church and clergy independent of the laity. It was also made possible for the laity to
endow the Church on a much larger scale than had hitherto been
possible, a measure intended to strengthen the Church's economic
position. A similar measure was the imposition of a tax (Peter's
Pence) payable to the Holy See. Other legislation, especially relating
to marriage, helped to strengthen the Church's position at the expense
of the civil power.

Another important consequence of Nicholas Breakspear's visit was
the calling-together of 'all the bishops in the country and the twelve
wisest men from each diocese'. Since the presence of the temporal
leaders at this meeting may be taken for granted, the 'twelve wise
men' must have been representatives of the *Bonde*. Thus this meeting
was a gathering representative of the country as a whole and the first
of its kind to be held in Norway.

These events helped greatly the cause of King Inge's party, but
they also helped to provoke the crisis which had never been far away.
Events were set in motion after a turbulent meeting of the three kings,
Sigurd, Øystein, and Inge, in Bergen in 1155, when, prompted by his
most powerful supporter, Gregorius Dagsson, a big landowner and
noted warrior from the south-west, Inge took up arms against his
brother Sigurd and Sigurd was killed. For the next two years Inge
maintained an uneasy peace with Øystein, but in 1157, he too was
killed. Even so, Inge's way to becoming sole king of Norway was not
clear. In the same year Øystein's supporters hailed Håkon Sigurdsson
(Håkon II), the ten-year-old illegitimate son of Sigurd II, as king,
and later Håkon was also accepted as king by the people of Trøndelag. In 1159 Håkon's forces were defeated by those of Inge at Gautelv
in the biggest battle Norway had seen for many years. But Håkon
escaped and he and his forces continued a threat to Inge. In 1161
they succeeded in killing Gregorius Dagsson in a skirmish and somewhat later they defeated and killed Inge in Oslo. Håkon was now the
only king in Norway and was hailed as such in Nidaros.

But Håkon and his supporters were not to enjoy power for very long. The party which had supported Inge now found in Erling Skakke, a son-in-law of Sigurd Jorsalfarer, a gifted leader. At a meeting in Bergen they agreed to continue the fight against Håkon. They found that Erling's five-year-old son, Magnus Erlingsson (Magnus IV), had the best title to the throne and hailed him as king. Erling then left with his men for Denmark to seek the support of his kinsman King Valdemar the Great. Valdemar agreed to provide the forces necessary to win Norway for Magnus and in return Erling promised that Viken should again pass to the Danes; it seems that he also promised that Valdemar should enjoy suzerainty over Norway as a whole. Battle between the forces of Håkon and Erling was not long delayed. Håkon was killed and Magnus, the son of Erling, was hailed as king of all Norway, though Håkon's men soon found a new pretender in the boy Sigurd Markusfostre, another son of Sigurd II. However, eventually he too was disposed of and at last Erling Skakke's party had the power fully in their hands. But difficulties remained. Magnus's right to the throne (through the female line) was dubious, and the promises which had been made to Valdemar about Norwegian territory were unacceptable to most Norwegians. It was at this point that the increased power and ambitions of the Church were to play their part.

The archbishop of Nidaros, Øystein Erlendsson, had been appointed by King Inge in 1157, though he was not consecrated, by Pope Alexander III, until 1161. The circumstances of his appointment by the temporal power were, strictly speaking, against the archbishop's principles and no doubt, in a sense, he resented this. But he was also alive to the realities of civil power, and as a member of a prominent Trøndelag family, he was not sympathetically inclined towards Erling Skakke and his son Magnus. But, in the event, he decided to do a deal with Erling. In return for giving the archbishop a free hand in the matter of church fines – in effect, through currency changes to double them – Erling secured the support of the Church for Magnus as king of Norway. At Bergen in the summer of 1163, with grand ceremonial, Magnus was anointed and crowned king by Archbishop Øystein.

This pomp and ceremony was something new in Norway, as was the concept: 'Magnus by the Grace of God, king of Norway'. In a statement which Magnus issued at the time of his coronation he declared that he intended to govern the kingdom as the deputy of Saint Olav and promised that at his death, his crown should be offered to Saint Olav and be placed in the Cathedral of Nidaros. There are a number of things here which are worthy of note: Magnus's anointing tended, and was no doubt intended, to obscure misgivings which still existed as to the legitimacy of his title to the throne; his statement that he held the kingdom on behalf of Saint Olav *perpetuus rex Norvegiae* implied that he was not holding it under the suzerainty of Valdemar the Great; nor, since Saint Olav was both a saint and Norway's eternal king, did it mean that Magnus was submitting himself completely to the Church.

Magnus's crowning was also used to lay down rules governing succession to the throne. In future there was to be only one king, the monarch's eldest legitimately born son, but with provision for the election of other candidates, the election to be carried out by a committee on which delegates of the *Bonde* were also to serve on a representative national basis. The old practice of choosing a king by acclamation at one of the *Ting* was to go. This meant in effect that popular acclaim would be replaced by appointment by a committee on which the lords spiritual and temporal would clearly have the main say.

Government was also to become more centralized. In legal matters the popularly appointed Law-speaker was to be replaced by *lagmenn* (law-men) appointed by the king, whose interpretation of the law, by virtue of the authority their office gave them, soon came to be regarded as having the force of judgement. The Church, too, was also to get her own ecclesiastical courts; she also attempted to assert the right to try all cases involving the clergy. Local administration, which during the period of civil strife had tended to degenerate into chaos, was now to be put on a new basis. Royal functionaries, *syslemenn*, took over the duties of both *lendmenn* and *årmenn* in certain districts, especially those which had been opposed to Magnus, and the loyal *lendmenn* were much more closely tied to the monarchy when they returned home than they had been before. An increase in the use of writing for the administration of affairs also made for the growth of a central administrative apparatus. In defence, too, the old system of *leidang*, which was little suited to the needs of land warfare, began to be replaced by a tax which the peasants paid in lieu of doing service. In consequence the armed forces tended to become more centralized, less connected with the people, and more aristocratic in character.

This grand apparatus of state was nevertheless doomed to failure. In the same year as Magnus's coronation, King Valdemar of Denmark began hostilities against Erling Skakke, who, eventually, was obliged to concede Valdemar the overlordship of Viken. In Norway itself rebellion broke out in 1165 and various pretenders to the throne staked their claims. In 1176 Øystein, a son of King Øystein Haraldsson, was acclaimed in Trøndelag, but he and his supporters, the *Birkebeiner*, so-called because of their use of birch-bark to make good deficiencies of their footwear, suffered a crushing defeat at the battle of Re (near Tønsberg) in 1177. But Øystein was to be succeeded by a man with an outstanding talent for leadership: Sverre Sigurdsson, who in a few years was to bring down in ruins the kingdom which Erling Skakke had built up for his son Magnus.

## King Sverre

According to his saga, Sverre was born about 1150 in the Faroe Islands, where he was brought up by the bishop of the Faroes, a brother of his mother's husband. Sverre was trained for the Church, but when he was in his early twenties, his mother came to the Faroes from Bergen, where she and her husband were living, and told Sverre that his father was King Sigurd Haraldsson. Doubt has been cast on this possibility, but it is clear that Sverre believed it implicitly.

At some time in the mid-1170s Sverre came to Norway and met up with the *Birkebeiner*. His and their odyssey from this point, their long marches through trackless forests, their battles, and their defeat and felling of Erling Skakke at the battle of Kalvskinnet near Nidaros in 1179, makes a story as fantastic as the circumstances of Sverre's own birth were enigmatic. It is clear, however, that after this battle Sverre was the master of Trøndelag and was accepted as such; in 1180 the archbishop of Nidaros, Øystein, fled to England from where he pronounced an anathema over Sverre. But King Magnus did not give up on the death of his father; he still controlled the major part of the kingdom and a superiority in forces and equipment. What he lacked were Sverre's personal attributes and his military talent; indeed, Sverre was probably the most capable military commander Norway had ever seen. He harried Magnus whenever possible and even penetrated his headquarters in Bergen, capturing Magnus's crown, sceptre, and coronation robe. But his most brilliant victory came at the decisive battle of Fimreite in July 1184 when, though heavily outnumbered, he inflicted a crushing defeat on his enemies in which Magnus and most of his followers perished. As was his practice, Sverre was magnanimous towards his enemies, though not many of them survived. In fact the old aristocracy which had supported Magnus had been decimated in his battles with Sverre. Their offices were now filled by Sverre's own men, many of whom had come up from the ranks of his ragged *Birkebeiner*. Many new faces appeared in the higher echelons of Norwegian society, but the social structure which Erling Skakke had imposed on it was consolidated rather than liberalized by Sverre's campaigns.

Many of the original *Birkebeiner* had been social and economic outcasts, often victims of the pressure on land which had been building up for some time. Though much new and often inferior land had been cleared and existing farms divided, there was still not enough agricultural living space for the rapidly increasing population. At the same time economic pressures often obliged farmers to mortgage or sell their farms to pay their debts, usually to big landowners or to the Church. Often they continued to work on their own farms as tenants, and thus the class of *leilendinger* (tenant farmers) increased rapidly. The outlook for the younger sons of independent small farmers and tenant farmers was bleak, and to join the ranks of the *Birkebeiner* opened enticing prospects, since they had nothing to lose and possibly much to gain. At the same time it gave them the opportunity of getting back at the rich. The economic situation in Norway was one in which the rich became richer and the poor poorer: big estates developed; the Church grew richer and was able to found monasteries and nunneries; there was sufficient surplus wealth to make possible the development of towns.

In the event, Sverre's victories did nothing to change this situation; his *Birkebeiner* merely took over from the men they had conquered. To begin with, after the death of Magnus, Sverre's government was of an authoritarian kind in which state and Church joined hands. Archbishop Øystein had made his peace with Sverre and had returned to Nidaros, but there were, nevertheless, serious underlying differences between them.

After Øystein's death in 1188 his successor, Archbishop Erik Ivarsson, at once took a tougher line, insisting that the Church should enjoy all the rights which had been established during the reign of King Magnus. The break between them came over the question of the size of the archbishop's bodyguard (*hird*). Sverre insisted that it be reduced to the number of men provided by law, and declared that if his demand was not met, he would proscribe all those members of the *hird* who were in excess of that number. At this ultimatum Archbishop Erik and his retainers left Nidaros and took refuge with Archbishop Absalon at Lund (then in Denmark). But the Norwegian bishops did not follow their superior into exile and in 1194 Sverre persuaded them to anoint and crown him king of Norway. In Lund Archbishop Erik excommunicated Sverre and later in 1194 Pope Celestine III excommunicated the bishops who had anointed Sverre.

The struggle between Church and state which now ensued reflected, in local terms, the struggle between Church and state which was a common European phenomenon at the time and which derived from Pope Gregory VII's claims for the freedom of the Church and her autonomy *vis-à-vis* the civil power. It also sprang from deep-seated antipathies towards Sverre's *Birkebeiner* who, in spite of the fact that Sverre's regime had consolidated the position of the landed classes, were still regarded by the old aristocracy as parvenus and jacks-in-office. This view was held particularly in Viken, where the depredations of the original *Birkebeiner* were still remembered, and uprisings against Sverre had been a recurrent phenomenon ever since he came to power; in fact, at times, rival kings had held complete sway in Viken and Sverre had been powerless to remove them. Although resentment against the *Birkebeiner* helped motivate these uprisings, they also derived from economic and social tensions which were particularly acute in this region.

It was in this situation that the *Bagler* party emerged, so-called from the Norwegian word for a bishop's crook. Their leader, Nikolas Arnesson, bishop of Oslo, was a clever tactician who had already taken part in an uprising against Sverre but had recanted. He had subsequently taken part in Sverre's crowning and had continued as bishop after the Pope had excommunicated the Norwegian bishops. In 1195 he went to Denmark and the next year raised a force of rebels which was to give the *Bagler* party power in eastern Norway for some twenty years. In Rome the new Pope, Innocent III, fulminated against Sverre and even urged the kings of Denmark and Sweden to take military action against him. Thus on all sides church resistance to Sverre stiffened and eventually all the Norwegian bishops deserted him. Nikolas Arnesson was quick to exploit the situation and skilfully mobilized religious zeal, social fears, prejudices, and discontent into a united opposition against Sverre. The whole of Viken and the eastern upland area came under *Bagler* control and even in other parts of the country their influence was strong. Sverre still showed all his old skill as a commander and as a clever propagandist, as his *Speech against the Bishops* shows, but his position was a difficult one and he was obliged to be on the defensive. The struggle between the two sides was still going on when Sverre died on 9 March 1202, but soon after, on the accession of his son Håkon (Håkon III), tension relaxed. Archbishop Erik and the Norwegian bishops returned and reached an agreement with Håkon. The Church was to be restored to her earlier freedoms and privileges, and in return she would render loyal duty to Håkon. But strife between the *Birkebeiner* and *Bagler* was not yet at an end. After Håkon's death in 1204, it flared up again and though peace was eventually signed between the two parties, Norway was governed from 1208 to 1217 as two separate kingdoms, each with its own monarch, Inge Bårdsson and Filippus. When both kings died in 1217, Håkon Sverresson's thirteen-year-old son, Håkon (Håkon IV), was accepted as king of Norway by both parties. Thus strife between *Birkebeiner* and *Bagler* was finally at an end, but peace between them had not come simply because of Håkon's accession. As ruling groups both were threatened by the less privileged. Already in 1213 the peasants in Trøndelag had risen in armed revolt against their *syslemenn* and had to be put down by force. In 1217, as a consequence of the agreements which had been concluded between

*Birkebeiner* and *Bagler*, the peasants in eastern Norway and Viken revolted. This time the dissident elements formed themselves into a group led by Sigurd Ribbung called *Ribbunger*, which operated with great success in eastern Norway, thanks largely to the support they enjoyed amongst the local populations who sympathized with their cause. But when Sigurd Ribbung died in 1226, the *Ribbunger* degenerated into a robber band and lost local support. Their last leader was, in fact, hanged by the peasants in 1228. At long last the age of civil strife seemed to be at an end.

## Period of Greatness

Against the background of recent Norwegian history, the choice of Håkon Håkonsson as king did not augur well for the peace of the realm. Håkon was of illegitimate birth and the claim that he was the son of King Håkon Sverresson rested solely on the evidence of his mother, Inga from Varteig, when, in 1218, she convinced the archbishop and bishops of the truth of her story by successfully submitting herself to the ordeal of carrying a hot iron without getting burnt (*Jernbyrd*).

There were also other possible pretenders to the throne, including Skule Bårdsson, a half-brother of King Inge Bårdsson, who had governed the country during Inge's last illness and had continued to do so after Håkon had been acclaimed king in 1217. At the same time, Skule had been given a third of the kingdom as his personal fief. The clergy in Nidaros wanted Skule as king; Skule himself had proposed Guttorm, the illegitimate son of Inge Bårdsson; but the *Birkebeiner* had insisted on Håkon. The *Birkebeiner* got their way and in 1223 Håkon's right to the throne was confirmed at a meeting of Notables in Bergen, though Skule still retained his third of the kingdom. In 1225 Håkon married Skule's daughter Margrethe, an act which was intended to set a seal on their friendship. Nevertheless, in 1233 Skule was relieved of his administrative functions, though he continued to enjoy the revenues of his fief, and in 1237 he was given the title of *Hertug* (Duke). But being deprived of power left Skule dissatisfied and goaded him into armed rebellion against Håkon, and in 1239 he was acclaimed king in Trøndelag. After a number of battles he and his forces were eventually defeated by Håkon, and Skule himself was killed in 1240. In 1247 Håkon was crowned in Bergen by a representative of Pope Innocent IV after long negotiations with the Holy See because of Håkon's illegitimate birth; at the same time the practice of *Jernbyrd* was abolished. In 1260 it was laid down by law that Norway should be governed by a sole king and that the king's eldest son should be first in line of succession.

In spite of its unpropitious start and Skule's rebellion, Håkon's reign lasted until his death in 1263, forty-six years in all, which together with the reign of his son Magnus Lagabøter (1263–80), constitutes the period in which medieval Norway achieved her finest flowering. Norway at last began to take her place in the community of European civilization and culture. Large sums were spent on the building of cathedrals and churches; artistic activities flourished; European fashions and manners were assiduously studied and followed; translations of French romances of chivalry replaced the old sagas; the so-called *Konungs skuggsjá* (*The King's Mirror*) provided a manual of polite behaviour and civilized conduct; administrative and legal practice was refined and codified; and the king of Norway entered into polite relations with his royal confrères in other European countries.

This cultural flowering was closely connected with the consolidation of the power of state and Church. Economic power had become concentrated in the hands of the temporal and spiritual upper class and it was their surplus revenues which made cultural advance possible. These advances were not, however, matched by an increase in the country's productivity. Thus it was the peasants who really paid. The number of independent farmers decreased; more and more farms were either mortgaged in whole or in part; and it has been estimated that by about 1300 only a quarter of the farming land in the country was actually owned by the peasants. The rest was held by the Church, often in the form of small parcels, or it was owned by the Crown or by other big landowners.

Nevertheless, the peasantry was not so depressed in Norway as it was in the other Scandinavian countries and in most of Europe at the time, nor were the Norwegian landowners independent feudal lords of the type known elsewhere. This was in large measure due to the nature of the country. Norwegian farms were scattered, villages did not exist, and rural communities were not susceptible of being brought under the sway of the lord of the manor or, indeed, of being protected by him. Castles, apart from those owned by the king and some of the bishops, were a rarity in Norway. A consequence was that Norwegian landowners had a greater feeling of common interest with their fellow-landowners and a greater attachment to the Crown than was the case in countries where the lord of the manor enjoyed far more local autonomy. It led in the thirteenth century to the Norwegian upper classes being drawn closely into the administration of the state.

One aspect of the period of greatness, which was also an expression of its inclusive aims, was the consolidation of the Norse empire overseas. In Sverre's time Jämtland in Sweden became part of Norway; Orkney and Shetland were in varying degrees under Norwegian rule; in 1262 Iceland accepted Norwegian sovereignty, as did Greenland.

It was, in fact, while returning from an expedition to assert his over-lordship over the Hebrides that Håkon died–in Orkney just before Christmas 1263. The battle of Largs, which had taken place two months earlier, and after which both sides claimed victory, seems to have been a petty affair–a sad anticlimax after the grandiose pre-parations which Håkon had made for the expedition and which autumn storms and unwilling conscripts brought to a disappointing end.

The legal reforms which culminated under Håkon's successor Magnus V, called Lagabøter (Lawmender), had already begun during the meeting of Notables after Håkon's coronation in 1247. The effect of these changes was to transfer legislative power from the local *Ting* to central civil and ecclesiastical authorities. In 1273, at another meeting of Notables, Magnus presented his new law book, which was partly based on earlier legal codes, especially the Gulating Law, but written in much more specifically legal style. In the follow-ing years this *Landslov* was given legal force at the *Frostating*, the *Gulating*, and the *Eidsivating* (centred on Eidsvoll in eastern Norway), and it was soon recognized as the official legal code all over the country. Concurrently with this *Landslov* a new *Bylov* (town law), which also superseded earlier codes, was brought into effect. Magnus also produced a new law relating to members of the *hird*. This law provided for a hierarchy among them, based on a European pattern, with titles including *Hertug* (duke), *Jarl* (earl), *Ridder* (knight), and *Baron* (baron). Each member of this hierarchy was to have his special privileges and had to take an oath of loyalty; and certain classes had the duty of maintaining and placing at the disposal of the king a certain number of armed men.

In legislation involving ecclesiastical matters some agreements had been reached between King Håkon and the Church at the 1247 meeting of Notables, and in the years immediately following we hear of agreement between the king and the archbishop on a new canon law. However, the Church was still dissatisfied with her legal position *vis-à-vis* the state, especially that the Crown had not renounced its legislative, judicial, and taxation rights in ecclesiastical matters. All this came to a head during Magnus Lagabøter's reign after Jon Raude had succeeded to the archbishopric of Nidaros in 1268. At a meeting of Notables in Bergen in 1273 the archbishop put forward demands relating to the judicial authority of the Church and also attempted to revive without success an earlier demand that the king of Norway should be elected and that the Church should have a decisive voice in the election. The 1273 meeting resulted, neverthe-less, in the conclusion of an agreement between Church and state under which both king and archbishop set their seals. However, complications ensued because of fresh demands from the archbishop and the agreement does not appear to have been put into effect. Later, further negotiations led to an agreement being signed in Tønsberg in 1277. Magnus acceded to many of the demands which the Church had made. In doing so he incurred the displeasure of the aristocracy, a situation which was to lead to open conflict after his death in 1280.

As a condition of crowning Magnus's twelve-year-old son, Erik (Erik II), as king of Norway the archbishop demanded that the privileges which (he maintained) the Church had been granted by the agreement of 1277 should be confirmed. The Norwegian nobility agreed to this, but after Erik's coronation they repudiated the concessions, saying they had been made under duress. They were, in fact, determined to maintain the supremacy of the state *vis-à-vis* the Church and excommunication by the archbishop did not deter them. Many of the privileges which the Church had been granted were now withdrawn, the canon law was revoked, and the clergy were required to submit themselves to royal authority or be outlawed. The archbishop and two of his bishops now left the country, but after Jon Raude's death a compromise was reached between the two parties in 1290. Nevertheless, the whole affair had left a legacy of anti-clerical feeling in Norway which was to persist for some time.

Another important feature of this period was the growth of the towns and of overseas trade. This derived in part from the emergence of a landowning class with surplus wealth to spend and also from an increase in the taxes which were paid to state and Church, much of which came in the form of farm products, skins, or fish, and from which there was always a considerable surplus for sale in the towns or abroad. Bergen had become the biggest of these towns and it was the only town with a trade, the trade in dried fish from north Norway, that was independent of the trade deriving from goods paid as taxation. This growth in trade had brought with it an increase in the merchant class (usually estate-owners) and in the artisan class. It had also led to an increase in the regulating activity of the state, as shown in the town laws of the 1270s. Artisans were required to live in certain areas of the town so that their activity might be controlled, and only those owning property or holding an important lease of property were qualified to become burgesses.

To begin with, most thirteenth-century foreign trade was with the British Isles, much of it being in the hands of the bishops and monasteries; the biggest trader of the period was, in fact, the archbishop of Nidaros. The principal carriers were merchants from abroad who brought with them (especially) luxury wares which they exchanged for the natural products of the country. This state of affairs was due both to the superior vessels which the foreign merchants were able to equip for the export trade and to their greater expertise in the conduct of business.

Towards the end of the first half of the thirteenth century Norway's overseas trade began to acquire a distinct bias towards the German towns along the Baltic coast, especially Lübeck. This followed partly from German expansion in this area and partly from an increased need in Norway for corn. The Germans had corn, but they needed fish, something the Norwegians could supply in abundance. The volume of trade became so great as to warrant special agreements between Norway and Lübeck. In 1250 these agreements were confirmed in a treaty. As time went on, the Lübeck merchants managed to acquire more and more privileges in Norway; they settled in Bergen and bought property there; and in a new treaty signed in 1294 even Norwegian law was revised to accommodate their demands. The fact is that Norway had now become completely dependent on supplies of corn from Lübeck, and any resistance to the demands of the Lübeck merchants led to their cutting off supplies which Norway was unable to obtain in sufficient quantities elsewhere. This development broke traditional links with the British Isles. Further, in drawing Norway politically towards the South and East, it boded ill for the future.

# Chapter 5

# Decline and Loss of Independence

---

## Norway in Decline

THE REIGN OF MAGNUS LAGABØTER'S SON, Erik Magnusson (Erik II; 1280–99), was undistinguished. He was succeeded by his brother Håkon Magnusson (Håkon V), a much abler man, whose destiny it nevertheless was to preside over the beginning of his kingdom's decline.

At the start of his reign Håkon had inherited a situation in which the authority of the monarchy over the nobles had declined. His brother, Erik, had lacked the ability to maintain the Crown as the central symbol of authority, and Håkon himself had brought with him the legacy of unpopularity he had acquired when, as Duke Håkon, he had been obliged to deal both with rebellious noblemen and with disgruntled peasants. Håkon was, nevertheless, determined to re-establish the royal authority. In 1308 he abolished the titles of earl and *lendmann* and withdrew a number of privileges which the nobility enjoyed. To achieve his aims he developed the central administrative and financial apparatus of the kingdom and established control over local administration. He also brought new men into his Council, especially from *Østlandet* (the south-eastern region) where he had particular influence, and he obtained the permission of Pope Clement V to reorganize the so-called Chapels Royal, which were to provide for the training, at schools established in Oslo and in Bergen, of scribes and others needed in the royal service. Finally, he built the fortresses of Akershus, Båhus, Tunsberghus, and Vardøhus, garrisoning them with well-trained troops as part of a modernization of the national defence. The fortress at Vardø was intended to be a bastion against the Russians and also a focal point in an attempt to establish Norwegian authority over Finnmark. This attempt was only partially successful, even after a border treaty had been signed with the Russians in 1326.

Håkon's achievement in adding to and consolidating the apparatus of state was not inconsiderable, but inner tensions had not been removed, and when they were coupled with tensions generated from without, the consequences were destined to prove fateful. Events in Sweden and Denmark brought things to a head.

Duke Erik of Sweden, a brother of King Birger, had become the unofficial leader of the Swedish nobility and also of a group of disaffected Danish nobles. To further his aim of consolidating the nobility of the North, he had sought Håkon's support. As it happened, Håkon needed at this time to assure himself of Sweden's goodwill because of a dispute with Russia. In 1302 his infant daughter Ingebjørg was betrothed to Erik. Two years later, however, Erik quarrelled with Birger and had to flee to Norway, whence he continued his Nordic intrigues. In 1318 Erik met his death at the hands of his brother, and Birger was swept off the Swedish throne. Duchess Ingebjørg (Erik's widow and Håkon's daughter) was left in power with Magnus, her two-year-old son by Erik, as heir to the Swedish throne. In 1319 Håkon V died and the child Magnus also inherited the throne of Norway. Later the same year Magnus was elected king of Sweden. It was agreed by both countries that during Magnus's minority each kingdom should be governed by a Council, it being understood that when Magnus had sons of his own, Norway and Sweden would get their own monarchs.

However, Ingebjørg, aided by a Danish knight, Knut Porse, still nourished the dreams her husband had had of a united Scandinavian kingdom and used her position to try and achieve this end. She aimed first to acquire the province of Skåne, then a part of Denmark. Their intrigues had disastrous financial consequences for Norway and, as a result, Norwegian Notables meeting in Oslo in 1323 agreed to put Erlend Vidkunsson, a leading nobleman, in charge of Norwegian affairs. He excluded Knut Porse from all power in Norway and pursued a policy of neutrality towards the two other Scandinavian countries. However, when Magnus (Magnus VI) assumed power in 1332, policies were abruptly changed. One of his first acts was to implement his mother's plan to acquire Skåne by means of a loan from Lübeck. Soon the nobles rebelled against Magnus's arbitrary methods of government and managed to assert their own authority. As a result Magnus agreed, in 1343, that his three-year-old son Håkon should become king of Norway and promised to hand over the royal power to him when he reached the age of majority in 1355. Soon after this the Swedes agreed that after Magnus's death they would elect his eldest son, Erik, as king of Sweden. Both in Norway and in Sweden it was agreed that the union between the two countries should then be dissolved.

However, before the end of Magnus's reign decline accelerated and developed rapidly into disaster. During 1349–50 the Black Death raged in Norway. It was a calamity of unparalleled magnitude for the country. The plague had been brought to Norway by a British ship in the summer of 1349 and spread rapidly over most of her territory. According to Icelandic annals two-thirds of the population of Norway perished from it, a statement which records relating to changed economic conditions seem to confirm. It has been estimated that even 200 years after the Black Death one-quarter of the farms in Norway were still deserted. The fact that it took Norway so long to recover was due to the preponderant role animal husbandry had played in Norwegian farming, and in consequence the difficulties of providing sufficient winter fodder for the animals when the labour force was so drastically reduced. This, in its turn, led to a dramatic drop in livestock and, as a result, famine conditions for those who had survived the plague. Another possible factor contributing to the slowness of recovery was a change for the worse in climatic conditions in the fourteenth century.

This painful recovery and the catastrophically depressed economy had far-reaching social and political consequences. It was now no longer possible for the economy to provide the margin necessary to maintain the upper strata of society and only a few very large landowners survived the catastrophe. While the Norwegian aristocracy had once been comparatively broadly based and had exercised their influence in local affairs, now it was the king's officials, the *syslemenn*, who wielded authority, often over very large areas. It was a situation which made both for less efficient and for more arbitrary government. The fact, too, that income from taxes was greatly reduced and that the king had arbitrarily and illegally imposed new taxes to maintain his revenues caused dissatisfaction which was directed especially at the local administrators. Available national funds were scarcely adequate for the maintenance of a skeleton administrative apparatus and there is evidence that even members of the royal family had insufficient to eat.

The Church in Norway, though equally hard hit, made a better recovery than the state. She was quick to reorganize on the basis of a reduced number of clergy and a reduced population. Her grip on the people had, in fact, increased as a result of the Black Death, and her international organization meant that her identity was not threatened by outside influences as was the identity of the state.

In the temporal sphere, not only was the monarchy half-Swedish but many of the leading aristocratic families in Norway had intermarried with the Swedish aristocracy, which often led to their estates falling into Swedish ownership. Thus it was not only the Black Death which led to the decline of Norway, but also the decay of Norwegian institutions which, as we shall see, led to Norway falling easy prey to the Danes in the sixteenth century.

Håkon Magnusson (Håkon VI) succeeded to the throne in 1355 as had been agreed, but it was some time before he was able to exercise authority over the whole country, and even when he did, his

Council as an organ of central power had none of its old effectiveness. It included not only Norwegians but also Swedes with estates in Norway and Danes who had been appointed to Norwegian bishoprics; foreigners also had important positions in the king's immediate entourage and his letters were often written by Swedes. Moreover, in spite of the measures which had been taken to ensure that Håkon was exclusively king of Norway, the idea of union between the Scandinavian countries persisted; indeed, at one stage (in 1362) Håkon was proclaimed king of Sweden. In 1363, as part of a settlement with King Valdemar Atterdag of Denmark, Håkon agreed to marry Valdemar's daughter, Margrethe; but a break with the Swedes put paid for the time being to thoughts of a triple monarchy, though Håkon had not given up his claim to Sweden. In fact, this claim later led to war with Sweden, which was still in progress when Håkon died in 1380.

In the meantime Olav, Håkon's infant son by Margrethe, had been elected king of Denmark in 1376 after Valdemar's death in the previous year, and in 1380 he also became king of Norway as Olav IV. He was then ten years old. No formal union was established between the two countries, but his mother exercised a dominating influence both in Norway and in Denmark. Like her late husband, Margrethe also had ambitions in Sweden. Thus it was a sad blow to her when Olav died in 1387 at only seventeen, since the whole basis of her power in the two countries rested on her position as the king's mother.

## The Kalmar Union and Danish Overlordship

The legal heirs to the thrones of Denmark and Norway were now members of the Mecklenburg family, but in spite of this Margrethe managed to retain power in both countries and get Erik of Pomerania, the five-year-old son of her sister, accepted as heir to both thrones. Erik (Erik III) was acclaimed king of Norway in 1389, but it was Margrethe who continued to govern; in Norway in Erik's name, in Denmark in her own. Sweden's turn came next and after a struggle with the Mecklenburgs (Albrecht of Mecklenburg was king of Sweden), Margrethe managed to impose her will. When peace had been concluded in 1395, her nephew Erik was hailed king both of Denmark and Sweden. Thus he was now king of all three Scandinavian countries. When Erik reached the age of majority in 1397, Margrethe called together Notables from all three countries to a meeting in Kalmar in Sweden where Erik was crowned with great ceremony. Afterwards, a document was drawn up providing for the permanent union of Denmark, Norway, and Sweden; but it was never given legal force.

Erik had followed Margrethe's policies while she was alive and continued them after her death in 1412. For Norway this had meant the virtual disappearance of any specifically Norwegian central administration. Power was concentrated in Denmark and Margrethe's policy in all three kingdoms had been to appoint foreigners who were completely dependent on her to occupy important positions, and otherwise to move her provincial governors continually from one post to another. Erik was a less gifted administrator and manipulator than his aunt. He also had warlike tastes and engaged for over twenty years in hostilities with the counts of Holstein over Schleswig. He also did battle with the German Hansa. All the time the Norwegians had to contribute to his war chest and received nothing in return except that in 1428 and 1429 Bergen was attacked and plundered by the Germans.

Dissatisfaction with Erik's regime first came to a head in Sweden in 1434 when Engelbrekt Engelbrektsson led a rising of peasants and miners against the tyranny of Erik's foreign administrators. Peasants in Norway soon followed suit and for similar reasons, but though some amelioration was obtained, the risings which took place in 1436 and 1438 were abortive. In fact, the Norwegian aristocracy who for a time governed the country benefited from the peasant rebellions rather than the peasants themselves.

The small degree of success which these rebellions had achieved was due in part to Erik's difficulties both in Scandinavia and abroad – he had been defeated by the Hansa and the Holsteiners, and by the rebels in Sweden over the succession to the throne. In 1436 he fled to the island of Gotland in the Baltic and there set himself up as a pirate. Finally he was deposed and Duke Christopher of Bavaria (a nephew of Erik) was elected king. In this situation the Norwegians showed great uncertainty, but eventually in June 1442 they, too, elected Christopher as king. Unlike Erik, Christopher was crowned separately in the three countries and no act of union was concluded between them. In each Christopher was very much in the hands of his Council. In Norway it attempted to curb the activities of the Hansa, which now began to have the same grip on Oslo and Tønsberg as it had on Bergen, but eventually, because of Christopher's financial dependence on the Hansa, the Council had to give in.

Christopher died in January 1448. In Sweden a Swedish nobleman, Karl Knutsson Bonde, succeeded in getting himself made king, and in Denmark Count Christian of Oldenburg was elected. Both monarchs now wooed Norway. The Norwegian peasants were, it seems, in favour of a Norwegian king for Norway, but the aristocracy, both temporal and spiritual, were very much Scandinavian-minded, and both the Swedish and the Danish kings had supporters in Norway. In the event, both were made kings in Norway; Christian was elected king at a meeting in Oslo in June 1449; Karl was crowned king in Nidaros later the same year. But eventually Christian's supporters and his forces prevailed and he was crowned sole king of Norway (Christian I) in Nidaros Cathedral in 1450. After the coronation a treaty was signed between Denmark and Norway in Bergen which provided that both countries should have one king in perpetuity, but that they should in every respect be equal in position within the union and that they should enjoy their ancient rights and freedoms and be governed by their own laws.

However, the members of the king's Council in Norway probably had no very clear idea of what the ancient rights and freedoms of Norway were. Its chairman was a German whom Christian I had made archbishop of Nidaros and other councillors were foreigners who had married into Norwegian families. Soon Christian was appointing foreigners to important positions in Norway and even deciding Norwegian matters at meetings of his Danish Council. Nor did he shrink from appropriating Norwegian funds for Danish purposes. In 1469 he pledged the old Norse colonies of Orkney and Shetland to the Scottish king, James III, as security for his daughter's dowry, a pledge which was never redeemed and the islands remained permanently under Scottish or British rule. It was also during Christian's reign that communication with Greenland was severed. From about 1476 there was no contact between Greenland and Europe for about 250 years. Iceland, too, because of neglect from Scandinavia, became during the fifteenth century dependent on the British and the Hansa for contact with the outside world. Norway lapsed more and more into feudalism; only the Church managed to preserve something of a distinctively Norwegian character.

Christian died in 1481 and in May that year the Danes elected his son Hans as king. The Norwegians were not immediately ready to accept him, but did so in 1483 after assurances had been given that Norwegian rights would be re-established and the activities of the Hansa curbed. Hans was more punctilious in keeping promises than his father had been. But, in the event, and in spite of a new economic, political, and cultural climate in the world outside, Norway did not benefit. The economy was still far too dependent on the Hansa, and the national will, vitiated by the many foreigners who occupied leading positions, was too feeble to take advantage of the new situation.

But the Norwegian spirit was not completely dead; once again, it needed events in Sweden to activate it. In 1497 Hans had had himself crowned king of Sweden by force of arms; but his reign was short-lived. In 1500 rebellion broke out and the Danes were forced out. This uprising and its success encouraged similar action in Norway led by Knut Alvsson, a rich and influential noble, who had himself taken part in the Swedish uprising. At one point it looked as if he would become the leader of a nationwide rising, but when Knut's principal opponent, the Dane Henrik Krummedike, managed to obtain reinforcements, Knut appears to have thought it advisable to sue for peace. It was during these negotiations, conducted under a flag of truce, that Knut and those accompanying him were treacherously murdered. As Ibsen wrote in his poem *På Akershus* (*At Akershus*), 'Knut Alvsson's death blow was a blow at Norway's heart.' After this the rebellion collapsed, though discontent continued to smoulder. Hans thought it advisable that he should be represented in Norway by the heir to the throne, Duke Christian.

Christian came to Norway in 1506 and soon set in motion a vigorous policy of Danicizing the country. He resisted all Norwegian claims to special rights and surrounded himself with Danish advisers and administrators. His rule was authoritarian and arbitrary, and intolerant of any sign of Norwegian nationalism. Attempts at revolt he put down mercilessly. But he did try to enforce control of foreigners in Norway, and in Bergen he gave Dutch merchants the same right to trade as the Hansa.

After Hans's death in 1513, Christian II again made it clear that Norwegians had no special claims to appointment to leading positions in their own country. However, Christian was himself very much in the hands of the Danish nobility. To counter this, he sought support and found advisers among the bourgeoisie. They included a Dutch-woman, Sigbrit Willums, mother of his mistress, Dyveke, whom he had met in Bergen. Christian's policies and personal conduct did not endear him to the Danish nobility, but relations with Sweden proved his undoing. Like his father, Christian was determined to bring Sweden under his sway and in 1520, after the so-called Bloodbath in Stockholm, he at last managed to break Swedish resistance and get himself crowned king. But, again like his father, his tenure of the Swedish throne was short-lived. Soon the Swedes were in revolt under the young Gustav Vasa. Lübeck joined them, and then the Juttish nobility rebelled and brought in Christian's uncle Duke Frederik of Holstein as king. In 1523 Christian fled and sought refuge with his brother-in-law, the Emperor Charles V.

In Norway, taxes had reached unheard-of levels to pay for Christian's war in Sweden and all government was completely in the hands of the Danes who had their orders from Copenhagen. Christian's fall was not an altogether unmixed blessing for the Norwegians. He had done his best to keep his tax-gatherers (against whom Norwegian resentment was focused) under control, and the advent of Frederik meant that the nobility were once again able to assert themselves. However, just at the moment when complete submission to Frederik seemed inevitable, a new Norwegian leader emerged. He was Olav Engelbrektsson who in April 1524 had returned to Norway from Rome where he had received Pope Clement VII's blessing as archbishop of Nidaros. Olav at once called together a meeting of the Norwegian Council of State to consider the election of Frederik as king of Norway. The Council agreed in return for certain guarantees, including safeguards for the rights of Norwegians.

Frederik fell in with most of these demands, but only because he himself was in a difficult position. But as he grew more secure so did his government in Norway become more despotic. Finally Archbishop Olav broke with Frederik, gathered together armed forces, and began negotiations with the exiled Christian II. Christian managed to equip a large fleet with Dutch help and in October 1531 made for Norway; but because of a storm, only a small part of his force reached Oslo. After an unsuccessful attempt to capture the fortress of Akershus, he was obliged to sue for peace and was captured and imprisoned. The Norwegians had no alternative but to acclaim Frederik (Frederik I) as king.

However, Olav's efforts had had some effect, for when Frederik died in 1533, the concept of Norway as a separate kingdom was still alive. Once again Olav called together the Norwegian Council of State and representatives of the burghers and peasants to discuss the election of a new monarch. In Denmark claims were being made on behalf of three possible pretenders, including the captive Christian II. Eventually, after a period of civil war (the so-called Count's War; *Grevefeiden*) the supporters of Frederik's eldest son, the Protestant Duke Christian of Holstein (Christian III), won the day. Olav was in a difficult position. He had hoped for a Catholic king and had believed that the Emperor Charles V would help Christian II's son-in-law, Count Friedrich of Pfalz, to win back his father-in-law's throne. But the tide of events was against Olav. In August 1536 the Reformation came to Denmark, the bishops were imprisoned, and Christian III ordered the archbishopric of Nidaros to be subdued by force. Olav mobilized his forces, but seeing that resistance would only lead to Norway being ravaged by Christian's army, he fled to the Netherlands where he died the following year. In a statement of October 1536 Christian III declared that Norway should in perpetuity form a part of Denmark under the Danish Crown as a Danish province.

### Norway – A Province of Denmark

Christian III's declaration about Norway's future sounded drastic, but this did not mean, of course, that the Norwegian way of life and Norwegian institutions suddenly ceased to exist; Norwegian law,

Norwegian judicial and governmental practice, and Norwegian language and culture remained. Political sovereignty had been lost and the Norwegian Council of State had been abolished, but this, in reality, was only the *coup de grace* delivered to an institution which, because of the weakness of the Norwegian nobility and now deprived of its ecclesiastical members, had little chance of being effective.

The imposition of the Reformation had more drastic consequences. Unlike other European countries, the Reformation had been little prepared in Norway. The country still lay on the fringe of Europe. Its population was still overwhelmingly peasant, conservative in its beliefs and customs, and it lacked the town bourgeoisie which had been the mainspring of the Reformation elsewhere. Thus it took some time to weaken opposition and not until after 1600 did the Lutheran faith begin to be accepted, though it took even longer before it gained a real grip on the peasant mind.

The introduction of the Reformation was also a powerful instrument in establishing Danish influence in Norway. The bishops and many of the clergy (especially as time went on) were Danish; the Bible, the catechism, and the hymnal were also in Danish. Together they were mainly responsible for establishing the hegemony of the Danish language. Christian III also appropriated church property and income, which he shared with the Danish nobles who had helped him to power. After 1537, for some time to come, the most important provincial governors in Norway were Danish. The administration of the two countries became more and more centralized and decisions on purely Norwegian affairs were taken in Copenhagen.

Dissatisfaction in Norway with Christian's government and with that of his successor, Frederik II (1559–88), soon led to peasant risings, notably in Telemark in the 1540s and in Trøndelag in the 1570s. Arbitrary taxation was the principal grievance and the peasantry were successful in their insistence that the principle embedded in old Norse law, no taxation without consent, be maintained. Indeed, peasant resistance to new taxes was as much, or even more, a question of principle than of the amounts involved. It did not, in fact, take the Danish kings long to discover that Norway had to be governed in her own way. Gradually she got her individual organs of government which gave her a considerable degree of political independence from Denmark.

Danish-Swedish antagonisms, which had been in abeyance while there had been a threat from the heirs of Christian II, were soon revived when Charles V concluded peace with Christian III in 1544, thus dropping the claims he had made on behalf of Christian II's heirs. Once again Norway was the bone of contention between Denmark and Sweden. In 1563 hostilities commenced between the two countries. The Swedes occupied the province of Jämtland and the Trondhjem area for a time, and later they extended their occupation to the whole of *Østlandet*. Norway had to suffer the ravages of the mercenary troops who formed the bulk of the armies. Eventually the Swedish forces were thrown out, partly thanks to Norwegian volunteers, though the peasants had resisted conscription. The war ended in 1570 without any territorial changes being made, but it also had consequences for the Danish attitude to and government of Norway. In 1572 a *Stattholder* (Governor-General), Povel Huitfeldt, was appointed for Norway with authority over the bishops and all other officials, and with the duty to hold so-called *Herredager* to hear complaints and to dispense justice according to Norwegian law, i.e., Magnus Lagabøter's *Landslov*. This had been translated into Danish and in 1604 was to form the basis of Christian IV's *Norske Lov* (Norwegian Law).

This changed attitude of the Danes was due partly to their fears of Swedish designs on Norway and partly to a changed Norwegian economic climate. It meant that by the end of the sixteenth century Norway had once again the appearance of a kingdom which, though governed by the Danes, was administered as a separate entity with its own institutions, with its law held in respect, and with its own aristocracy given due honour.

Norway had at last begun to recover from her period of decline and during the seventeenth century progress continued at an ever-increasing tempo. One sign of this was the rapid growth in population. It is estimated that in 1665 the population was about 440,000, whereas in 1500 it could scarcely have been more than 180,000. There was also a marked increase in trade, especially in timber, prompted by the invention of the water-driven saw and the need for timber in Europe, and in fish, due to the appearance of herring in vast quantities off the Norwegian coast. Mining, too, was also developed by the exploitation of the deposits of iron, copper, and silver in different parts of the country, and especially by the founding of the Røros copper-works in 1644 and the Kongsberg silver-works in 1624. The standard of living of the ordinary peasant and fisherman rose, though taxes increased and the class of depressed agricultural workers (*husmenn*) became significantly more numerous in the seventeenth century.

The bourgeoisie were responsible for the increase in trade and reaped the chief benefits. Trade had hitherto been very much in the hands of foreigners, but Norwegians themselves now began, to some extent, to come into their own, especially through the development of the herring industry. The power of the Hansa had declined and many Germans who had worked in Bergen under the aegis of the Hansa were now either obliged to become Norwegian citizens or did so of their own accord. However, other foreign merchants settled in Norway, so that the Norwegian merchant class still included very many foreign names. In fact, the king encouraged foreigners to come to Norway, for they brought with them much needed capital, expertise, and enterprise. Together with their Norwegian colleagues they made the bourgeoisie the most important social class. New trading centres also grew up, especially the so-called *Ladestedene*: Bragernes (later Drammen), Moss, Halden, Larvik, Arendal, and Mandal. This was the age of mercantilism when trade was encouraged, controlled, and protected by the monarch through the medium of privileges, monopolies, and customs dues.

This period of renaissance was presided over during the first half of the century by the energetic and temperamental Christian IV (1588–1648), himself very much a child of the age and the most active of the Danish kings of Norway. He visited the country thirty times, travelling as far north as Finnmark, and took a personal part in the administration of justice. He was also deeply committed to Norwegian economic development. He founded the towns of Kongsberg, Christiansand, and the new capital Christiania, which was built on a new site after medieval Oslo had been ravaged by fire in 1624. He injected life into the system of representation by Estates (*Stender*), which now included clergy and the bourgeoisie as well as the nobility, reorganized the administration, including that of justice, and provided the possibility of appeal to a *Herredag* over which he himself often presided.

But Christian IV's reign also had its other side. In 1611 he declared war on Sweden (the so-called Kalmar War) and demanded that Norway should conscript and equip 8,000 peasants. It ended in 1613 in Christian's favour, though the outcome had been decided on other fronts. Its importance for Norway had been to show the country's military impotence. During the years which followed, plans were discussed for making more satisfactory arrangements and in 1641 a new system of conscription was agreed on. This was just as well, for Sweden, now a great power, attacked Denmark in 1643. The Norwegian army, under the leadership of Hannibal Sehested, the Norwegian *Stattholder* and a son-in-law of Christian IV, acquitted itself well, but Denmark was defeated and at the Peace of Brömsebro of 1645 the Norwegian provinces of Jämtland and Härjedalen were handed over to Sweden.

The war had cost a great deal and taxes were high in Norway; even after the Peace of Brömsebro, Denmark and Sweden were still suspicious of each other and a state of military preparedness was maintained. All this led to a far greater degree of administrative independence in Norway including, for a short period, the establishment of a separate Norwegian treasury into which all the revenues of state were paid. All this owed much to the energetic Sehested, whose position depended very much on the authority he derived from Christian IV.

Christian's successor, Frederik III (1648–70), aspired to make Denmark and Norway an absolute monarchy. He had admired Sehested's autocratic rule and saw in it a model for his own personal rule in Denmark. He was, however, a clever tactician and did not wish to antagonize the nobility. Eventually he supported them in their demand for Sehested's removal. In the meantime the apparatus of state continued to be strengthened both in Norway and in Denmark.

In 1657 war broke out again between Denmark and Sweden. Once more the Norwegian army, this time under the Norwegian Jørgen Bjelke, acquitted itself with distinction and won back Jämtland and Härjedalen. But elsewhere the Swedish forces were superior and at the Peace of Roskilde in 1658 the Trondhjem area (*Trondhjems len*) and the province of Båhus, together with certain Danish territories, passed to Sweden. Swedish ambition for territorial gain was, however, not yet satisfied and later the same year the Swedes attacked again, but this time, with the help of a Dutch fleet, the Danes threw them back. The Swedes then turned their attention to Norway, but Norwegian troops won back the Trondhjem area and in the south at Fredrikshald (Halden) they resisted a prolonged siege by the Swedes who eventually, in 1660, had to withdraw. At the Peace of Copenhagen the same year, the Trondhjem area once again became part of Norway, though Jämtland and Härjedalen remained Swedish. The year 1660 was also, for other reasons, to be a turning-point in Danish and Norwegian history.

## Absolutism

After the end of the war the Danish Council of State called together the Danish Estates to discuss the reduced condition of the kingdom. In September 1660 representatives of the nobility, clergy, and burghers met in Copenhagen; the peasants were not represented and the nobility had as many representatives as the clergy and the burghers put together.

Though the nobility, through their membership of the Council of State, their governorships, and their ownership of land, still occupied a very powerful position, this was less than before; the Council of State had lost much of its old power, and the nobility's prestige had not been increased by their conduct during the war. Correspondingly, the power of the monarch, Frederik III, had increased and his personal courage during the war had made him more than ever a national symbol. He was warmly regarded by the burghers and the clergy, and strongly supported by them. Both these groups were also led by men of calibre; the burghers by the burgomaster of Copenhagen, Hans Nansen, and the Clergy by the bishop of Zealand, Hans Svane. The burghers in particular were intent on reducing the power and privileges of the nobility. In this they found a powerful ally in the deposed Hannibal Sehested, who, with Nansen and Svane, supported by other leaders of the burghers and clergy, proposed to the Estates that the monarchy should in future be hereditary. This was a proposal which, if accepted, would have deprived the Council of State of its power to elect the king and to impose conditions on his election. Naturally, it infuriated the nobility; but the king, after wavering for some time, finally came down on the side of the burghers and clergy. In July 1661, only a month after the meeting of the Estates was dissolved, a document was issued called *Enevoldsarveregjeringsakten* in which the monarch was made absolute. Representatives of the different Danish Estates were required to sign it. This they did, and in August 1661 the Norwegian Estates were called together in Christiania to sign the document and to acclaim the king as absolute.

The new system led to a far-reaching reorganization of the central administration of the two kingdoms. Affairs of state were departmentalized into so-called 'colleges', each with its president, but with the power of ultimate decision reserved for the monarch. Among other things a High Court replaced the old *Herredag* for the administration of justice. The new system was designed, both in theory and in practice, to make the monarch supreme and to prevent any one individual or department acquiring an overriding influence in affairs of state.

For Norway the new arrangements meant, in principle, that the country was incorporated into the administrative structure of the Danish kingdom as a whole, though in the *Kongelov* (Royal Law) of 1665 there was no suggestion that Norway was not a kingdom. Any form of separatism was, of course, anathema to the absolute monarchy, but Norway did get some institutions of her own. A High Court (*Overhofretten*) for Norway was established in Christiania to replace the *Herredag*, from which appeal could be made to the High Court in Copenhagen. Norway also had a *Stattholder*, as the monarch's personal representative, whose function it was to exercise a general supervision over the work of civil servants and state enterprises, and to send in reports to Copenhagen on the state of the economy. The administrative units in Norway were now termed *Amter* (counties) with salaried *Amtmenn* as their chief administrative officers, but with rather less authority than the old *Lensherre* and with no duties or authority in the military sphere.

The activity of the state grew continually and entered every department of life with an ever-increasing number of functionaries, and although more and more members of the bourgeoisie entered state service, it remained rigidly hierarchical. Though there were abuses, the Crown managed, by and large, to keep its functionaries under control, probably more so than in most other countries. The crying need of the state was for increased revenues to fill its empty coffers and to pay off the national debt. One means of doing this was for creditors to be paid by being obliged to take crown land at a very high valuation in payment, and much crown land in Norway was disposed of in this way. A new system of land taxation (*matrikkel*) was worked out for Norway and came into force in 1669, but although it was an improvement, it still contained injustices and caused taxation to fall unduly heavily on the peasantry.

In 1664 Ulrik Frederik Gyldenløve, the illegitimate son of Frederik III, became *Stattholder* in Norway. He soon realized that Norway's problems were different from Denmark's. She needed governing in a different way. In particular he believed that the peasantry, whom he regarded as being the heart-blood of the country, should be relieved from their heavy burden of taxation and be more protected from exploitation by officials and landowners. At the same time he believed that Norway's defences should be improved. However, it was not until Christian V became king in 1670 that Gyldenløve, who had returned to Denmark in 1667, was able to get some of his plans for Norway realized. Now he succeeded in getting the Norwegian army and navy strengthened and, to reduce the burden of taxes, the number of civil servants and the salaries of the highest-paid officials cut. In 1673 Gyldenløve returned to Norway, anticipating that war would break out again between Denmark and Sweden. When it did in 1675, his work to strengthen the Norwegian armed forces bore fruit. At the battle of Kvistrum in 1677 the Norwegian army scored an important victory over a superior force of Swedes. When the war ended in 1679, without any territorial changes, Gyldenløve returned to Denmark, where he continued his efforts for reform in Norway. In particular he urged the preparation of a new legal code for Norway and in 1680 a commission was appointed to prepare a draft. In 1687 their efforts resulted in the promulgation of Christian V's *Norske Lov* (Norwegian Law). Though in its final form this was not as 'Norwegian' as its authors had intended, it was a great step forward. The measures taken by the government in Copenhagen to protect the Norwegian peasants against the depredations of landlords and officials also reflect the influence of Gyldenløve's ideas. The taxes and duties which rested on the Norwegian peasantry were many and various, including the duty of military service and of providing hospitality and transport for officials on their journeys about the country. But most burdensome of all were the fees the peasants had to pay, especially to lower-paid officials, for services rendered and for which there were no fixed scales. In 1684–85 ordinances were promulgated, with the object of preventing the misuse by officials of their right to perquisites. Similarly, an ordinance was enacted to protect tenants from exploitation by landlords, which had become particularly acute after the transfer of crown land at high valuation to creditors during the period 1660–79. Like other good pieces of legislation passed during the period of absolute monarchy, its provisions were not always observed, but at least the state had made the position of rapacious landlords and others much more difficult.

The centralizing activities of the state extended particularly to the control of trade. Every town was given a prescribed area within which it was permitted to trade and competition between towns for the home trade was discouraged. Controls had the effect of hampering the natural growth and movement of trade in a period of rapid internal and external development. It was a policy intended to cushion the merchant class and, at the same time, because of the privileged position merchants enjoyed, to encourage foreign merchants to settle in Norway and to take Norwegian citizenship. These measures succeeded and many foreign merchants came to Norway, but although they became Norwegians, it did not mean that Norway had liberated herself from the grip which foreign merchants and foreign capital had on Norwegian trade. The root of the trouble lay in the lack of credit facilities in Norway for the financing of trade, but although Gyldenløve had proposed the creation of such facilities, credits were not made available by the government, who were quite content with the revenue from customs dues which increased trade was bringing in.

Soon after Frederik IV (1699–1730) succeeded to the throne, Gyldenløve resigned as *Stattholder*. The office was not filled, but also in 1699 Frederik Gabel, the son of one of Frederik III's ministers, came to Norway with the title of *Vice-Stattholder*. Gabel worked for a more independent position for Norway within the Dano-Norwegian kingdom, but the proposals he made for more autonomy were unacceptable to Copenhagen. The government did, nevertheless, agree to establish a central administrative organ for Norway which was to exercise a tighter control over the activities of officials and citizens than was possible from Copenhagen. The so-called *Slottsloven* of Akershus, established in 1704, was a body consisting of five members and invested with the same authority as the *Stattholder* had previously enjoyed; the *Vice-Stattholder* was to be its chairman. It constituted, in fact, a Norwegian government in embryo but, regrettably, Gabel died soon after it was set up and the other members were not of the calibre to assert its authority *vis-à-vis* Copenhagen.

One of the reasons that had induced the Danes to permit the setting-up of the *Slottsloven* was fear of war with Sweden. Sweden had possessions in north Germany which by their very existence were a threat to Denmark's southern border, but when the Swedes formed an alliance with the dukes of Gottorp, who had extensive lands in Schleswig and in Holstein, the peril increased. In 1700 Frederik IV decided that the time was opportune to attack these Gottorp territories, calculating that the Swedes had their hands full elsewhere. But the whole campaign misfired and it was only the intervention of England and Holland that prevented the Swedish king, Charles XII, from marching on Copenhagen. However, Charles XII's defeat at Poltava in 1709 and his subsequent exile in Turkey encouraged Frederik to try again, but he did not find it as easy as expected to crush what was left of the Swedish army. As part of this campaign it was intended that the Norwegian army should invade Sweden to draw Swedish troops away from Skåne, but owing to poor planning, nothing came of it and, in the event, some 5,000 of the best Norwegian troops were sent to Denmark to take part in the campaign there. In the meantime Charles XII was on his way back from Turkey, determined to conquer Norway as a substitute for the territories Sweden had lost in north Germany. In 1716 his forces invaded Norway and occupied Christiania, but they could not take the fortress of Akershus and were obliged to withdraw. Charles now turned his attention to the town of Frederikshald (Halden) and its fortress of Frederiksten so as to secure them as a base for future attacks. After a bitter struggle he took the town, but the fire-power of the fortress was too great for his forces and they had to withdraw. However, a Swedish fleet was on its way with the guns and ammunition Charles required for the siege. It was then that Peder Wessel Tordenskiold, the celebrated Norwegian naval hero, performed his most famous deed. With a tiny squadron of ships he sailed into Dynekilen (a short fjord off Strömstad in Sweden) and destroyed the Swedish fleet. Charles had to retire, but in 1718 he invaded Norway again with a new army and was soon besieging Frederiksten. The Swedes made steady progress and the outworks of the fortress were breached. But while he was on a tour of inspection Charles was struck in the temple by a bullet and killed (30 November 1718). Whether the bullet came from the fortress or from somebody on his own side has been a matter of continuing speculation. On his death, the Swedes lifted the siege and returned home. To the north, in Trøndelag, the Swedish forces under General Armfeldt which Charles had sent against Trondhjem, decided to retire, only to be decimated in the winter storms during a march over the mountains from Norway into Sweden. In 1720 peace was at last signed in the North.

The absolute monarchy in Denmark-Norway concerned itself with every aspect of the citizen's life and especially with his religious life. Strict Lutheran orthodoxy was the rule of the day. However, there were occasions, especially from the end of the seventeenth century, when economic and other worldly considerations coalesced with the concern of the state for the spiritual welfare of its citizens. This showed itself, particularly, in missionary activity in Finnmark in north Norway and in Greenland during the early eighteenth century. In 1715, during the war with Sweden, the government decided that something must be done to bring Christianity to the Lapps. Finnmark was an area that had long been disputed between Denmark and Sweden and the Dano-Norwegian kings had continually made attempts to establish their sovereignty more firmly over it. When the Swedes began to build churches in the area, the government were agreed that efforts should be made both to spread the gospel and to maintain Norwegian sovereignty there. A Norwegian clergyman, Thomas von Westen, was selected for the task, which was paid for by contributions from all the churches in the country. Von Westen was the leader of a group of pietistic clergymen, calling themselves *Syvstjernen* (The Pleiades), and he proved himself a missionary of genius. He spoke fluent Lappish and had an extraordinary capacity for making contact with the Lapps and for presenting Christianity to them in a way they could understand. The Greenland mission, on the other hand, owed its origin to Hans Egede (1686–1758), also a clergyman. He knew of the old Norse colony and was determined to bring the gospel to their descendants and to the Eskimos. To do this he enlisted the support of merchants in Bergen and in 1720 a Greenland Company was founded which was to exploit her fur-trading potential and, at the same time, to convert the natives to Christianity. Hans Egede was to spend the winter there and build a missionary station on the coast which could also be used as a trading centre. This he did, but as a trading venture the undertaking was a disaster and it took Egede eight years before he converted the first Eskimo. But he persisted with his missionary work and when he returned to Copenhagen after fifteen years, his son stayed behind. However, this missionary work in Finnmark and in Greenland gave little economic benefit to Norway, since a monopoly on the trade in both areas was given to a Dane.

Under Christian VI (1730–46), pietistic tendencies in the state Church became intensified. In 1735 a new Lord's Day Observance Act (*Sabbatsforordning*) was introduced, prescribing severe penalties for neglect of church attendance, though in Norway these regulations were not taken too seriously. Nor, to begin with, did the new Pietism have the same effect in Norway as elsewhere in northern Europe. The Norwegian peasantry were still very much rooted in their old, almost medieval, ways and continued to be so even well on into the nineteenth century. A more important consequence of the state's intervention in religious matters was the introduction of compulsory confirmation in 1736. This necessitated the provision of some form of elementary education and in 1739 an Education Act (*Forordning om Skolevesenet*) was passed. It was to apply both to Norway and to Denmark, but in Norway, because of economic difficulties and resistance from the peasantry, the provisions of the Act were slow to take effect. In general, instruction was organized in the form of *Omgangskoler*, schools with the teacher going from farm to farm to take classes. It was intended that children between the ages of seven and twelve should attend school for from six to nine months of the year and receive instruction in religious knowledge and reading. In places where the provisions were put into effect they also learnt, in most cases, writing and some arithmetic.

During the first half of the eighteenth century the centralizing tendencies of the state were intensified to concentrate trade more and more in Copenhagen. In the past, the government had insisted on the towns as the centres of trade, Now it was the capital, Copenhagen, which was to be given overriding commercial importance. Trade was to be organized in large companies, supported by the government, each with its monopoly over a given area. Copenhagen was also to be a centre of the transit trade for the Baltic and an entrepôt for the import of certain goods for internal use; here they would attract much lower customs dues. Later, certain Norwegian towns were also given this particular privilege. The same centralizing tendency also showed itself in the organization of industry, in that the considerable sums set aside by the government to subsidize the manufacturing industries were used to support industry in Copenhagen, where it was also protected by customs barriers and monopolies. Norway was, of course, brought into this trading system and, as a consequence, the favourable tariffs accorded to Danish goods hindered the free development of trade between Norway and foreign countries. The lack of capital and credit facilities was also a continuing problem in Norway and when Denmark got her own issue-bank in 1736, it did little to ease the Norwegian credit situation. Proposals that Norway should get her own bank were rejected in Copenhagen.

The central government's corn policy also affected Norway adversely. The import duty on foreign corn had always been high, but in 1735 a ban was imposed on the import of any foreign corn to southern Norway. This meant, in effect, that the cost of living in Norway was increased for the benefit of the Danish landowners and the Danish merchants and shipowners who controlled the export of corn. On the other hand, Norwegian iron was given a monopoly of the Danish market, but if it exceeded a certain price, the Danes were permitted to import from Sweden, a provision which did not apply to Norwegian imports of corn from Denmark, where there was no maximum price. The whole policy of turning Copenhagen into an entrepôt adversely affected Norway, where it had been usual and natural to trade with those countries which took Norwegian exports. In fact trade with foreign countries was much more important to Norway than internal trade, and a further consequence of the central government's policy was that a decrease of imports into Norway naturally led to a decrease in exports.

A further feature of government during this period of mercantilism was the measures taken to ensure that raw materials were, as far as possible, processed at home. In Norway this led to the setting-up of a number of small factories. In particular, the processing of salt was encouraged and, more important, the manufacture of glass, which led to the founding of the well-known Hadeland glass factory in 1765.

Christian VI continued his father's policy of keeping his civil servants well under control and of severely punishing corruption and dereliction of duty. Nevertheless, the power of the bureaucracy grew and in Norway the post of *Stattholder*, which had become less effective, was abolished in 1739, thus removing the monarch's personal representative. After Christian's death in 1746, power passed completely to the civil service. Both Christian's successors, Frederik V (1746–66) and Christian VII (1766–1808), were incapable of effective government; Christian VII soon lapsed into insanity. During the first half of the eighteenth century the Danish civil service had been recruited principally from Germany and now some of its most powerful members, such as A. Moltke and J. H. E. Bernstorff, were Germans. Few of them understood the special problems of Norway and these were often overlooked. However, a *Vice-Stattholder* for Norway was appointed in 1750 to redress this situation, but even he could not prevent the government from pursuing a taxation policy which was so much resented that in 1765 it led to the so-called *Strilekrigen*, an uprising of fishermen and small farmers in the Bergen area. This was the most serious challenge to the authority of the government during the absolutist period.

In 1762, because of Denmark's serious financial situation, direct taxation over the whole kingdom was drastically increased, to twice its previous level. In Norway, both the method of calculating this increased taxation and the means used to collect it led to great dissatisfaction and hardship, especially among the small farmers and fishermen along the west coast. In March 1765 they gathered in Bergen to protest to the provincial governor and, failing to obtain satisfaction, took matters into their own hands. The uprising did not amount to much more than a riot, but the government sent out troops, severely punished the ringleaders, and insisted on the taxes being paid. Nevertheless, they did learn the lesson of the episode and subsequently sent abler civil servants to Norway so that they might be better informed on Norwegian conditions.

Towards the end of the 1760s power in Denmark had been gained by Johann Friedrich Struensee, a German from Halle and personal physician to Christian VII. Struensee was dedicated to the ideals of the French encyclopaedists and a firm believer in autocratic government, provided it served the cause of equality and freedom. He drastically reorganized the administrative machinery, keeping the direction of affairs in his own and a small cabinet's hands. The affairs of Norway and Iceland he assigned to a separate department of state, which meant that they were likely to receive more skilled and knowledgeable attention than they had in the past. In economic matters he was a physiocrat, believing in full freedom for trade and industry. Thus he was opposed to the prevailing system of privileges, monopolies, and state support. Among other things he abolished the Danish corn monopoly in Norway. He also instituted freedom of the press and passed other measures in line with the spirit of the Enlightenment. Struensee's many and rapid reforms naturally made him enemies and his liaison with Caroline Mathilde, the queen of the deranged Christian VII, scandalized the country. He fell from power as a result of a conspiracy in January 1772, was imprisoned, and soon afterwards executed.

## National Resurgence and European Embroilment

The late eighteenth century was a period of increasing Norwegian national awareness and economic growth. One of the objects of the Royal Society which had been founded in Trondhjem was to promote the writing of Norwegian history, and one of its founders, J. E. Gunnerus, also worked for the founding of a Norwegian university. In Christiania the demand was put forward for a Norwegian bank. These and many other ideas were discussed and written about. The freedom granted to the press released a flood of pamphlets and articles, many of them critical of the union between Norway and Denmark and the constraints it placed on Norwegian development. Even in Denmark, especially in the wake of anti-German feeling after Struensee's fall, admiring voices were raised in praise of the steadfast Norwegians, of whom the *Odelsbonde* (yeoman farmer) became the type.

This new confidence had as its background Norway's general economic growth. One aspect of this was the growth of population. In 1665 it was roughly 440,000, in 1723 it was 530,000, in 1769 it had risen to 723,618, and by 1801 it was 883,487. In particular the towns grew rapidly, from a total population of 30,000 in 1665 to 77,545 in 1801. However, the majority of the population still lived in the country and the way of life of the rural dwellers, like their agricultural methods, had not changed much over the centuries. Little had been done to improve the yield of the soil and when bad years came, it meant starvation for both man and beast. The well-meaning efforts of some members of the official classes to introduce more rational and intensive methods of agriculture had not had much success with the mass of the peasantry. Another feature of the development of rural life in eighteenth-century Norway was the increase in the number of *husmenn* (smallholders or landless agricultural labourers); their numbers had in fact become so large as to represent an important change in the structure of rural society. By 1801 the number of *husmenn* with land had risen to 48,700 and those without land to 42,500, an increase which occurred principally in eastern Norway where it was in part due to an increase in the size of farms, which in turn increased the need for agricultural labourers. A concomitant of this situation was the emergence of a new class of big farmers with money to spare for consumer goods.

Though the larger number of *husmenn* meant that there had been a considerable increase in the area of cultivated land, the government was not very happy about the concentration of agricultural land into fewer hands, and in 1771 it enacted a new law governing *Odelsrett* (odal freehold) which was designed to lessen the restrictions on the sale of *Odelsgårder* (farms held on odal freehold). The government also supported initiatives to clear common land and other unused land, to create more farmsteads, especially in eastern Norway. But these efforts, because of peasant conservatism, were only partially successful.

In Denmark the fall of Struensee was followed by a period of reaction and the new government under Ove Høegh Guldberg returned to a policy of centralizing all trading activity in Copenhagen, reintroducing monopolies (the corn monopoly among them) and giving the state an active role in the stimulation and direction of business. In 1784, however, Guldberg himself fell in a *coup d'état* which gave power to the growing number of his opponents.

The new regime reverted in many respects to the policies of Struensee. Trade was liberalized; the play of market forces was to replace state control; monopolies were abolished; and the state withdrew from participation in business. The new customs regulations which the government introduced in 1797 were among the most liberal in Europe at the time. For Norway, this meant that the monopolies on trade in Finnmark were abolished; it also meant that the merchants of Christiania, Bergen, and Trondhjem lost the privileges they had hitherto enjoyed under the system of monopolies. However, the liberalism of the Copenhagen government did not extend to acceding to Norwegian demands for their own bank and university.

These measures and the intellectual liberalism which went with them did not mean that there were not depressed, and oppressed, sectors of the population in Norway. In spite of economic growth the situation of the *husmenn*, the fishermen, and the servant class was often wretched. Their dissatisfactions were to show themselves in the so-called Lofthus rising, named from Christian Lofthus (1750–97), a farmer from near Lillesand in southern Norway. Lofthus had ventured to engage in trade, though in doing so he had infringed the trade privileges which had been granted to the town of Arendal. Proceedings were instituted against him and as a result he was ruined. But this calamity had opened his eyes to the injustices which the small farmers, workers, and seamen suffered at the hands of the ruling classes. In 1786 he went to Copenhagen to put his case to the crown prince and later, to accumulate more evidence and gain more support, he travelled around Norway holding meetings. This exposed him to arrest for unlawful assembly, but a rising of the peasants forced the local authorities to rescind the order for arrest and to allow them to put Lofthus's case to the government in Copenhagen. The government decided to set up a commission to investigate the case and to pass judgement, but although it was composed of liberally-minded men, Lofthus was sentenced to life imprisonment. When this news got around, there were protests and minor uprisings in many parts of southern and south-eastern Norway. These risings, the most extensive during this period, and other more minor episodes showed that something of a proletariat was beginning to emerge in Norway. They also showed that this proleteriat could find a spokesman and was not afraid to take action in defence of what it regarded as its rights.

It would nevertheless be unfair to judge the official classes in Norway too harshly on the basis of such episodes. By the standards of their time they were probably better than in most countries. There is also evidence that in the 1790s they became much more Norwegian in their orientation, even those who had been born in Denmark. Norway had become the country in which they wished to live, whose institutions they supported, and whose cultural heritage they helped to preserve. The spirit of the Enlightenment was strong, especially among the clergy, who were often more concerned with preaching morality and the merits of reason than with sin and salvation. This rationalist approach often accorded ill with the traditional beliefs of their peasant parishioners and failed to satisfy their need for a more inward religion.

This need, however, was soon to be met by one of the most remarkable religious talents Norway has produced: Hans Nielsen Hauge (1771–1824). Hauge was a farmer's son who, after he had been converted in 1796, began to travel the country preaching the repentance of sins and salvation through God's grace. His adherents, calling themselves 'Friends', grew in number and formed themselves into exclusive sects. As well as being an evangelist of genius, Hauge had many practical talents and was a good businessman who, with funds subscribed by his followers, started many enterprises. His preaching activities, including attacks on the state Church, soon made him many enemies and in 1804 he was imprisoned under the so-called *Konventikkelplakaten* of 1741, which prohibited laymen from holding religious services. He was released from prison for a time in 1809 in order to help increase salt production during the blockade of Norway, but he was not entirely free until 1814. He was then forbidden to preach, but the movement he had founded continued to play an important role in the religious and political life of Norway during much of the nineteenth century.

The conclusion of the war with Sweden in 1720 inaugurated a long period of peace for Denmark-Norway. Relations with Sweden were now unwarlike and in 1734 a treaty was signed between the two countries which led to the setting-up of a boundary commission to define the border between Norway and Sweden. During the Seven Years War between Britain and France, from 1756 to 1763, the country maintained neutrality. Denmark and Sweden signed a neutrality pact and operated together a neutrality control in the Kattegat. For a time after the *coup d'état* of Gustav III of Sweden in 1772 and later, in 1783, the old Swedish hostility to Denmark and Swedish ambitions in Norway flared up again, but the danger of war passed. However, when Gustav attacked Russia in 1788, Denmark-Norway was bound by treaty to go to Russia's aid, which they did, but Prussia and Britain forced the two parties to conclude peace, though not before there had been relatively severe Norwegian casualties which caused much dissatisfaction in Norway, and which Gustav later tried to exploit for separatist ends.

After the assassination of Gustav III in 1792, the Danes and the Swedes renewed in 1794 their alliance of neutrality. But when in 1801 the alliance was extended to include Russia and Prussia, Britain regarded this as a challenge and demanded that Denmark should withdraw. When she refused to comply, the British sent a fleet to

Copenhagen under Parker and Nelson to force a withdrawal. The battle of Copenhagen which followed had the desired effect, but not before a gallant fight had added a stirring chapter to the annals of the Dano-Norwegian fleet.

After the battle of Copenhagen events moved quickly in the North. In Norway the six years immediately following were a period of unparalleled prosperity in the export trade, with prices booming. Shipping was in its heyday and the Napoleonic Wars (Britain had declared war on France in May 1803) created a tremendous demand for timber, iron, and cargo space. Norwegian agriculture, on the other hand, was in a perilous state. Bad harvests, aggravated by neglect created by the boom conditions elsewhere, led to famine in the years 1800–03. But worse was to come. In 1807 the course of the war between Britain and France persuaded Napoleon to force Denmark-Norway into his continental system. The British, however, were determined that they should not close their ports to them, and they acted promptly. In August 1807 a large British fleet sailed to Copenhagen and demanded the handing-over of the Danish fleet. When this demand was rejected, Copenhagen was bombarded for three days. Eventually the Danes capitulated, and their fleet was taken away. After this Denmark-Norway went over to Napoleon and declared war on Britain.

This declaration of war had immediate and catastrophic consequences for the Norwegian economy which depended on overseas trade, and many of the country's essential needs, especially corn, had to be imported. War with Britain meant the loss of markets which had become even more important as a result of the earlier boom period, and the export of corn from Denmark ceased as soon as war broke out. A so-called Government Commission (*Regjeringskommisjonen*) was set up in Norway to deal with the situation, but because of the lack of proper directives from Copenhagen and the civil-service caution of its members, it failed to act with the urgency the situation demanded. A so-called *Provideringskommisjon* was also established to deal with a food shortage, but the difficulty was to raise enough money to secure the supplies that were needed. Credit facilities were not available and since all corn export to Norway had been in the hands of the Danes, the Norwegian merchants did not have the experience or the connections to obtain supplies. The situation was made worse by the failure of the harvests of 1807 and 1808, when corn grown in Norway failed to ripen. During these years all sorts of substitutes were tried, including the use of meal made out of birchbark.

In the midst of all this Sweden came into the war on the allied side. The Norwegian army was in no way equipped to defend the country, but in minor encounters the Norwegian soldiers acquitted themselves well. Fortunately, there was no great enthusiasm in Sweden for the war. But as time went on, the economic consequences for Norway became more and more ruinous. The Danish king, Frederik VI, insisted that all British property in Norway should be confiscated, even though the Norwegians had credits in England worth far more.

At this point a gifted leader emerged in Norway: Count Herman Wedel Jarlsberg (1779–1840). He had become a member of the Government Commission in 1808 and had soon made his influence felt. He was determined to make the Commission an independent organ both in its policy and in its attitude to Denmark. Events in Sweden, however, really saved the situation. A *coup d'état* in 1809 had removed Gustav IV from the throne and immediately there was a *rapprochement* with Norway-Denmark. Prince Christian August of Augustenborg, commander of the Norwegian troops in southern Norway, was made crown prince of Sweden and thus heir to the Swedish throne (Carl XIII, who succeeded Gustav IV, was without heirs) and Danish fears that the Norwegians might seek a union with Sweden caused Frederik VI to agree to Norway being released from the continental system. At this the British agreed to lift their blockade on the basis of a licence system and once again trade in Norway began to flourish. But Count Wedel Jarlsberg still pursued his aim of greater Norwegian independence and believed that this could be best achieved by a union with Sweden. Among other things he was responsible for the founding in 1809 of *Selskabet for Norges Vel* (Society for the Good of Norway) to promote economic and educational advance. The society also made plans for a Norwegian university and collected funds for its establishment. In 1811 these plans were placed before Frederik VI in Copenhagen by Wedel Jarlsberg, who argued the case so well that the king finally agreed.

In 1810 Christian August (or Karl August, as he had become known in Sweden) died suddenly. To replace him the Swedes chose, by a curious twist of history, Jean-Baptiste Bernadotte, one of Napoleon's marshals, in the hope that he would win back Finland, which they had lost to Russia in 1809. But Bernadotte had other views. He thought it would be difficult for Sweden to defend Finland against Russia in the long run and decided it would be better to seek an agreement with Russia, which would provide for Norway to be handed over to Sweden. In 1813 the matter was settled by agreement with Russia and Britain. As a result the British once again began to blockade Norway as part of the attempt to force Norway into union with Sweden. Trade between Norway and England came to a halt, as did the import of corn, and once again shortages in Norway were aggravated by a bad harvest.

In these circumstances the Danes decided, in May 1813, to send
the heir to the Danish throne, Prince Christian Frederik, to Norway.
Now it was not only a question of famine and economic ruin, but of
the future of the monarchy itself in Norway. Christian Frederik, it
was believed, was the man who had the best chance of saving Norway
for the house of Oldenburg. He had many qualities to recommend
him and was determined to do his best for Norway. In December the
same year, a meeting of seventy-two of the richest men in the country
was called to found a Norwegian bank and a considerable sum of
money was raised. However, events abroad had already determined
Norway's fate. In October 1813 Napoleon had been decisively defeated at Leipzig, and Bernadotte, or Carl Johan as he was called in
Sweden, who had taken part in the campaign, now moved his forces
northward ready to secure Norway. At the Peace of Kiel, signed on
14 January 1814, Denmark was obliged to hand over Norway to
Sweden. Thus the union between Norway and Denmark, which had
lasted for more than 400 years, was at an end.

# Chapter 6

# Union with Sweden

## *The Constitution and Union with Sweden*

THE PROVISIONS OF THE TREATY OF KIEL could not have been unexpected in Norway; in fact, the principal reason for Christian Frederik's dispatch to Norway was to prepare, as best he could, to meet the eventuality that Norway would be handed over to Sweden.

The tense situation which prevailed in Norway at the beginning of 1814 was one which suited Christian Frederik's temperament and, as soon as the terms of the treaty were known, he set off on a journey through the country to agitate against them and to work up feeling against Sweden. As crown prince he regarded himself as the legitimate heir to the throne of Norway and even thought of having himself acclaimed king in the Cathedral of Nidaros. However, although he was received with enthusiasm on his journeys, he found that the Norwegians were not in favour of continuing the absolute monarchy. Leading Norwegians believed that since the Dano-Norwegian king, Frederik VI, had renounced his sovereignty over Norway, this had now reverted to the Norwegian people themselves and they could dispose of it as they thought fit.

On 16 February 1814 a meeting of leading officials and citizens was called at Eidsvoll in eastern Norway. Three days later Christian Frederik issued a proclamation to the Norwegian people, to be read in all churches, urging them to assert and defend the independence of Norway, and inviting them to pledge themselves to do this on oath. The proclamation and the taking of the oath activated the national will and focused the cause of independence on Christian Frederik. At the same time delegates were appointed from each district in Norway to take part in an assembly of Notables which was also to be held at Eidsvoll.

Misgivings at the steps which had been taken were, however, expressed, notably by Count Wedel Jarlsberg who believed that Norway should accept union with Sweden and that to refuse to do so would involve the country in war with Sweden and lead it into head-on collision with the great powers who had been the signatories of the Treaty of Kiel. It was also pointed out that if Christian Frederik, heir to the Danish throne, became king of Norway, the country would eventually be brought into a union with Denmark again.

In March 1814 the party favouring independence sent Carsten Anker, the owner of the estate at Eidsvoll at which the Notables were to meet, to England with a view to putting the Norwegian case to the British government. He met Lord Liverpool, the Prime Minister, privately but the British view was that the Norwegian campaign for independence had been engineered by the Danes and that Britain must fulfil her obligations under the Treaty of Kiel. Anker, however, was given to understand that the British government would do all it could to secure the best possible conditions for Norway in a union with Sweden when that was brought about.

In April 1814, 112 representatives, consisting of 37 farmers, 16 businessmen, and 59 members of the official classes assembled at Eidsvoll from all parts of the country except Nordland and Finnmark. It was soon seen that the delegates were divided into two parties: those who supported the idea of an independent Norway headed by Christian Frederik and those who believed that union with Sweden was unavoidable and must be accepted. In the event it was the independence party which won the day. But abroad pressures were building up the whole time to make Norway accept union with Sweden. Denmark was forced to sever connections with Norway; the Swedes urged Britain to renew the blockade of Norway, and the Swedish crown prince, Carl Johan, was soon expected back from the continent with the Swedish army.

Nevertheless, the delegates at Eidsvoll continued with the work of drafting a constitution for the new Norway and by 2 May 1814 a revised draft was ready. The assembly was fortunate in having many legal members who were skilled in drafting and familiar with the liberal constitutions of the time, especially the American constitution of 1787 and the Spanish constitution of 1812. Discussion of the draft started immediately and on 17 May 1814 it was signed by the members of the assembly and promulgated.[1] On the same day Christian Frederik was elected king of Norway.

[1] The Norwegian constitution (*Grunnloven*) of 17 May 1814 provided for a complete division between the executive and legislative powers, the former being vested in the sovereign, the latter in the *Storting* (National Assembly).

The king's person being sacred, the responsibility for executive action was in the hands of a Council of State (*Statsråd*) or government appointed by him. Members of the Council of State were required by the constitution to speak their minds on any issue that came before them and were subject to impeachment and trial by *Riksrett* (the Constitutional Court of the Realm) if they failed to register their protest should the sovereign act unconstitutionally. They were not eligible to become members of the *Storting*.

The *Storting* was to be elected by Norwegian male citizens who had reached the age of 25 and who satisfied property or other qualifications; the elections were to be conducted by a system of electoral colleges devised in such a way as to give the towns one-third of the mandates and the country districts two thirds (the so-called *Bondeparagrafen*). The *Storting*, which was to be elected and to meet every three

At the same time the powers were taking steps to see that the provisions of the Treaty of Kiel were implemented. In mid-May they sent a commission to Copenhagen where Frederik VI was able to convince them that he had taken all necessary steps to bring about an implementation of the treaty, including the threat to disinherit Christian Frederik. In June the commission went on to Norway where a special British representative, I. P. Morier, had already preceded them. Morier had obtained information about the state of Norwegian opinion, but he had also made it clear to the Norwegians that the British government was prepared to give full support to Sweden in the matter of the union. This, and the arrival of the commission which also insisted that the conditions of the Treaty of Kiel must be fulfilled, was a sad blow to the hopes of Christian Frederik. He realized that his chances of being able to retain his throne were very small, but he was determined to do his best for the Norwegians. He insisted that as he had been elected by the Norwegian *Storting* in accordance with the constitution, he could not renounce the throne without summoning a meeting of the *Storting*, but declared that he would only do so on condition that the internal independence of Norway in a union with Sweden was maintained.

The commission promised to put his views to Carl Johan, but the latter refused to accept them and at the end of July 1814 began hostilities against Norway. It was a very one-sided contest, but the Norwegians, in spite of inferiority in numbers and material, gave a good account of themselves. Christian Frederik had soon to sue for

---

years–normally not for more than three months–was to divide itself into two sections: the *Lagting* (consisting of one-quarter of the members) and the *Odelsting* (consisting of three-quarters). Bills were to be proposed in the *Odelsting* and if approved sent to the *Lagting*. If the *Lagting* rejected a bill on two occasions, it was to be referred to the whole *Storting*, where a two-thirds majority was necessary. The sovereign could refuse his consent to any measure passed, but if it was passed three times in succession in unchanged form at the three-yearly meetings of the *Storting* it became law without his consent; thus the sovereign's veto was only a suspensive one.

The members of the *Lagting*, together with those of the Supreme Court (*Høyesterett*), were to constitute the *Riksrett* whose function it was to judge members of the king's Council of State, the Supreme Court, and the *Storting* for acts involving dereliction of duty.

Changes in the constitution were to require the consent of two thirds of the *Storting*.

[*Note*. The following are the main changes in the constitution or in constitutional practice since 1814: the *Storting* to meet every year (*årlig Storting*) and to sit as long as its members deem necessary (1869); the king accepts the principle of appointing a government which has the confidence of the *Storting* (1884); universal suffrage for men (1898); abolition of indirect election to the *Storting* through electoral colleges (1905); women receive the vote (1907), and on same terms as men (1913); introduction of proportional representation (1919); reduction of voting age to 23 (1920), 21 (1946) and 20 (1969); the *Storting* to be elected for a four-year period (1938); abolition of *bondeparagrafen* providing for a fixed division of seats in the *Storting* between town and country (1952).]

peace, but Carl Johan, too, was anxious to get matters settled without further bloodshed or delay. Though he did not succeed to the throne until 1818, Carl Johan was already, in effect, Head of State and realized that to conquer Norway would take time and perpetuate antagonisms. Moreover, the Congress of Vienna would soon be held to settle the state of Europe and his own position, as a parvenu among the princes of Europe, was still uncertain. A meeting between the parties was called at Moss in south-eastern Norway and on 14 August 1814 the so-called Convention of Moss was signed. It provided that in a union with Sweden, Norway would retain her constitution and her *Storting* subject only to such changes as were made necessary by the union. In a secret paragraph in the agreement, Christian Frederik promised to abdicate when the details of the union had been arranged.

When the provisions of the Convention were made public, they gave no pleasure either in Norway or Sweden. Many Norwegians saw it as a defeat and many Swedes regarded it as a sell-out. Thus, the subsequent discussions to define the precise relationship of the two countries within the union were delicate. That the final result was as satisfactory to the Norwegians as it was, was due principally to the statesmanship of Carl Johan who understood that the Norwegians had to be wooed and won. On the Norwegian side, the fact that Norway retained so much internal independence owed a great deal to skilful and firm negotiating by W. K. Christie. On 10 October 1814 Christian Frederik formally abdicated. The final details of the union were worked out and on 4 November 1814 the Norwegian *Storting* elected the king of Sweden, Carl XIII, as king of Norway. In Sweden, the precise conditions of the union, over which there was still considerable dissatisfaction, were incorporated in a document called *Riksakten*,[1] which was also later approved by the *Storting*.

### Internal Problems and Disputes with Sweden

A union with Sweden had not been what the majority of Norwegians had wanted, but it must have been a source of satisfaction and relief to them that they had achieved a measure of self-government without further bloodshed, and after the tensions of recent years they began to look forward to a resumption of normal life.

There were, however, many problems ahead. In the first place it was to be no easy task to get a stable economy after the distortions it had suffered during the war years and in the boom years immediately

---

[1] Among other things the *Riksakten* provided for a Norwegian minister of state (*Statsminister*) and two councillors of state (*Statsråder*) to be in attendance on the king while he was in residence in Stockholm. They were to have seats and a vote in the Swedish Council of State when matters affecting both kingdoms were being transacted.

preceding them. The monetary system was in chaos and in order to raise the necessary backing for the new Bank of Norway, which was founded in 1816, the *Storting* had to impose a special silver tax; but the response from the people was poor and often recalcitrant. Confidence in the new bank was weak and eventually the plan to give the currency silver or gold backing had to be dropped, with the result that it was unstable for a long time to come. In fact, the Bank of Norway, which, as we have seen, had long been one of the Norwegians' main aspirations, was something of a disappointment. The fact that its head office was located in Trondhjem—to remove it from the political influences of the capital—meant that it was not in close touch with business. It failed to satisfy the need for credit facilities for trade and industry, and it limited its operations principally to providing mortgages.

Problems arising from the union with Sweden were also not slow to appear. One of the provisions of the Treaty of Kiel was that Norway should be responsible for paying a share of the national debt of Denmark-Norway. The Norwegians resisted this, believing that, since Norway had been exploited by the Danes during the period of the union, it was Norway who should receive compensation from Denmark; indeed, to prove their point, Nicolai Wergeland, the father of the poet Henrik Wergeland, published in 1816 a book entitled *Danmarks politiske Forbrydelser mod Kongeriget Norge* (*Denmark's Political Crimes against the Kingdom of Norway*). Norway also made the counter-claim against Denmark that the old Norwegian colonies of Iceland, Greenland, and the Faroes, which had not been part of the transfer to Sweden in 1814 and had remained as part of Denmark, should be handed back to Norway. However, it was Sweden's responsibility to see that the provisions of the Treaty of Kiel were carried out as far as they concerned Norway, and after the matter had been discussed by Denmark, Sweden, and the great powers who were the guarantors of the treaty, Carl Johan insisted that Norway should pay the sum that had been agreed on, especially as during the negotiations he had resisted threats of direct action from the other powers and had done his best to reduce the Danish demands. Thus he was furious when the *Storting* now suggested that Sweden ought to shoulder part of the financial burden.

Carl Johan's dissatisfaction with the Norwegians was not limited to this. He was displeased at the degree of independence they were showing, especially as it went against his own aim of a gradual merging of the two kingdoms. In 1815 the *Storting* had passed a bill abolishing all noble titles and privileges in Norway. The king had refused to sanction this bill, but it was passed again by the *Storting* in 1818, and again the king refused to sanction it. If the *Storting* passed it again in 1821, it would, according to the constitution, become law even if the king again refused his consent. It would mean that the provision in the constitution that the king only had a suspensive veto would have been established in practice, a provision to which Carl Johan had objected most strongly. Nevertheless, in spite of threats and the king's promise that he would sanction the bill in 1824 should it be passed again, the Norwegians went ahead and passed the bill for the third time in 1821. This, together with the Norwegians' recalcitrance over the payment of their share of the national debt to Denmark, brought Carl Johan to the brink of armed intervention in Norway. To prepare the way he had sent a note to the great powers complaining of certain of the provisions of the Norwegian constitution, but the response of the powers did not encourage him – they wanted, above all, peace. But when Carl Johan began to concentrate Swedish troops on the Norwegian border and ordered military manoeuvres just outside Christiania, and a Swedish fleet appeared in harbour, the Norwegians gave way to the extent of paying to Denmark the sum which had been agreed upon as their share of the national debt of the joint kingdom.

There were also political troubles in Norway itself. In 1818 peasants in eastern Norway, disgruntled about taxes and the economic difficulties, and supposing that the new constitution and officialdom were responsible, believing, too, that the personal rule of the monarch would be better, started to march on the capital. Their demonstration seems to have fizzled out half-way and although the government did not take this episode very seriously, it did lead to a proposal from Christian Magnus Falsen (one of the authors of the constitution) that the number of peasant representatives in the *Storting* should be reduced. This proposal was rejected, as were attempts by Carl Johan to get the constitution amended so as to give the monarch more power. In fact the constitution of 17 May 1814 was becoming more and more the symbol of Norwegian freedom and independence, and any attempt to tamper with it was regarded as sacrilege.

Norway's economic problems were basically part of the wider, European, economic difficulties of the post-Napoleonic War years and related especially to the economic difficulties of England. They also stemmed from the earlier distortion of the economy during the war years and from the cutting of economic ties with Denmark. However, a factor of major importance was the setting-up of tariff barriers in England. When, on the outbreak of war in 1807, export of timber from Norway to England had stopped, British capital developed the Canadian timber industry. Now it had to be protected by tariffs, which were so high that it even became profitable to send

Norwegian timber to Canada for trans-shipment back to Britain. Not only did it create difficult times for the Norwegian timber merchants but also for all those associated with the trade, especially the shipping industry. The major part of the Norwegian merchant fleet had been engaged in this trade, but now when cargoes for England were no longer there, tonnage fell dramatically. The British Navigation Acts also adversely affected Norwegian shipping and, although an increase in the timber trade between Norway and France provided some relief, it was not until the abolition of the Navigation Acts in 1849 that Norwegian shipping really got back on its feet again.

In the decade that followed, tussles between the king and the *Storting* continued. Indeed, they characterized the whole period of the union between Norway and Sweden until the dissolution in 1905. Often, these disputes reflected a developing political awareness. Other points of irritation turned on matters of prestige. Though the constitution emphasized that Norway was an independent kingdom with full equality with Sweden, various aspects seemed to imply that Norway had an inferior status. The post of *Stattholder* in Norway could be held by a Swede; the Norwegian man-of-war flag was the Swedish flag with the union sign superimposed on it; and although the merchant flag was Norwegian, it could not be used south of Cape Finisterre and in the Mediterannean because of the threat from North African pirates. In these waters Norwegian ships had to use the Swedish flag in order to obtain the immunity from pirates which the tribute paid by the Swedes to the North African states ensured.

A much more serious and lasting cause of dissatisfaction was the fact that foreign and diplomatic representation for Norway was in Swedish hands. In the early years it was realized that a separate Norwegian foreign service was not a practical proposition, but there was latent dissatisfaction with these arrangements and this flared up in 1827 in connection with the so-called Bodø affair. It concerned the illicit activities of some British merchants in Bodø in north Norway. When the Norwegian authorities took action against them, they retaliated by using violence, and on their return to England complained to the British authorities, representing themselves as peaceful traders who had been wronged and maltreated. The British took up the matter with the Swedish foreign office which agreed to pay compensation for the alleged wrongs these so-called traders had suffered. The decision was regarded by the Norwegians as a gross betrayal of their interests and they complained bitterly to the Swedes, demanding that the Norwegian representatives in Stockholm should in future always be present when foreign affairs relating to Norway were discussed. It led in 1835 and 1836 to Carl Johan making concessions to Norwegian demands both for Norwegian participation in decision-taking on foreign affairs and on the appointment of Swedes who were also to act as Norwegian consuls. In 1838 the Norwegians were also given permission to use their merchant flag south of Cape Finisterre. Relations between the two countries had improved, for although all matters of order and precedence in documents, etc., relating to the two countries had not been settled to the Norwegians' satisfaction, Carl Johan was given a great welcome when he came to Christiania in 1838.

## Political Development and New Legislation

An important feature of Norwegian political life in the decades immediately following 1814 was the emergence of the peasants as a political force. Hitherto, the farmers had tended to regard politics as the sphere of the official, landowning, and merchant classes, but now they began to see that the way to achieve their principal objective—a reduction in taxation—was through political participation in the *Storting* and in local government. This programme was naturally an attractive one and it was supported by all sectors of the farming community. Liberally-minded men of other classes also believed that active peasant participation in politics was essential to Norway's future wellbeing. This was also the period of National Romanticism, a movement which assigned a high place to the peasant and his culture, the living link between the medieval period of greatness and the present day. Henrik Wergeland, who was one of the early champions of the peasant, was also active in the work of popular enlightenment on their behalf. The periodical *Statsborgeren* (*The Citizen*), with which he was associated, put forward the point of view of the peasant and, at the same time, directed much criticism at the official classes. In 1830 John Neergaard published his so-called *Olaboka* in which peasant demands were put forward in a form which would appeal to the rural electorate. Neergaard also travelled the country speaking and agitating on behalf of the peasant cause. How effective this campaign was is shown by the success of the peasants at the *Storting* elections of 1832 when 45 of the 95 representatives elected were farmers. Among them was Ole Gabriel Ueland, who was destined to become one of the chief leaders of the farmers' party.

The importance which the *Storting* attached to local affairs was shown when in 1833 it approved a bill embodying a new law relating to local government. There had since the eighteenth century been some machinery for the expression of local opinion and since 1814 a number of proposals had been made to extend and codify the arrangements. It was, however, the farmers themselves with the help of a leading liberal, J. A. Hielm, who eventually produced a draft which became the basis of the new law. This provided for the establishment of local councils (*Formandskaber*) in counties, parishes, and towns. These councils were to be vested with both financial and executive powers. There were, however, some controversial features in the bill and it did not receive the royal assent until 1837. In the meantime tension between the *Storting* and the king had increased, and in 1836 Carl Johan had used his powers to dissolve it. However, it was soon recalled again, but not before the chief Norwegian minister in Stockholm, Severin Løvenskiold, had been impeached under the constitution by *Riksrett* for failing to protest against the king's action. But, as we have already noted, tensions eased and in the last years of his reign Carl Johan achieved a genuine popularity in Norway. When he died in 1844, grief was widespread and heartfelt.

During these years conservative forces had once again got the upper hand in Norway with power concentrated chiefly in the hands of the official classes in Christiania. A typical and highly influential representative of this trend was Anton Martin Schweigaard, whose hand can be seen in much of the important legislation enacted around this time. In the economic field their policy was to allow the free play of market forces, which won the support of the peasants who had always resisted the granting of monopolies or privileges. In 1839 a law was passed which provided for the abolition of guilds; in 1842 the law relating to the conduct of trade was liberalized, as was the schedule of import tariffs, making them more favourable to the consumer at large.

The increase in the volume of internal and external trade led to demands for better communications. In 1845 a department of the interior was established, and in 1851 legislation was passed providing for the building, maintenance, and financing of new roads; the new department also established the principles, especially in respect of gradients, on which new roads should be built. In the same year, also, a plan for railway development was approved. A British company was to undertake the work with Robert Stephenson, a son of George Stephenson, as chief engineer and on 1 September 1854 the first section (68 kilometres), connecting Christiania with Eidsvoll, was opened. At the same time a start had been made on building an electric telegraph system, the first line between Christiania and Drammen being opened in 1855. The postal service was modernized and the need for the expeditious and reliable delivery of mail also led to the development of better communications, especially by the introduction and improvement of coastal mail-steamer services.

These improvements were also paralleled by a greater sense of social responsibility. This showed itself in new legislation designed to control the private distilling of spirits which, since 1816 when the monopoly had been abolished, had given rise to serious social prob-

lems. Temperance societies were established with official encouragement to combat the drink problem; the criminal law and the treatment of prisoners was made more humane; and the sociological
surveys carried out by Eilert Sundt are monuments of their kind,
reflecting contemporary interest in the social conditions of the underprivileged sections of the community.

However, the temper of the ruling classes was still authoritarian,
as was shown by the treatment meted out to the leaders of the so-
called Thrane movement. Its leader, Marcus Thrane, had established
a Workers' Union (*Arbeiderforening*) in Drammen in 1848 and had
begun to publish a journal, *Arbeider-Foreningernes Blad*. He then
organized a petition to the king, which received 13,000 signatures,
supplicating, among other things, for an extension of the franchise,
better primary schools, and better conditions for *husmenn*. It is
interesting to note that, like Lofthus before him, Thrane believed
that the best way to bring the grievances of the underprivileged to
public notice was by a direct approach to the king. No action was
taken at the time, but in 1851 the new and more radical *Storting* set
up a committee to consider the petition. The Workers' Union, in
order to put pressure on the *Storting*, called at the same time a meeting in Christiania of its representatives, an assembly which became
popularly known as *Lilletinget* (Little *Ting*) by contrast to *Storting*
(Big *Ting*). Its activities and the disturbances which occurred in
some places alarmed more moderate elements and encouraged the
more reactionary members of the government to take action. The
*Storting* decided to shelve the petition without further debate and the
government ordered that the activities and membership of the
Workers' Union should be investigated. As a result, no less than 133
people were found guilty in 1854 of conspiring against the security of
the state. Marcus Thrane was given a prison sentence of four years.

*Pan-Scandinavianism*

In foreign affairs the years immediately before and after mid-
century were characterized by a feeling of solidarity between the
three Scandinavian countries. Both Sweden-Norway and Denmark
had a common interest in maintaining neutrality and in collaborating on any measures that might be necessary to ensure this. In
particular, the Danes, who felt threatened by the possibility of a
revolt of the German populations in Schleswig and Holstein and
consequent embroilment with Germany, were enthusiastic Pan-
Scandinavianists. The solidarity between the three countries was,
however, more apparent than real and a misleading appearance had
been given to it by the junketings of the Scandinavian students and
academics who had been holding meetings each year to give expres-

sion to their brotherly feelings and their belief in the Pan-Scandin-avian idea.

The first test of Scandinavian solidarity came in 1848 when, under the influence of the February revolution in Paris, rebellion broke out in Schleswig-Holstein, and was immediately supported by Prussia and the German states. In the face of this threat, the Danish army in the south withdrew, but at the request of Frederik VII of Denmark, King Oscar I (1844–59) of Sweden-Norway promised 15,000 men if Denmark proper should be attacked. Norway was to contribute 3,000 men to this force, a proposal to which the *Storting* agreed with some reservations. In the event, the Danes, helped by the political intervention of Tsar Nicholas I, managed to deal with the situation themselves and the Swedish-Norwegian forces were not called upon, though some Norwegian and Swedish volunteers took part in the actual fighting.

Somewhat unaccountably, the outcome of the war seemed to the Pan-Scandinavianists to be a triumph for their movement and in Norway the writers J. S. Welhaven, Andreas Munch, Henrik Ibsen, and Bjørnstjerne Bjørnson affirmed their strong support of it. The new king of Sweden-Norway, Carl XV, who succeeded in 1859, was also enthusiastic for the Pan-Scandinavian idea. The cumulative effect of all this was to lull Denmark into a feeling of false security in her relations with Schleswig and Holstein. It seemed to the Danes that the support of Sweden-Norway was assured in the event of any future conflict; in actual fact, when a treaty of alliance was proposed between the two countries, the greatest misgivings were expressed both in Stockholm and Christiania.

In 1864 things once again came to a head over Schleswig-Holstein when Prussia and Austria declared war on Denmark. Carl XV wanted to help, but the government and people of Sweden were opposed, and the reaction of the *Storting* was also extremely cautious. To the adherents of the Pan-Scandinavian movement this was sheer treachery. Ibsen and Bjørnson declaimed against the decision not to help; indeed, Ibsen's play *Brand* was born directly out of this situation. Now, however, it was revealed for all to see that the Pan-Scandinavian movement never had been much more than a student, academic, and literary movement. It was a spent force. In-deed, Sweden-Norway had already shown in the mid-1850s that they were prepared to follow a policy of *Realpolitik* in foreign affairs. When they left the position of strict neutrality, they veered towards Britain and France. After the Crimean War, the so-called November Treaty (*Novembertraktaten*) of 1855 was signed, under which Sweden-Norway agreed not to concede any of their territory to Russia, while Britain and France gave guarantees of help in the event of a Russian attack.

*Sverdrup's Rise to Power*

In domestic politics the 1850s in Norway saw the emergence of Johan Sverdrup (1816–92) as a political leader. Sverdrup, a lawyer from Larvik in southern Norway, realized that if Norwegian political life was to develop, the *Storting* must become the supreme centre of government, wielding both legislative and executive power. The first step in this direction was to co-ordinate the opposition forces in the *Storting* and give them a programme to work for. A major difficulty in welding people and opinions together was that the means and media for commanding influence and chanelling opinion were lacking. The electoral law of 1828 had even forbidden electioneering and, although this law had been abolished, such activity was still thought to be hardly respectable. Moreover, the opposition factions lacked a press through which they could make their opinions known, and although Sverdrup and the peasant leader Ole Gabriel Ueland tried to get a newspaper going, it was not a success.

However, when the *Storting* reassembled in 1859, Sverdrup and Ueland, together with Johannes Steen (1827–1906), a future leader of the Liberal (*Venstre*) Party, produced a seven-point programme designed to provide the basis for the establishment of a *Reformforening* (A Reform Society). The programme included among other things proposals that the *Storting* should be convened every year instead of every three years, as was provided by the constitution, and for the introduction of a jury system in criminal cases. However, though this programme was supported by many deputies, they resented the idea of being bound by party policy on a given issue, an objection which reveals the state of political development in Norway at the time and which led Sverdrup to insist that the political situation did not call for the founding of a debating society but a political party. That there was a need for solidarity was shown in connection with the *Juryloven* (Jury Law) which, though passed in 1857 by a large majority, was refused sanction by the government. Co-operation with the peasant politicians was not easy, especially because of their determination to resist any increase in the apparatus of state or of state expenditure. Indeed, on financial grounds, they even changed their minds over the desirability of introducing the jury system. But Sverdrup persevered and managed to find common ground with the peasant party and Ueland on the question of revision of the law governing conscription and in opposing an increase in the size of the army and length of military service. Sverdrup saw that such an increase would also mean an increase in the power of the king and a closer integration of the two countries in the union. Both were contrary to his overall political programme of weakening the union and increasing Norwegian independence of Sweden.

In 1865, on the initiative of the peasant leader Søren Jaabæk (1814–94), a group calling itself *Bondevennerne* (Society of Friends of the Peasants) was founded in Mandal in southern Norway. The movement, which provided a new local focus for political activity, grew rapidly, especially in the southern and eastern regions. The movement's journal, *Folketidende*, which Jaabæk founded in the same year, and which was said to have had some 16,000 subscribers, campaigned incessantly for a reduction in the apparatus of state and in state expenditure, especially in the salaries paid to state officials. Jaabæk also engaged in direct electioneering and this, too, stimulated political life and discussion in the country districts. However, as a result of his miserly policies, a proposal that the *Storting* should meet each year, because of the additional expense involved, failed to receive the necessary two-thirds majority when it was put to the vote in 1866. But Sverdrup continued to persevere, basing his political position more broadly in order to command wider support. In 1868 Jaabæk agreed to accept his leadership for the achievement of common aims and now supported both the proposal for a yearly sitting and the law providing for the introduction of the jury system, in return for Sverdrup's support on a number of issues of peasant interest.

The introduction of annual meetings of the *Storting* from 1870 was a great step forward. The development of popular education had also contributed to a greater political awareness. In 1848 an Act providing for at least one school in the towns (*Kjøpsteder*), with compulsory attendance from the age of seven until confirmation, and in 1860 a new Education Act relating to rural schools had been passed, based on a scheme worked out by the educationalist Hartvig Nissen, who had also planned changes in the pattern of grammar-school education.

In 1859 Carl XV had promised the Norwegians that the post of *Stattholder* would be abolished. The office had always aroused the resentment of the Norwegians who saw in it a symbol of overlordship, though during 1836–56 it had been held by a Norwegian. However, when the *Storting* actually abolished the office in December 1859, their action aroused tremendous protest in the Swedish *Riksdag*. The Swedish government maintained that the *Stattholder*'s post could not be abolished without a joint decision of both Sweden and Norway. At the same time the Swedes demanded that a committee should be set up to look into the terms of the union with a view to revising them. Thus, what had begun as a relatively minor matter now developed into a threat to the very independence of Norway within the union. The Swedish government made it clear to the king that they regarded the acceptance of their views of this issue as a matter of confidence in them.

In these circumstances Carl XV tried to placate both sides, but in doing so he leant towards the Swedish side. In April 1860 the *Storting* agreed on the text of an address to the king, maintaining that the Norwegians had the sole right to propose changes in their own constitution and rejecting the Swedish proposals for revision and the assumptions on which these proposals had been based. But the Swedes were not prepared to let the matter rest there. In 1861 the Swedish prime minister, Louis de Geer, proposed to the joint Swedish-Norwegian Council in Stockholm that a committee should be set up with a mandate to propose just those things which the Norwegians had so unanimously rejected in their address. Meanwhile Norwegian opinion had become less firm and changes in the Norwegian government had brought in as premier the respected Frederik Stang (1808–84) who was not opposed to a revision of the terms of the union, at least in principle. In 1863 the matter was taken up again in the *Storting*, with the result that a Union Committee was set up with Ueland among its members. The committee carried out its work in the shadow and aftermath of the Prussian and Austrian attack on Denmark, and fears that danger from the great powers made closer union with Sweden inevitable. In 1871 they submitted their report to the *Storting*. It was signed by all the Norwegian members of the committee and was approved by the king and government. In the *Storting* the report seemed sure of support from many quarters, though the death of Ueland in 1870 had weakened those prospects somewhat. In the event, however, violent opposition to it developed, especially from a former minister, Ketil Motzfeldt (1814–89), who had been dismissed from the government in 1861. Sverdrup also entered the lists against the report and his speech against it during the three-day debate was decisive in getting it rejected by 92 votes to 17.

Sverdrup's next step was to introduce legislation which would oblige the members of the king's *Statsråd* (council of state or government) to attend sessions of the *Storting* and be answerable to it for the manner in which they discharged their duties. This was a matter which had been discussed many times before. In 1824 it had been rejected because, it was argued, the presence of members of the king's Council in the *Storting* would increase royal influence there. Later still it was argued that their presence would make for better communication and understanding between the *Storting* and the king's ministers. For others the separation of the two bodies was essential for the balanced conduct of affairs; the king's Council, it was argued, was a guarantee should radical tendencies in the *Storting* get out of hand; moreover, many people had a strong mistrust of parliamentary government. However, in 1872 the *Storting* passed, with the necessary two-thirds majority, the bill requiring the presence of the members of the *Statsråd*, but Carl XV refused to sanction it. It was also approved in 1874 and 1877, and in 1880 the bill came up again for a further reading. On the second of these occasions a slight change had been made in the bill. Now it was to be approved for the third time in an unchanged form. It was clear that it would now be passed again and thus would become law whether it received the royal assent or not. The king, Oscar II (1872–1907), supported by leading jurists, held that in matters affecting the provisions of the constitution he had an absolute veto. His forthrightness enraged the *Storting*, which on 17 March 1880 passed the bill by 93 votes to 20. Not unexpectedly the government refused to give the bill legal force. They also made difficulties in other matters, including the refusal to pay a grant of 20,000 *kroner* to rifle associations and to give administrative effect to a *Storting* decision on railway development. In the circumstances the only way out of this difficulty was for the *Storting* to impeach the ministers by *Riksrett* for dereliction of duty.

The start of proceedings was postponed until after the new *Storting* elections, in the hope that the king would appoint new ministers with whom the *Storting* could collaborate. But this attempt at compromise failed. The king and government were adamant. Frederik Stang resigned as prime minister and the king appointed Christian Selmer, one of his most uncompromising ministers, in his place. The *Storting* now had no option but to proceed with the *Riksrett*. Selmer was removed from office in 1884 and fined, as were other members of the government. A new right-wing government was formed under Christian Schweigaard, but the *Storting* insisted on their attendance in the chamber to answer questions. This led to an untenable situation and after some further manoeuvring the king was finally obliged to call in Sverdrup to form a government.

*Economic Development and Social Change*

This political ferment was matched in the economic and cultural fields. In shipping the turning-point was the abolition of the British Navigation Acts in 1849, which, together with the abolition of a similar law in Holland, had a startling effect on the growth of Norwegian tonnage. In 1850 it had amounted to 288,633 tons and by 1880 had grown to 1,510,699 tons, thereby making the Norwegian merchant fleet the third largest in the world after those of Britain and the United States of America. Not only was this growth in itself a tremendous stimulus to trade, but the earnings of the merchant fleet abroad were an important factor in the economy as a whole.

However, the lack of credit in Norway for financing new trade ventures was still a serious problem. In all major undertakings, especially the improvement of communications, the state had to take the lead and make itself responsible for the raising of capital abroad, or it had to act as guarantor for loans. But gradually the banking service within the country was expanded. In 1851 a Mortgage Bank (*Hypotekbanken*) was established to take over the mortgage concerns of the Bank of Norway, which in future was to concentrate more on supplying credit to business. In 1848 the first joint stock bank had been founded in Christiania and gradually the number of such banks grew to fifty-five by 1899. At the same time the number of insurance companies and the range of their affairs grew to match the increase in the volume of trade and business.

The second half of the century also saw radical changes in the relationship between town and country. By 1900 28 per cent of the population lived in the towns by comparison with 12.2 per cent in 1845, a process hastened by the advent of steam power, which allowed industry to be placed in the economically most advantageous places. The number of factories grew, especially those engaged in the textile trade, and Christiania became the largest industrial town in the country and the centre of communications. However, fish and timber, together with shipping, continued to be the main supports of the economy. In the herring and cod fisheries new methods brought notable advances and Svend Foyn's invention of the harpoon-gun revolutionized whale-fishing and brought rich profits. The export of timber trebled from the 1830s to the 1870s, after which it declined as other materials came more widely into use, but at the same time the production of wood-pulp and cellulose began to grow into an important industry.

Earlier efforts to improve agricultural methods were given more direction by the founding of agricultural colleges, notably in 1854 when the *Storting* voted the money to found a State Agricultural College (*Landbrukshøgskole*) at Ås, thus providing a centre for agricultural research. However, farming still wrestled with many economic problems. Profits were often not enough to cover the cost of new machinery and other modern improvements. The change from a natural to a money economy had also made for a surplus population in the country districts, a problem which was relieved to some extent by large-scale emigration[1] to North America in the second half of the century and by the growth of the new industries. All in all, it was a period of drastic change in rural life with far-reaching consequences for rural economy, culture, and mode of life. These changes, together

---

[1] After the start in 1825 with the emigrant ship *Restaurationen* (see above, p. 30), Norwegian emigration to the United States really got underway in the 1840s and continued on an appreciable scale almost up to World War I. The number of emigrants fluctuated with economic conditions, rising when times were good and falling when they were bad. In 1882, a record year, some 29,000 Norwegians emigrated, and in 1910 a census showed that there were over 400,000 persons of Norwegian birth in the United States.

with economic and political unrest, provided a rich field for documentation and artistic expression by the great writers of the period, especially Ibsen, Bjørnson, Kielland, Lie, and Garborg.

## Political Life and Relations with Sweden

There were high hopes of Sverdrup's new government. But affairs of state did not proceed smoothly. Ministers were divided politically and there was personal hostility between them. Many resignations and changes followed, which soon led to criticism of Sverdrup himself, who seemed incapable of welding his government into a team. Moreover, the first reform which the new government carried through aroused disapproval. In 1884 the franchise was extended to include all men above twenty-five who had a certain minimum income, but this minimum was fixed so high that most working-class men were excluded. Sverdrup's opposition to a lowering of this income requirement provided his critics with a continuing source of complaint. Also, the new Army Act of 1885, though reducing the period of military service, contained other features which exposed the government to criticism. However, at the *Storting* elections held the same year, Sverdrup's *Venstre* Party gained a great victory, winning 84 seats. Their opponents of the party of the Right (*Høire*) only got 30 seats.

In 1885 the *Storting* debated an application from the writer Alexander Kielland for a writer's pension (*diktergasje*). Kielland, whose work contained many attacks on the established Church and on sectarianism, was a controversial figure, especially detested by low-church elements, from whom *Venstre* derived much of its support. Sverdrup decided to leave the decision to the *Storting*, but this did not save him from bitter Liberal criticism when the application was rejected. Many people believed that this was an issue on which the government should have formed an opinion.

Relations with Sweden also brought further criticism. After accommodating Norwegian demands for equal representation on the foreign affairs committee, the Swedes now demanded (Sverdrup appears to have agreed) that the foreign minister of the two countries should be Swedish. Sverdrup had achieved great popularity because of his success on the equal representation issue; but when the concession about the nationality of the foreign minister became known in Norway, it aroused great anger. Sverdrup then attributed responsibility to Ole Richter, the Norwegian minister of state in Stockholm, who later committed suicide because of the opprobrium to which he had been exposed. But the whole affair increased the credibility gap between Sverdrup's public utterances and his actual deeds.

Division in the ranks of *Venstre* became glaring during the debates on a bill to establish so-called Congregational Councils (*Menighetsråd*) in the state Church. The bill aroused great controversy and was defeated by a large majority in the *Storting*. A demand was now made that Jakob Sverdrup, nephew of Johan, who was the minister responsible for the bill, should resign. Johan Sverdrup rejected this demand. The result was that in 1888 *Venstre* divided into two factions – the so-called *Rene Venstre* (Radical Left) and the *Moderate Venstre* (Moderate Left). It was impossible for the party to retain power and at the elections in the same year the party of the Right (*Høire*) became the largest party with 51 seats. The Radical Left got 38 and the Moderate Left 25 seats. Sverdrup fell and in 1889 a government of the Right was formed under Emil Stang (1834–1912), a son of the former prime minister.

The party of the Right had been somewhat unwillingly constituted after the events which led up to 1884 and Sverdrup's accession to power. Emil Stang had been the driving force in creating it and found support chiefly among the bourgeoisie and the official classes. Its policy, like that of the farmers' party earlier, centred very much on a reduction in state expenditure and activity.

On taking office Stang had inherited a strained situation in relation to Sweden, but he did his best to reduce tension, having some initial success when the free trade agreement between the two countries was extended after Sweden had begun to adopt protectionist policies. However, the continuation of this agreement turned out to be less advantageous to Norway than it had seemed. *Venstre* was critical of it because they saw in it a link holding the union together. Stang also sought to reach final agreement with Sweden on Norwegian participation in the foreign affairs committee, especially on whether the foreign ministry should be reserved for a Swede. It looked as if a settlement was going to be reached. But then the Swedes made public certain reservations about Norway's legal rights to increased representation on the committee. The Norwegians were indignant. Violent criticism of the Norwegian minister of state in Stockholm and of Stang's government followed. He and his colleagues felt obliged to resign. They were succeeded in 1891 by a Radical Left government under Johannes Steen.

The same year *Venstre*'s election manifesto promised that Sweden would be pressed both for a satisfactory settlement of the foreign affairs issue and for the establishment of a separate Norwegian consular service. A satisfactory settlement clearly meant a separate Norwegian foreign minister. The election resulted in a great victory for the radical Left, which gained 65 seats and subsequently called itself simply *Venstre*. It also gave the Steen government an absolute majority in the *Storting*.

The government decided that they would first do battle on the consular service issue. Here, they felt, they were on firmest ground. They also believed that Norwegian businessmen and exporters would support them, especially as Norway had economic interests in areas where they were in direct competition with the Swedes, a situation which made the presence of Norwegian consuls particularly desirable. Steen and his colleagues decided that they would treat the matter as a purely Norwegian one and approved expenditure of 50,000 *kroner* on measures necessary for the setting-up of a Norwegian consular service. The king refused to sanction this and the Steen ministry resigned. Emil Stang also refused to form a government unless the king agreed to sanction the expenditure. However, both in the country and in the parties there was inadequate support for persisting with this hard-line policy. In 1893 Stang formed a minority government of the Right. These uncertainties were also reflected in the results of the *Storting* elections in 1894, when *Venstre's* majority was reduced. The Stang government felt it necessary to resign; but *Venstre* refused to take office on the conditions the king wished to impose, namely that they should not take any unilateral action in matters affecting the union. Feeling was running very high in certain quarters in Sweden and strong measures against the Norwegians were being urged. Norway was exposed to the danger of war, for which she was little prepared. In the circumstances, the politicians agreed to climb down and to negotiate with Sweden on points of difference. In the autumn of 1895 a coalition government was formed under a conservative, Francis Hagerup (1853–1921).

The Norwegians' determination to be masters in their own country was not, however, changed. Both in 1897 and in 1900 *Venstre* was returned with large majorities. In 1897 Hagerup's government was succeeded by one under Steen. Relations with Sweden had been relatively peaceful since 1895, though the committee which had then been set up in an effort to reach agreement had achieved nothing. A bill providing for a Norwegian flag without the union sign on it was passed for the third time in 1898 and became law without the king's sanction. Norwegians realized, after the humiliation of their retreat in 1895, that Norwegian defence had to be built up if the country was to be in a stronger negotiating position. Even *Venstre* concurred in this policy and large sums were spent on modern armaments and defence works. Other legislation passed during this period included an extension of the franchise–in 1896 in local elections; and in 1898 all men over twenty-five were given the vote in *Storting* elections. The educational system was also reorganized. The grammar schools were linked with the elementary schools in a unified system; the school curriculum was also modernized.

The 1890s also saw the full emergence of the Labour Party (*Arbeiderpartiet*) and the trade union movement in Norway. The Labour Party, founded in 1887 by Christian Holtermann Knudsen and a Dane, Carl Jeppesen, sought in particular to detach the working classes from *Venstre* and get them to support their own social democratic policies. It did not have any great success, but its agitation brought social problems more into prominence and led to the passing of legislation relating to child labour, inspection of factories, and workmen's compensation. The Labour Party also played some part in union affairs. Basically it believed that the union should be dissolved, and that this would benefit both Norwegians and Swedes. It also hoped that solidarity with Swedish workers would help the situation, and indeed Swedish labour leaders did do their best to calm warlike tempers in Sweden. However, even Norwegian Labour leaders were just as convinced as the leaders of the other parties that Norway must rearm and defend herself by armed force if necessary.

In Norway, as elsewhere, the trade union movement had its origins among the more skilled workers, for whose services there was an increasing demand and who were in a strong negotiating position for higher wages; thus the printers' union, founded in 1872, was the first trade union in Norway. But it was during the great economic expansion of the 1890s that the movement really got going, so much so that in 1899 the Norwegian trades union congress (*Den faglige Landsorganisjon*) was founded.

## 1905

It must have been clear to both Norwegians and Swedes that their unsatisfactory relations within the union must sooner or later lead to crisis if nothing was done to improve them. In 1902 the Swedish foreign minister, Alfred Lagerheim, took the initiative to bring the two countries together, partly in the belief that Russia had evil designs on the Scandinavian peninsula and thus Swedish-Norwegian solidarity was more important than ever. He proposed that a union committee should investigate the possibility of establishing separate consular services within a common diplomatic service. The Norwegians agreed to this, but the ensuing negotiations proved difficult. In March 1903 a compromise solution to the various problems was issued in the form of a so-called 'communiqué'. This document proposed that separate consular services should be established, each to be responsible to an authority in its own country. The relationship of the consuls to the foreign minister of the two countries should be subject to laws, so-called *likelydende lover*, applying to both countries, which could not be changed or abolished without the consent of both countries.

In Norway these proposals created a deep division in *Venstre*. The radical wing had always regarded the consular issue as being the first step towards a separate Norwegian foreign service with its own foreign minister. Thus they regarded the present proposals with the deepest suspicion. The right-wing elements believed, on the other hand, that the Swedes had made all the concessions they could be expected to make and that a settlement should now be concluded on the basis of the Swedish proposals. The dispute led to ministerial resignations and many prominent members of *Venstre* went over to the Right. In addition to their present dissatisfaction many of the right-wing *Venstre* men were also disenchanted with the increase in state expenditure which had taken place under *Venstre* and feared that spending on defence would increase if Norway went it alone. This, too, made them all the more ready to negotiate with Sweden.

At the *Storting* elections in 1903 a coalition of the Right and dissident *Venstre* men obtained 63 seats, *Venstre* proper 49, and the Labour Party 5; this last figure owed very much to the socialist agitation in north Norway of a clergyman, Alfred Eriksen. In the circumstances a coalition government was formed with Hagerup as premier. He was, it seems, determined that the provisions of the 'communiqué' should be given effect. By May 1904 the Norwegian government had its draft for the proposed *likelydende lover* ready. But in the meantime the Swedes had begun to drag their heels. There were two reasons for this; Russian defeats at the hands of the Japanese made agreement on defence grounds seem less urgent, and there had been a resurgence of Swedish ill-will towards Norway. Moreover, the resignation of Lagerheim had cleared the way for the Swedish 'hard-liners' and their policies. When the Swedish government eventually produced their draft laws in December 1904, they contained a number of clauses which would have made the Norwegian consular service dependent on the foreign minister. The Norwegian government at once demanded the removal of these clauses, but the Swedes were only prepared to negotiate on points of detail and not on the substance of their proposals.

The Swedish change of front infuriated both political parties in Norway and both agreed that it would have serious consequences for the continuance of the union. It was not, however, so easy to secure agreement on what should actually be done. *Venstre* and public opinion, whipped up by the press, were for taking immediate action to give the Norwegian proposals legislative effect. Hagerup and the Right were for allowing a period to elapse before pushing the matter through. In both cases the crucial point would come when the king used his veto, if he did. The resignation of two prominent *Venstre* ministers, Christian Michelsen and J. Schøning, brought things to a head. Their departure made Hagerup's position untenable, and a new government under Michelsen was formed. On 15 March 1905 Michelsen declared in the *Storting* that the government was determined to set up a Norwegian consular service and to assert Norwegian sovereignty in a free and independent kingdom. On 5 April the Swedes offered to negotiate on the basis of a foreign minister for the two countries who could be either a Swede or a Norwegian, and separate consular services with the foreign minister's control limited to consular relations with foreign powers. Reasonable though these proposals may seem, they accorded ill with the strength of Norwegian feeling. The offer was regarded as a tactical move designed to split the parties in Norway, unify Swedish opinion, and to influence foreign opinion against Norway. The Norwegian rejection of the offer brought tempers in Sweden to boiling-point.

In May 1905 the bill providing for the establishment of a Norwegian consular service was passed by the *Storting*. It had been drafted in such a way that, had it not been for the whole background of the affair, royal sanction would not have been impossible. But in fact the king, Oscar II, had no choice. It had always been maintained in Sweden that any unilateral action by the Norwegians would be unlawful. So strong were Swedish feelings that any retreat by the king was out of the question. The king's refusal led at once to resignation of the three Norwegian representatives in Stockholm. On their return to Christiania it was clear that a break with Sweden must follow. On 7 June 1905 Michelsen made the government's proposals public. It would resign, but since the king would be unable to obtain an alternative government, the royal power would be regarded as having lapsed. This power would then revert to the *Storting*, which would authorize the Michelsen government to continue as a provisional government. At the same time Oscar would be asked to appoint one of the princes of the house of Bernadotte as king of Norway. The *Storting* agreed unanimously to these proposals, except that the five socialist members voted against the proposal to obtain a new monarch from Sweden.

In Sweden the government took the Norwegian *fait accompli* relatively calmly, though Oscar was deeply hurt. Both he and the Swedish prime minister urged that force should not be used. The Swedish *Riksdag*, especially the upper chamber, and press reacted violently and warlike noises were made. But the more peaceful factions prevailed and it was agreed that as a condition of negotiating on the dissolution of the union, the Norwegians should be required to hold a plebiscite and that, among a number of other points, certain Norwegian fortresses should be dismantled. The possibility of holding a plebiscite had, as it happens, already been discussed in

Norway. On 13 August 1905, 368,208 people voted for the dissolution and only 184 against.

This was massive confirmation of the Norwegian national will for independence, but the union had not yet been legally dissolved. The Swedes made it clear that this would not happen until the Act of Union had been abrogated by the *Riksdag*. If the Norwegians wanted this, they must ask for it. For the Norwegians to accept would, of course, have called into question the validity of the decision they had taken on 7 June. If they agreed, the Swedes might even refuse to abrogate the Act of Union and thus prevent the union from being dissolved; it would even give them the right to maintain it by force.

In these circumstances the Michelsen government temporized. At secret sessions of the *Storting* Michelsen proposed that they should invite the Swedes to co-operate by abolishing the Act of Union and that the government be authorized to start negotiations with the Swedes on the various matters which would arise out of the dissolution. This proposal was agreed to with some dissent and on 31 August 1905 negotiations began in Karlstad in Sweden. The Swedish demand that Norwegian fortresses along the common border, especially those of Fredriksten and Kongsvinger, should be dismantled soon led to difficulties and on 7 September negotiations were suspended to allow Michelsen to consult the *Storting*, where feeling was running high. Michelsen also used the pause to canvass support abroad for the Norwegian case, and Russia and France brought pressure on the Swedes to concede the Norwegian demands. The situation appeared critical, but after the negotiations were resumed, the Swedish position became less intransigent. The Swedes agreed to allow Norway to retain the fortresses of Fredriksten and Kongsvinger, and on 23 September 1905 an agreement was signed which, by and large, gave the Norwegians what they wanted. There were some dissenters in the *Storting*, but the agreement was ratified by a large majority. The *Riksdag* also ratified the agreement and Oscar abdicated the throne of Norway.

It had already become clear that Oscar would not agree to any member of his house becoming king of Norway, since this would seem to sanction Norwegian action on 7 June. Thus a new candidate for the Norwegian throne, Prince Carl of Denmark, had already been approached before the Karlstad agreement had been signed. Apart from his obvious advantage in language and common cultural background, Carl also enjoyed the prestige of being married to Maud, third daughter of King Edward VII of Great Britain. As in 1814, the Norwegians were anxious for England's blessing on their new arrangements. The Norwegian government had also been given to understand that if Carl became king of Norway, the British would do their best to see that the November Treaty of 1855 (see above, p. 129) would also apply to the new independent Norway. Before accepting the Norwegian throne Carl asked for a plebiscite, to ascertain whether the Norwegian people wanted him. There was some republican feeling, but when the vote was taken, 259,563 voted for Carl and a monarchy and 69,264 against. On 25 November 1905 the new king, who had assumed the title Haakon VII and had accorded his two-year-old son the name Olav, arrived in Christiania.

# Chapter 7

# Norway an Independent Country

*A New Working Day*

CHRISTIAN MICHELSEN'S COMMENT that it was a 'new working-day' that faced the country in 1905 after the abolition of the union, captured the imagination of his compatriots and it seemed that the stage was set for a new and prosperous epoch.

Economic progress, especially in the fishing industry and in shipping, gave cause for optimism, but it was the belief in Norway's future as an industrial country that produced the most sanguine hopes. This optimism derived especially from her potential for the development of hydroelectric power by harnessing her numerous waterfalls. No one saw this potential more clearly than the Norwegian engineer Sam Eyde (1866–1940), who had already established a considerable engineering concern with ramifications throughout Scandinavia. About the same time, a Norwegian scientist, Kristian Birkeland (1867–1917), had discovered a method of releasing nitrogen from the atmosphere by the use of electricity. Eyde was quick to see that this discovery could be exploited inexpensively by the use of hydroelectric power. With the aid of Swedish and French capital he bought up a number of the most important waterfalls and in 1905 *Norsk Hydro*, destined to become a vital industrial concern, was founded. Two years later the production of calcium nitrate began at Notodden in Telemark and later, when the waterfalls at Rjukan had been harnessed, production was greatly increased. In fact the period 1905–14 was one of industrial revolution. The number of workers in industry rose from 86,500 in 1905 to 144,000 in 1913; production increased correspondingly and progress was especially noteworthy in the paper-pulp, cellulose, and paper industries.

Such rapid economic progress and consequent changes in social patterns brought problems. An indication of new political currents was seen at the 1906 elections when the socialists increased their number of seats to ten. But problems arising out of the exploitation of the country's natural resources provided the burning political issue of the day. Many foreigners had already seen that Norwegian forests, waterfalls, and ore deposits were potentially valuable. A large number had been bought up cheaply by foreign speculators before the Norwegians realized what was happening. In 1906 the government proposed temporary legislation to make such purchases subject to buyers first having been granted a concession by the government. However, these proposals did not go far enough to satisfy the radical wing of *Venstre* and as a result they broke away and formed their own group. The remainder of *Venstre* which supported Michelsen's coalition government then formed itself into a so-called Liberal Left (*Det Frisinnede Venstre*). As a result of these dissensions Michelsen was succeeded as Prime Minister in October 1907 by Jørgen Løvland and he, in 1908, by Gunnar Knudsen. In 1909, after contentious debate, the concession laws were passed by a small majority. They were now made applicable also to Norwegian citizens and companies, and included the provision that the concession and the property appertaining to it would revert to the state after a period of fifty to sixty years.

The battles over these concession laws led to the 1909 *Storting* elections being bitterly contested. They resulted in a victory for the Right and the Liberal Left (*Det Frisinnede Venstre*), and a government was formed under Wollert Konow. But his administration was a disappointment to its supporters; the coalition did not work well, and nothing was done to revise the concession laws–indeed they were carried a step further. And when Konow, at a meeting of representatives of the *Landsmaal* language movement, declared his support for the movement, it was too much for his political associates and he was obliged to resign. At the next elections in 1912, *Venstre* was once again a united party and secured a great victory, obtaining 70 seats. The socialists also took a great leap forward, obtaining 23 seats, almost as many as the Right and their supporters put together, a development which was also paralleled by an increase in trade union membership, from 17,500 in 1905 to 67,000 in 1914, most of them belonging to unions affiliated to the Norwegian T.U.C.

Industrial conflicts were also beginning to occur in Norway. To counter these, attempts were made to introduce legislation providing for compulsory arbitration; but they failed, partly because of the workers' confidence in their own strength and partly because of a marked swing further to the Left in their political sympathies. The future socialist leader Martin Tranmæl saw the workers' situation in terms of the class struggle and social revolution, even advocating violent action. Nevertheless, in spite of this extreme movement, the period 1905–14 was one of improved living standards and shorter working hours for many workers. Progress was also made in the field of social legislation, most importantly by the establishment of a national health service to cover the needs of workers below a certain level of income.

*Norway and World War I*

Norway's preoccupation since 1814 with her own affairs and with relations with Sweden, and since 1905 with getting the new ship of state on to a right course, had made non-involvement in the disputes of the outside world a natural corollary. Neutrality was regarded as the best and only policy for Norway. This desire was also recognized by the great powers. In 1907 Great Britain, France, Germany, and Russia signed a treaty with Norway in which they guaranteed her territorial integrity.

Nevertheless, the Norwegians took steps to improve their armed forces; in 1911 a new Army Act was passed and in the following year additional funds were voted by the *Storting* for the navy. On the outbreak of World War I in August 1914, Norway at once mobilized her navy and coastal defence forces, and made it clear that she not only wished to maintain her neutrality but was also prepared to defend it. This, however, did not prevent sentiment in the country being by and large on the side of the Western Allies.

The war situation also stimulated co-operation between the three Scandinavian countries and this in turn reduced the ill-will and suspicion which had characterized Norwegian-Swedish relations since the break in 1905. On 8 August 1914 Norway and Sweden signed an agreement affirming their intention both to preserve their neutrality and not to go to war with each other. Scandinavian solidarity was also expressed in December 1914 when the three Scandinavian monarchs met in Malmø in Sweden and again, in 1917, in Christiania.

The British blockade of Germany soon had consequences for Norway. The volume of Norwegian fish exports to Germany attracted British attention and, to begin with, they dealt with the problem by outbidding the Germans. In so doing, they got more fish than they wanted. But later the British refused to continue the export of coal and oil to Norway unless fish exports to Germany were stopped. Ultimately a secret agreement was concluded between the two countries which stated that the British would buy up surplus Norwegian fish at maximum prices, provided that exports to Germany were kept to a minimum. British economic pressure also led to the Norwegians being obliged to prohibit the export of copper pyrites. The Germans were highly dissatisfied with the consequences, but there was on the Norwegian side rising indignation at German ruthlessness in waging submarine warfare against both enemy and neutral shipping alike. However, in spite of these difficulties Norway managed to hold some sort of balance in her trading between the Allies and the Central Powers, and the first two years of the war were golden ones for her economy. Speculation was rife and rich dividends went to those who could successfully provide for the needs of the warring nations and for their compatriots at home. But in the last two years of the war unlimited German submarine warfare and British determination to keep prices down whenever possible reduced Norwegian freedom of action in the economic sphere. In the first part of 1917 Norwegian shipping losses and the consequent loss of life were particularly high. There were demands that merchant ships should be armed but, in the event, it was agreed with the British that their ships should take over the transport of cargoes from the United Kingdom to Norway, while a similar number of Norwegian ships should be chartered to the British and sail under the British flag, so that they could be armed. The introduction of the convoy system also cut shipping losses in the second half of 1917 and in 1918. Nevertheless, supplies to Norway from overseas had been seriously affected by the war at sea, as also by the entry of the United States into the war. In 1917 a trade mission, headed by Fridtjof Nansen, went to the United States to negotiate supplies for Norway. They found that agreement was not easy to reach. The Americans demanded big cuts in Norwegian exports to Germany, something which the Norwegians were unwilling to carry too far for fear of reprisals. By 1918 food supplies had become so run down in Norway that rationing had to be introduced, and in April 1918 the Norwegian trade mission signed an agreement with the United States in which they accepted most of the American demands.

The direction of political affairs in Norway during the war remained in the hands of Gunnar Knudsen and his *Venstre* government. Knudsen's policy was one of economic liberalism with as little interference from the state as possible. But in war conditions the government was nevertheless obliged to extend considerably the apparatus of state and to impose the controls which became necessary. It was also drawn into the sphere of industrial relations. Wages and salaries had not kept pace with the rate of inflation and this affected especially workers in industry and those on fixed wages. Moreover, when they compared their depressed living standards with the wild extravagances of the speculators, whose activities during this so-called *jobbetiden* were a national disgrace, unrest followed. In 1916 the employers declared a lock-out and Knudsen responded by pushing a bill through the *Storting* which imposed compulsory arbitration, though this was opposed by the unions. There was also considerable social unrest in the final years of the war and to counteract this the government was obliged to grant large subsidies to keep the price of food and other necessities down. It was also obliged to support the fishing industry which, after the British had stopped buying surplus Norwegian fish, had fallen on evil times. These outlays and the other costs which the war imposed, including the cost of maintaining neutrality precautions, meant that state expenditure reached astronomical proportions, which the prevailing rates of taxation failed to cover. As a result the Norwegian national debt rose from 357 million *kroner* in 1914 to 1,130 million *kroner* in 1920.

## The 1920s and 1930s

When World War I ended, Norway was one of the creditor nations. Income from shipping had throughout the war given the country a surplus on its balance of payments. But though, relative to its size, it had acquired enormous assets, these were, by and large, used neither wisely nor well. The situation perfectly demonstrated the phrase 'easy come, easy go' and before long the country's balance of payments deficit had gone deeper into the red than it had formerly been in the black.

The speculation fever of the war years had created a mentality which saw business enterprise as a lottery rather than as solidly based growth–particularly damaging in a country like Norway where the industrial revolution was only in its infancy. Difficulties in obtaining new machinery and raw materials during the war had naturally inhibited new investment and had diverted funds into existing investment channels or into temporary projects, thus making for inflation without adding to the country's basic wealth. In fact at the end of the war the real productive capacity of the country had declined. Now new machinery and ships had to be acquired, most of them from abroad, to provide the necessary renewals in industry and to replace the one and a half million tons of shipping which had been lost during the war. Consumer goods of all kinds also had to be imported in large quantities to replenish depleted stores.

By 1921 Norway found herself in the grip of an economic depression on a grand scale. The decline in world trade had caused production in most Norwegian exporting industries to fall catastrophically. The demand for shipping fell correspondingly and by 1921, 1,300,000 tons of Norwegian shipping were laid up. Share prices fell and many banks found themselves in difficulty, including some of the biggest. State support became necessary and in 1923 a bill providing for the public control of banks was passed. Nevertheless, in spite of these measures, one of the biggest banks, *Handelsbanken*, went bankrupt in 1924, although it had received state support, some of it secret. The Norwegian currency also had a chequered career in the post-war years. In 1919 the government had decided not to tie it to gold, and as the price of gold rose, the Norwegian *krone* lagged behind. The evil consequences which deflation was having for the economy led to thoughts of a return to the gold standard. However, in the meantime the value of the *krone* rose, largely due to the activities of foreign currency speculators. By 1927 it had been pushed up to parity and in 1928 Norway went on to the gold standard. But this upward revaluation also had disastrous consequences for many businesses and for farmers and smallholders with loans to repay. It also led employers to try to reduce wages which now, by international standards, were very high. The result was industrial strife and large-scale unemployment, which was higher in the years 1926–28 than it had been in the immediate post-war crisis years. The need for public assistance grew proportionally and taxes increased correspondingly. Many local authorities also found themselves in serious difficulties and some of them had to be put under government administration.

Changes in the pattern of economic life during the war and the difficulties of the immediate post-war period had made for individual uncertainty and profound changes in Norwegian social and cultural life. The Russian revolution in 1917, too, had, as elsewhere, political repercussions in Norway, especially on the development of the Norwegian Labour Party. As we have seen, even before the war Martin Tranmæl had been urging the workers not to shrink from revolutionary methods, including sabotage, as the way to social revolution. These influences were such that in 1918 a congress of the Labour Party approved by 159 votes to 126 a resolution in which the party reserved to itself the right to use 'revolutionary action in the struggle for the economic liberation of the working classes.' At the same time, the party had agreed to affiliate itself to the so-called Zimmerwald International and later it joined the Third International which had its headquarters in Moscow. However, many members, especially the older ones, could not go along with this policy and a division grew up between those who believed that a democratic majority was the way to power and those who subscribed to the doctrine of the dictatorship of the proletariat. In 1920 the Norwegian trade union movement also identified itself with the views of the radical wing of the party.

It was, however, the so-called 'Moscow Theses' which led to a split in the party. These theses had been adopted in Moscow in 1920 at a meeting of the Third International and all affiliated parties were required to subscribe to them. The social democrats in the Labour Party found them unacceptable and they formed their own group, and even in those sections of the party which accepted them there was very little enthusiasm for them. Russian demands for a centralized party discipline accorded ill with the leading personalities in the Norwegian Labour movement and at a congress in 1923 matters came to a head. A majority of the delegates present were unwilling to accept demands which had been made by the executive of the

Third International and by voting to reject them, they had automatically excluded themselves from membership of that body. The minority, which had been willing to accept the demands, then formed themselves into a separate Communist Party with Olav Scheflo (1883–1943) as leader. Thus the Norwegian Labour Party had fragmented into three groups: the Norwegian Labour Party, the Norwegian Social Democratic Labour Party, and the Norwegian Communist Party. At the 1924 elections they received 24, 8, and 6 seats respectively.[1]

At the 1927 elections the Labour Party, collaborating with the Social Democrats, made a real breakthrough. They obtained 59 seats and thus became the biggest party in the *Storting*, although they did not have an overall majority. Their policies were now more broadly based, with a programme of reform which also attracted the small farmers and fishermen as well as the industrial and white-collar workers. The changed character of the party was shown in 1928 when it agreed to form a government under Christopher Hornsrud, although it had hitherto been a principle not to accept power until it had an overall majority in the *Storting*, lest it should compromise its socialist policies. However, this first Labour government in Norway fell to a vote of no confidence after fourteen days in office.

The post-war years also saw the formation of the Norwegian Agrarian Party (*Bondepartiet*) which in 1921 gained 17 seats in the *Storting*, principally at the expense of *Venstre*. It derived its membership mainly from farmers who were opposed to *Venstre*'s free-trade policies and wanted tariff protection against imports of food from abroad. The Agrarians also wanted a reduction in state expenditure (rather like Ueland and Jaabæk before them), including that on cultural matters, demanding what they called a 'cultural pause' (*Kulturpause*). The farmers also saw with a jaundiced eye the growth of the trade union movement and the rising wages of workers in industry, developments which made for discontent among agricultural workers. In general, too, the Agrarian Party provided a focus for those forces which were somewhat narrowly nationalistic in their outlook.

The Wall Street crash of 1929 also had repercussions in Norway. In the second half of 1930 unemployment rose and by 1933 100,000 people were out of work. Shipping, in particular, was badly hit by the reduced demand for tonnage. But partly because of the batterings the Norwegian economy had received earlier in the decade, it was not so badly hit as in many other countries. Nevertheless, things

[1] One gets a good idea of the agitations and oscillations of the extreme Left at this period from the periodical *Mot Dag*, the organ of a movement of the same name, consisting of intellectuals and workers, led by Erling Falk (1887–1940).

were bad enough and at one point one-third of all trade unionists in
the country were out of work. Industrial conflict on a large scale was
inevitable, especially when the employers tried to reduce wages, and
it is from this period that the most notorious incident in the history of
Norwegian industrial relations dates, the so-called Menstad battle
(*Menstadslaget*) of 1931. During a lock-out, workers at the installations of *Norsk Hydro* had declared all transport to and from *Norsk
Hydro*'s quays at Menstad, between Skien and Porsgrunn, to be
'black'. When they tried to implement this by force, one of their
trade union leaders was arrested and police reinforcements called in.
These measures enraged the workers and on 8 June 1931 columns of
protesters converged on Menstad. The barricades which had been
set up were stormed and several policemen were seriously injured.
On the orders of defence minister Quisling armed troops and naval
vessels were sent to the area to keep the peace. It was an unpleasant
episode which made a deep impression on the Norwegians.

In September 1931 Britain was forced to leave the gold standard
and soon after Norway had to follow suit. Some Norwegian banks
found themselves in difficulty and government support became
necessary, but in 1932 the economic tide at last began to turn. World
markets became more promising and for the rest of the decade the
economy showed an upward trend, although unemployment
continued at a high level.

Apart from the fortnight of Labour administration in 1928
Norway had been governed since 1920 by minority *Venstre* or Right
ministries, with support from other parties: *Venstre* under Johan L.
Mowinckel held office in 1924–26 and 1928–31.

In 1931 the Agrarian Party took office after Mowinckel had fallen
over the question of a concession to the so-called De-No-Fa Company
which was under the control of Unilever. But the new government
did not fare well. It had to grant a concession to De-No-Fa on worse
terms than had previously been rejected, and this, together with its
handling of a dispute with Denmark over Norwegian rights in
eastern Greenland, did not encourage confidence. Eventually, the
Greenland issue had to be referred to the International Court at The
Hague, which in 1933 gave judgement for Denmark. But the government's difficulties also derived from the behaviour of its defence
minister, Vidkun Quisling, both because of his Fascist sympathies,
already discernible at this stage, and because of a violent attack he
made on Labour in the *Storting* in 1932, including accusations, which
he later failed to substantiate, that Labour was planning armed
revolution. It was, however, the Agrarian Party's miserly attitude to
state expenditure, especially on unemployment relief and on the
social services, which caused the government to fall in 1933 during a

budget debate. It was succeeded by a *Venstre* government, again under Mowinckel.

There was great ferment in the Labour Party during the 1930s. The continuing high rate of unemployment led to the conclusion that an economy planned and controlled by the state was the only solution. Labour now believed that this should be achieved by a gradual process of reform – the old revolutionary slogans had passed from the party vocabulary for good. In 1933 it had gone to the polls under the banner of 'the whole nation at work!' and, at the same time, had produced a three-year plan for economic development. The election result was a great Labour victory: it gained over 40 per cent of the vote and increased its representation in the *Storting* from 47 to 69 seats. It did not, however, come to power until 1935, after the defeat of the Mowinckel government, when Johan Nygaardsvold (1879–1952), who was destined to be prime minister of Norway for the next ten years, and his government inaugurated a long period of Labour power.

In foreign affairs the dispute with Denmark over Norwegian fishing rights in east Greenland was the only matter of any consequence to arise. In general co-operation between the three Scandinavian countries, which had been so close during World War I, was intensified between the wars. In foreign affairs, especially, they presented a united front. Their foreign ministers met regularly and they pursued a common policy at the League of Nations. Norway even acquired some overseas territory: in 1920 she had been given sovereignty over Spitzbergen, confirmed in 1925 when the territory was renamed Svalbard; she also occupied the islands of Jan Mayen in the North Atlantic and Bouvet Island and Peter I Island in the Antarctic; an area of the Antarctic continent was also taken into Norwegian possession.

*Norway Neutral and Invaded*

As in 1914 Norway immediately issued a statement proclaiming her neutrality when World War II broke out in September 1939. Though Nazism and its methods were generally detested by the Norwegians and the threat they represented, especially to small countries, was recognized, 125 years of peace had led to the tacit assumption that it was unthinkable that Norway would become involved in a war. Indeed, there were some Norwegians who believed that the country was in less danger of being drawn in than it had been in World War I.

Thus the steps taken at the outbreak of war to defend Norwegian neutrality were far from adequate. The Norwegian fleet was mobilized, but it had few modern vessels; only about 7,000 men were called up in the army, even though the country's defence plan required 20–30,000; coastal defences were only partly manned; and, in general, the Norwegian armed forces lacked modern equipment and adequate training.

For many years defence had been neglected. The belief that it could not happen here, that a declaration of neutrality and member-ship of the League of Nations would be enough protection, coupled with the influence of the pacifist movement and an innate distrust in many quarters of the armed forces, led to the defence budget being cut to the bone. Only a small proportion of those actually liable for military service were called up and purchases of equipment were kept to the barest minimum; indeed the defence plan which had been approved in 1933 reduced the role of the Norwegian armed forces to nothing much more than border defence. Warnings of these deficiencies were given in the years immediately preceding the war and some additional funds were made available, but on a very small scale. In 1939 Norwegian defence was one of the weakest in Europe.

The first difficulties for the Norwegians during the war came from the Allied side. The British complained that their ships had been sunk by the enemy in Norwegian territorial waters and that German ships were making use of these waters for the transportation south of iron-ore from the port of Narvik in north Norway. The British pro-posed that the Norwegians should lay out minefields to force the German ships out onto the high seas. The so-called *Altmark* affair also bore on this problem. In February 1940 the *Altmark*, an auxiliary vessel serving the German pocket battleship *Graf von Spee*, had sought refuge in Norwegian territorial waters, in Jøssingfjord near Egersund in south-western Norway. The vessel was on its way to Germany with some 300 captured British seamen on board. The Royal Navy sent vessels into the fjord to release the prisoners, a mission which was successfully accomplished. Two small Norwegian naval vessels which were nearby protested, but did not open fire. Later the Norwegian government sent a strong protest to the British. It was a situation which dissatisfied all parties: the Norwegians because of the incident itself; the British because they believed the Norwegians were unable to prevent an abuse of their territorial waters; and the Germans be-cause they believed the Norwegians lacked the will to assert their neutrality.

However, although incidents of this kind showed that Norway was in an exposed position, the Norwegian government continued in its belief that Norway would not be drawn into the war and even contemplated reducing the size of the forces which had already been called up. Yet, at this very time, the German forces which were soon to attack Norway and Denmark were being assembled in German harbours. A sinister aspect was that Quisling had been in Berlin in 1939. Yet even when warnings of these preparations began to filter through, the Norwegian government discounted them. They were in fact more preoccupied with Allied mine-laying along the Norwegian coast, about which they agreed to send a strong protest to the British. On the same day that this protest was sent, 8 April 1940, German naval units and transport ships were on their way to Norway carrying the forces who were to occupy the country. In fact a German transport ship had been sunk off Lillesand in southern Norway and survivors from it had stated that they were on their way to Bergen in order to protect Norway from the British. Even this news provoked very little reaction from the Norwegian government and no mobilization order was issued. A few hours later the invasion had begun and later the same night the German minister in Oslo sent a note to the Norwegian government: the Germans were only proposing to occupy strategic points so as to prevent them falling into the hands of the British.

In this situation, on the initiative of the President of the *Storting*, C. J. Hambro, the Norwegian government, members of the *Storting*, and the king and crown prince, left Oslo for Hamar. There the *Storting* met and at a later meeting held at Elverum agreed to appoint a delegation to meet the Germans. The *Storting* also agreed, again on the initiative of Hambro, to give the government full powers 'to take whatever decisions might be necessary to ensure the best interests of the country'. This so-called *Elverumsfullmakt* (Elverum Mandate) was a highly important decision, since it provided the Nygaardsvold government with the authority for its later decision to leave for England and to continue to act there as the government-in-exile.

On 10 April the German minister in Oslo arrived at Elverum and presented his country's demands. These went further than the previous ones, including the demand that Quisling should be prime minister; Quisling had, in fact, already proclaimed himself premier over Norwegian radio and had urged that there should be no resistance to the Germans. The assistance which Quisling had given with the invasion and his party's support of Hitler and Nazism were now to be rewarded. At this point Quisling's so-called *Nasjonal Samling* (National Unity) Party represented only 1·8 per cent of the electorate and had no members in the *Storting*. The demand that he should be prime minister stiffened the resistance of the Norwegian government and at a meeting in Trysil they unanimously rejected the German demands. The Germans replied with bombing attacks on the area. The fight was now officially on, although there had already been resistance to the invaders, notably when the German heavy cruiser *Blücher* was sunk by coastal batteries at the entrance to the Oslo fjord, an action which had an important delaying effect on the invasion. In the north at Narvik two ancient Norwegian destroyers had heroically defied the enemy. But in general 9 April 1940 was a sad day for the Norwegian armed forces. Most of their naval and army units had been put out of action and most strategic points were in enemy hands. Only pockets of resistance remained.

In these circumstances the subsequent battle with the invaders was destined to be very one-sided. Many believed that capitulation was the only sensible course, others that Allied help must come immediately if resistance was to be of any avail.

On 14 and 15 April Allied troops were landed at Åndalsnes and at Namsos, south and north of Trondheim respectively. At the same time Norwegian troops in eastern Norway managed to group themselves into small pockets. A principal objective was to prevent the northward advance of the Germans towards Trondheim. British troops were sent southwards from Åndalsnes to reinforce the Norwegians there, but the combined forces were inferior to the Germans both in numbers and equipment, and were pushed back. By the end of the month, in spite of many gallant episodes, the battle in southern Norway was as good as over. Further north the British troops who had been landed at Namsos did not fare any better and soon had to be evacuated. A crucial factor was that the British were hopelessly inferior to the Germans in air support. As a result of the British presence the towns of Åndalsnes, Namsos, Steinkjer, Mosjøen were reduced to ashes by German bombing.

There remained the Narvik front in the far north. Because of the shipments of iron-ore from Narvik the Allies took this area very seriously. In the days immediately following the invasion the Royal Navy was in action off Narvik and destroyed German naval units there. The Norwegian forces in this area were also stronger than in other parts of the country and were well led. A combined force of Norwegians, British, French, and Poles was assembled and began to advance on the town. The Germans were thrown back and on 28 May Narvik was occupied. But by this time, with the progress of the German offensive in western Europe, the Norwegian campaign had become a sideshow for the Allies. Their forces were ordered to withdraw from Norway, and the Norwegians were left in the lurch. The king and the Norwegian government, who had been evacuated to north Norway, now took the hard decision to leave their country and to continue the fight from England. On 7 June 1940 they left on board a British cruiser.

*Resistance at Home and Abroad*

The German insistence that Quisling should be prime minister was their first great blunder in Norway. It united the Norwegian government and hardened their resistance. Quisling's own radio proclamation had the same effect on the Norwegian people at large. Now that German aims had become clear to them, the Norwegians knew where they stood. Even the pro-German elements in Norway realized that the sponsorship of Quisling had been a mistake.

There was, however, great fear in the country that affairs would degenerate into chaos. In these circumstances the members of the Norwegian High Court took the initiative and on 15 April 1940 they appointed an Administrative Council (*Administrasjonsrådet*) to be responsible for the administration of the occupied part of Norway. It was emphasized that this was to be a purely administrative organ and that it was in no way intended to usurp the authority of the *Storting*. The establishment of the Council restored confidence. It was a body which could resist demands from the occupying power and it provided a focus for the vast majority of loyal Norwegians who gave it their support.

The Germans were not, however, content to let power revert to Norwegian hands. Towards the end of April Hitler appointed a Nazi, Josef Terboven, as *Reichskommissar* in Norway. Terboven was to be directly responsible to Hitler, and for the next five years he was, in many ways, the scourge of the country. On 13 June 1940 he demanded that the *Storting* should meet at Eidsvoll to depose the king and elect a new government. These demands were considered in agonized discussions among the Administrative Council and by leading members (the *Presidentskap*) of the *Storting*. These were dark days for western Europe. The British had been forced off the continent and the French had capitulated. Belief in an ultimate Allied victory was not strong. Finally the *Presidentskap* agreed to recall the *Storting* and propose acceptance of the German demands. They also agreed to call on King Haakon in England to abdicate. The king replied over the B.B.C. that he would abdicate if a majority of the Norwegian people wanted it, but would not do so on the basis of the present procedure which was contrary to the constitution and which had been forced on the Norwegian people. In the event, the *Storting* was not recalled and instead it was agreed that a Council of State (*Riksrådet*) should be set up. The Germans made it clear, however, that it was they who were to decide how many members this Council should have and who its members were to be. They insisted that it should contain a member of the *Nasjonal Samling* Party (*NS*), though Quisling himself, of whom Terboven had a low opinion, was to be sent to Germany. But Quisling had many powerful friends in Germany, and Terboven was obliged to modify his attitude towards him. Now the Germans demanded that many more members of *NS* should have seats on the proposed Council of State. This was resisted by the Norwegians and eventually negotiations broke down. In the meantime the *Storting* had met in its parliamentary groups to discuss the situation and those present had voted by a small majority to suspend the royal functions. Terboven now decided to take the matter into his own hands. On 25 September 1940 he announced on the radio that in future each department of state in Norway was to be under a minister appointed by himself, the majority of whom would be members of *NS*.

Suppression of all free and democratic expression soon followed. The political parties and their organs were dissolved; local administration was brought under central control; the press and radio were muzzled and many newspapers ceased publication; members of *NS* were placed in key positions in those organizations which continued to exist. Attempts were also made to force civil servants and public employees, including teachers, to toe the *NS* party line, in particular by demanding from them a declaration of loyalty to the new political order, accompanied by threats as to the consequences if they refused. This demand was often parried by an alternative declaration being prepared and signed by those who had been threatened. Attempts were also made to undermine the rule of law by the promulgation of decrees, but when *NS* tried to take over control of the High Court, its members resigned. In February 1941 the Church also took a stand against arbitrary and unlawful rule. In fact everywhere, often in quite small ways, the Norwegians were demonstrating their national solidarity. Clandestine newspapers began to appear; resistance began to take on more organized forms; members of *NS* were ostracized.

As time went on, the situation became more tense and in September 1941, using a strike of engineering-workers as a pretext, Terboven proclaimed a state of emergency in Greater Oslo. Hundreds of arrests were made and two trade union leaders, Viggo Hansteen and Rolf Wickstrøm, were taken off and shot. The Norwegian T.U.C. was Nazified and the Rector of the University of Oslo arrested. A concentration camp was set up at Grini just outside Oslo and a reign of terror ensued with a growing number of arrests and executions. In the spring of 1942 the village of Telavåg on the island of Sotra outside Bergen was burnt to the ground, its men deported to Germany, and its women and children interned as a reprisal for incidents arising out of the harbouring of Norwegians who had come back to Norway from England. Eighteen Norwegians were executed in Ålesund for attempting to escape to England. All radio sets were called in, but enough Norwegians managed to retain them to get news from the B.B.C., which was then circulated in the form of clandestine news-sheets, the number of which increased enormously.

It was a situation which stimulated the closer integration of the various civil organizations opposed to the occupation, and it led to the setting-up of a central secretariat in Oslo.

Though the intervention of Terboven in September 1940 had given the trappings of power to *NS*, Quisling was far from satisfied. The Germans had not constituted him as the official Norwegian Führer and the presence of Terboven and the continued existence of the post of *Reichskommisar* were thorns in his flesh. What he wanted was supreme power for himself, including the right to conclude peace with Germany and then to mobilize the Norwegians on the German side. Terboven had always been sceptical about Quisling and he doubted whether he commanded enough influence to wield authority. He regarded Quisling's mobilization plan as something which would simply create trouble for the occupying power. But Quisling's influence in Germany won the day and on 1 February 1942 he was appointed 'Ministerpresident' of Norway. The way was now clear to form an *NS* government of Norway. However, Terboven still remained as *Reichskommissar*.

This was the chance Quisling had been waiting for and he had his plans ready. They included a general Nazification of educational, political, and organizational life, peace with Germany, an alliance with the Axis powers, and mobilization. He began by requiring all boys and girls between the ages of ten and eighteen to join the *NS* youth organization and all teachers to join an official teachers' organization; this teachers' organization was to be the model for other organizations, which in their turn were to form the basis of a national assembly, a so-called *Riksting*. The teachers had already opposed attempts at Nazification in the schools and they were well drilled. Their protests against these measures were met with threats of dismissal and when these had no effect, the schools were closed. Drastic action soon followed from *NS*, supported by the occupying power. 1,300 teachers were arrested and sent to the Grini concentration camp, and later some 500 of them were transported in slave-ship conditions to Kirkenes in north Norway. But terror did not work. Protests came from the Church and when they were disregarded, the bishops resigned. They were replaced by *NS* bishops and the bishop of Oslo, Bishop Berggrav, was arrested. *NS* also set up an organization for lawyers similar to that for teachers, but it suffered the same fate; 95 per cent of the lawyers refused to join it. Later attempts to impose similar organizations on the trade unions and other groups also failed. It was clear that Quisling and his party had no real authority.

However, the situation remained grim. Thousands of Norwegians were arrested and sent to Grini or to concentration camps in Germany, including several hundred students. Pressure was put on the Norwegians to provide workers for German defence works in Norway. A compulsory labour service (*Arbeidstjeneste*) had been introduced for all young men and this became a burning issue in 1944 when it was believed that plans were being made to mobilize young Norwegians for service with the German army on the eastern front. These suspicions were confirmed when Quisling issued an order for the mobilization of certain age-groups for labour service. Only a very few of those who were called up actually reported for duty, and thousands of young men went into hiding in the forests. The Home Front grappled successfully with the enormous problems this raised and many of the young men were got over to Sweden where they were organized in police units.[1]

In addition to the purely civil underground organization which grew up in Norway during the war, there were also a number of underground military organizations, some of them dating back to the 1940 campaign when groups got together for work behind the German lines. The essential distinguishing feature of the military organizations was that they were in possession of arms and took steps to build up stores of weapons for future use. During the winter months of 1941 most of these groups were gathered together into one organization, called *Milorg*, with its own council and secretariat. Its activities naturally attracted the attention of the Gestapo, many members were arrested, and others had to flee the country. Within the organization discussions turned chiefly on the role it was to play

---

[1] The formation and training of Norwegian police units in Sweden began semi-officially in 1943 as a means of occupying in a more satisfactory way some of the 10,000 Norwegian refugees who found themselves in Sweden at the end of 1942. To begin with, Norwegians of military age were called to 'health camps' where they received basic courses in physical training, drill, map-reading, etc., and in police work. Later they received training in the use of weapons. In November 1943 the scheme received the official blessing of the Swedish prime minister and foreign minister, with the reservation that the regular police force trained in this way should not exceed 1,500 men and the reserve force not more than 10,000 men. The force was only to be used in Norway in the event of a German capitulation there. The whole scheme was, of course, a clear breach of Swedish neutrality, but by 1943 the Swedish position *vis-à-vis* the Germans, who were now on the defensive, had changed radically. Previously the Norwegians had complained bitterly that the Swedes had departed from neutrality to the advantage of the Germans when (until August 1943) they permitted the transit of German forces and war material through Sweden to north Norway, and even between Trondheim, Narvik, and Oslo via Sweden. In fact during the first three years of the war Swedish concessions to the Germans gave both the Norwegians and the Allies much to complain of; but the Swedes always pleaded that their neutrality had to take account of the prevailing circumstances. Sweden was, nevertheless, indispensable to Norway during the war as a place of asylum. It is calculated that some 50,000 Norwegians fled to Sweden, some few of whom (especially in 1940) were refused entry. Swedish organizations provided large-scale humanitarian aid to Norway and towards the end of the war the Swedish government granted considerable credits to Norway which were later made a gift.

in the event of an Allied invasion of Norway or of an evacuation of the German forces. There were differences of opinion within *Milorg* as to what this role should be and there were also differences with the civil resistance groups. Relations with the Norwegian authorities in the United Kingdom and with the British were also, to begin with, confused and there was a lack of mutual confidence. Another complicating factor was that the British also had their own secret organizations which mounted operations in Norway and about which, on security grounds, the Norwegian organizations were often uninformed. However, with the establishment of regular channels of contact between Norway and the United Kingdom, either via Sweden or across the North Sea to Shetland by the 'Shetland Bus', and after a Norwegian military High Command had been set up in London at the beginning of 1942, understanding and co-operation between the different parties improved. Supplies of arms and instructors came over to Norway from the United Kingdom, radio stations were set up, and couriers ferried to and fro; and a continuous flow of invaluable intelligence was passed to London. Naturally, all these undertakings involved the greatest danger and difficulties, and time and time again a carefully and laboriously built up group was infiltrated by the Gestapo and its members arrested. But a number of important acts of sabotage were carried out in Norway in conjunction with Norwegians sent from the United Kingdom, most notably the destruction of installations at the heavy water-plants at Rjukan in southern Norway.

In England King Haakon and the Nygaardsvold government continued to represent free Norway to the outside world. Their task was to mobilize Norwegians and Norwegian resources outside Norway on behalf of the Allied cause and for the ultimate liberation of Norway. Both economically and politically the position of the Norwegian government-in-exile was strengthened enormously by the fact that when the Germans invaded Norway, the greater part of the Norwegian merchant fleet of 4·8 million tons was abroad. This tonnage was immediately requisitioned by the government and placed under the administration of a central organization called *Nortraship*. During the war half of this was to be lost and some 3,600 Norwegian merchant seamen were to lose their lives. Norwegian army and naval units were also soon established in the United Kingdom. A number of ships of the Norwegian navy had come to Britain at the time of the Norwegian capitulation in 1940 and as the war went on, many Norwegian naval officers and seamen made their way to Britain, so that by 1943 the Norwegian navy in Britain had seventy ships fighting on the Allied side. Some Norwegian planes also came over in 1940, but the Norwegian air force had to be built up from scratch. Many of its personnel were trained at 'Little Norway', which was set up in Canada. In addition to these forces were the Norwegian police units in Sweden (see above, p. 158), formed from among Norwegian refugees there. When Norway was liberated in 1945 they comprised 13,000 men.

It was, of course, inevitable that difficulties should arise between the Nygaardsvold government in London and the Norwegian organizations in occupied Norway. There were also many Norwegians in Norway who were critical of the government-in-exile holding it responsible for Norway's unpreparedness. In fact, during the first years of the occupation, confidence in the government's ability to understand the problems of those who were still in the country was not high. Nevertheless, it was realized that Haakon and the government were the rallying-point for Norwegian resistance both at home and abroad, and as time went on, the government's credit grew. There were indeed those who believed that some at least of Nygaardsvold's ministers should be included in a new government after the liberation of Norway. On the other hand, the *Storting* of 1936 was held in low esteem because of its attitude in 1940 when a majority had voted for depriving king and government of their functions. Points of view continued to diverge on the steps to be taken to re-establish central and local government after the liberation. It was agreed that it was important to convince the Allies that these were problems which the Norwegians could solve by themselves and that there would be no need for an Allied administration to take over. Another important problem was the setting-up of a judicial apparatus to deal with Quislings and other traitors. Eventually it was agreed that when the Germans capitulated, the Home Front leadership should appoint temporary heads of each government ministry who would function until such time as the government in England could send over some of its own number to take charge.

In the autumn of 1944 German troops in northern Finland began to retreat southwards through Finnmark in north Norway. In doing so they adopted a scorched-earth policy to hinder the advance of the Russians. As a result, the towns and almost all human habitation in Finnmark and in the northern part of the county of Troms were laid waste. The inhabitants of these areas were herded to assembly points, put on board fishing-boats, and evacuated to the south. Many feared that this destruction was a foretaste of what would happen in other parts of the country as the Germans withdrew. Another question was whether the Germans would continue the fight in Norway after their forces had capitulated elsewhere. They were in a very strong position with an army of 350,000 men, many naval units, good defensive positions, and (unlike the Norwegians) adequate supplies. In the event, both these dangers passed. They capitulated on 7 May 1945 and thus gave the signal for rejoicing, the like of which Norway had never seen before.

Norwegians in German concentration camps had already been freed as a result of an initiative taken in Stockholm by the Norwegian diplomat Niels Christian Ditleff, who had enlisted the aid of Count Folke Bernadotte, of the Swedish Red Cross. Thousands of Norwegian prisoners now streamed out of the concentration camp at Grini and the capital was in a state of non-stop jubilation. On 13 May Crown Prince Olav arrived back in Norway together with a delegation of the Nygaardsvold government, and on 30 May the remaining members of the government returned. Finally, on 7 June 1945, five years to the day since he had left Tromsø for England, King Haakon arrived back in Oslo.

# Chapter 8

# Post-War Norway

---

*Domestic Affairs*

AFTER THE CAPITULATION of the Germans on 7 May 1945 the change of government proceeded smoothly, thanks to the careful arrangements made in advance by the Norwegian government in London and the Home Front leadership in Norway. Members of the Home Front occupied key buildings and installations and helped the police in the arrest of collaborators; positions in the civil administration and in government departments were taken over by candidates who had been appointed in advance; and the Home Front leadership headed by Paal Berg, a High Court judge, took up the mandate they had received from the Norwegian government in London to act in a caretaker capacity.

The question soon arose as to whether members of the *Storting* should be recalled. They had been elected in 1936 and, since no elections had been held during the occupation, their four-year period expired in 1940. The legal position was not clear and, in addition, the 1936 *Storting* was not in good odour with the public because of the large number of members who had voted to suspend the royal functions in 1940. In the event, it was decided that the assembly should be recalled, although this was little more than a formality since it was realized that it had no real mandate to legislate.

In the meantime the Nygaardsvold government had returned from London and on 12 June 1945 it resigned. In the first place the king asked Paal Berg to form a provisional government, but owing to difficulties with the party leaders he gave up the attempt and the task devolved on Einar Gerhardsen, the newly elected chairman of the Norwegian Labour Party, who had been active in the Home Front and who had just returned after almost four years in German captivity. His government, which was completed on 22 June 1945, consisted principally of people who had been prominent in the Home Front, although most of them had political affiliations, including six who were members of the Labour Party.

This caretaker government had a ready-made programme which had been agreed on by all parties in Norway immediately after the liberation; it was in essence the programme which had been prepared and discussed during the winter of 1944–45 with a view to having a reconstruction policy ready as soon as the war was over. Its most important feature concerned future economic policy which, it was agreed, should seek to find a balance between free competition and planned economy. Industrial disputes were to be settled without recourse to strikes or lock-outs, a provision which was soon to be tested by the demands for higher wages to meet the over 50 per cent rise in the cost of living which had taken place during the war.

One feature of the immediate post-war political scene was the emergence of the Communist Party; Gerhardsen's caretaker government contained two Communists. Before the war the party's influence had been practically nil, with no members in the *Storting*, but their underground wartime activity and the prestige the Soviet Union enjoyed in Norway immediately after the war meant that the Communists were now regarded as a political force to be reckoned with although their actual strength was unknown. At all events their potential was sufficiently highly regarded for the Labour Party to negotiate with them with a view to the two parties joining forces to contest the *Storting* elections scheduled for early October. As it happened, these negotiations, after some initial agreement, came to nothing, but the results of the elections showed that there had been a marked swing to the Left: The Labour Party increased its number of seats from 70 to 76 (an absolute majority) and the Communist Party won 11 seats. The results for the other parties were: Conservatives (*Høyre*) 25 (at previous election 36); Liberals (*Venstre*) 20 (23); Agrarian Party (*Bondepartiet*) 10 (18); Christian People's Party (*Kristelig folkeparti*) 8 (2). On 5 November 1945 a Labour government, headed by Gerhardsen, took office.

The prosecution of Quisling and other traitors aroused wide public interest in the immediate post-liberation period. Charges were brought against some 50,000 people, most of whom were petty offenders. It was the sentencing of such people that aroused most debate; one section of opinion urging moderation, the other complaining that sentences were too mild. On the whole, the courts followed a middle way, though, whatever the sentence, the stigma of having been *NS* during the war was one which still clings to the offender. There was little dissent about the punishments meted out to the principal offenders, of whom twenty-five were executed, including Quisling and two of his ministers.

The country had been impoverished by the war and the occupation. Apart from the destruction caused by the bombing of towns in 1940, the wholesale destruction in the province of Finnmark in 1945 during the German retreat, and the losses suffered by the merchant marine, production had fallen and the means of production were in a sad state of disrepair. The need for consumer goods of all kinds was enormous. The monetary system, because of the increase in the supply of paper money during the war was in disorder – the value of banknotes in circulation in 1945 being five times greater than in 1940. They threatened inflation and prompt counter-measures were called for. On 22 September 1945 old banknotes were called in and new ones to the value of 60 per cent were issued, the remaining 40 per cent being retained as a frozen credit; in the event, notes valued at some 120 million *kroner* were not returned, in all probability representing funds held by Germans and war profiteers. Moreover, a law had been passed in July requiring all property in whatever form to be registered; this had been done with a view to taxing any increased value which had accrued during the war. It was held that individuals should not profit from Norway's wartime impoverishment.

The overriding need to stabilize conditions in Norway, coupled with the common programme which had been agreed on immediately after the liberation, meant that political life tended to be uncontroversial. Any debate which involved differences of opinion turned mainly on the question of how far state direction of the economy should go. On 8 May 1945 a provisional decree known as Lex Thagaard (after the head of the Directorate of Prices; *Pris-direktoratet*) had given the government very wide powers, both to control prices and to regulate production and distribution. In fact the decree provided for governmental intervention in almost every area of economic life. Some objected to its provisions, but the majority held that it was necessary to prevent economic chaos after the liberation. Originally intended to apply until the end of 1946, it was extended to 1 July 1947; meanwhile the government was to propose new provisional legislation. These proposals were seen to be based by and large on Lex Thagaard and the government indicated that they intended to propose further legislation of a similar, though more permanent, kind. These proposals called forth strong protests both from the parties of the Right and Centre and from industry. Such dissatisfactions, the shortage of foreign currency which for a time led to many restrictions, and complaints from the farmers over low prices were reflected in the results of the local elections on 20 October 1947 when there was a marked swing to the Right and Centre.

In July 1948 the report of the *Storting*'s protocol committee, which had been inquiring into the behaviour of government ministers at the time of the German invasion, was published. This matter had already been investigated in 1946 by a committee of inquiry which had assembled much material and had been very critical of leading ministers including Nygaardsvold. The task of the protocol committee had been to decide whether there were grounds for impeaching any of the ministers before the *Riksrett* (see above, p. 121) for dereliction of duty. A majority of the committee, while agreeing with the criticisms made by the 1946 committee, submitted that there was no case for impeachment; a minority, consisting of members who belonged to the non-socialist parties, believed there was a case, but that it should not be pursued. The protocol committee was also critical of the so-called Administrative Council (*Administrasjonsrådet*) (see above, p. 155), and of members of the *Storting* for their negotiations with the Germans on the deposing of the king and the government, and on the setting-up of the Council of State (*Riksrådet*; see above, p. 155) in 1940. Military leaders and county governors (*fylkesmenn*) were also criticized, but the members of the High Court were praised. The report provoked lively debate, partly on party lines, which together with the political reaction earlier in the year when a number of generals had asked to be relieved of their duties because of disagreements with the minister of defence, showed that the opposition were beginning to prepare for battle at the 1949 *Storting* elections.

Political debate immediately before the 1949 elections turned principally on the government's economic policy. The parties of the Right and Centre were critical, demanding a liberalization of the economy. But in spite of an active electioneering campaign on their part the Labour Party increased its number of seats from 76 to 85; the results for the opposition parties were: Conservatives 23 (25), Liberals 21 (20), Agrarian Party 12 (10), Christian People's Party 9 (8). The sensation of the election was the complete defeat of the Communist Party which lost all eleven of its seats. Two factors were principally responsible for the changed situation: the Communist *coup* in Czechoslovakia in 1948 had lost the Norwegian Communists the support they received in 1945; while the Labour Party (the principal beneficiary of the communist defeat) had managed to improve its standing since the local elections in 1947 thanks to the improved economic situation, for which Marshall Aid was partly responsible. Though there were still many difficulties, it was clear that the Norwegian working classes felt themselves better off than ever before.

The Korean War in 1950 not only prompted the government to propose a sharp increase in the defence budget but it also lent urgency to proposals for strengthening the law relating to treason and for the enactment of new laws to operate in time of war or when the country was threatened with war. The proposed increase in the defence budget was relatively uncontroversial, but the proposed new laws provoked intense debate. Since the beginning of World War II a need had been felt for legislation which could expedite defence arrangements in the event of war or the threat of war, and deal with the activities of fifth-columnists. The invasion of Norway came before anything could be achieved, but in 1948 a committee of experts was set up to propose legislation. Their recommendations were ready in March 1950, before the Korean War had begun, and came before the *Storting* in a practically unchanged form in August. They included provision for the government to be invested with wide-ranging powers, including the setting-up of special tribunals to try traitors, the internment of suspects, and the control of the press. The circumstances in which these powers could be used were also wide and this soon aroused protest, some believing that a government might invoke them to deal with a purely internal situation. There was also strong criticism of the proposed special courts, which were to deal summarily with cases of treachery either by imposing the death penalty or by acquittal (in which case the accused could be passed on to another court); the power of internment without trial; and the control of the press. After much debate these provisions were deleted from the draft text, although the law which was eventually approved gave the government full powers to take whatever steps were necessary to protect Norway's interests in time of war, or when threatened with war, or when her security was in danger; the last two contingencies were closely defined. The powers which this law gave, constituted in fact the kind of mandate which the Elverum Mandate of 1940 (see above, p. 153) had given.

Otherwise the government's problems in 1950 were very much on the economic front. The devaluation of the *krone* in September 1949 (at the same time as the devaluation of the pound) meant that, with the increase in the cost of imports, the government found it impossible to maintain its policy of keeping the cost of necessities down through price control and subsidies. The price of many commodities rose rapidly, that of margarine and coffee almost doubling. Demands for higher wages inevitably followed. At the same time Norway was faced with a balance of payments deficit, but though this was for the time being largely offset by Marshall Aid funds, it could not be overlooked that this aid was due to cease in 1952. The government also had to find the money to meet the increased cost of defence. In the circumstances it was decided to cut back on investment. But there was little inclination to introduce really tough economic measures, though one of the leading exponents of a planned economy in Norway, Ole Colbjørnsen, complained that life since the war had been characterized far too much by 'leisure, holidays, absenteeism, and pleasure' and that the Norwegian worker did not work hard enough.

The Labour government was nevertheless still firmly in the saddle. The results of the 1951 local elections showed that there was no slackening in the massive support the party had received at the 1949 elections. Thus it seemed incomprehensible when Gerhardsen suddenly resigned on 13 November 1951 and was succeeded by Oscar Torp. Gerhardsen's own explanation was that he was tired and wished to be relieved of the burdens of office. Since he first took office as prime minister in 1945, he had become a popular figure and something of an institution; yet there is much to suggest that beneath his forthcoming exterior he was not ideally suited to the rough and tumble of political life or to the glare of publicity which went with his office.

Earlier in 1951 the *Storting* had approved plans for the building of a state aluminium plant in Sunndalsøra in the county of Møre og Romsdal which was to take advantage of the extensive exploitation of the hydroelectric potential of the adjacent Aura river region. Plans were also put forward for the development of north Norway over a ten-year period, principally by the creation of a special fund, to be used to finance industrial undertakings and provide the region with a more varied economy; to develop communications and power supplies; and to provide more educational opportunities. All these plans went ahead in spite of opposition criticisms that the large-scale investment required would overstrain resources, that the terms on which a loan had been obtained for the building of the aluminium plant were unfavourable, and that the plans for north Norway had been inadequately thought out.

Since 1945 the political parties had by and large been agreed on foreign, defence, and social policies. The only major differences between them sprang from the question of economic planning. These differences came to a head in March 1952 when a report from the Committee for Prices and Rationalization (*Pris- og rasjonaliserings-komiteen*), also known as the Sjaastad Committee from its chairman Gustav Sjaastad, was published. The committee had been set up in 1947 to investigate how the state could most effectively co-operate in the rationalization of economic activity, and to make proposals for legislation to control prices and profits. A minority of its members favoured temporary legislation to control prices, but the majority made proposals for laws to control prices, competition, and the organization and development of economic activity. In fact the proposed legislation gave the government very wide powers not only to control the economy but also to intervene in the activity of individual industrial undertakings. The detailed proposals included control of dividends, which in any case were not to be higher than 5 per cent; the right to expropriate industrial concerns if their activity was damaging to the public interest; powers to decide whether new industrial enterprises should be started; and a whole range of controls for existing industry.

The publication of the report led to a storm of protest. As a result the government stated that it would not propose any general legislation on the rationalization of industry, but only such legislation as became necessary for the control of individual industries. It did, however, on 12 September make proposals for a permanent law to govern prices, to replace the provisional Lex Thagaard which was still in force. These proposals went nothing like as far as the proposals of the Sjaastad Committee and, in some respects, less far than the Lex Thagaard, but they included a Sjaastad proposal that a higher dividend than 5 per cent should not be paid without special permission. After further debate this 5 per cent limitation was dropped; instead the *Storting* was to fix dividend levels annually. The new law, which still gave the government extensive powers to regulate prices, came into effect on 1 January 1954.

Another controversial matter which came before the *Storting* in 1952 concerned election regulations. Since 1919 Norway had used a system of proportional representation, employing the so-called d'Hondt method. For a variety of reasons this system favoured the largest parties; thus at the 1949 elections the Labour Party, which polled 45·7 per cent of the votes and, proportionately, should have had 68 of the 150 seats in the *Storting*, actually got 85. Change was not easy: the constitution would have to be amended, and there were geographical, political, and technical problems to be solved. Though there was agreement that the situation was unsatisfactory, there was a division of opinion as to what should actually be done. In the event, the so-called *Bondeparagrafen* (see above, p. 120) of the constitution was abolished and the number of electoral districts (*valgdistrikter*) was reduced from twenty-nine to twenty so that they corresponded to the number of counties (*fylker*), except that the towns of Oslo and Bergen constituted separate electoral districts. At the same time the so-called Laguë's method of proportional representation was introduced, which gave results less favourable to the largest parties than the d'Hondt method. These changes meant a sacrifice for the Labour Party, of particular interest in view of the forthcoming elections in 1953; it was seen that the new system would give the opposition parties a much better chance of challenging Labour's absolute majority.

In the event, although Labour's seats dropped from 85 to 77, they actually increased their share in the poll from 45·7 to 46·7 per cent. The other parties, except the Liberals and the Conservatives, also increased their share, and all parties except the Liberals obtained more seats. The final results were: Conservatives 27 (23), Liberals 15 (21), Agrarian Party 14 (12), Christian People's Party 14 (9), Communists 3 (0)—a victory for Labour which, though the new electoral system still favoured them, would have received 92 seats under the old. Their success must be ascribed to their supporters' satisfaction with socialist policies, including a tax structure which strongly favoured the lowest-paid; price subsidies which kept down the cost of necessities; and the development of social welfare. Moreover, a favourable economic situation made for full employment and many workers, especially in fishing and agriculture, were better off than they had ever been before. Another factor in Labour's success was that the parties of the Right and Centre did not, either individually or collectively, present any clearly formulated alternative programme, or inspire confidence that they had leaders of calibre or that they could collaborate in the exercise of power.

In 1953, after previous surpluses, there was a deficit of 839 million *kroner* on the balance of payments, followed in 1954 by a deficit of 1,127 million *kroner*. The cost of living index for the year went up by some 6 per cent. On the other hand, Norway had one of the highest investment rates in Europe (about 28 per cent of the national product), and production increased in 1954 by 4 per cent over 1953. However, it was clear that the economy had become overheated and that a steep rise in prices was threatening Norway's competitive position abroad. Not unexpectedly, the government came in for a great deal of criticism: from the workers because of price rises; and from industry and the opposition who blamed the whole situation on the government's economic policy. The situation also seems to have made for tensions and disagreements within the government ranks. In January 1955, in a general reshuffle, Oscar Torp resigned and was succeeded by Gerhardsen. Measures to deal with the economic situation soon followed: bank-rate was increased from $2\frac{1}{2}$ to $3\frac{1}{2}$ per cent, a measure which Labour governments had previously refused to take; the reserves which the banks were required to maintain were increased; and credit was restricted. Special steps were also taken to curb price rises—particularly important as many wage settlements were tied to the cost-of-living index—and these were for the time being successful. The deficit on the balance of payments was also reduced, though this was partly due to favourable terms of trade and an increase in freight rates, which meant that earnings from the merchant fleet rose considerably. However, during 1956 the prices-wages spiral continued, with the government struggling to keep the situation in check by subsidies and other controls.

There was much discussion before the 1957 elections about the possibility of electoral co-operation between the four parties of the

Right and Centre (the Conservative, Liberal, Agrarian, and Christian People's), principally to see whether they could agree on some common electoral programme and whether they could agree not to put up competing candidates in some electoral districts to avoid splitting the vote to Labour's advantage. Very little came out of these discussions. There was some co-operation between Conservatives and Agrarians in two electoral districts and between Conservatives and Liberals in one other, but even this caused much dissension within the parties.

The elections resulted in a new victory for Labour: an increase in seats from 77 to 78. The results for the other parties were: Conservatives 29 (27), Liberals 15 (15), Agrarians 15 (14), Christian People's 12 (14), Communists one (3). The election showed that confidence in Labour was undiminished, in fact their percentage of votes cast (48·3) was for the first time bigger than all the votes cast for the parties of the Right and Centre (48·1). A special feature of the result was the spectacular decline in communist support. The party lost about a third of its votes, roughly the number which Labour gained. At the 1945 election it received almost 12 per cent of the votes, now it had got only 3·4. A contributory factor in this decline was undoubtedly the Soviet intervention in Hungary in 1956.

Apart from the continuing problem of inflation the internal political scene between the 1957 and 1961 *Storting* elections was pretty featureless. There had, however, been disagreements within the Labour Party on foreign policy which were destined to have serious consequences. For many years a small left wing of the party, opposed to Norway's membership of NATO and the increasing cost of defence, had demanded more radical social and economic policies. During the 1950s this group started publishing its own journal, *Orientering*, which made sharp attacks on Norwegian foreign policy in general and on the foreign minister, Halvard Lange, in particular. In 1960–61 the movement received fresh impetus from the protest demonstrations against atomic weapons which were held in Norway and in other western European countries. The *Orientering* group seized in particular on the refusal of the Labour leadership to repudiate the stationing of atomic weapons on Norwegian soil, although a motion to this effect had been passed at a Labour Party conference in 1957. Leadership and government declared that they would not permit such weapons on Norwegian territory but, nevertheless, reserved the right to review this policy if major international changes threatened Norway's security. The left-wing activists took this to mean that the government was 'leaving the door ajar' for atomic weapons. Bitter conflict ensued at the 1961 Labour Party conference, but eventually a compromise formula was arrived at: the party's policy was that no atomic weapons should be permitted in Norway; but Norway could, through her constitutional organs, decide at any time on steps necessary to preserve her security and independence. This formulation was agreed to by the vast majority of conference representatives, but immediately afterwards dissident elements together with others who were opposed to atomic weapons met and on 16 April 1961 founded the Socialist People's Party (*Sosialistisk folkeparti*).

Though it was clear that this splinter-group would make some mark on the September elections, there was general astonishment when it succeeded in winning two seats. This success also put it in a controlling position in the *Storting*, the final position of the other parties being: Labour 74 (78), Conservatives 29 (29), Liberals 14 (15), Centre (*Senterpartiet*, formerly *Bondepartiet*) 16 (15), Christian People's 15 (12), Communists nil (1). Thus Labour and the parties of the Right and Centre had 74 seats each.

Apart from the votes it lost to the Socialist People's Party, support for the Labour Party in general receded, its percentage of the total poll falling to 46·8 per cent as compared with 48·3 in 1957. There seemed, nevertheless, to be no real alternative to a Labour government in spite of the Right and Centre parties' parity. In 1960 and 1961 there had been much talk of 'co-operation at the centre', and for more than a year the Liberal, Centre, and Christian People's parties had had discussions about a common policy should the Labour Party lose its overall majority. But nothing concrete emerged from these discussions, except a clear indication that in all three parties there were powerful factions opposed to co-operation. However the Gerhardsen government's position had changed. No longer could it rely on its overall majority to pass any measure and ride out any storm. But, since the Socialist People's Party was well to the left of Labour, its two members would vote with the opposition, and thus defeat the government, only in exceptional circumstances.

To begin with, the new government proceeded smoothly but in 1963 the political climate changed. One reason for this was that discussion on Norway's entry into the Common Market lapsed after de Gaulle had vetoed British membership and, consequently, Norway had not gone ahead with her application. This meant that, since the opposition parties had been divided over Norway's entry, political debate once more became polarized into government and opposition. A number of other issues arose on which there were sharp clashes between government and opposition. The first was in February over the appointment of a member of the Labour Party and prominent trade unionist as head of the State Police Academy (*Statens politiskole*);

the opposition criticized this as a political appointment, maintaining that there were better-qualified candidates for the post, but a vote of no confidence failed. The next clash occurred in June and concerned a state enterprise: the construction at Mo i Rana of a plant for the production of coke from Spitzbergen coal, which had cost much more than originally estimated. There was sharp criticism of the minister of industry and allegations of bad planning and management; again the government managed to survive a vote of no confidence. Shortly after this a new crisis developed over safety precautions at the state coal-mines at Ny-Ålesund in Spitzbergen.

The so-called King's Bay Mining Company at Ny-Ålesund had originally been a private company, but was taken over by the state in the early 1930s. In 1948, 1952, and 1953 there had been explosions in the mines, with a total loss of forty-three lives. In 1956 the *Storting* had agreed to the modernization of the mines, on the express condition that everything possible should be done to prevent accidents in the future and that proper security precautions should be enforced. Nevertheless, on 5 November 1962 another explosion occurred with the loss of twenty-one lives. The report of a committee of inquiry appeared in June 1963, just before the *Storting* was due to begin its summer recess, and contained severe criticism of the management and supervision of the mines both at local and governmental level. The industry minister resigned and the *Storting* unanimously agreed to meet for a debate during the summer; in the meantime the government was to obtain additional documentation.

In the first place the matter was considered by a special committee of the *Storting*; but it soon became apparent that it had become a political issue. The Labour members of the committee argued that as the cause of the accident could not be established, it was impossible to lay the blame on individuals; but the opposition members maintained that the government had been negligent and had not implemented the *Storting* decision of 1956. They proposed a vote of no confidence in the government. When the *Storting* debated the issue on 20–23 August these arguments were repeated, the government reproaching the opposition for wishing to make political capital out of an accident. However, when the *Storting* divided, the motion was carried by 76 votes to 74, the two Socialist People's Party members voting against the government. The Gerhardsen government immediately resigned.

The question now was whether the Right and Centre parties would be able to form a government in view of their known differences. To the surprise of many these were rapidly overcome, and on 27 August 1963 a coalition government of the Conservative, Liberal, Centre, and Christian People's parties took office with John Lyng of the Conservative Party as prime minister. Feeling in the Labour Party was running high over what had happened, but the leadership decided to bide its time and, in the first place, asked the new government to produce a policy statement which the *Storting* could debate before the local elections on 23 September. When this statement was produced on 16 September it turned out to be a very neutral document, proposing no radical changes, and was characterized by the compromises the four coalition parties had been obliged to make to reach agreement. Labour immediately replied by producing its own programme, including proposals for a new national pension scheme, four weeks holiday established by law (instead of the existing three weeks), a shorter working-week, and provision for further state control in a number of areas. During the *Storting* debate on 18–20 September Labour moved that the government should adopt Labour's policy statement as a basis for government. The two Socialist People's Party members, who, nevertheless, produced a policy statement of their own, added their support. The government, the Labour Party, and the Socialist People's Party all voted for their own proposals; thus none received a majority. Nevertheless, the Lyng government regarded this as a defeat, since there were two motions against its own policy statement which together commanded a majority of votes, and resigned. As a result, a new Labour government under Einar Gerhardsen was formed and took office on 25 September.

The crisis and brief change of government had two main consequences: it made for a radicalization of Labour Party policy, and it showed that in spite of their differences the four opposition parties could form a government. The whole episode stimulated political interest: at the local elections 81 per cent of the electorate participated. The Labour Party increased its share of the total vote to 45·79 per cent (43·74 per cent), which it regarded as a vindication of its conduct in the King's Bay affair.

Problems connected with the ministry of industry continued, however, to harrass the government. In October 1963 a ministry official was arrested and charged with the misappropriation of state property and other offences. The ministry was also criticized for its handling of agreements in connection with the building of a new aluminium plant, mainly financed by Swiss and French capital, at Husnes in Hardanger, on the grounds that Norwegian interests had not been properly taken care of. Criticism of the state coke plant continued and also of the costs associated with the state iron-works at Mo i Rana, which continued to soar; figures were also produced to show that the works would continue to operate at a loss. As a result of these criticisms the government in the autumn of 1963 set up a committee of inquiry into the work of the ministry. Its report appeared some nine months later and was critical of many aspects of the ministry's work. The government therefore made a number of proposals for reform.

1964 was generally a quiet year on the internal political front. The government made headway with its proposed earnings-based pension scheme and the *Storting* agreed to amend the law governing holidays so as to give all wage-earners the right to four weeks holiday (i.e. 24 working-days). By contrast, 1965 was the most dramatic in post-war Norwegian history: the year in which the Labour Party finally fell from power.

There can be no doubt that Labour's defeat in 1963 had a deep psychological effect on the Norwegian electorate. It showed that the Labour Party was not invincible after all, and that an alternative government was possible. Also, in spite of Labour's success at the 1963 local elections and the fact that Labour was back in power, the opposition's criticisms of the government's management of state enterprises had an undermining effect, especially when they were linked with dissatisfaction over high taxes, rising prices, a shortage of living accommodation, and shortcomings in the educational and telephone services. Both the opinion polls and the results of some local elections, which had been held in 1964 because of the revision of some local boundaries, showed that the popularity of the Labour Party was on the wane.

This situation naturally heartened the four opposition parties and encouraged them to arrange various forms of electoral co-opera-tion so as to avoid splitting the vote at the forthcoming *Storting* elections. They also took comfort from the fact that the Socialist People's Party was putting up candidates in many more electoral districts than at the previous election and that Labour had rejected any form of alliance with it. Thus it did not come as a complete surprise when at the elections in September 1965 the number of seats held by Labour was reduced from 74 to 68. The Socialist People's Party retained its two seats, the Communists again failing to get any candidates returned. The results for the parties of the Right and Centre were: Conservatives 31 (29), Liberals 18 (14), Centre 18 (16), Christian People's 13 (15)–a total of 80 seats.

This time the four coalition parties agreed that their prime minister should come from one of the Centre parties. With the Conservatives as the largest party in the group they were anxious to avoid being dubbed a right-wing, Conservative-dominated govern-ment by their political opponents. The choice was between the leaders of the Liberals and the Centre Party, and eventually Per Borten of the Centre Party was chosen, both because of his political moderation and also because his party lacked extreme fringes likely to offend the susceptibilities of, particularly, the Conservatives and the Christian People's Party.

Since the Norwegian budget is approved in the autumn for the following calendar year, it was not until autumn 1966 that the Borten government was able to show whether it intended to pursue any radically different fiscal policies. When budget proposals were announced, it was seen that, apart from some minor changes, they were the mixture very much as before; in fact even the opposition maintained that there was no essential change from the budgets they themselves had put forward. The whole period of the Borten administration until the elections in 1969 was unexciting. There were no major trials of strength between it and the opposition. The most important piece of legislation to be carried through was the national insurance scheme (*folketrygden*), to replace previous schemes relating to old age, children's, widows', and mothers' pensions and rehabilitation assistance, which took effect from 1 January 1967.

Nevertheless, the results of the September 1969 elections were awaited with great interest. Would the coalition retain power or would the Labour Party make a comeback? During the election campaign the coalition parties managed to present a common policy on all matters of substance, though rivalries were apparent over co-operation on representation within the electoral districts. Labour concentrated on putting over an electoral programme which provided a distinct alternative to the coalition, and in particular listed the reforms it would carry through during the first hundred days of office if it were returned to power. The Socialist People's Party was in sad disarray before the elections, partly because of internal dissension, but also because its leader, Finn Gustavsen, had decided not to seek re-election.

The result showed a marked increase in the support for Labour, which gained 74 seats, six more than in the 1965 elections. The Socialist People's Party lost its two seats and the coalition parties received 76 seats, distributed as follows: Conservatives 29 (31), Liberals 13 (18), Centre 20 (18), Christian People's 14 (13). Votes were cast by 83·6 per cent of the electorate, which now included twenty-year-olds, the age limit having been reduced from twenty-one. The coalition parties had retained power, but their greatly reduced majority of only two seats meant that the need for solidarity between them was greater than ever, especially as Labour was very much on the offensive and seized every opportunity of exploiting the weaknesses which from time to time showed up in the coalition. A number of changes in the composition of the government, still under Per Borten, also gave the impression that they derived from disagreements within the four parties. A major subject of debate in the first half of 1969 was the proposal for the introduction of a value-added tax and the changes in the country's tax structure which would flow from it. Differences between government and opposition turned mainly on the tax percentage to be levied. Eventually in June a 20 per cent tax was agreed on by the *Storting*, the reform to take effect from 1 January 1970.

In March 1971, as a result of a leak of information in connection with Norway's negotiations for entry into the Common Market (see below, p. 187), Per Borten resigned as prime minister and, since it was not found possible to form a new government from the Right and Centre coalition, a minority Labour government took office on 17 March under Trygve Bratteli. His government has, of course, not been able to propose legislation of a controversial kind: in fact the *Storting*'s most important legislative since the Bratteli government took office has been a lowering of the minimum age for the state old-age pension from seventy to sixty-seven, to take effect from 1 January 1973.

## FOREIGN POLICY

Before World War II the overriding aim of Norwegian foreign policy was to maintain neutrality, but to combine it with membership of the League of Nations and the support of collective action, provided this did not seriously jeopardize neutrality. Thus Norway supported sanctions against Italy during the Ethiopian War in 1935–36.

### Norway and the U.N.

In 1945 Norway signed the charter of the United Nations as one of its founder members, and membership of that organization has been one of the cornerstones of Norwegian post-war foreign policy. At the U.N. Norway has been a consistent supporter of the principle that membership should be open to all sovereign states irrespective of their political systems, and thus has always supported membership for the People's Republic of China. Norway has also advocated disarmament subject to the establishment of an effective control system; the banning of nuclear tests in the atmosphere; and the conclusion of agreements to prevent the further spread of nuclear weapons. In colonial matters Norway supported in 1960 the General Assembly's Declaration on the granting of independence to colonial peoples and territories, and its representatives have spoken against the South African administration of South-West Africa and Portuguese administration in Angola and Mozambique. Norway has also refused to recognize the Smith regime's unilateral declaration of

1 Adolf Tidemand: *Catechization in a Norwegian Country Church* (1847)

2 Carl Johan (Jean-Baptiste Bernadotte), king of Norway and Sweden (1818–44)

3 Carl XV, king of Norway and Sweden (1859–72)

4 Meeting of Notables at Eidsvoll in 1814 at the time of the promulgation of the Norwegian constitution

5 Edvard Munch: *Girls on the Bridge* (1893)

6 Johan Christian Dahl: *Stalheim* (1842)

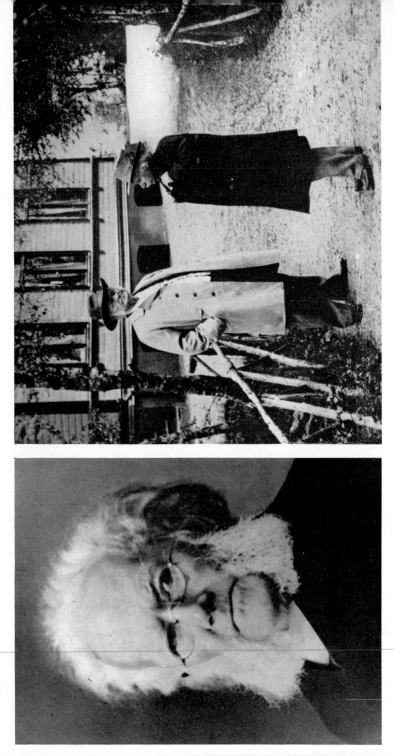

8 The writer Bjørnstjerne Bjørnson (*left*) and the composer Edvard Grieg at Trollhaugen (Grieg's home near Bergen)

7 Henrik Ibsen

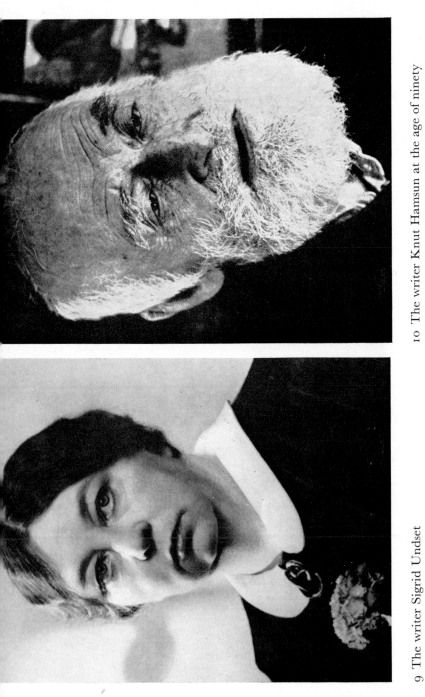

9 The writer Sigrid Undset

10 The writer Knut Hamsun at the age of ninety

11 The mining town of Røros in the nineteenth century

12 Karl Johans gate showing the Royal Palace, about 1900

13 Nansen's *Fram* in the polar ice 1895

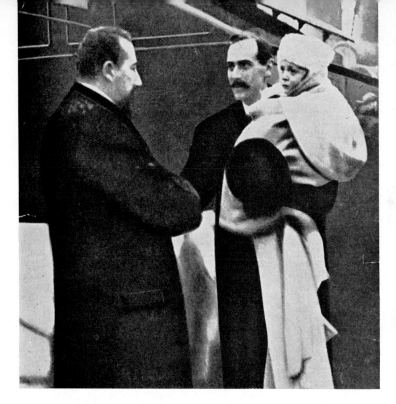

14 King Haakon, carrying Crown Prince Olav, greeted by Prime Minister Christian Michelsen on his arrival in Christiania on 25 November 1905

15 Demonstration by strikers in Christiania in 1924. The placards read (*left*): 'Nickel and bank swindlers go free. Striking metal workers given sentences'; and 'A leech is better than a strikebreaker'

16 Narvik in flames after a German air attack in 1940

17 Members of the Administrative Council during a meeting with the German minister to Norway in 1940. Gunnar Jahn, Director of the Central Office of Statistics (*1st left*); (*5th left in front, in morning dress*) Curt Bräuer, German minister; (*6th left between* Bräuer *and* Christensen) Didrik Arup Seip, Rector of Oslo University; (*7th left*) I. E. Christensen, Governor of Oslo and the county of Akershus; (*right holding white paper*) Paal Berg, President of the High Court of Justice

18 King Haakon and Crown Prince Olav taking refuge in a forest during the German bombing of Molde in 1940

19 Quisling (*right*) with Reichskommisar Terboven (*centre*) arriving at Akershus castle on 1 February 1942 at the time of Quisling's appointment as 'Minister-president' of Norway

20 Haakon VII's monogram painted on a wall in Drammen in 1941

21 Johan Nygaardsvold, prime minister of Norway 1935–45

22 Einar Gerhardsen, prime minister of Norway 1945–51 and 1955–65, showing Oslo to British Prime Minister Harold Macmillan during a visit to Norway in 1960

23 Per Borten, prime minister of Norway 1965–71

24 Trygve Bratteli, prime minister of Norway 1971–

25 Gustav Vigeland's *Fountain* and *The Monolith* in Frogner Park, Oslo

26 The campus of the University of Oslo at Blindern, showing Arnold Haukeland's sculpture *Air*

27 Bergen, the harbour area

28 A farm in Romsdalen

29 The Cathedral of Nidaros at Trondheim

30 Hammerfest

31 Timber being sprayed prior to processing

32 Mo i Rana, the state iron-works

independence in 1965 and has joined in economic sanctions against Rhodesia.

In Middle East affairs Norway was one of the countries which in 1956 proposed the establishment of the United Nations Emergency Force (UNEF) to supervise the cessation of hostilities after the Suez crisis and to provide a peace-keeping force in the Gaza strip; subsequently Norwegian troops formed part of this force and, in the early 1960s, of a similar force in the Congo. Norway has also provided personnel for the United Nations Truce Supervision Organization (UNTSO), of which General Odd Bull of Norway became chief-of-staff in 1963. In the relief sphere Norway has provided assistance to the Palestine Arab refugees by making annual contributions to the United Nations Relief and Works Agency (UNRWA), and has also made other financial contributions to the work of the U.N. Together with Finland, Norway was the first country to purchase United Nation bonds in 1962, a measure which was designed to alleviate the financial crisis in which the U.N. found itself, mainly because of the failure of some members to contribute to the cost of peace-keeping operations in the Middle East and the Congo. In 1965 Norway also made a voluntary contribution of 5 million *kroner* to U.N. funds, and has established a permanent peace-keeping unit, designed for service with the U.N., which can also be used as an international emergency force to assist after earthquakes and other natural disasters.

Norway has also been high on the list of those countries giving financial support to U.N. programmes of assistance to developing countries, including support of the U.N. Conference on Trade and Development (UNCTAD). In 1962 the *Storting* agreed to levy a tax of 0·25 per cent on taxable incomes to provide funds for this purpose. Moreover, Norway has since 1952 been operating a scheme in the Indian state of Kerala for the promotion of off-shore fishing, including the training of Indians. In 1962 the *Storting* set up Norsk Utviklingshjelp (The Norwegian Agency for International Development; NORAD) to co-ordinate its aid programmes. This organization, sometimes in co-operation with the other Nordic countries, has established or participated in a number of aid projects in different parts of the world, including a share in operating, with Denmark and Sweden, a national medical centre and hospital at Seoul in Korea. In 1963 the *Storting* agreed to the establishment of a Norwegian Peace Corps for service in developing countries. For 1972 the *Storting* has voted a budget of 376 million *kroner* for development aid, and aims by 1974 to devote 0·7 per cent of the country's gross national product to this purpose.

*Norway and NATO*

The occupation of Norway during the war and her participation on the Allied side had strengthened the country's traditional ties with the West. They had also fostered goodwill towards the Soviet Union, whose troops had taken part in the liberation of Norway, and had changed relations with the other Nordic countries, especially with neutral Sweden.

After the war Norwegians were agreed that Nordic co-operation should be maintained, but there was also a strong feeling that to return to the pre-war isolationism in foreign affairs was unrealistic. During the immediate post-war years when disagreements between the great powers divided Europe into two opposing blocs, Norway saw her role as a 'bridge-building' one. Her own exposed strategic position should any conflict arise between East and West was an additional reason for this. In 1947 Norway participated in the negotiations for a large-scale loan to Europe under the Marshall Plan, and in 1948 she supported Ernest Bevin's plan for extended co-operation between the countries of western Europe in a Western union.

The Communist *coup* in Czechoslovakia in February 1948 led the Norwegians both to strengthen their defences and also to reassess their foreign policy. It was now felt that the country could no longer rely for its security on the United Nations and that steps must be taken to make other arrangements to secure this; an added reason was the possibility that the Soviet Union might offer to enter into a military agreement with Norway (see below, p. 181).

First, the idea of a Nordic defence agreement was taken up and high level discussions were held in the spring of 1948. In September a meeting of Nordic foreign ministers agreed to the setting-up of a Scandinavian Defence Commission. Meanwhile, however, discussion in the press had already revealed differing views on the form any defence agreement should take. In Sweden the idea of an independent Nordic defence system commanded most support; in Norway there was a widely-expressed desire for co-operation with wartime allies in the West. When the findings of the Defence Commission became known early in 1949, it was seen that the defence of Norway and Denmark needed to be considerably strengthened and that a Nordic defence system would require military assistance from outside in the first phase of any attack. The difficulty in meeting the first of these needs was that the United States would only aid those countries which were co-operating with her in defence matters, while as far as military assistance from outside was concerned, the Swedes were unwilling to enter into any alliances with countries outside Scandinavia. Representatives of the Nordic countries met several times, but Swedish insistence that Norway and Denmark should immediately improve their defences (only possible with aid from the United States) and that the Nordic countries should in every way conduct themselves as neutrals, precluded agreement. While these negotiations were taking place, Norway and Denmark were secretly informed that they would be invited to join the Atlantic pact.

The breakdown of the negotiations for a Nordic defence agreement, the bad state of East-West relations (the Berlin blockade), made the need for a decision on Norwegian defence policy imperative. The Soviet Union's antagonism to a Nordic defence agreement had been made abundantly clear. The Soviet ambassador in Norway now delivered a warning to the Norwegian government against joining the North Atlantic Treaty Organization and an exchange of notes followed. The Russians argued that Norwegian membership of NATO would lead to foreign air and naval bases being set up on Norwegian territory. But the Norwegians were not deterred. On 1 February 1949 they stated that they had no intention of allowing foreign bases on their soil as long as they were not attacked or exposed to threats of attack. Intense discussions in the *Storting* followed in which Foreign Minister Lange played a leading part. When a vote was taken, there was an overwhelming majority in favour of Norway joining NATO. On 4 April 1949 Lange signed the treaty in Washington.

As the discussions on a Nordic defence agreement had shown, Norwegian defence was regarded as highly deficient, and when Norway joined NATO, there was much to make good. In the years that followed, large consignments of equipment and weapons came from the United States. In order to integrate them into an overall defence plan, a far-reaching reorganization of the armed forces also took place. Many defence installations, including airfields, naval bases, telecommunication links, and depots were constructed, principally with American financial support. The Northern Europe Command of NATO was established at Kolsås near Oslo, but in peacetime Norwegian forces are not under NATO command except, since 1961, for a part of the air force.

The February 1949 declaration had not satisfied the Soviet Union and, from time to time since, accusations have been made that Norway had agreed to put her territory at the disposal of the armed forces of 'the aggressive North Atlantic bloc'. This has always been denied by the Norwegians who have nevertheless argued that the declaration does not preclude Norwegian forces from participating in NATO exercises or units of the armed forces of allied countries from visiting Norway for short periods. Norway has also stated that she does not intend to permit the storage of nuclear weapons or the installation of firing-bases for medium-range rockets on her territory.

Norwegian membership of NATO has not been an uncontroversial issue and from time to time opposition to it has erupted into public demonstration. At Easter 1958 the Socialist Students' Society presented Labour with a demand that it should veto in the Council of NATO the supply of atomic rockets to West Germany. In itself this demand was not remarkable, but the startling thing was that the resolution had been signed by a majority (45 out of 78) of the Labour members of the *Storting*. It looked as if the government's NATO policy could force a palace revolution. However, it turned out that the support of some of the parliamentary dissidents was a lapse soon regretted; others had been lukewarm or opposed to Norway's membership of NATO; and others again believed that the Western powers should be more ready to negotiate with the Eastern bloc. On its side the government reaffirmed its support of NATO, but seemed to make some concession to its critics by stating that when the Council of NATO again discussed atomic and rocket armaments in Europe, the matter would be referred to the *Storting*. This concession, if such it was, was immediately neutralized by a statement from the foreign minister: a Norwegian veto on atomic weapons for West Germany would in effect be tantamount to a withdrawal from NATO. The question of stationing atomic weapons in Norway was also a subject of protracted debate in 1960. Although the government agreed not to permit them, as we have seen (see above, p. 170), the Socialist People's Party was formed as a result of the affair. Together with the Communists it was bitterly opposed to Norwegian membership of NATO and indeed to the whole of Norwegian post-war foreign and defence policy.

Debate on Norwegian membership of NATO escalated in the autumn of 1967 partly through the activity of an organization operating under the slogan 'Norway out of NATO!' whose aim was to prevent a renewal of Norwegian membership when the initial twenty-year period expired on 24 August 1969. A number of publications argued the case for and against, including one from the government which stated that there was no real alternative. It rejected the idea of a Scandinavian defence arrangement as unrealistic. The government also emphasized that through her membership Norway could influence the common policy of the member countries and thus contribute both to the defence objectives of NATO and also to the work of trying to reduce tension between East and West. During the *Storting* debate on 13–14 June 1968 a motion that Norway should leave NATO was supported by only six members. The backing which Norwegian membership of NATO had both in the *Storting* and in the country was strengthened in the summer of 1968 when Czechoslovakia was invaded by forces of the Warsaw Pact countries.

In May 1970 the *Storting* again debated Norwegian membership of NATO and there was again overwhelming support for continuing the association. However, the Labour opposition and the Liberals argued that the government should take the initiative to get Greece expelled. The coalition was embarrassed that one of its own parties had associated itself with the opposition, but a crisis was avoided. But in the autumn of the same year, an opposition motion that Norway should use her influence to have deliveries of arms to Greece stopped was approved. Proposals were also put forward that Norway should raise the matter of Portugal's colonial policy in the Council of NATO, that a better method of regulating trade with East Germany should be found, and that Norway should try to get a European security conference arranged. The government declared that these proposals constituted a vote of no confidence in its conduct of foreign affairs and that they would be resisted. An uncomfortable situation was resolved when it was agreed to refer everything to the foreign affairs committee of the *Storting*.

*Other Foreign Matters*

Foreign affairs other than those connected with membership of international organizations have tended to be of somewhat teacup proportions, though they throw interesting sidelights on Norwegian attitudes in international relations.

In 1947 the Soviet Union expressed the wish to conclude an agreement with Norway on the defence of Spitzbergen. This had first been raised in 1944 when the Russians questioned the validity, in the war situation, of the Spitzbergen Treaty which had been concluded in 1920, especially as two of the signatories, Italy and Japan, were enemy powers; the Soviet Union had not become a party to the treaty until 1935, but had recognized Norwegian sovereignty over the islands in 1924. In 1944 the Norwegians agreed that the situation had changed, but pointed out that Article 9 of the treaty prohibited defence works or other warlike installations on the islands. However, after further discussion the Norwegian government in London indicated that it would be willing to issue a joint declaration with the Russians, to include the question of defence, but made it clear that any new arrangement would have to be approved by the other signatories (Denmark, France, Holland, Sweden, the United Kingdom, and the United States of America) and by the Norwegian *Storting*. Nothing came of this, but in the latter part of 1946 the Russians raised the matter again at foreign minister level. Discussion in 1947 showed that both the *Storting* (with the exception of the Communists) and public opinion were strongly opposed to any defence agreement with the Russians over Spitzbergen, though there was a willingness to discuss other matters connected with the islands, especially Russian mining interests there. Further initiative was left to the Russians, but this was not taken.

In 1947, too, a crisis developed in Norway's relations with Spain. There had always been a great deal of anti-Franco sentiment in Norway, which from time to time resulted in demonstrations, including a refusal by dockers to unload Spanish ships. In 1946, as the result of an initiative which Norway took together with some other countries, the General Assembly of the United Nations passed a motion recommending member states to withdraw their ambassadors from Madrid. At the same time the Norwegian government reduced the number of licences issued for trade with Spain, notwithstanding strong Spanish-Norwegian commercial ties. Other countries, however, including some which had voted for the United Nations resolution, were not slow to turn this situation to their own advantage by capturing Norwegian markets in Spain. The Spanish government also threatened to ban Norwegian ships from Spanish ports if the Norwegians persisted in their attitude. In the circumstances the Norwegian government decided to take steps to normalize relations in spite of protests from the Communists and radical circles that it was giving way to Fascist threats and selling its principles for economic advantage.

In 1951 a long-standing dispute with the United Kingdom on fishing limits was finally resolved. Originally the dispute had concerned Norway's entitlement to a three- or four-mile fishing limit; but since 1935 it had turned principally on the positioning of the base-lines from which fishing limits were calculated. In that year the Norwegian government had decided that in north Norway these base-lines were to be drawn across the entrances to wide fjords and bays, a principle from which the British dissented. Eventually, in 1949, the United Kingdom brought the matter before the International Court at The Hague which, after hearing lengthy submissions, found in favour of Norway.

In 1960 a very sharp edge was put on the criticisms which the Soviet Union had made of Norway's membership of NATO by the U.2 affair. This began on 1 May 1960 when the Russians shot down an American reconnaisance aircraft over the Urals. It transpired that it had orders to land at Bodø in north Norway after its mission had ended. The episode led to the Russians accusing the Norwegians of participating in American aerial espionage and to threats that Norwegian air bases used for this purpose would be destroyed. The

Norwegian government replied that it had no knowledge of American flights over Soviet territory and had never given permission for Norwegian air bases to be used for flights which violated the airspace of other countries. The Norwegians later protested to the American ambassador in Oslo about the incident. After an exchange of notes the Russians accepted the Norwegian explanations, but warned of dire consequences should the episode be repeated. On 1 July another incident occurred in which an American reconnaisance plane was shot down over the Barents Sea near the Kola peninsula. The Russians alleged that the plane had violated their territory and that the pilot had instructions to land at a Norwegian base if necessary. Again the Norwegian government denied all knowledge of the affair: there was no arrangement for American planes to make use of Norwegian air bases. The Russian reply was so truculent that the Norwegian government declined to reply to it. Relations between the two countries thereafter remained cool. In a speech in the *Storting* in October Halvard Lange made it clear that although Norwegian public opinion was disturbed by what had happened, the government did not think that Norway was exposed to the threat of attack. (This was a clear reference to the possibility of invoking NATO aid.) Nevertheless, if the Soviet Union continued her threatening attitude, the government would have to reconsider its policy.

In 1967 the question of the delivery of a patrol boat to Greece aroused passions in the *Storting*. The government maintained that under international law it was bound to allow delivery, an interpretation which the socialist opposition found unacceptable. Though a vote of no confidence failed, the debate highlighted the *Storting*'s and the government's disapproval of the Greek military regime and its policies. This also showed itself when the Norwegian government, together with the Danish and Swedish governments, protested to the European Commission for Human Rights that the Greek government had violated the European Declaration on Human Rights on a number of points.

In October 1967 the war in Vietnam figured prominently in the debate on the speech from the throne. A motion that the government should inform the United States administration that the bombing of North Vietnam should stop unconditionally was eventually referred to a committee of the *Storting* for reformulation in more general terms. After a sharp debate the committee's recommendations were adopted. However, the whole affair led to anti-American demonstrations which were also used to attack Norwegian membership of NATO.

## Nordic Relations

Though the idea of a defence agreement between Denmark, Norway, and Sweden came to nothing, co-operation in other spheres has been extensive. In 1952 Denmark, Sweden, Norway, and Iceland set up the Nordic Council (*Nordisk Råd*) consisting of members of the parliaments of the member countries, to act as a consultative body for the exchange of ideas and the encouragement of inter-Scandinavian projects of common benefit. Though the council statutes do not exclude defence and foreign policy, these are not in practice discussed. In 1955 Finland also joined the council.

Meetings are also attended by government ministers, usually the prime ministers and foreign ministers. Thus it is a high-level body and it has already achieved much. In the field of communications, postal, telegraph, and telephone services have been co-ordinated and freed from restrictions and formalities; efforts have been made to standardize traffic regulations; and Scandinavians can travel in member countries without a passport. The labour market is also largely free. Steps have been taken to standardize practice in public administration and in the administration of justice. In the sciences, humanities, and technology joint institutions have been established. On 15 March 1971 a cultural agreement, backed by large-scale funds, was signed, to take effect from 1 January 1972.

During the negotiations in GATT (General Agreement on Tariffs and Trade) on tariff reductions (the so-called Kennedy Round), concluded in May 1967, the Nordic countries participated as one delegation.

### ECONOMIC CO-OPERATION

Norway's outward-looking policy after World War II in relation to the United Nations and NATO has also been matched by commitment to the idea of European economic co-operation.

Norway was one of the fourteen countries which in 1947 accepted the American offer of economic aid under the Marshall Plan and thus joined the Organization for European Economic Co-operation (OEEC), set up in 1947 to work out how this aid should be applied and to help co-ordinate the economic policies of the member states. When OEEC was superseded in 1960 by the larger Organization for Economic Co-operation and Development (OECD), Norway also became a member.

## EFTA

One of the consequences of the Treaty of Rome, signed by the governments of Belgium, France, Holland, Italy, Luxembourg, and West Germany on 25 March 1957 and the setting-up of the European Economic Community was the United Kingdom's opening of negotiations with these countries to create a free-trade area which would include both EEC and the other western European states. Though this idea found support, especially outside EEC, negotiations with the Six came to nothing and were broken off in November 1958. Soon afterwards the United Kingdom, Austria, Portugal, Switzerland, Denmark, Norway, and Sweden opened negotiations for the creation of a free-trade area of their own, and in November 1959 they signed an agreement establishing the European Free Trade Association (EFTA) to take effect from May 1960; Finland became an associate member in 1961. The free-trade arrangements excluded most agricultural and fishing products, but member states agreed to aim at an expansion of trade in these areas through bilateral arrangements.

EEC and EFTA did much to stimulate Norwegian overseas trade. In 1959, 29 per cent of Norwegian trade in goods was with EEC and 37 per cent with EFTA; in 1969 the figures had risen to 30 per cent with EEC and 48 per cent with EFTA, the increase with EFTA being largely due to an increase in trade with the other Scandinavian countries, which rose from 16 per cent in 1959 to 28 per cent in 1969.

Apart from the objective of establishing free trade in industrial goods over a ten-year period (actually achieved by 1 January 1967), the EFTA countries aimed at establishing a wider economic community together with the EEC. The failure in 1962 and 1967 to achieve this latter objective led to Denmark, Norway, and Sweden taking the initiative to see whether economic co-operation within EFTA could be intensified; but owing to a conflict of interests between members and the United Kingdom's difficult economic situation, little was achieved. The Nordic countries then turned to the possibility of extending economic co-operation between themselves.

## NORDØK

The proposal for extended Nordic economic co-operation (Nordisk økonomisk samarbeid; NORDØK) was made at a February 1968 meeting of the Nordic Council in Oslo when it was agreed to recommend members to implement the proposal. This would strengthen EFTA and pave the way for a wider European economic community. In April 1968 the Nordic prime ministers, having defined a number of areas in which economic and other forms of co-operation could be extended, appointed a committee of government officials to prepare a report. This committee made an interim report in January 1969, from which it was apparent that on a number of matters agreement had not been reached. The premiers, however, felt that the committee should complete its work and at the same time produce a draft treaty. The principal feature of the report and the draft treaty of July 1969 was a proposal to establish a Nordic customs union; but there were still a number of unresolved problems. It was now decided that future negotiations should be conducted by a government delegation from each of the countries led by its prime minister. These began in Oslo in November 1969. At one stage the Finnish government showed signs of wavering, but in Reykjavik on 7 February 1970, at a meeting of the Nordic Council, the premiers announced agreement on the contents of a draft NORDØK treaty and stated that this would be put before their national assemblies as soon as possible. It was hoped that the treaty could take effect from the summer of 1970.

However, on 24 February the Finnish government decided to postpone the question of signing the treaty, because of impending elections, and on 24 March hope that the treaty could take effect was dashed when the Finns finally decided not to sign. The principal reason for this decision was the belief that as Denmark and Norway were preparing to negotiate for membership of EEC, the whole basis for the treaty and thus the future of NORDØK were uncertain. At the opening of the newly elected Finnish parliament on 6 April 1970, President Kekkonen gave a detailed account of the reasons which had led to the Finnish decision. The NORDØK idea has been regarded as shelved.

*EEC*

A fusion of the two European economic blocs had always been the aim of the EFTA countries. In July 1961, with the support of the ministerial council of EFTA, the United Kingdom and Denmark announced their intention to ask EEC to start negotiations for their admission to the community. In April 1962 Norway, too, applied after the *Storting* had approved a government proposal that negotiations should be started. In their application, however, the Norwegians expressed the hope for a satisfactory solution to the special problems which their geographical situation and economic structure posed. In the event, these negotiations came to nothing; the French veto in 1963 of the United Kingdom's application meant that the applications of Denmark and Norway were not proceeded with. In 1967, this time joined by Eire, they applied again, the *Storting* approving the Norwegian government's decision to do so by 136 votes to 13. But once again the bid for membership failed because of the French veto. De Gaulle's departure in April 1969 soon led to a new climate of opinion in France and a desire to carry European co-operation further by developing EEC and by the inclusion of new members. A French plan for future development was approved in principle at a meeting of the Six at The Hague on 1–2 December 1969. This was an important turning-point in EEC's relations with prospective members and in June 1970 new negotiations were begun. On 25 June 1970 the *Storting* voted by 132 votes to 17 for a renewal of negotiations.

During the whole of this period there had been lively debate in Norway on the Common Market issue. Especial concern was expressed about the consequences EEC membership would have for Norwegian agriculture and fisheries, and the government repeatedly stated that special arrangements of a permanent kind would have to be made to protect them. It was argued that Norwegian agriculture has to contend with unfavourable natural and climatic conditions, and that whole communities, especially in north Norway, depend for their very existence on inshore fishing.

In the autumn of 1970 the opponents of Norwegian entry organized a so-called Popular Front (*Folkebevegelse*) to agitate against it and received substantial support from the farmers' organizations. Substantial opposition to membership within Prime Minister Borten's Centre Party (*Senterpartiet*) was also apparent. Indeed, it was even suggested that differences within the government over the Common Market could jeopardize its continuance in office. When Borten's government did fall on 2 March 1971, the indirect reason *was* the Common Market. On Friday, 19 February 1971 the newspaper *Dagbladet* published the contents of a confidential report to the government on the Common Market from Jahn Halvorsen, the Norwegian representative in Brussels. On the following Monday Borten stated in a newspaper interview that it was quite fantastic to believe that he or any member of his government was responsible for the leak of information. Two days later he stated categorically that *Dagbladet* had not received its information from him. However, on Friday 26 February he admitted to his foreign minister that during a journey to Copenhagen on 15 February he had shown Halvorsen's report to Arne Haugestad, the chairman of the Popular Front movement; he had, however, received an assurance from Haugestad that he was not the source of *Dagbladet*'s information. Later the same day the prime minister issued a press statement admitting his indiscretion and on 2 March gave a full account of the affair in the *Storting*. Immediately afterwards he resigned. The episode was a painful one. It was no secret that Borten had been lukewarm about EEC and had even been accused of double-dealing.

In contrast to the uncertainties within the Centre Party, the Labour leaders and top trade union officials have supported Norwegian entry, as has Norwegian industry. Since taking office on 17 March 1971 the Labour government under Trygve Bratteli has strongly argued the case for Norwegian membership, outlining the benefits it will bring to Norwegian industry; but it has repeated that special arrangements must be made for Norwegian agriculture and fisheries. As Foreign Minister Andreas Cappelen indicated in a speech in Brussels on 30 March 1971, the government also sees membership of the Common Market as an opportunity to pursue its political ideals within a European forum.

In May 1971 the *Storting* approved expenditure of $1\frac{1}{2}$ million *kroner* to provide the public with information on all aspects of entry. The pollsters have also been busy canvassing the opinion of the man in the street. Their results have shown that the 'don't knows' still form the largest percentage of those interviewed, with the anti-marketeers in the lead among those who have made up their minds. The 'noes' also have it in the polls on replies to the advisory referendum on entry which the government has agreed to hold in the autumn of 1972. In Brussels the Norwegian negotiators are still trying to get better terms from the Six for their fisheries than those which Denmark, Eire, and the United Kingdom have agreed on.[1]

Those opposed to Norwegian entry form a somewhat hetero-geneous group. There are those on the extreme political Left who are, in principle, against any closer association between the countries of western Europe; there are others who are uncertain, sceptical, or even fearful as to how Norway would fare economically in the com-munity; and there is a third group which is opposed to entry on 'national-romantic' grounds, believing that Norway would lose her national sovereignty, identity, and character if she joined. Those who argue for membership maintain that there is no real alternative, not even the maintenance of the *status quo*. Norwegian industry, it is said, must depend more and more on exporting if the country is to prosper. This will mean the development of more industry dependent on research, technical skills, and good management, and less depend-ence on industries based on natural resources, especially as these are approaching maximum exploitation. It is also argued that prospects for the development of new industries and for the exploitation of North Sea oil and gas would be enhanced if Norway were a member of EEC. As for sovereignty, pro-marketeers argue that the transfer of authority in certain areas to an enlarged Common Market would not involve any real loss of sovereignty since Norway, more than most countries, is already dependent on decisions taken in other, bigger, countries. Membership of the community would, it is argued, give Norway more influence on decision-taking in larger countries, and that it is an advantage for a small country when large countries are also bound by rules which have been agreed on in common.

[1] On 22 January 1972 Norway signed the Treaty of Accession to EEC, it being understood that no change detrimental to vital Norwegian interests would be made in the special arrangements for the protection of her fisheries when they expire on 31 December 1982.

# PART THREE

# The Language Question and the Literature

# Chapter 9

# The Language Question

*Two Languages and their Background*

EVEN THE SLIGHTEST ACQUAINTANCE with Norway is almost certain to have brought the foreigner into contact with the language question and the disputes arising from it. It has now been a controversial issue in Norway for more than a century and the bitter quarrels it has engendered are still not resolved. Norwegians will assure the foreigner that they no longer know what Norwegian is or how it is spelt, statements which greatly exaggerate the realities. One does not, nevertheless, have to be an expert linguist to detect some of the manifestations of this situation. They are obvious from the appearance of public notices, for example in the spelling of the words *Røkere* and *Røykjarar*, both meaning *Smokers*.

The fact is that Norway has two official language forms: the one called *Bokmål* (lit. the language of the book); the other *Nynorsk* (New Norwegian). Both these language forms are closely related and both are mutually comprehensible. There is a very large overlap between them, their main differences being in orthography–and hence also in pronunciation; and there are also differences in vocabulary, although these are continually being eroded. The aim of official language policy is to bring the two forms together into a Common Norwegian (*Samnorsk*). A further complicating factor is that the spelling of both language forms has been revised on a number of occasions during this century.

The history of the language question in Norway belongs chiefly, and especially for our present purpose, to the nineteenth and twentieth centuries; but in order to put the matter into perspective one must refer briefly to earlier developments. In the twelfth and thirteenth centuries the language of Norway and of the Norwegian colonies to the West was the Old Norse of the sagas, the Eddaic lays, and the scaldic poems. Most of this literature was written down in Iceland, but the differences between the Old Norse of Norway and Iceland were small. Indeed, there were also differences in the written language in Norway itself, differences which reflected the moves of the royal Court and chancellery from Trondhjem to Bergen and then to Oslo. It meant that prominence was given in turn to the dialects of Trøndelag and western and eastern Norway.

In the fourteenth century the written tradition in Norway became far less secure. This was due in large measure to the high mortality rate among the clergy during the Black Death (1349–50), but also to changes which had occurred in the spoken language, especially the decay of case endings and the substitution of other grammatical features which began to be reflected in the written language. The political situation and the unions with Sweden and Denmark also meant that Swedish and Danish began to exercise an influence on Norwegian. The influence of Swedish is particularly noticeable up to 1450; and after that of Danish, especially in official documents. Soon after 1500 the bishops of Oslo and Nidaros used only Danish, and because of the increased influence of German, many German elements came into the language. In private letters, however, Norwegian maintained its position somewhat better.

These factors, coupled with the lack of any strong Norwegian literary tradition during the fourteenth and fifteenth centuries, meant that Danish became first the predominating and soon the only written language of Norway, especially from the time of the Reformation. This process had also been helped on by the prestige which the language forms of south-eastern Norway enjoyed after Oslo became the capital, especially as they had developed in a number of respects parallel with Danish. However, Norwegian continued to be the spoken language of native-born Norwegians, though the dialect forms into which Old Norse had split often differed considerably. Thus one can say that the Middle Norwegian of the period *c.* 1370–1525 was followed by Danish as the written language of the country and New Norwegian (as philologists call it) as the spoken language–the use of the term *Nynorsk* dates from 1929 (see below, p. 201). There was at this time no written form for New Norwegian. The spoken language now differed so much from the old written norm that the difficulty in reading the old laws led to their being translated into Danish.

The influence of Danish in Norway was reinforced by the advent of printing. Denmark got her first printing press in 1480, but Norway had to wait until 1643. This meant that the literature of the Reformation in Danish flooded into Norway: the Danish translation of the Bible; the catechism, hymnals, volumes of sermons, and other edifying works. The fact, too, that Copenhagen was the cultural centre of the two countries and the seat of their only university, from which after 1629 all members of the clergy had to graduate, made for an overall Danicizing of the Norwegian upper classes. The most distinguished writer in eighteenth-century Danish literature was Ludvig Holberg (1684–1754), a Norwegian who spent most of his life in Denmark and wrote in Danish. When compulsory confirmation was introduced in 1736, it meant that all classes in Norway had to be able to read at least a modicum of Danish.

Nevertheless, during this Danish period, interest in the spoken language in Norway was kept alive by a number of enthusiasts, especially clergymen. Many collections of Norwegian words with Danish translations were made, among them Christen Jenssøn's *Den Norske Dictionarium* of 1646, Bishop Erik Pontoppidan's *Glossarium Norvagicum* of 1749, and Laurents Hallager's *Norsk Ordsamling* of 1802. Occasional poems were also written in Norwegian dialects, many of them by clergymen, some of whom were not always completely at home in the dialect they were using. More serious and valuable attempts to use dialects as literary media were made by Thomas Rosing de Stockfleth (1742–1808) in his *Heimatkomsten* (*Return Home*; 1798) and by Edvard Storm (1749–94) in his *Døleviser* (*Dale Ballads*), which were printed in Hallager's collection of 1802. Purely Norwegian elements can also be detected in the work of those Norwegians who wrote in Danish, including Ludvig Holberg. Towards the end of the eighteenth century such elements were used for patriotic effect in the poems written by members of *Det Norske Selskab* (The Norwegian Society) in Copenhagen.

Norwegians also used their own pronunciation when reading Danish aloud, imposing as far as possible on the written Danish forms the characteristic intonation and other phonetic features of Norwegian pronunciation. In this way a curious reading pronunciation of Danish grew up in Norway, especially in church. It meant also that, especially among the upper classes, a stiff Danicized pronunciation would be used on formal occasions, i.e. in sermons and speeches, and a more dialect-coloured speech in everyday contexts. However, this situation did lead, especially during the eighteenth century, to the written language exercising an influence on pronunciation. This was particularly so among the upper classes, who developed what came to be regarded as a norm of cultivated pronunciation.

The growth of Norwegian national consciousness in the late eighteenth century had repercussions on the way Norwegians regarded their own language. Soon after the turn of the century the question of establishing a written norm for Norwegian was raised and when the university in Christiania was founded in 1811, impetus was given to this idea, since it was envisaged that research into the Norwegian dialects would be one of its tasks.

When, as a result of the Treaty of Kiel (see above, p. 118), the union between Norway and Denmark was dissolved in 1814, the position of Danish in Norway as the written language was still supreme. Indeed in the years immediately following 1814, as a result of the growth of education, its position was strengthened, since all school reading material was in Danish. Moreover, the schools at this time aimed at teaching as pure a Danish as possible and Norwegian words and forms were regarded as incorrect or as provincialisms to be avoided. Nevertheless, the question did arise as to what the language of the country should be called. Eventually, a compromise solution was found by calling it *Modersmaalet* (Mother Tongue), though an amendment to the constitution of 1814 (of 4 November 1814), consequent on the union with Sweden, prescribed that affairs of state should be conducted in Norwegian – a provision which may, however, have been designed to exclude the use of Swedish.

Opinion on the language question in the first decades of the nineteenth century can also be judged from the criticisms which were levelled against writers like Mauritz Hansen and H. A. Bjerregaard (1792–1842) for having introduced purely Norwegian words into their works. Their critics regretted this also because they believed it would lead to a loosening of the cultural ties between Norway and Denmark. Differences between the pronunciation of Norwegian and Danish continued, however, to be very great, though the spread of literacy meant that the unnatural Norwegian reading pronunciation of Danish became more widespread. As with the written language, Danish pronunciation was regarded as the ideal. Norwegian actors were severely criticized for the pronunciation they used on the stage and were unfavourably compared in this respect with the Danes who, in fact, dominated the Norwegian theatre at the time.

## Towards Language Reform

In the 1830s a different view of the use of purely Norwegian-language elements was put forward by the poet and publicist Henrik Wergeland (1808–45). In a dissertation, *Om norsk Sprogreformation* (*On Norwegian Language Reform*), written in 1832 and published in 1835, he argued that written Norwegian should admit those purely Norwegian elements which Norwegians used naturally. He also maintained that the dialects should not be regarded as inferior and argued that an independent people must have its own language. On stylistic grounds, too, Wergeland urged, Norwegians should use a written form that was natural to them: democracy and the spread of education demanded that the written language should correspond much more closely to the spoken language of the people. Wergeland put his principles into practice in his writings, especially in his work for popular enlightenment, and was criticized for doing so. His efforts did not lead to any immediate language reform, but they were important for having stated the case that Norwegian must develop away from Danish. Wergeland prophesied that by the end of the century Norway would have her own written language.

In the 1840s the National Romantic movement got underway, of which one of the principal manifestations was the collecting of folk-tales and ballads, which were now written down for the first time. Since this folk-literature had been preserved in oral tradition by dialect-speakers, the difficulties of giving it written form highlighted the differences between the written and spoken languages. Asbjørnsen and Moe (see below, p. 226) solved this problem in their collections of folk-tales by using the outer garment of Danish orthography and declension – also for the many purely Norwegian words and expressions they used. But they also included many purely Norwegian syntactical features and, since it was impossible for them to give some purely Norwegian words an appropriate Danish form, they established a Norwegian spelling for them which later became part of the written language. Although today their versions of the Norwegian folk-tales look very Danish, they did provide the basis for development away from Danish in a purely Norwegian direction.

Concurrently with the publication of the collections of Asbjørnsen and Moe, two other lines in Norwegian-language development were gathering impetus. The first was the researches of Ivar Aasen (1813–96) into the Norwegian rural dialects; the second the campaigning of Knud Knudsen (1812–95) for a Norwegianization of the current written language.

Aasen began in 1841 with an account of his own dialect of Sunnmøre. His work attracted the attention of the Royal Society in Trondhjem (see above, p. 26) which invited him to compile a grammar and dictionary of the dialects of Norway. Aasen accepted and spent some four years travelling the country to collect material. In 1848 he published *Det Norske Folkesprogs Grammatik* (*A Grammar of the Norwegian Folk Language*) and in 1850 *Ordbog over det Norske Folkesprog* (*Dictionary of the Norwegian Folk Language*). During his survey Aasen had covered many different dialects, but the crucial problem was, as he realized, to decide which was the appropriate spelling norm to adopt, since the success of the language movement would depend very much on how far his orthography found acceptance. Aasen did not finally decide on the forms which were to be normative until he published new editions of his grammar (1864) and of his dictionary (1873); although he had already in 1853 published a volume called *Prøver af Landsmaalet i Norge* (*Specimens of Landsmaal in Norway*), which gave examples both of dialects from different parts of the country and of some pieces in a language form that Aasen called common *Landsmaal*.

Thus a new language form, *Landsmaal*, had been launched, but with a somewhat ambiguous title, since *Landsmaal* may mean both 'the country language' and 'the language of the (whole) country'. Subsequently Aasen wrote poetry and a play in his *Landsmaal*, and, although he realized that this new written language needed further refining, he confidently believed that he had created a serviceable linguistic instrument for his compatriots which sooner or later would become the language of the country. In establishing his norm, Aasen had tried to make it as widely applicable to the different dialects as possible and always chose the form which would have the greatest unifying power. In the event, his *Landsmaal* corresponded most closely to the dialects of western Norway. In compiling his dictionary he gave priority to purely Norwegian words and eschewed as far as possible loan-words and forms derived from Danish and German.

Knud Knudsen, a master in the Cathedral (Latin) School in Christiania, developed an interest in the language question as a result of the difficulties his pupils had with Danish spelling, and he came to the conclusion that this must be modified so that it resembled Norwegian pronunciation more closely. Knudsen had a practical teacher's point of view and believed that Aasen's plan to create a new national written language on the basis of dialects was too great an undertaking to be accomplished at one go. His plan was, as he explained in his *Det Norske Målstræv (The Norwegian Language Struggle*; 1867), to work step by step for the Norwegianization of the current Dano-Norwegian. His campaigning for orthographic changes bore some fruit first in 1862 and later in the 1870s and '80s. In 1866 J. Aars's *Norske Retskrivnings-Regler (Spelling Rules for Norwegian)* was published –a book that was used in the schools and, as new editions of it appeared containing fresh spelling changes, one that gradually became accepted as the norm of the written language. But the chief item in Knudsen's programme of reform, the substitution of the unvoiced consonants *p, t, k* for the voiced *b, d, g* of Danish, was not carried through until after his death. Knudsen also believed that it was necessary to combat the influence of Danish on spoken Norwegian. The fact that the Danes dominated the theatre in Norway tended to make a Danicized pronunciation of Norwegian fashionable, especially among the upper classes in the towns who believed it to be superior. Knudsen associated himself with Bjørnson and Ibsen in combating this influence and in his book *Den landsgyldige norske uttale (A Norwegian Pronunciation Valid for the Whole Country;* 1876) he argued that there was no difficulty in establishing a norm of cultivated Norwegian pronunciation, and that there was no need to have recourse to Danish for its improvement. Knudsen was also an advocate of the Norwegianizing of the written language by the substitution of Norwegian words for loan-words, and to this end he compiled a massive dictionary called *Unorsk og norsk (Un-Norwegian and Norwegian;* 1881) in which he proposed Norwegian equivalents for foreign words, some of which were neologisms of his own devising.

Knudsen's aim of Norwegianizing the current written language had already (as we have seen) been given some effect in the folk-tales of Asbjørnsen and Moe, but the peasant tales (*Bondefortællinger*) which Bjørnson published in the 1850s carried this further. It was realized, and Bjørnson was criticized for it, that he had created a language form which was not only different from Danish in vocabulary and orthographical detail, but which also had a completely different stylistic appeal. Ibsen, too, Norwegianized the language in his plays from this period as a result of his contacts with Knudsen (Knudsen was language consultant at *Kristiania Norske Theater* while Ibsen was there), especially in *Peer Gynt* (1867).

The Pan-Scandinavian movement, too, believed that the three Scandinavian countries should aim at a common orthography. In 1869 a meeting was held in Stockholm, which Ibsen and Knud Knudsen attended as Norwegian delegates, to discuss the problem. The meeting made a number of proposals for change which, while they did not lead to any official alteration in Norwegian spelling, were subsequently adopted by Ibsen and Bjørnson in their works, and some of the suggestions made found their way into the spelling reforms which were later adopted in Norway.

The advent of the realist movement in literature in the later decades of the nineteenth century also had consequences for the Norwegianizing of the written language. This was especially true in the drama, where the demand that dialogue should be true to life led to a much more widespread use of the whole spectrum of everyday speech for the purposes of characterization.

At the same time *Landsmaal* had been making headway. In 1858 the writer and journalist Aasmund Olafsen Vinje (see below, p. 228) declared publicly that he would in future no longer use the current Dano-Norwegian language, but would write exclusively in *Landsmaal*. To further this end he founded the periodical *Dølen* (*The Dalesman*), written mainly by himself in the new language form. Vinje did not, however, dare to be, as he himself put it, *heilnorsk* (completely Norwegian). His version of *Landsmaal* retained certain Danish features and he never succeeded in establishing an orthographic norm.

Vinje was succeeded in his championship of *Landsmaal* by Arne Garborg (see below, p. 246), a more notable writer, who also began his writing career in the Dano-Norwegian language, but taught himself to write *Landsmaal*. Garborg's influence in the gradual acceptance of *Landsmaal* was considerable, both by virtue of his standing as a writer and also because of his success in refining *Landsmaal* into a literary instrument suitable for all uses. His version of it was both more Norwegian and more certain in its orthography and declension than Vinje's had been, and his example gave rise to a whole school of end-of-century *Landsmaal* writers. The movement also got a periodical when *Fedraheimen* began to appear in Christiania in 1877.

## Language Reform and Politics

It was not long before the language question came into the political arena. *Venstre* supported the Norwegianization of the current written language and in 1878 a motion, proposed by Johan Sverdrup (see above, p. 130), that instruction in the schools should, as far as possible, be in speech form which the children themselves used was later adopted by the primary schools. This meant a change from the old pedantic Danish reading style, but it also raised the question of what the spoken norm should be. In 1887 the Ministry of Church and Education recommended that it should be on the basis of the cultivated speech (*dannede talesprog*) of the different parts of the country. In 1885 the *Storting* agreed that steps should be taken to give *Landsmaal* the same position in the schools as the current Dano-Norwegian had. This decision was embodied in the Primary Schools Act (*Folkeskole-loven*) of 1892 which prescribed that all pupils should learn to read both language forms. It was left to local option which form should be used for written work. By the turn of the century some 200 schools in rural areas had opted for *Landsmaal*. The decision that cultivated but natural speech should be the norm to aim for in the schools led to difficulties when pupils read aloud, since it meant that they had to pronounce their Danish text in a different, though for them more natural, way from the spelling on the printed page. This led to demands from the teaching profession that the spelling must be reformed, and these demands became more and more insistent as time went on. The school reader edited by Nordahl Rolfsen and published in 1892 made some attempt to introduce a more Norwegian spelling for some words. The fact, too, that a reading knowledge of *Landsmaal* was now required in all schools meant that schoolchildren were becoming more accustomed to seeing Norwegian spelling forms in print. But the problem of teaching the written language in the schools still remained; in fact it was made worse by the new flexibility of the printed word. As a first step towards a solution it was agreed that the new forms which had been included in Rolfsen's reader should also be permitted as optional spellings in written work in schools. But this only led to further confusion. In *Landsmaal*, too, demands that a spelling norm should be established were also heard. In 1899 a committee of which Garborg was a member made proposals for a *Landsmaal* spelling norm to be used in schools, and in 1901 a word-list compiled by Matias Skard was officially approved for school use.

The whole situation was one in which passions were easily aroused, especially over the various proposals for the reform of Dano-Norwegian. There were also tensions between the champions of Dano-

Norwegian and *Landsmaal* who organized themselves into hostile camps. In 1899 the so-called *Rigsmaalsforeninger* (Societies for the Protection of *Rigsmaal*, as they called Dano-Norwegian) which had been formed led to the founding of *Rigsmaalsforbundet* (the *Rigsmaal* Alliance) in 1909. In 1906 *Noregs Maallag* was founded to further the cause of *Landsmaal*.

The dissolution of the union with Sweden in 1905 and the stimulus it gave to national consciousness seems to have helped crystallize the efforts to reform the spelling of Dano-Norwegian. In 1907 proposals for spelling changes were approved. A principal feature of these was the substitution of the unvoiced *p*, *t*, *k* (the so-called 'hard' consonants) for the Danish voiced *b*, *d*, *g* (the so-called 'soft' consonants), a reform which, as we have seen, had been one of the main aims of Knud Knudsen. These new forms were to be mandatory on government offices and on the schools, but they were also soon adopted by the press, commerce, and publishing houses. Though there had been protests and forebodings, the comparatively rapid adoption of the new spellings showed that they had not gone beyond what most people were ready to accept. They also established the principle that it was the spoken language on which spelling reform was to be based. These reforms did, nevertheless, create a situation which has been a continuing one ever since: they made for variations in spelling and provoked the first plaintive cries from the Norwegians that they no longer knew how to spell their own language. Problems of how to deal with the orthography of Norwegian writers of the nineteenth century and earlier also arose. To read them in the original spelling created confusion in the classroom, but on the other hand, to normalize them led to accusations of improper interference. The difficulty was that if spelling was normalized, it often also became necessary to make changes in vocabulary and syntax, and this soon led to the charge that the style of writers was being tampered with and that the whole Norwegian cultural tradition was being put in jeopardy.

The idea had been present that reforms in the spelling of Dano-Norwegian and *Landsmaal* should pave the way for an eventual unification of the two language forms into a single Norwegian language. Knud Knudsen had been a spokesman for this idea, but now it was cogently argued by Moltke Moe (1859–1913), one of the chief architects of the 1907 reform, that the aim must be to create what he called a *Fælles norsk* (Common Norwegian), an aim which looked forward to the *Samnorsk* movement of the 1950s. In 1908 a three-man committee was set up to consider this aspect and in the following year they published a lengthy report; but its only immediate effect was to lead to a few minor changes in *Landsmaal*.

In the years immediately following the 1907 reform, the language question remained the subject of lively debate. In 1912 it even led to the resignation of the prime minister, Wollert Konow. In 1913, following a request from prominent educationalists, the ministry appointed a six-man committee to look into the problems of spelling reforms in both language forms, but it failed to accomplish anything. In 1916 it was reconstituted and in the following year submitted a report which was to become the basis of a new spelling reform for both languages. This was promulgated by the *Venstre* government on 21 December 1917. These reforms carried the process of Norwegianizing Dano-Norwegian a stage further. Among other things the feminine gender was introduced into the written language for certain words (the feminine had always been a regular feature of Norwegian dialects) and alternative forms were permitted for certain verb-endings; the letter *å* was substituted for *aa*. The committee's report was also much concerned with the problem of harmonizing the two language forms and in its proposals it attempted to do this as far as was possible.

The proposals immediately let loose a storm of protest from the supporters of Dano-Norwegian, including a number of leading Norwegian authors, among them Knut Hamsun (see below, p. 250). He embodied his protest in a scathing pamphlet called *Sproget i Fare* (*The Language in Danger*; 1918), in which he emphasized that language is a living thing and not to be tampered with by academics whose only need for language is to have an instrument to make themselves understood. In general, too, the new orthography met far more opposition than the 1907 reform and came much more slowly into general use. One consequence of lasting importance of this opposition was the setting-up of the *Riksmålsvernet* (the Defenders of *Riksmål*), consisting of a body of leading men in the educational and literary worlds who constituted themselves as a kind of academy of *Riksmål*. One of their first acts was to decide to launch a dictionary of *Riksmål*. This began to appear in 1930 and was completed in 1957, providing the only standard Norwegian dictionary in the language. Ironically, it used the orthography of 1917.

Various developments arising from the reforms which had been carried through, or inspired by the spirit of reform, are worth noting. From 1913 it was possible for *Storting* deputies to have their speeches printed in *Landsmaal*, and a decree of 1925 required government offices to reply to letters in the language form in which they were written. The practice of Norwegianizing geographical and place names became common. In 1917, by government decree, 189 place names were Norwegianized. From 1918 the Danish word *amt* (county) was replaced by the Norwegian *fylke*, and the names of the counties were not only respelt but in some cases given a name culled from the early period of Norwegian history. Thus Bratsberg county was renamed Telemark; Søndre Bergenhus was renamed Hordaland. In 1925 Christiania was given back its old name of Oslo; in 1926 Fredrikshald was renamed Halden; and in 1930 Trondhjem was changed to Nidaros, though subsequent protests from the inhabitants led to Nidaros being abandoned in 1931 for Trondheim, a Norsified version of the old name. In 1926 foreign geographical names were also modified, both to bring them into line with the new spelling and also to remove traces of Danish or German influence in them.

The names of the two language forms themselves also underwent change. Written Danish in Norway, also in its modified forms, had officially been called *Det almindelige Bogsprog* (Common Book Language) during most of the nineteenth century. In 1899 Bjørnson had made use of the term *Rigsmaal* (later *Riksmaal* and now *Riksmål*; National Language) to describe it, an appellation which had been used before but which now gained currency, although the supporters of *Landsmaal* protested. As we have seen, the description *Landsmaal* (later *Landsmål*) went back to Ivar Aasen. In 1928, during the drafting of a revision of the school law, the ministry proposed that *Bokmål* (Language of the Book) should be the future official description of *Riksmål*. This proposal brought sharp criticism from the *Riksmål* camp, and the *Landsmål* supporters also objected to the continuing use of the description *Landsmål*, saying that the two language forms should be called Danish and Norwegian respectively. After much debate the terms *Bokmål* and *Nynorsk* (to replace *Landsmål*) were officially adopted in 1929 as the names of the two language forms. The first, especially, was a misleading description which was never accepted by the *Riksmål* men, and gave rise to much future dissension.

During the first two decades of the century the language question had continued to occupy the politicians; but it was not until the Labour Party began to gather strength in the 1920s that political discussion of the language question began to take on a new direction. Now it began to be debated in relation to the class struggle. The Labour Party's chief spokesman and theoretician in this debate was Halvdan Koht (1873–1965), then professor of history at the University of Oslo and later to become foreign minister. Koht advocated that what he called *Folkemålet* (the Folk Language) should be the basis for future language reform, and after the Labour Party's election victory in 1933 the *Storting* agreed to set up a new language committee to make recommendations for the coalescing of the two language forms on the basis of Norwegian folk-speech (*på norsk folkemåls grunn*). At the same time, it was asked to make proposals for a reduction in the number of alternative word forms in both languages.

*A New Orthography*

In 1934 a committee was appointed and it presented its report on 8 January 1936. It soon became clear that it had found some difficulty in reconciling the two parts of its mandate. The requirement that its recommendations should make for the unification of the two language forms often meant the removal from one or other of them of words or grammatical forms which were well established, and to find substitutes which would be accepted in both language forms was not easy. Indeed, in order to achieve this unity the committee sometimes found it necessary to propose additional alternative lexical or grammatical forms, but this naturally conflicted with the second part of its mandate. Another difficulty was with the concept *Folkemålet* itself, with the presupposition that such an entity existed. There were many dialects in Norway, each representing a speech norm, but folk-speech as such could only mean a selection from them.

The committee's proposals meant that for *Bokmål*, many lexical and grammatical forms formerly regarded as dialect or *Landsmål* were now established in it as the only ones officially allowed. Among them was the requirement that the feminine gender should now be compulsory for some 400 nouns and optional for a number of others. With regard to *Nynorsk* the committee's proposals made for a stabilizing of the orthography, and for the establishing of a single lexical form for many words, but as with *Bokmål* the most radical changes proposed were in matters of grammatical form.

Criticisms of the proposals came from both language camps, those from the champions of *Nynorsk* being the most vociferous. They were particularly dissatisfied with the changes proposed in grammatical forms, many of which were hallowed by tradition and the work of Ivar Aasen. The *Bokmål* camp regarded the imposition of folk forms such as the feminine gender as out of keeping with the stylistic needs of, as they regarded it, the language of culture. Teachers also protested that the permissiveness of the optional forms would lead to chaos.

As a result of these criticisms the committee issued a supplementary report to take account of them in so far as they did not run counter to their basic concepts. The most important difference in this supplementary report was a change of attitude towards the optional forms. Originally the committee had believed that the availability of these forms would be beneficial, in that they would lead people to think about the language they were using and choose the form which for them was the most natural. Now it agreed that there must be a selection from these optional forms for use in textbooks and issued a directive for the use of textbook-writers urging them to adopt, as far as possible, forms which were common to both languages. The committee also retreated at a number of points on its proposals for changes in *Nynorsk*.

However, controversy was far from being at an end and the ministry decided not to promulgate the new spelling until it had received the approval of the *Storting*. Its opponents now began to campaign for its rejection or postponement. On 25 June 1937 the *Storting* debated the matter for a whole day. At the end a motion for postponement was defeated by a narrow majority, but a motion for rejection of the proposals lost heavily by 37 votes to 112. After some further revision the government decreed that the new spelling should have effect from 1 July 1938.

The new orthography, the use of which was mandatory on teachers and government offices, had the disadvantage of being to some extent a construct. The forms prescribed did not coincide with the actual speech of any one social group and officially approved word-lists had to be published to guide Norwegians as to the correct spelling of their language. Apart from the obligatory forms which they contained, these word-lists also gave an optional form of equal status for many words, and for some others they gave a so-called side-form (which was also allowed in written work in schools). On the other hand, many forms in current use were excluded from the list and their use in school written work was disallowed. The optional forms continued to call forth protests from teachers and publishers of textbooks, who repeated their demands for the establishment of a textbook norm. In March 1939 a small committee was, in fact, set up to work out such a norm, but when its report appeared it was only given advisory status.

The new orthography was, however, given a great fillip by its adoption by the city of Oslo and the city school authority. Many street names in Oslo were changed to bring them into line with the new spelling, especially by the substitution of the feminine gender for the common gender in the suffixed definite article in the word for 'street', which thus became *gata* instead of *gaten*. In the schools the Oslo authorities decided to adopt textbooks which, as far as possible, made use of orthographic forms common to both languages. As a result of this, and because of the importance of the Oslo area for the textbook market, schoolbooks written in a very radical kind of *Bokmål* began to appear. This meant that many town children used textbooks written in an orthography and containing forms which were very different from the language they used at home. It was a situation which was to provide much fuel for future controversy.

It is not surprising that, with the uncertainty created by the new orthography, manuals of correct style and usage soon began to appear. The authors of the new orthography had not laid down any stylistic guidelines, though it is clear they hoped that a new and natural style would emerge from the situation they had created. The pundits of style now urged in their manuals that Norwegian should be written in a simple and natural way, and that the spoken language should always be kept in mind, though not slavishly followed. Some of them attacked current *Bokmål* style as being un-Norwegian and undemocratic. It was high time, they argued, that in the written language Norwegian folk-style really came into its own. It was advice which, though it may have made for a more everyday and natural style of writing, did at the same time make for less precision, fewer nuances, and a greater wordiness by recommending the circumlocutions of everyday speech rather than the concentrated grammatical constructions of literary style.

The sharpest reaction both to the new orthography and to the pundits came, somewhat unexpectedly, from the poet and essayist Arnulf Øverland (see below, p. 261), hitherto regarded as one of the more radical members of the Labour Party. In a flaming speech early in 1940 he cried a plague on both houses, asking whether the Norwegian language had been abolished and sharply attacking the idea that the speech of the Oslo proletariat should become the language of Norway. And it was there that debate on the language question had to rest for some time to come. The invasion of Norway in April gave the Norwegians other things to think about, including Øverland whose anti-Nazi poems led to his imprisonment in German concentration camps.

When the invasion came the new orthography had been in operation for over two years and had already begun to take effect, in both its moderate and radical forms. One consequence of the reforms had been an increase in the number of rural schools which had opted for *Nynorsk*, and this had given *Nynorsk* a lead over *Bokmål* in the rural areas. Once the occupation got under way the Quisling regime soon found that the language question was of concern to them, especially as it gave them the opportunity to discredit Halvdan Koht (foreign minister in the Norwegian government-in-exile), who had been one of the chief architects of the 1938 reform and who was much criticized for his handling of Norwegian foreign affairs immediately before the invasion. They set up a committee to devise a new orthography which, it was decreed, should take effect from mid-1942. This orthography, a hotch-potch aimed at appealing to conservatives in both language camps, was largely ignored in the schools. The Nazi-controlled press praised it, but a projected series of new textbooks using the new forms never really got off the ground thanks to the passive resistance of those concerned in their production.

After the liberation of Norway in May 1945 the orthography of 1938 was reinstated as the official norm for both language forms. But it was not long before debate on the implications and implementation of the new spelling was resumed. The teachers reiterated their pre-war demanded for a textbook norm and on 31 January 1948 a committee was set up to make proposals for such a norm in both language forms. Soon after the liberation, too, suggestions were made by supporters of both language forms that some sort of language academy should be set up. The discussions which followed convinced the ministry that this was the way to deal with the language question in future. In February 1949 the church and education minister announced in the *Storting* that his department had put work on a textbook norm in hand and, at the same time, he proposed the establishment of a standing language commission (*Språknemnd*).

## A Language Commission and Language Battles

At the end of March 1949 a working committee was set up to make proposals as to the constitution of the proposed commission. Its report appeared in July of the same year. In brief, it stated that the function of the commission would be to advise the authorities and the public on language matters, and to promote the fusion of the two language forms on the basis of Norwegian folk-language (*på norsk folkemåls grunn*); among specific tasks, the commission was to be responsible for the preparation of a textbook norm. It was to consist of twenty-six members, including an equal number representing each language form, to be nominated by educational and scholarly bodies, the press, the society of authors, and broadcasting.

The proposal that Norwegian folk-language should be a basis of reform was at once attacked; indeed, one member of the working committee had dissented from it and wrote a minority report. Of the institutions who were to nominate members of the commission, the universities were critical of certain powers which the ministry were to have over nominations and refused to co-operate unless these were changed. Some of the other bodies were also divided in their views.

As a result of these criticisms the ministry made some changes in the proposals, but without conceding anything of substance. In the meantime public discussion of the language question was rising to fever pitch, with Arnulf Øverland again leading the attack. In the autumn of 1949 parents in the Oslo area organized themselves into a group to protest at the language forms which were being used in their children's schoolbooks, a movement which grew and soon spread to other Norwegian towns. The parents kept up a continuous pressure on the authorities both by public meetings and in the columns of the conservative press. In March 1950 the protest movement got another organ of publicity when *Riksmålsforbundet* began to publish a monthly magazine called *Ordet* (*The Word*) designed to further the cause of *Riksmål* and to be a literary journal demonstrating the merits of that language form. It was edited by the poet and essayist André Bjerke (see below, p. 267) and supported by a number of other prominent writers who were opposed to the official language policy, among them Øverland and Sigurd Hoel (see below, p. 261).

Another reaction was the publication in 1950 by the *Riksmålsvernet* of a word-list containing many of the forms which had been excluded in the 1938 orthography but which, according to the compilers of the list, were still in common use. Such words were marked in the list by an asterisk referring to a footnote which informed the reader that such forms were common in *Riksmål* (they rejected the term *Bokmål*), but were forbidden in written work in the schools.

In the meantime the proposals for the establishment of a language commission remained, until November 1951, in the committee stage when they were presented to the *Storting* in majority and minority versions. Somewhat earlier in the same year a change in language practice, not directly connected with the proposal to set up a language commission, was approved by the *Storting*. This involved a change in the method of counting numbers over twenty. Hitherto, Norwegians had followed the Danish and German practices of saying the digit before the decade, e.g. five and twenty. Now they were to follow the British and Swedish practice and say twenty-five. The change was relatively uncontroversial at the time and was made mandatory on schools, government offices, and the broadcasting service from 1 July 1951, though certain complications ensued, due in some degree to spelling changes of the numerals seven and twenty which had been stipulated in the 1938 reform. Partly because of this but mainly by force of habit very many Norwegians still use the old system of counting.

The prospect that the majority version of the report on the establishment of a language commission would be approved by the ministry—it corresponded closely to the ministry's own thinking—led to a concentrated effort by the protest groups to influence public opinion against the proposals. Their propaganda, mounted in impressive style, declared that the commission was going to unite *Bokmål* and *Nynorsk* into one language form to be called *Samnorsk* (Common Norwegian), thereby extinguishing, so they said, the language of culture. The parents' action group (*Foreldreaksjonen mot samnorsk*) collected over 90,000 signatures to back this protest. In December 1951 the *Storting* debated the matter for two days and when a vote was taken, the majority proposals were adopted.

The business of nominating the members of the Language Commission was not accomplished without arousing controversy within the nominating bodies themselves, most notably in the Society of

Norwegian Authors (*Den Norske Forfatterforening*). Here, a minority led by Arnulf Øverland decided that they would have nothing to do with the Language Commission and argued that it was contrary to the constitution of the society for it to do so. They felt so strongly about things that they seceded from the society and formed their own Authors' Society of 1952 (*Forfatterforeningen av 1952*), and brought a court action (which they lost) against the old society to restrain it from nominating representatives.

On 3 April 1952 the Language Commission (*Norsk Språknemnd*) met for the first time and was soon asked by the ministry to make proposals to solve the textbook norm problem. The commission soon realized that this was going to be a long job, though at the time it is doubtful whether anyone envisaged that it would be January 1958 before its proposals were published. During these years controversy over the language question continued unabated. The parents' action group continued their campaign against *Samnorsk* and in May 1953 they began publishing a fortnightly newspaper, *Frisprog* (Free Language), to further their cause. Almost at the same time *Riksmåls-vernet* decided to create a new academy to be called *Norsk Akademi for Sprog og Litteratur* (Norwegian Academy for Language and Literature). It elected Øverland as its president and had as its objects the protection of *Riksmål* from encroachments, especially from compulsory fusion with *Nynorsk*, and sponsorship of publications designed to promote *Riksmål*. Later in the same year parents were urged by *Frisprog* to take direct action over spellings used in their children's schoolbooks and to amend them to forms which they regarded as acceptable. The government's language policy, it was argued, was a violation of parental rights, the Norwegian constitution, the Education Act, and the International Declaration of Human Rights. To achieve their ends a court action was to be the next step.

However, before this happened, the ministry made a concession. In April 1954 it agreed that textbooks using 'moderate forms' would in future be made available and approved. This meant, as far as Oslo was concerned, a retreat from the position which the school authorities had adopted in 1939 when they cast their vote for the more radical forms. Now, a middle-of-the-road policy was to apply and this was soon reflected in school textbooks.

This concession mollified the parents to a certain extent but not the *Riksmål* militants. Their leading members travelled the country on recruiting campaigns for the cause and were continually on the attack both in print and speech. The normalization of the orthography of Norwegian *belles lettres*, especially the works of the great writers of the nineteenth century, was a source of continuing controversy which led in 1954 to the Authors' Society of 1952 threatening certain publishers with legal proceedings. Pamphlets continued to proliferate and in 1955 the periodical *Ordet* launched a series of publications under the general title 'Language and Style' to further the cause of *Riksmål*. Radio listeners also organized themselves into a society to keep an eye on language usage in radio programmes.

In January 1958 the Language Commission made public its proposals for a new textbook norm, presenting them in a 140-page document of large format. Its principal task had been to propose a reduction in the number of optional spellings and thus make for greater stability in orthography and remove the need for parallel editions of texts. In the event, the commission's proposals were in no way drastic. In *Bokmål* the status of some of the optional spelling forms for a number of words was reduced to that of a subsidiary form (*sideform*), the other form then becoming the obligatory one. Some minor spelling changes were also introduced and a somewhat complicated set of rules governing the use of the feminine gender were formulated. In *Nynorsk* vowel changes were proposed for a large number of words to bring them into line with *Bokmål*. Consonants were also doubled in some words with a similar end in view. But the number of permitted optional forms in *Nynorsk* was increased rather than reduced.

These proposals pleased neither the *Riksmål* nor the *Nynorsk* party. Both believed that the changes proposed did violence to the established norms and to the literary tradition which the two language forms embodied. Many of the earlier arguments were once again rehearsed both inside and outside the *Storting* where they were the subject of a lengthy debate. However, in October 1958 the *Storting* gave its approval to the commission's proposals and in April 1959 they were promulgated after a number of minor changes had been made. Later the same month a list containing the spelling changes from those given in the 1938 orthography was published. The new norm, *Ny Læreboknormal 1959* (The New Textbook Norm; 1959), was then published in both *Bokmål* and *Nynorsk* in the form of word-lists for the guidance of the public. Some of these word-lists contained all the permitted forms, others only the so-called 'moderate forms', others the so-called 'radical forms', so that people could take their pick according to their linguistic taste.

In 1959 an organization calling itself *Landslaget for Språklig Samling* (The Society for Language Unification) was formed to promote the fusion of the two language forms and to provide a third force in the language battle which, hitherto, had been dominated by the militant *Riksmål* and *Nynorsk* organizations. The new society has commanded a certain degree of support and has issued a number of publications including proposals for a common orthographic norm to cover both language forms. However, since the publication of the textbook norm, the movement for language fusion seems to have lost ground. During this time the *Riksmål* faction, in particular, has lost no opportunity to keep up its pressure and has backed it by a number of well-written publications. In 1959 a Norwegian version of *My Fair Lady* provided the translator André Bjerke (a well-known poet and champion of *Riksmål*) with a chance to lampoon official language policy and to aver that in Norway it was Eliza Doolittle and not Professor Higgins who laid down the norms of the spoken language. *Riksmål* criticism was also directed at the language policy of the Norwegian State Radio where, it was alleged, both members of the staff and other broadcasters were pressured into the use of radical forms. The most celebrated episode in this aspect of the language controversy involved the insistence of a member of the staff of the meteorological office on using certain forms which were not officially permitted, especially the form *sne* (snow) instead of the official *snø*, when broadcasting weather forecasts. Eventually, because of his persistence, he was relieved of his broadcasting duties. He then brought a suit against his employers on the grounds that he had been discriminated against because of the language form which was natural to him. The court ruled that the action against him had no basis in law, a decision which was acclaimed by the *Riksmål* movement as a great victory.

In the meantime the Language Commission worked on, especially its secretariat which, among other tasks, acted as language advisor to a wide range of public and private institutions. It also established co-operation with the other Scandinavian countries in language matters, acted as consultant to the publishers of school textbooks, and issued a number of publications of its own. However, it soon became clear that its work was not going to have any radical effect on the language situation in Norway. Another thing was that a new wind of toleration began to blow. In 1964 the minister of church and education, himself a *Nynorsk* supporter, set up a new language committee to discuss the language situation and prepare measures for the conservation of the Norwegian linguistic heritage as a whole. This committee, known as the Vogt Committee after its chairman Hans Vogt, then Rector of the University of Oslo, included two members of the *Riksmål* faction, something which had never happened before on official committees. In 1966 the Vogt Committee made its recommendations which included proposals for a reorganization of the Language Commission, the dropping of the commission's mandate to promote a fusion of the two language forms on the basis of the Norwegian folk-language, and suggestions that there should be a return to some of the traditional forms which had been dropped at the time of the 1938 spelling reform. Popularly the Vogt Committee became known as *Språkfredkomitéen* (The Language Peace Committee). Its recommendations have led to plans to replace the Language Commission (*Språknemnd*) by a Language Council (*Språkråd*). Another development which indicated that a climate of greater tolerance had developed was the reuniting in 1966 of the two Authors' Societies into one.

The squabbles over the language situation may seem to the outsider to be of teacup proportions and a wasteful expenditure of time, money, and energy in a country with a population of barely 4 million. Arnold Toynbee saw the whole movement as a wrong-headed combination of archaism and nationalism. It is, nevertheless, difficult to see how the language battle could have been avoided, given the Norwegian historical and linguistic background and the nature of the national renaissance in the nineteenth century. The language battle has, in fact, had its distinctly positive and beneficial sides. The spelling of Norwegian, whatever Norwegians may say at times about their difficulties, has become very much more phonetic than it was at the turn of the century. This has also helped the achievement of a more natural norm of cultivated pronunciation since it has removed the spoken language from the influences which the printed word could exercise on it. Not that there is any norm of pronunciation in Norway with the prestige which Received Pronunciation has in English. The differences in the pronunciation of Norwegian between the different parts of the country and especially between the east and the west have meant that no one norm for the whole country has been able to develop. However, the prestige of town norms of pronunciation has, with increasing urbanization, risen continually, especially in the south-east, the most densely populated area.

As in the nineteenth century, an important influence on Norwegian language development has been the practice of the country's leading writers. Generally speaking they have tended to go their own way both in the use they have made of forms and vocabulary taken from the dialects and in their choice of a radical or conservative orthography. Whatever their differences, imaginative writers have been a major influence in making *Bokmål* a much more flexible literary instrument than it was formerly. This applies especially to writers like Knut Hamsun (see below, p. 250) and Sigurd Hoel (see below, p. 262) whose prestige and stylistic qualities have had the same influence on language development in the twentieth as Asbjørnsen and Moe, and Bjørnson, had in the nineteenth century. *Nynorsk* has also benefited from the fact that some of the country's leading writers have used it, especially Olav Duun (see below, p. 255) and Tarjei Vesaas (see below, p. 265). Like their *Bokmål* colleagues they have felt free to make use of their own dialects in their works, though they have by and large conformed to the current official orthography. The prestige they have commanded has been an important factor in the development of *Nynorsk* as a literary language, though this has not led to a wider use of *Nynorsk* in other fields. Statistics relating to the use of *Nynorsk* in primary schools show that while, in 1946, 31.9 per cent of them used *Nynorsk* as their principal language, the figure had fallen to 17.9 per cent in 1970. There is no doubt that *Nynorsk* has been losing ground. Only about 10 per cent of books published in Norway are in *Nynorsk* and in other areas the use of *Nynorsk* is only a small fraction of the use of *Bokmål*. Progressive urbanization is no doubt one of the principal reasons for this, and in spite of what writers like Duun and Vesaas have done on behalf of *Nynorsk* and although *Det Norsk Teater* in Oslo exists for the specific purpose of furthering *Nynorsk* on the stage, and is well supported, it does not influence the number of people who actually use *Nynorsk* themselves. In the spoken language it seems likely that the town norms, especially those of the Oslo area, will continue to make progress at the expense of *Nynorsk* and the dialects. In the written language, though it is still an open question, it also seems likely that some modified form of *Bokmål* will eventually become the sole language form of Norway, but the achievement of this still seems to be a very long way ahead.

# Chapter 10

# Literature from the Old Norse
# Period to the Advent of Realism

THERE ARE TWO COMPLICATIONS in dealing with Norwegian literature before 1800. Firstly, most of the literature of the medieval period, which we call Old Norse and which Norwegian literary historians treat as part of Norwegian literature, was in fact written down in Iceland. Secondly, most of the literature written by Norwegians during the Danish period from the sixteenth century to 1814 was written in Danish and forms part of the corpus of Danish literature. However, in the case of Old Norse literature, not only did the Icelanders, during their Commonwealth period (930 to the 1260s), continue to feel a strong attachment to Norway, but the Norwegian national renaissance of the first half of the nineteenth century drew so much of its inspiration from the medieval history of Norway, which was also mainly written down in Iceland, and from the literary tradition which the two countries had in common, that the renaissance itself would probably have been unthinkable without it. Much the same may be said of the literature of the Danish period, for to omit the name of Ludvig Holberg (see below, p. 220) from any consideration of the history of Norwegian literature would create a lacuna which Norwegians would find intolerable.

## THE OLD NORSE PERIOD

The earliest communications preserved to us from the forbears of the Norwegiar. people are runic inscriptions scratched on rock, stone, or other material. Like such inscriptions found in other countries the runic inscriptions of Norway can scarcely be called literature. Most of them consist of communications of a factual or commemorative kind, though the Eggjum stone found in Sogn in western Norway in 1917 and thought to be from about A.D. 700 gives sufficient evidence of imaginative power and artistic form in the some 200 runes it bears to make it a precursor of the Eddaic lays and scaldic verse.

### Eddaic Poetry

The Eddaic lays are a collection of ancient poems dealing with the mythical gods and heroes of Scandinavian antiquity. The majority of them are found in a collection called the *Elder or Poetic Edda*, a name used to distinguish them from the *Younger or Prose Edda*, written by a known person, Snorri Sturluson (see below, p. 216), and which have come down to us in an Icelandic manuscript of the thirteenth century. They had, however, been preserved by oral tradition, some for several hundred years, before they were given written form. Most scholars are agreed that some of the lays are from pagan times, and that others reflect the advent of Christianity, while others again are from as late as the thirteenth century. Some were composed in Iceland, but others had their origin in Norway; one lay is believed to have originated in Greenland, and it is not impossible that some may have been composed in other Norwegian colonies.

The first poem in the *Edda* manuscript is called *Vǫluspá* (*Sibyl's Prophecy*). In it a prophetess gives an account of Northern cosmology, including the creation of the world out of the void of Ginnunga-Gap, the life of the gods, the origins of strife, and how Odin breathed life into the first human pair, Ask and Embla. The World Ash, Yggdrasill, spreads its evergreen branches over the whole world, its roots leading to the kingdom of the gods, the giants, and the dead. The poem ends with prophecies of the future, of Ragnarǫk the twilight of the gods, but from which a new world will arise. *Vǫluspá* is the most important of the lays of the gods, though others add to our knowledge of Northern mythology. Sometimes these lays have a didactic aspect. This is especially so in *Hávamál* (*Sayings of the High One*), also one of the notable lays of the *Edda*, where the first 80 stanzas are devoted to advice on how one should conduct oneself in life, dispensing wisdom in epigrammatic form. In other lays Odin and the gods are depicted in their relationships with people, frequently in everyday situations, and sometimes comically. In fact the lays of the gods range in character from high and mystical seriousness to earthy humour; some are in dramatic form and may have been used in this way.

Some of the lays of the *Edda* dealing with the legendary heroes of the past go back to early Germanic originals from the time of the Migration of Peoples, others date from about 1200 or later. Their heroes are endowed with all the qualities the Norsemen placed highest: freedom from fear, courage, and the capacity for great deeds which would secure for them the immortality of posthumous fame. Sometimes the gods come to the aid of the hero; sometimes the heroes are of divine origin; often they are stylized supermen lacking the more human traits of the gods. The actual historical events which form the background to some of the heroic lays are treated with the greatest freedom. Among them is *Vǫlundarkviða* (*The Lay of Vǫlund*), treating a subject (Wayland the Smith) known in other countries, and a majority of them have Sigurd the dragon-slayer, the Siegfried of the *Nibelungenlied*, as their central hero.

## Scaldic Verse

Like some of the lays of the *Elder Edda*, much scaldic verse had been handed down by oral tradition for long periods before it was given written form. It is known that Germanic princes had scalds at their Courts whose job it was to compose and recite lays in honour of kings, princes, and chieftains, praising them for their courage and generosity. The scaldic art was also practised and developed in Norway and Iceland, and it is from this area that the main corpus of scaldic verse has been preserved. It was on account of its value as historical material that scaldic verse was written down and many saga-writers made use of it in their sagas. Scaldic verse usually differs very much from the lays of the *Elder Edda*, especially because of the complicated verse forms it employs and the extensive use it makes of kennings. Scaldic verse, unlike the anonymous lays of the *Edda*, is generally by known authors and the names of some 250 scalds have come down to us, though the greater part of their work has been lost. The oldest extant piece of scaldic verse is by Bragi Boddason, who lived in the first half of the ninth century. Some of the best-known scaldic lays relate directly to historical events and personages: the Lay of Harald (*Haraldskvæði* or *Hrafnsmál*) by Þorbjǫrn Hornklofi tells of the battle of Hafrsfjord (see above, p. 73); *Eiríksmál*, from an unknown hand, celebrates Erik Bloodaxe (see above, p. 73); *Hákonarmál*, by Eyvindr Skáldaspillir (tenth century), one of the most remarkable specimens of scaldic verse, is a memorial lay commemorating the death of Håkon the Good (see above, p. 73). Eyvindr was the last Norwegian scald of importance. Subsequently, the scaldic art became the preserve of the Icelanders with Egill Skalla-Grímsson (*c.* 910–90) as its most distinguished practitioner. His strikingly original lay *Hǫfuðlausn* (*Head-ransom*), with which he saved his life when he fell into the hands of Erik Bloodaxe in England, and his *Sonatorrek* (*The Irreparable Loss of his Sons*), written as a memorial lay over the death of his sons, are his great works. Ibsen had Egill in mind when he created the character of Ørnulf in his play *Hærmændene paa Helgeland* (*The Warriors at Helgeland*; 1858).

The whole art of the scald was so rooted in pagan beliefs, in its diction, imagery, ideas, and kennings, that the coming of Christianity to the North naturally had important consequences for it. Some scaldic verse had already reflected the battle between the old and the new faiths and, in spite of its pagan affiliations, even an ardent Christianizer like King Olav Haraldsson supported the scaldic art and even practised it himself. In fact scaldic poetry showed a remarkable capacity for self-renewal and adaptation to the new conditions. This showed itself especially in the work of Sigvatr Þórðarson (*c.* 995–1045), an Icelander at King Olav's Court who wrote a lay on the battle of Nesjar (see above, p. 76) and found a theme for scaldic verse in the journeys he made on behalf of the king. He also incorporated outspoken advice to the young King Magnus (the Good) in a lay called *Bersǫglivísur* (*Plain-speaking Verses*). From this time onwards Christian motifs were frequently used by scalds and after the death of King Olav many scaldic lays were devoted to him. This type of scaldic poetry reached a high point in the lay *Geisli* (*The Sunbeam*) dedicated to Olav and composed by Einarr Skúlason (*c.* 1100–60), the greatest scald of the twelfth century; and in the visionary poem *Sólarljóð* (*Song of the Sun*), from an unknown hand, we get a Christian parallel to the lay *Vǫluspá* of the *Elder Edda*.

Scaldic poetry continued to be written on into the fourteenth century, but mainly as an antiquarian pursuit. However, about the middle of the century a monk, Eysteinn Ásgrímsson, wrote a religious lay *Lilja* (*The Lily*), dedicated to the glory of God, Christ, and the Virgin Mary, which is generally rated as the finest of the Christian scaldic lays.

### THE SAGAS

Like the lays of the *Elder Edda* and the poems of the scalds, the prose sagas were not written down until much later than the events they describe, probably not until the thirteenth century, though opinions are divided as to the extent to which some sagas are based on oral transmission. But whereas the Eddaic and scaldic lays drew on a common Germanic heritage, the sagas drew their material from the histories of the early kings of Norway, the events of the Viking Age, the settlement of Iceland and life there. An indispensable precondition for the writing-down of the sagas, as with the Eddaic and scaldic lays, was the introduction of the Latin alphabet into the North with the coming of Christianity.

### The Sagas of the Kings

As we shall see, the majority of these sagas of the kings of Norway were written down in Iceland. Early in the twelfth century Sæmundr Sigfússon (1056–1133), whose name was often connected with the *Elder Edda*, in the belief that he had either written it or collated it, wrote a short work in Latin on the Norwegian kings, and Ari Þorgilsson (1067–1148) included, in the lost first edition of his *Íslendingabók* (*Book of the Icelanders*) written in the 1120s, a list of the kings of Norway up to this time, thus providing a useful chronological basis for later historians.

There were also some historians writing in Norway itself. In the second half of the twelfth century a monk Theodoricus wrote a chronicle in Latin dealing with the Norwegian kings from Harald Fairhair to about 1130, and there is a somewhat later Latin chronicle from an unknown hand, *Historia Norvegiae*, written for foreigners, which first came to light in 1849 and which deals, among other topics, with the early kings of Norway up to Olav Haraldsson.

But it was in Iceland, with the successors of Ari Þorgilsson, that the writing of Norwegian history really got underway. About 1160 Eiríkr Oddsson wrote his *Hryggjarstykki* (possibly meaning *Backbone piece*), contemporary with the events it describes, and about the same time sagas were also written on Saint Olav and on Olav Tryggvason. In 1185 Karl Jónsson, abbot of the monastery of Þingeyrar, came to Norway from Iceland to write the first part of the Saga of King Sverre (*Sverris Saga*).

In 1190 an unknown author wrote in Old Norse a history of the kings of Norway, later called *Ágrip* (*Summary of the History of the Kings of Norway*) which, it is believed, originally covered the whole period of the history of the Norwegian kings up to 1177, but the first and last parts have been lost. About 1220 another account appeared, later known as *Morkinskinna* (*Rotten Skin*), originally covering the period from Magnus the Good (1035) up to the battle of Re in 1177, but the end has been lost. Here, we find for the first time the characteristic features of saga-writing as they later developed, including a welding of events into an artistic whole and the use of scaldic lays and other anecdotes and short stories to give the whole account of life. (One of these short stories, that of Auðunn and the polar bear, is among the most notable examples of Old Norse literary art.)

The most comprehensive and detailed of these early historical sagas is the manuscript, later called *Fagrskinna* (*Fine Skin*), which was written about 1230 and covers the whole period of Norwegian history from Halfdan the Black to the battle of Re in 1177. The author made use of earlier manuscripts and scaldic lays, but his work has not the same artistic merit as *Morkinskinna*.

But these manuscripts and a number of others were really only preparatory work for the greatest of the writers of historical sagas, Snorri Sturluson (1178/9–1241) whose *Heimskringla*, covering the history of the kings of Norway from the beginning up to the battle of Re, must be accounted one of the monuments of world literature.

Snorri, who was born in Iceland, and eventually became the richest man in the country, had already distinguished himself as a scald when he visited Norway in the years 1218–20. On his return to Iceland he completed his *Prose Edda*, an *Ars poetica*, designed as a manual for the guidance of aspiring scalds and written, it seems, in the belief that the scaldic art was in decline and that an account of the scald's mythological and metrical stock-in-trade was urgently needed.

The close study of the work of the scalds which the writing of his *Prose Edda* involved also brought Snorri into intimate contact with incidents from Norwegian history as they were recorded in the scaldic lays, and this may have given him the idea of writing his history of the Norwegian kings. Snorri certainly realized the value of the scaldic lays as historical source material, and though, as he says in his preface to *Heimskringla*, the scalds were laudatory in their attitude to the kings and chieftains they wrote about, they would not include things which everybody present would know were untrue, for that would be 'mockery and not praise'. Thus, in *Heimskringla*, Snorri made great use of scaldic material and also of earlier historical sagas, but he applied to them both his critical sense and wide scholarship. Not that he shuns the use of purely legendary material and, like his contemporaries, he made free use of invented dialogue in his accounts of historical personages; but he succeeded, with his unique blend of critical scholarship and narrative and compositional skill, in bringing the early history of Norway to life in a way that had never been achieved before and producing a work which was to have consequences for Norwegian history many hundreds of years later.

## The Sagas of the Icelanders

Another category of sagas, the sagas of the Icelanders, those dealing with life in Iceland during the centuries immediately following the settlement of the country, though a highly important part of the general corpus of the medieval literature of Iceland, do not have the same relevance to Norway as the historical sagas do. Indeed it is uncertain whether these sagas were known in Norway at the time. The relevance they do have to Norway derives more from the general ethos they generate than from the actual material they contain, and this, together with their stylistic qualities, exercised an influence on Norwegian literature in the nineteenth and twentieth centuries. The historical novels of Sigrid Undset (see below, p. 254) and the stylistic qualities of Olav Duun (see below, p. 255) are in their different ways literary heirs of the sagas of the Icelanders.

## Later Saga and Other Writing

In 1264–65 the Icelander Sturla Þórðarson (1214–84) composed, at the behest of King Magnus Lagabøter, the saga of Håkon Håkonsson (*Hákonar saga Hákonarsonar*). It added to the body of historical writing on the kings of Norway and like *Sverris saga* it was a contemporary account. Otherwise the literature written in Norway at this period consisted mainly of translations, either of works of edification, especially *Gammel norsk homiliebok* (*Norwegian Homily Book; c.* 1200), or of foreign romances (*Riddarasǫgur*) among them *Percevals saga,* a prose version of Chrétien de Troyes's epic, and *Karlamagnús saga,* partly based on the French *Chanson de Roland.*

The *Fornaldarsaga* (*Saga of Ancient Times*), a type of saga which developed in Iceland about the middle of the thirteenth century, should also be mentioned here, though there appears to be no evidence that any of them were written in Norway. By contrast to the Icelandic family sagas, these sagas make no pretence of being true, though there may be a core of historical fact in them. They may be regarded as historical novels or romances, intended to entertain, usually set in the remote Germanic past and often in Norway, and giving idealized pictures of the heroes and events they describe. Noteworthy *fornaldarsǫgur* are the *Vǫlsunga saga* (*The Saga of the Volsungs*), to which Ibsen's *The Warriors at Helgeland* is indebted, and *Friðþófs saga,* set in Sogn in western Norway.

There was, however, one definitely Norwegian work of stature written at this time, *Konungs skuggsjá* or *The King's Mirror.* The book takes the form of a dialogue between father and son, in the course of which the father gives an *exposé* of the life of the merchant, including much information about the world at large; the duties of the courtier and the mode of conduct expected of a gentleman; and a large section devoted to the rights and duties of the monarch, which provides the principal subject of the book. Though obviously modelled on similar works written in other literatures, the unknown author of *The King's Mirror* gives his account of the state of Norwegian culture and his ideals in the mid-thirteenth century in an original and personal way.

Translations of foreign romances continued to be made on into the fourteenth century, but with Norwegian decline and the Black Death all literary activity came to an end, and, until well on into the sixteenth century, nothing of note was written in Norway. The disintegration of the old written language meant that with the advent of Danish political supremacy and the coming of the Reformation, the literary life of Norway was ripe for takeover by the Danish language. It was only through the oral transmission of folk-ballads, stories, and legends that an independent Norwegian literary tradition was kept alive, but it was not until the nineteenth century that the majority of this folk-literature was written down for the first time.

## THE DANISH PERIOD

As we have seen (above, p. 101), the establishment of Danish power in Norway and the imposition of the Reformation came at a period when Norway was at her lowest ebb. Culturally, too, the situation was no better. Indeed it was made worse when, after the Reformation, churches were plundered of their works of art and manuscripts, and even torn down to provide building material for defence-works in Denmark. The *Chronicle of Hamar* (*Hamarkrøniken*), written about 1550, gives a melancholy picture of the plight of Norway at the time. The Reformation also led to the establishment of the Danish language as the written language of Norway (see above, p. 192).

It took a long time for the new ideas of the Renaissance to reach Norway and then their effect was slight. European humanism did, however, have some impact, though in a specifically Norwegian way, in the work of the so-called Bergen humanists. Bergen was the largest, most prosperous, and culturally most advanced town in Norway at the time. The presence of the German Hansa in the town also represented a challenge which stimulated Norwegian national feeling. Most prominent of these Bergen humanists was Absalon Pederssøn Beyer (1528–75), who after studies in Copenhagen and Wittenberg returned to teach at the Cathedral (Latin) School in Bergen and later advanced to high ecclesiastical office. Among other things he was responsible for the first known theatrical performance in Norway, given by the boys of the school, something we learn in his journal, the so-called *Bergens Kapitelsbog*, a unique and personal account of life in Bergen during 1552–72 which he began in Latin and continued in Danish. However, Absalon's principal work was his *Om Norigs Rige* (*Concerning the Kingdom of Norway*), written in 1567, a compilation based on a wide study of the source material and which deals both with the contemporary local scene and with the sagas of the kings of Norway. Everywhere in his account Absalon reveals his many-sided interests and his deep sense of the values of the past. Though often copied and widely read, his history was not printed until the late eighteenth century, and then only parts of it.

Absalon's younger contemporary, Peder Claussøn Friis (1545–1614), was a lesser man, a learned cleric whose scientific, topographical, and historical interests were characteristic of his time. His most important work was his translation of Snorri Sturluson's *Heimskringla* and other royal sagas which were published in 1633 under the title *Norske Kongers Chronica* (*The Chronicles of the Norwegian Kings*). Its republication in 1757 in a somewhat revised edition had an important influence on the growth of Norwegian national feeling in the latter part of the eighteenth century. Apart from these one or two outstanding names, the general level of culture remained low in Norway during the sixteenth century. The so-called Oslo humanists, of whom Jens Nilssøn (1538–1600) and Hallvard Gunnarssøn (d. 1608) were the most prominent, wrote mainly in Latin.

The seventeenth century saw the advent of the Baroque to the
North. Its most noteworthy representatives were the Swede Georg
Stiernhielm (1598–1672) and the Dane Thomas Kingo (1634–1703).
Much was also written in Norway during this century: devotional
works; great quantities of occasional verse; history and topography;
but most of it was soon forgotten. Dorothe Engelbretsdatter (1634–
1716), who enjoyed a high reputation in her day, is still commemorated in the histories of Norwegian literature for her lachrymose *Siælens
Sang-Offer* (*Song Offerings of the Soul*; 1678), but the only really important name of the period is that of Petter Dass (1647–1707). He
was born in Alstahaug in north Norway of Scottish descent and after
studies in Copenhagen eventually returned to his native parish to
become its all-powerful priest. There he wrote his major work,
*Nordlands Trompet* (*The Trumpet of the North*), in which he describes
and celebrates the province of Nordland and the life there in the
lusty, resounding Baroque verse of which he was a consummate
master. Though the work includes such matters as geography, topography, and ethnology, everything is seen from a personal point of
view imbued with devout belief and vividly brought to life by
apposite digression and description. *The Trumpet of the North* was first
printed in 1739 after Dass's death, as was much of his other work,
which is mainly of an edifying kind.

At the turn of the eighteenth century Norwegian intellectual and
cultural life was at a low ebb, as it was in Denmark where hair-
splitting pedantry was the order of the day. Renewal in both countries
had to wait for Ludvig Holberg, the greatest name in the North
during the eighteenth century. He was born in Bergen in Norway,
but spent most of his life in Denmark, becoming a professor at the
University of Copenhagen and eventually a Danish baron. He has
naturally been claimed by both Danes and Norwegians as their own,
but it is clear that his literary output which, as well as the comedies
for which he is best known abroad, includes essays, satires, and many
volumes of history, belongs to the corpus of Danish literature. Norwegian scholars have been quick to find Norwegianisms in his written
Danish and reflections in his work of his early years in Norway–in
Gudbrandsdalen, in Bergen (he wrote a book on Bergen), and in
Christiansand–but his specific importance for the development of
Norwegian life and culture lies principally in the influence his work
had on the members of *Det Norske Selskab* in Copenhagen in the late
eighteenth century, thus acting as a direct stimulus to the awakening
of the Norwegian national consciousness. In the nineteenth century,
too, the influence of Holberg is traceable in Vinje, Ibsen, and in the
essays of Nils Kjær.

In the late eighteenth century the Northern countries were particularly exposed to the new impulses which the Enlightenment and pre-romanticism brought from England, France, and Germany. In Sweden the period produced the greatest Rococo poet of the North, Carl Michael Bellman (1740–95), and in Denmark the poet and dramatist Johannes Ewald (1743–81), but in Norway the only writer of any stature was Christian Braunman Tullin (1728–65). Unlike most of the other Norwegian-born writers of the period, who migrated to Denmark, Tullin continued to live in Christiania. His principal work is the typically Rococo poem *Majdagen* (*May Day*; 1758), which was highly praised by his contemporaries, celebrating the Norwegian landscape, albeit a cultivated landscape, for didactic ends. Elsewhere his poems reflect the influence of Rousseau, criticize contemporary materialism, and in a prize poem of 1763 he adumbrates a world-view where everything from the angels above to the lowliest serpent has been appointed its place by the wisdom of the Almighty. In his essays, posthumously published, he also clearly shows himself as an heir to the Holbergian tradition, especially in his view of the importance of agriculture and the peasant.

Signs of the late eighteenth-century cultural upsurge in Norway (see above, p. 26) were the founding of the Royal Scientific Society in Trondhjem; the extent and quality of the topographical literature on Norway which was appearing; and Gerhard Schøning's massive *Norges Riiges Historie* (*The History of the Kingdom of Norway*; 1771–81) – the title itself a declaration that Norway was still a kingdom.

Norwegian writers in Copenhagen were also enjoying literary success, especially Niels Krog Bredal (1732–78) with his play *Tronfølgen i Sidon* (*The Succession in Sidon*; 1771) and Johan Nordahl Brun (1745–1816) with his tragedy *Zarine* (1772). They began to feel themselves as a group, not only nationally but also in their opposition to the German-dominated (by Klopstock) Danish literature of the time. They organized a literary club, eventually called *Det Norske Selskab*, to devote themselves to literary chit-chat and conviviality round the punch-bowl, but they also published three volumes of verse. However, only one of the club's members, Johan Herman Wessel (1742–85), was outstanding as a writer.

Wessel was the equivalent of a 'failed B.A.' of the University of Copenhagen and subsequently led a Bohemian existence, inadequately supporting himself by casual teaching and literary hackwork. He had, however, a highly developed and inventive satirical talent which he used with rapier-like precision in his verses, epigrams, and comic short stories, giving apt expression to the spirit of *Det Norske Selskab*. But his name is immortalized in the annals of Norwegian literary history by his mock tragedy *Kierlighed uden Strømper* (*Love without Stockings*; 1772), written in impeccable alexandrines where the loss of a pair of stockings sets the whole apparatus of high tragedy in motion, and probably intended as a parody of the epigonous tragedies written in the French classical style by his fellow-countrymen Nordahl Brun and Claus Fasting.

However, from the point of view of literary development at the time, the members of *Det Norske Selskab* represented a conservative, even reactionary, force in relation to the newer literary currents in Denmark, of which Johannes Ewald was the foremost representative. Nevertheless, some of the literary efforts of the society's members and of some other Norwegian writers, though in no sense great literature, had important consequences for the growth of Norwegian national feeling. Among those who wrote in a patriotic vein was Hans Bull (1739–83) who praised the Norwegian yeoman farmer (*Odelsbonden*) and the glories of Norwegian scenery in his poems. He also established the Dovre mountains as a prime symbol of Norwegian sturdiness and nationhood, a symbol which was taken up by other Norwegian poets, so much so that it soon degenerated into a cliché; later it was savagely satirized by Ibsen in *Peer Gynt* in the scenes in the hall of the mountain king (*Dovregubben*). Bull's contemporary Johan Nordahl Brun had already inaugurated the Norwegian saga-drama with his play *Einer Tambeskielver* (1772), which contained so much patriotic red meat that the authorities in Denmark were offended and he failed to get it produced there. His patriotic poem *For Norge, Kiæmpers Fødeland* (*For Norway the Fatherland of Giants*), called by Wergeland 'a Norwegian Marseillaise', became one of the best-known and most sung ditties in the country. Claus Frimann (1746–1829) celebrated the peasants and fishermen of Norway in his lively and down-to-earth verses *Almuens Sanger* (*Songs of the Common People*; 1790) and *Den syngende Søemand* (*The Singing Seaman*; 1793). Edvard Storm made use of the dialect of Vågå in his *Døleviser*, the most important contribution to verse in dialect which had so far appeared in Norway, and at roughly the same time Thomas Rosing de Stockfleth wrote his poem *Heimatkomsten* in a dialect from Gudbrandsdalen.

### LITERARY RENAISSANCE

The years immediately before and after 1814 (see above, p. 122), charged with political and economic problems, provided very shallow soil for literary creativity. It has been said that the formulation of the Norwegian constitution of 1814 was the greatest creative achievement in Norway at this period. However, in spite of the many tribulations, intellectual life was carried on, and often in the spirit of *Det Norske Selskab*, though that body had been dissolved in 1813. During the years 1816–20 Johan Storm Munch (1778–1832) published a periodical called *Saga* in which he included translations from the sagas and articles on Norwegian language and history. Other scholars, too, devoted themselves to research into the past history of Norway, often producing results unflattering to the Danes. Another impressive achievement was Jens Kraft's monumental work on the topography of Norway, *Topografisk-statistisk Beskrivelse over Kongeriget Norge* (6 volumes, 1820–35).

In the field of *belles lettres*, such as they were, the two principal names were Henrik Anker Bjerregaard (1792–1842) and Mauritz Hansen (1794–1842). Bjerregaard, the author of Norway's first national anthem, *Sønner af Norge (Sons of Norway)* with music by Christian Blom, also wrote the operetta *Fjeldeventyret (The Mountain Adventure*; 1824), set to music by Waldemar Thrane, and the historical play *Magnus Barfods Sønner (The Sons of Magnus Bareleg*; 1829). Like the literary products of some of his lesser colleagues, both these works appealed in their different ways to Norwegian national sentiment; the former putting dialect-speaking Norwegian peasants on the stage for the first time, the latter treating a theme from the early history of Norway. Mauritz Hansen, who was highly regarded in his day, though he does not seem to have realized his full potential, inaugurated with his short story *Luren (The Shepherd's Horn*; 1819) the peasant story *(Bondefortelling)* in Norwegian literature, a genre which was later to become exceedingly popular. Elsewhere, Hansen's voluminous literary production, mainly novels and short stories, was much influenced by German and Danish romanticism, especially in its Gothic aspects, but he was the first real writer of imaginative prose modern Norway had produced.

## *Wergeland and Welhaven*

The ideas and the ideals of the Romantic movement were first brought to the North in a famous series of lectures at Copenhagen in 1802–03 by the Norwegian-born Henrich Steffens (1773–1845), who made his career in Germany and was closely associated with the Jena Circle. Yet the Romantic movement did not take Norway by storm as it did Denmark and Sweden. In fact it penetrated into Norway very slowly indeed, and then only when its force was practically spent elsewhere. Moreover, the sole Norwegian representative of romanticism of any consequence, Henrik Wergeland, was also very much an heir of the spirit of the Enlightenment. It is in the so-called National Romantic movement *(Nasjonalromantikken)*, which found its inspiration in the native and peasant culture of Norway, that the Romantic spirit found expression in Norway, but then in a form which was strongly suffused with poetic realism.

The life and work of Henrik Wergeland epitomizes in many ways the spirit of the new Norway in the decades which immediately followed 1814. He also set the pattern of the writer as a leader of public opinion, which was to become traditional in Norwegian letters, often to their disadvantage. We can perhaps see in this a continuation of the medieval concept of the scald as both poet and man of action.

Wergeland's literary output includes large-scale works in verse, plays, essays and sketches, and works of history. He also edited a number of periodicals intended for the enlightenment of the common people, the workers and the peasants, and he was otherwise incessantly engaged in publicist activity of one sort or another. He became the leader of the so-called 'Patriots' faction, for whom the cornerstone of the new Norway was the constitution of 1814, and the way forward a complete break with the hegemony of Danish literature and culture. Opposed to them was the so-called 'Intelligence Party', led by Wergeland's lesser contemporary, the poet and writer Johan Sebastian Welhaven (1807–73), which stood for a continuance of the cultural ties with Denmark and a programme of steady development rather than the noisy radicalism of Wergeland and his supporters. Together the two factions included many of the best intelligences in the country, and although their opposing programmes involved a vast range of political, social, and cultural topics relating to the new Norway (on which there was often disagreement within the factions themselves), one of their main differences concerned the role of creative literature and the writer in society.

It is clear that Wergeland's thought and work owed much to the literary and intellectual influences which had impinged on Norwegian cultural life from the outside world, from the French Enlightenment and from German and English romanticism. He was also deeply conscious of the historical position of Norway after 1814 and of how necessary it was for the country to derive strength from its medieval period of greatness, though not in any narrowly nationalistic or backward-looking sense. However, in his best poetry the prevailing perspectives are cosmic and divine, and the tone ecstatic. His universe is that of the spirit which invests the smallest thing or creature. Flowers are often the symbol of this, to which some of his shorter poems give exquisite expression. His major work in verse, the epic *Skabelsen, Mennesket og Messias* (*Creation, Man and Messiah*; 1830) dedicated to spokesmen of Truth, Freedom, and Love, develops its gigantic theme partly as a visionary poem and partly as an expression of the ideals embodied in the dedication. The work provides a conspectus of Wergeland's literary virtues and vices: his extraordinary vitality and felicity of language on the one hand and his cloudiness and tastelessness on the other; and also of the themes he developed elsewhere in his poetry.

Wergeland battled against tyranny and oppression not only in long poems like *Cæsaris* (1831–aimed at Tsarist oppression in Poland; *Spaniolen* (*The Spaniard*; 1833)–reaction in Spain; *Jøden* (*The Jew*; 1842)–discrimination against the Jews in Norway; and, implicitly, in poems like *Jan van Huysums Blomsterstykke* (*Jan van Huysum's Flower-piece*; 1840) and *Den engelske Lods* (*The English Pilot*; 1844), but also in real life, especially on behalf of the peasants. Indeed, as some of his short sketches show, he was a staunch adherent of the cult of the peasant as it had developed towards the end of the eighteenth century. In his plays, too, Wergeland takes up the cudgels against oppressors: against the British in India in *Den indiske Cholera* (*The Indian Cholera*; 1835) and on behalf of unmarried mothers in *Barnemordersken* (*The Infanticide*; 1835). Wergeland's personal life was tumultuous and full of conflict. His early death at thirty-seven and the pathos of his last illness, during which he composed some of his most memorable short poems, set a seal on his life and work which was to make him the first immortal of the new Norway.

The position which Welhaven enjoys in the history of Norwegian literature is enhanced by his and his party's polemics against Wergeland. At the same time, his literary qualities tend to be obscured by the greater talents of Wergeland. Welhaven started his writing career not only as a severe critic of Wergeland, against whom he wrote a polemical dissertation, but also as a scathing critic of the Norwegian society of his day in his poem *Norges Dæmring* (*The Dawn of Norway*; 1834). His own aesthetic, which also emerges from these criticisms, involved harmony, balance, and the recording of emotion recalled in tranquillity. The poet's craft was, according to Welhaven, to combine form with content in such a way that in so doing poetry shall perform the impossible and express the inexpressible. It is easy to see how Wergeland's extravagances of style must have annoyed Welhaven. In his own collections of poems he put his principles into practice in work frequently characterized by a great inwardness, sometimes inspired by nature and by a feeling of the immanence of the divine, and also by his unhappy love for Ida Kjerulf (a sister of the composer Halfdan Kjerulf). Welhaven also wrote, under the aegis of the National Romantic movement, a number of poems based on themes taken from the sagas, and from folk-tales and folk-beliefs. Welhaven was a sensitive writer, perhaps as typical in his way of the Norwegian spirit as Wergeland, both in relation to his time and in the careful artistry of his work.

## National Romanticism

The origins of the National Romantic movement can be traced back to the concluding decades of the eighteenth century. There were then various manifestations, already noted, of an interest in the specifically Norwegian inheritance in history, topography, and dialects. It was a movement which *Det Norske Selskab*, in its own way, carried further.

In the 1830s and especially in the 1840s this interest escalated through the stimulus given to it by Norway's new independence. In fact it developed into nothing less than a national 'breakthrough' (*Det nationale gjennembrud*), as Moltke Moe called it. It involved the recovery and refurbishing of the treasures of Norwegian language, folk-tales and poetry, folk-music, and research into Norwegian history. It also involved the glorification of Norway's scenic beauty and of the peasant and his way of life.

In 1833 Andreas Faye published his collection of Norwegian legends (*Norske Sagn*); in 1835 Henrik Wergeland issued a call for an independent Norwegian language in his *Om norsk Sprogreformation*; and in the years 1838–39 Jacob Aall published his translations of Snorri Sturluson's *Heimskringla*. In 1840 Jørgen Moe (1813–82) published a collection of songs, ballads, and verses in the Norwegian dialects, and in 1842–44, with Peter Christen Asbjørnsen (1812–85), their many collections of Norwegian folk-tales (*Norske Folkeeventyr*; 1842–44, followed in 1845 and 1848 by *Norske Huldreeventyr og Folke-sagn* (*Norwegian Fairy-stories and Popular Legends*), which Asbjørnsen published alone. In 1852–53 the collections of Norwegian ballads, *Norske Folkeviser*, made by Magnus Brostrup Landstad (1802–80) appeared together with a collection of folk-melodies for which L. M. Lindeman was responsible (see above, p. 58). In the field of language Ivar Aasen published in 1848 his grammar of the Norwegian folk-language and in 1852 his dictionary, (see above, p. 195), and later both verse and prose in his *Landsmaal*, including the verse cycle *Symra* (1863) and the play *Ervingen* (*The Legatee*; 1855). Finally, the historian Peter Andreas Munch published in 1840 his account of the ancient mythology of the North, and between 1851 and 1863 his massive history of the Norwegian people, *Det norske Folks Historie*. The influence of the National Romantic movement is also strong in the early work of Ibsen and Bjørnson, in the music of Grieg, and in the paintings of artists like Dahl, Gude, Tidemand, and others.

A consideration of the Norwegian ballads and folk-tales which were collected and given written form at this period after they had been preserved by oral tradition for hundreds of years takes us straight back to the Middle Ages, and especially to the period of Norwegian decline in the fourteenth and fifteenth centuries.

The ballad (*Folkevisen*) was a European phenomenon which came to the North from France via England and Scotland. It was intended both to be danced to and to have a narrative function. Those ballads which have come down to us may be roughly grouped according to their content, though there is a great deal of overlapping between them. Those dealing with trolls and legendary heroes (*Trollvisene* and *Kjempevisene*) are clearly connected in content with Old Norse legend and often with the *Fornaldarsaga* or with the heroic lay. The largest of these groups, the knightly ballads (*Ridderviser*), make use of material taken from the *Riddarasǫgur*. Sometimes the ballads are related to the sagas of the Norwegian kings, though Norway, by comparison with Denmark, has relatively few historical ballads. Other ballads deal with the conflict between Christianity and the powers of darkness, and there are also some purely religious ballads of which the most remarkable, indeed the most remarkable of all Norwegian ballads, is the visionary *Draumkvedet* (*The Dream Ballad*) which appears to be purely Norwegian. Characterization in the Norwegian ballads tends to be stylized and it is clear that those ballads which date from the thirteenth and fourteenth centuries were, both in content and in mode of presentation, intended to appeal to an upper-class audience. Later, those from the sixteenth and seventeenth centuries were aimed at the peasant community, even to the extent of making fun of the high-falutin language of the earlier ballads. Some of the Norwegian ballads were written down and even printed as early as the seventeenth and eighteenth centuries, but it was only when Landstad's collection and later the edition by Sophus Bugge of 1858 appeared that they were brought into the corpus of Norwegian literature.

The folk-tales (*Folkeeventyr*), though they may seem quintessentially Norwegian in their style and content, often have an international background with themes deriving ultimately from motifs that are found in ancient Indian, Arabic, and Greek literature. Traces of the *Folkeeventyr* can also be found in Northern mythology and in the sagas, but in their Norwegian form these motifs have become perfectly acclimatized. Nature and milieu are typically Norwegian and the point of view reflects the peasant community in which they take place. The trolls are Norwegian, so is Askeladden (a sort of male Cinderella), and the other characters; even the king is depicted as a well-to-do Norwegian farmer.

## THE ADVENT OF REALISM

In actual creative writing Norwegian literature was at a low ebb in the mid-nineteenth century. A great deal was produced by third-rate talents who have hardly survived, even in the Norwegian literary histories. Andreas Munch (1811–84), a rather bloodless Romantic with a wide-ranging production, was highly rated in his day and his novel *Pigen fra Norge* (*The Maid of Norway*; 1861) was even translated

into English, but with the advent of realism he became a back
number even in his own lifetime.

*Camilla Collett and Aasmund Vinje*

New currents were now flowing which were destined to mould a
new generation of writers whose concerns were to be very different
from the writers of the Romantic or National Romantic schools.
They included the revolutions of 1848 in Europe which, among other
things, provoked Ibsen to write his first play, *Catilina*. In Norway the
socialist movement of Marcus Thrane, with which both Ibsen and
Vinje had connections, also had indirect literary consequences. The
growth of Pietism in the Norwegian state Church; the philosophy of
the Dane Søren Kierkegaard; and the sociological investigations of
Eilert Sundt into Norwegian rural life–all, in their different ways,
entered into the fabric of Norwegian literature in the second part of
the nineteenth century.

In 1855 there appeared anonymously a work which showed
change was in the air. This was the novel *Amtmandens Døttre* (*The
Sheriff's Daughters*) by Camilla Collett (1813–95), the sister of Henrik
Wergeland, and also celebrated for her unrequited love for the poet
Welhaven, her brother's most bitter opponent. Camilla Collett was in
many respects a transitional figure in Norwegian literature. *The
Sheriff's Daughters*, in its passionate debate on the disabilities which
women of the official classes laboured under at the time in relation to
marriage, looks forward in an extraordinary way to the literature of
*Tendens* (social criticism) as practised, though with greater artistic
merit, by writers like Ibsen, Kielland, and Lie. At the same time, *The
Sheriff's Daughters* is in the Romantic tradition: the social and political
disabilities of women are not the crux of the matter. Rather it is love,
female love (*den kvinnelige kjærlighet*), which society prevents from
deciding who gets whom in marriage; the heroine in *The Sheriff's
Daughters* has to make do with an elderly Dean for a husband. However,
it is the social debate which *The Sheriff's Daughters* contains that makes
it a milestone in Norwegian literature; from the literary point of view
its technique is somewhat antiquated. Like everything Camilla
Collett wrote, this novel was founded on her own deep personal
experience and her own unhappy life. Her other literary work, which
takes the form of reminiscences or of discursive and polemical prose,
provides both an interesting conspectus of the Norwegian cultural life
of the period and also of her continuing efforts, partly inspired by
John Stuart Mill, on behalf of the Woman's Cause.

Another transitional figure of importance from this period is
Aasmund Olafsen Vinje (1818–70), though his interests were much
more diverse and his personality much more complex than Camilla

Collett's. In fact the whole of Vinje's career typified certain aspects of contemporary Norwegian life and culture, and his own personality had many traits which were typically Norwegian. The son of a cottar (*husmann*), the lowest grade of rural dweller, Vinje made desperate attempts in his early years both to educate himself and to make his way in society. He was in many respects the type of the *Bondestudent* (peasant student) *par excellence*. Eventually, after leading a Jack-of-all-trades existence, he became a student in 1850 and combined university study with journalism, taking a degree in law at the age of thirty-eight. In 1851 he was associated with Ibsen and Botten-Hansen in the publication of the critical journal *Andhrimner*, and during 1851–58 he was the Christiania correspondent of the Drammen newspaper *Drammens Tidende*. His articles brought him into prominence, but in 1858 he renounced the use of Dano-Norwegian and began to publish his own periodical, *Dølen* ,written in his own form of *Landsmaal*. It was now that the real Vinje emerged, both stylistically and in the free rein he was able to give to his, often highly contradictory, opinions on almost any subject under the sun. He elevated what he called *Tvisyn*, the ability to see both sides of any question, to a principle. Though this stance involved, no doubt, a certain lack of willingness to commit himself and led to his not being taken completely seriously, his object was to stimulate his readers to think for themselves. Certainly, he always took the language question seriously, and in his poetry there is an intense feeling for nature which reveals the depths that lay under his sceptical-ironical exterior. It is in his most successful work, *Ferdaminni fraa Sumaren 1860* (*Travel Memories from the Summer of 1860*; 1861), that Vinje's literary and other talents achieve their happiest synthesis and give the most complete expression of his personality. In it he records his wise, witty, and knowledgeable impressions of a journey he made to Trondhjem for the crowning of King Carl XV, interlacing them with some of his best-remembered verse. Vinje also published a book in English, *A Norseman's Views of Britain and the British* (1863), which he wrote after a study trip to England, again well informed and well observed, but somewhat critical of life in Britain.

*Chapter 11*

# Period of Greatness

---

WE ARE NOW APPROACHING THE PERIOD WHEN, graced by the names of Henrik Ibsen, Bjørnstjerne Bjørnson, Alexander Kielland, and Jonas Lie, Norwegian literature made its breakthrough on the European and world scenes. The genius of Ibsen provided a first-rate springboard for this conquering of new territory, but translations of the works of Bjørnson, Kielland, and Lie into foreign languages also contributed to making Norwegian literature known abroad as never before.

The new literature represented not only a flowering of the national renaissance which had begun with Wergeland and which the enthusiasms of the National Romantic movement had carried further. It also derived from the coincidence of trends which, while they were also European, had a special relevance to contemporary Norwegian life and culture. But most important of all was, of course, the appearance in Norway of creative literary talent of a very high order.

As has already been noted, romanticism in the European sense had hardly come to Norway at all. There had also been the roots of realism in the work of Asbjørnsen and Moe, and in the writings of Camilla Collett and Vinje. Thus the new European literary realism as represented by Dickens, Balzac, Flaubert, Zola, and Turgenev, and the work of thinkers and philosophers like Darwin, John Stuart Mill, and Herbert Spencer, fell on particularly receptive soil in Norway. At the same time the rise in Norway itself of an industrial society and of *Venstre*, and, at the same time, the disintegration of the old rural society, provided Norwegian writers with themes which coincided with the new currents from abroad. There were also two influences from Denmark which accorded perfectly with developments in Norway: firstly, the work of the literary critic Georg Brandes (1842–1927) with his demand that the task of the new living literature was to present problems for debate; and, secondly, the philosophy of Søren Kierkegaard (1813–55) which with its absolute demands appealed strongly to the fundamentalism which is endemic in the Norwegians.

*Ibsen*

Perhaps the most remarkable thing about Henrik Johan Ibsen (1828–1906), the dramatist, was his very existence, given the unpromising soil which the Norway of his day provided for the nurturing of dramatic genius. He was born on 20 March 1828 in the small provincial town of Skien in Telemark, the son of a spendthrift merchant whose financial indiscretions plunged his family into poverty. The traumatic effect of this on Ibsen the child was followed in his teens by apprenticeship to an apothecary in the even smaller coastal town of Grimstad, where Ibsen's poetic talents found their first expression in epigrams directed against the good citizens of the town and in poems with titles like *Resignation, Doubt* and *Hope*, and *The Corpse's Ball*, showing that Ibsen the radical talker, as he was reputed to have been at the time, was consumed with doubt and despair. The February revolution of 1848 inspired him to write a poem *To Hungary* (1849) and more importantly a tragedy on the Roman rebel Catiline. This subject also fitted in well with his Latin reading for the university entrance examination, for which he was preparing at the time. Today the interest of *Catilina*, which the generosity of a friend enabled Ibsen to get published in 1850 under the pseudonym Brynjolf Bjarme, derives principally from the presence in it, in embryo, of themes and situations which were to be characteristic of his later work; indeed, in a preface to the second edition of the play, published in 1875, Ibsen pointed to this fact himself. In *Catilina* the problems of vocation, the relationship between ambition and ability, the ideal in the context of society, and the idealist in his personal relations are set out for the first time. The play also provides in its two contrasting female characters the prototypes of the female characters in many of Ibsen's later plays.

The plays which followed *Catilina* were to be written very much under the aegis of the National Romantic movement, taking their themes from Norwegian history, ballads, and legends of the medieval period. In the meantime Ibsen had moved to Christiania with a view to studying medicine, a plan which in the event came to nothing. In 1850 he managed to get his next play, the one-act *Kjæmpehøien* (*The Warrior's Barrow*), performed. It was a trifle on a medieval Norse theme, remarkable in the context of Ibsen's work for its insistence on the primacy of the new idea or thing which, as elsewhere in Ibsen, always supplants the old; in this case paganism giving way before Christianity.

In the capital Ibsen had a better opportunity of contact with current developments and, among other things, he got involved in the socialist movement of Marcus Thrane, narrowly escaping arrest when the movement was put down by the authorities. He also wrote a short political satire, *Norma* (1851), based on the story of Bellini's opera, though in parody; and together with Botten-Hansen and Vinje published a critical and satirical journal, first called *Andhrimner* (after the cook in Valhalla) and then *Manden* (*The Man*).

In 1851 Ole Bull offered Ibsen a post, which he accepted, at the newly-founded *Det Norske Theater* in Bergen, of which Bull had been one of the chief promoters. Ibsen's duties do not seem to have been very closely defined, but he was to 'assist the theatre as a dramatic author' and write a new piece with a 'national' content to mark the anniversary of the theatre on 2 January each year. Ibsen stayed in Bergen until 1857 and the experience he gained there was indispensable to his development as a dramatist. He acquired a practical knowledge of the work of the theatre and of the work of other dramatists, and in 1852 he was sent on a trip to study the theatre in Denmark and Germany, where he got to know Hermann Hettner's recently published book *Das moderne Drama* (1852) which, with its insistence on psychological verisimilitude in historical drama, fitted in very well with Ibsen's own inclinations.

While he was in Bergen, Ibsen completed four plays: *Sancthansnatten* (*St John's Eve*; 1853), *Fru Inger til Østeraad* (*Lady Inger of Østraat*; 1855), *Gildet paa Solhoug* (*The Feast at Solhoug*; 1856), and *Olaf Liljekrans* (1857). Of these only *The Feast at Solhoug* enjoyed any success–indeed, the first and last of these four plays were fiascos and deserved to be, but *Lady Inger of Østraat*, though written very much after the recipe of Eugène Scribe, deserved a better reception than it got. It was, in many respects, the first real play Ibsen had written, and typically Ibsenist in its treatment of the 'call' and in its understanding of female psychology. *The Feast at Solhoug*, a lyrical play inspired by the Norwegian ballad, also looks forward, in its treatment of the two contrasting female types who are its principal characters, to the saga drama *Hærmændene paa Helgeland* (*The Warriors at Helgeland*; 1858), both of which were inspired by Ibsen's reading of the Norwegian ballads and the Icelandic sagas.

In 1857 Ibsen moved to Christiania to become director of *Kristiania Norske Theater*, which, like the theatre in Bergen, had been founded in 1852 to further the cause of a specifically Norwegian theatre. On the strength of this appointment Ibsen got married in 1858 but, in the event, the years in Christiania which followed were destined to be the most wretched of his whole career. In spite of his efforts to Norwegianize the theatre and in other cultural areas to free the country from Danish cultural hegemony–including taking the initiative in the founding of a new Norwegian Society–he experienced little but failure. The critics rated him low as a poet and dramatist; his play *The Warriors at Helgeland* had been rejected by the

Royal Theatre in Copenhagen; and his own theatre, which had always laboured under financial difficulties, finally went bankrupt in 1862.

Ibsen was now utterly depressed: in poor health, deeply disappointed, and financially embarrassed. His whole career seemed in jeopardy but, in the event, his situation led him to a close scrutiny both of himself and of the whole position of the creative artist in society. In 1870 he wrote in a letter: 'It was only after I was married that my life got a weightier content', something which is reflected in his long narrative poem *Terje Vigen* of 1862, while both the poem *Paa Vidderne (On the Heights;* 1860) and the play *Kjærlighedens Komedie (Love's Comedy;* 1862) treat the problem of the relationship of the creative artist to life, a problem which had been very much Ibsen's own and one which continued to recur in his work.

In some respects *Love's Comedy* is a harbinger of Ibsen's later social plays, with its satire of the conventions of the day as they applied to love, betrothal, and marriage. But the play plunges deeper in its juxtaposing of the aesthetic and ethical modes of existence (we may see here the influence of Kierkegaard), especially in relation to the hero of the piece, the poet Falk, whose philosophy of 'enjoy the moment' at the beginning gives way at the end to a resolve that he will *live* his poetry. But he also leaves his love, Svanhild, allowing her to contract a *mariage de raison* with an unexceptional, ethical man with a heart and a purse of gold. With her saga name (the Svanhild of the sagas was trampled to death under horses' hooves) it leaves open the question of her later fate and gives the comedy its *côté sombre,*

*Love's Comedy* was also a failure, but a meeting with Bjørnson in the summer of 1863 at a festival of song in Bergen raised Ibsen's spirits to such a degree that he completed in record time his next drama, the historical play *Kongs-Emnerne (The Pretenders;* 1863), set in the Norway of the thirteenth century. Like *Lady Inger* and *Love's Comedy, The Pretenders* carries further the treatment of the nature of vocation, exemplifying it in the characters of the three main protagonists in the play: King Håkon Håkonsson (see above, p. 88), the integrated personality who is at one with his kingly vocation to make the Norwegians a united people; Duke Skule, the talented, ambitious, but doubting and essentially barren man who can only steal Håkon's 'royal thought'; and Bishop Nikolas, the 'half man' in whom the disparity between ambition and ability is catastrophic. *The Pretenders* was a great advance on anything Ibsen had written before, and is one of the best historical plays ever written in Norwegian. It was performed with great success in Christiania in January 1864. In the meantime Ibsen had been awarded a travelling scholarship which, supplemented by private benefaction, enabled him to leave Norway in April en route for Italy. Twenty-seven years were to pass before he took up permanent residence in Norway again.

In spite of the distinct turn for the better in his personal circumstances, Ibsen nourished bitter feelings towards his compatriots at this time. He had been an ardent supporter of the current Pan-Scandinavian movement and the failure of Norway and Sweden to come to the aid of Denmark when she was attacked by Prussia and Austria in December 1863 shocked him deeply and convinced him that the Norwegians were strong only in words. The besetting national vice was, he believed, *halvhet*, or an incapacity for whole-hearted commitment to anything. Towards the end of 1863 he had composed a bitter poem called *En Broder i Nød (A Brother in Need)* on this subject, but the full expression of his indignation had to wait until the play *Brand* (1866).

In June 1864 Ibsen arrived in Rome. The new impulses which crowded in on him meant that at first his plans for a new work were uncertain. They included a play on the Roman emperor Julian the Apostate, which was finally realized in 1873 with *Emperor and Galilean*, but the naggings he had brought with him from Norway gained the upper hand. He began work on *Brand*, first as an epic poem which began with a poem addressed to *De Medskyldige* (Fellow Culprits). But during a visit to St Peter's the idea of how to treat the subject dramatically came to him (as Ibsen says in a letter) in a flash. Though *Brand* gives unequivocal expression to the indignation Ibsen felt towards his compatriots, the play also rehearses with infinitely more power earlier Ibsen themes, like the nature of vocation and the constitution of the aesthetic man. When the work appeared in 1866, it brought Ibsen immediate recognition in his homeland and in the rest of Scandinavia. The Norwegian *Storting* agreed to award him a state pension. This success led to Ibsen making remarkable changes in his personal appearance and manner; he even changed his hand-writing. His Bohemian days were now over and henceforth he took on the tight-lipped, scrupulously attired, and distant *persona* which we know from later photographs and paintings of him.

After *Brand*, his next play *Peer Gynt* (1867) came, as Ibsen himself wrote, 'as it were by itself'. In one sense *Peer Gynt* is the reverse of the medal of *Brand*, a practice which Ibsen was to follow in some later pairs of plays. For Brand's motto 'All or Nothing' we get Peer's 'Go round about'. *Peer Gynt* continues Ibsen's settling of accounts with his native Norway, both in terms of the national *halvhet* and also of the outgrowths of Norwegian National Romanticism in its chauvinistic and self-sufficient aspects. The Dovre mountains, which for the National Romantics were the very symbol of Norwegianness, are here the habitat of disgusting trolls whose motto 'Troll to thyself be enough' becomes Peer's own. But these features are only the bare bones of the matter. Never before had Ibsen's genius unfolded itself with such variety and richness, nor had he plumbed so fully the depths of the human situation. Peer's journey through life, though longer than Brand's, ends like his in the achievement of self-knowledge. Both plays seem to end with the promise of salvation for their heroes; for Brand in the realization that *caritas* was the missing ingredient in his 'All or Nothing' philosophy, and for Peer that it was in Solveig he had his empire (a romantic ending to an otherwise anti-(National)Romantic play).

*Peer Gynt* was to be Ibsen's last play in verse. When the Danish critic Clemens Petersen criticized it for not being poetry, Ibsen retorted angrily that if he was no poet, he would become a photographer, and in his pictures of life as it was, he would spare no one, not even the child in its mother's womb. As if to underline the change he was making, Ibsen moved in 1868 from Italy to Dresden, where he wrote his first modern prose play, *De unges Forbund* (*The League of Youth*; 1869). Of it Ibsen wrote that if *Peer Gynt* was a *vinrus* (heady on wine), then *The League of Youth* was reminiscent of *Knackwurst* and *Bier*. Certainly the piece is redolent of provincial life—Norwegian provincial life—with the phrase-mongering political carpetbagger Steensgaard as its central character. The implications of the piece for the rising *Venstre* Party were scathing and Norwegian nationalism is now shown in an almost farcical light. *The League of Youth* has something Holbergian about it; witty in dialogue and situation, and one of the best comedies ever written in Norway. At the same time, it is both a pioneer work of Norwegian realism and contains some typically Ibsen elements, especially in its characterization.

In 1873 Ibsen finally completed his two-part play, each with five acts, *Kejser og Galilæer* (*Emperor and Galilean*) which had been occupying him off and on for ten years and which, he always later insisted, was his most important play. In a letter to his publisher in 1871 he wrote that the play would give 'the positive view of life' which his critics had always been demanding from him. After the apparently anti-Liberal tendencies of *The League of Youth*, the rebel Julian of *Emperor and Galilean* seemed to take one back to Ibsen's very first plays, *Catilina* and *Lady Inger of Østraat*, but it also coincided with the revolutionary nature of some of the poems in the collection which Ibsen had published in 1871, especially *Abraham Lincolns Mord* (*Abraham Lincoln's Murder*), and in the poem *Til min Venn Revolusjons-aleren!* (*To My Friend the Revolutionary!* which) included the lines:

> I sørger for vandflom til verdens marken;
> Jeg lægger med lyst torpédo under Arken.

You deluge the world to its topmost mark;
With pleasure I will torpedo the Ark.

However, *Emperor and Galilean* does more than look back to earlier rebels and forward to the rebel figures who were to be in the forefront of Ibsen's plays for some time to come. It also brought into focus themes which had occurred before but which now were to be given far greater prominence, e.g.: the joy of life *contra* renunciation; freewill and determinism; the synthesis of the Third Empire (*Det tredje Rige*). In fact it is as a quintessential statement of Ibsenism that *Emperor and Galilean* has its importance; as a play for the stage it has been seldom performed.

In *Samfundets støtter* (*Pillars of Society*; 1877) Ibsen switches his social critique from the Liberals (of *The League of Youth*) to the right-wing 'Establishment' of a small Norwegian provincial town which, symbolized by its leading citizen Karsten Bernick, is a citadel of untruth and humbug. Ostensibly it operates in the service of society, but in reality only to further its own ends and retain power. Yet, at the end of the play the sinner, Bernick, is shown to be capable of redemption through (as in *Peer Gynt*) the good influence of a good woman. Technically, the play shows Ibsen's increasing mastery in integrating the past with the present, his so-called retrospective technique, but like *The League of Youth*, on which it is a considerable step forward, it is still predominantly local in its scope.

With *Et dukkehjem* (*A Doll's House*; 1879) Ibsen achieved European fame (or notoriety). Primarily it was the end of the play where Nora, the heroine, leaves her husband and children, marking her departure with a slam of the door, that really startled Ibsen's contemporaries. But the play itself, apart from providing the first of Ibsen's great female roles, also achieved a masterly technical concentration and economy, integrating the past with the present in a brilliant display of retrospective technique and illuminating such typically Ibsenist themes as heredity, the aesthetic man, and probing the whole question of the preconditions for the development of human personality.

The hubbub which *A Doll's House* provoked led directly to the composition of Ibsen's next two plays: *Gengangere* (*Ghosts*; 1881) and *En folkefiende* (*An Enemy of the People*; 1882). *Ghosts* is, in one sense, the reverse of the medal of *A Doll's House*; *An Enemy of the People* something of a self-satire, written after *Ghosts* had aroused an even greater furore than *A Doll's House*. In *Ghosts* the theme of heredity, which was secondary in *A Doll's House*, is brought to the forefront of the play and juxtaposed with the ghosts of 'old dead opinions and all sorts of old dead beliefs and the like' which inhibit people from developing and becoming themselves. But in the general gloom of the play there is also a vision of the joy of life which, as in *Emperor and Galilean*, may shine brightly or look tarnished. Bisecting the whole is the question of responsibility–to oneself and to others.

Doctor Stockmann, the ebullient but somewhat muddle-headed hero of *An Enemy of the People*, finds himself hounded out of his native town, to which he has returned after a number of years in the far north, for showing that the thermal baths on which the town's prosperity depends are polluted. It is a vigorous comedy of provincial life but savage in its satire of the 'compact majority' which, according to Doctor Stockmann (with whom Ibsen said he got on fairly well), is always wrong. The piece is notable, not only for the unfavourable light in which the majority is depicted, a criticism which looks forward to Johannes Rosmer's 'aristocratic radicalism' in *Rosmersholm*, but Doctor Stockmann's criticism of established truths that they 'seldom last more than seventeen-eighteen years' also continues the line from *Ghosts*.

Brand had been the Ibsen idealist *par excellence* with his demand for complete truth–All or Nothing. Lona Hessel in *Pillars of Society*, Mrs Linde in *A Doll's House*, and Doctor Stockmann had also been apostles of truth, though they were not of a Brand's heroic stature; indeed, Mrs Linde's decision to bring truth into the Helmer home has its dubious side, while Doctor Stockmann is, to a degree, a figure of fun. In *Vildanden* (*The Wild Duck*; 1884) the idealist, in the person of Gregers Werle, with his so-called 'Claim of the Ideal', has now degenerated into something of a caricature of Brand. It is not only that the validity of ideals or indeed of truth for all persons is called into question, but Doctor Relling, who in many respects is the *raisonneur* of the piece, maintains that certain people, like the play's Hjalmar Ekdal, need what he calls a Life-lie to carry them through life. When the play appeared, Ibsen's admirers were dismayed at his apparent renunciation of his earlier idealism. It would, however, be a mistake to think of *The Wild Duck* simply as a drama of ideas, for these have, in a sense, dropped into the background. The play is, above all, noteworthy for its remarkable gallery of appealing characters, nearly all of whom are invested with a tragic-comic aura; for the ambivalence, of which the wild duck is the central symbol, which invests it; and for the pervasiveness of its poetry. The irony of the piece is that it is Gregers Werle's own father (a background manipulator to whom Gregers is implacably opposed) who achieves the marriage in truth which Gregers has been trying to achieve for his Peer Gynt-like friend Hjalmar Ekdal.

In the summer of 1885 Ibsen spent several months in Norway, including a stay at Molde on the west coast. During his visit Ibsen

had been disagreeably impressed by Norwegian public life, and
these impressions were reflected both in a speech he made in Trondhjem, when he said that a new 'noble element' must come into
Norwegian public life, and also in his next play *Rosmersholm* (1886)
in characters like the conservative Kroll and the Liberal newspaper
editor Mortensgaard. But the public sector in the play is really only a
mechanism which sets in motion the private drama of the two central
characters, Johannes Rosmer and Rebekka West. In this drama
Rebekka's pagan vitality and Rosmer's humanism meet to coalesce in
a version of the Third Empire in which Rebekka, transfigured by the
Rosmer view of life, finds that her unscrupulous will to power is
broken, while Rosmer, whose programme it was to ennoble men's
minds, finds that he has lost his happy innocence. As elsewhere in
Ibsen, the complete synthesis is not for this world, and together
Rosmer and Rebekka find their end in the mill-race. The play is
noteworthy for revealing Ibsen's interest in irrational and hypnotic
influences: Rebekka's over Beate (Rosmer's dead wife) and over
Rosmer himself, and the pervading influence of the 'white horses' of
Rosmersholm.

In Ibsen's next play, *Fruen fra havet* (*The Lady from the Sea*; 1888)
these influences are brought into the foreground in the principal
female character, Ellida Wangel, an under-occupied doctor's wife
who is obsessed by the memory of a stranger, a seaman, with whom
she believes she has contracted a marriage years before when they
threw rings into the sea. The seaman has become for her the very
symbol of the sea itself, from which, living at the end of a fjord, she
feels herself cut off. The nature of her obsession is revealed when the
stranger reappears, but she fails at first to recognize him. When her
understanding husband allows her to choose 'in freedom and with
responsibility' whether to remain with him or go with the stranger,
she decides to remain, finding that all the time there had been tasks
awaiting her in the home. The thesis of the play, stated baldly, is
that one must acclimatize oneself; it is in the sphere of the home that
human vocation lies. Nevertheless, in other respects the play is
suffused with poetry and melancholy: one must renounce that great
free life 'out there' to which the shoals of fish in the fjord are swim-
ming and acclimatize oneself to the human habitat like the carp in
the fishpond in Doctor Wangel's garden.

With *Hedda Gabler* (1890) Ibsen again showed how well he kept
abreast of current trends, for in the character of Hedda, a kind of
decadent poet pressing a pistol into the hands of Løvborg, her would-
be Bacchant, and urging him 'to do it beautifully', he approaches the
*fin de siècle*. But the question is also implicit in the play as to how a
*supérieure dégénérée* like Hedda could function in the inhibiting world

of her father, General Gabler, or surrounded by the bourgeois mediocrity of her husband, Jørgen Tesman.

Since he left Norway in April 1864, Ibsen had lived in Italy and in Dresden and Munich. In 1891 he returned to Norway and took up residence in Christiania. There he wrote his four last plays: *Bygmester Solness* (*The Master Builder*; 1892), *Lille Eyolf* (*Little Eyolf*; 1894), *John Gabriel Borkman* (1896), and *Når vi døde vågner* (*When We Dead Awaken*; 1899), works which George Bernard Shaw described under the collective title 'Down Among the Dead Men'. Certainly, there is much in the first and last two of these plays to suggest that Ibsen's return to Christiania was also a meeting with his youth and that it led to his taking stock of his life and work.

In the years immediately preceding Ibsen's departure from Norway he had been much preoccupied, as the play *Love's Comedy* and the poem *On the Heights* show, with the relation of art and the artist to life. Now, in *The Master Builder*, he returned to this theme in the character of Halvard Solness, the master builder who has tried both building churches for God and homes for people and has come to the conclusion that neither is worth the candle and that both have been at the expense of his personal life and happiness. Many have seen in this juxtaposition of churches for God and homes for people a parallel to Ibsen's early verse plays and his later prose plays. The new house which Solness has built himself with a tower on is also reminiscent of the synthesis of the Third Empire; a resolution of the dichotomy between the idealistic heights and the human sphere below had been a recurring theme in Ibsen's work and one from which much of its dramatic tension derives. But in the play, a synthesis of the two, like its symbol the Third Empire, is really a dream and not realizable in this life. *The Master Builder* is also typical of Ibsen's work as a whole in that the past, though ineluctable, cannot be regained. When Solness, urged on by the youthful Hilde, tries to 'do it again' and climb to the top of his new house, he falls to his death while Youth, which he fought hard to keep out, moves in. Like other plays of the period, *The Master Builder* also shows Ibsen's interest in the hypnotic and the irrational–in Solness's power over Kaja and Hilde's over him, and Solness's belief in 'the helpers and servers'.

*Little Eyolf* does not have the same relevance to the question, the artist and life, as do the other three plays. Though it is a deeply serious play, the man with a vocation in it (Alfred Allmers) is something of a playacting Hjalmar Ekdal. Here, too, the theme of hypnotic attraction is treated in the eerie figure of the Rat Wife, also a 'helper and server', whom little Eyolf follows to his death in the fjord. The theme of sexual potency, something we also get in *The Master Builder* and in other plays, is also not far beneath the surface but, like *The Lady from the Sea*, the play is resolved in the human context when Alfred Allmers and his wife Rita find a vocation in work among the ragged children of the district.

In these last four plays the domestic life of the characters is bleak, but nowhere is it bleaker than in *John Gabriel Borkman*. It is also the play in which Ibsen achieved his greatest dramatic concentration and in which the past is brought so vividly into the present that it almost constitutes the whole play; the principal figures in it are ready to disintegrate at the slightest touch. John Gabriel Borkman is a sort of Nietzschean superman *manqué*, a Napoleon of finance who has been imprisoned for embezzlement before his great schemes even got underway. However, his greatest crime, we are given to understand, is not the one he was arraigned for in a criminal court, but that he had 'destroyed the love-life in a woman', by jilting the woman he loved to further his financial schemes. Nevertheless, John Gabriel seems to be more an artist than a business tycoon. He, the miner's son, has dreamed of freeing the hidden wealth from the earth and has sacrificed his own personal happiness and that of others to the dream. Again the situation is very much that of art *contra* life. In Ibsen's last play, the so-called dramatic epilogue *When We Dead Awaken*, the question of the artist and life gets quintessential expression. Rubek, the sculptor, has achieved world fame but at the cost of the bankruptcy of his personal life.

It is perhaps unnecessary to comment on Ibsen's standing as a world dramatist. As has often been said, he is one of the pillars on which drama rests. His work, in spite of its overall unity, has an extraordinary underlying complexity which makes any pigeon-holing of it misguided and any definitive critical structuring of it unlikely. At its best its richly bisecting frames of poetic and human reference, its wide-ranging resonances, and its masterly technical skill bear the hallmark of supreme literary greatness.

### Bjørnstjerne Bjørnson

While Ibsen had tended to remain a distant figure for the Norwegians and had taken comparatively little active part in public debate, his contemporary Bjørnstjerne Bjørnson (1832–1910) came, through his many-sided activities as writer, publicist, and orator, to symbolize for his compatriots the Norway of the second half of the nineteenth century in much the same way as Henrik Wergeland had done for the first half. Like him, Bjørnson was a typically Norwegian phenomenon, the poet-king *par excellence*, and even today in Norway Bjørnson seems to loom larger than Ibsen and to be more representative of the Norwegian spirit of his times. It is noteworthy that it is Bjørnson and Wergeland who figure prominently in the frescoes which adorn the much-decorated walls of the Oslo City Hall. Thus it is difficult to speak of Bjørnson's work as a writer without at the same time speaking of him as a publicist and man of action. He would have little patience with the idea of art for art's sake and all theory and abstraction were alien to his outward-going nature.

He first made his name as a writer with his stories of peasant life, especially *Synnøve Solbakken* (1857), *Arne* (1859), and *En glad Gut* (*A Happy Boy*; 1860), which artistically are among the best things he ever wrote. At the same time they were a milestone in the development of a more Norwegian literary language. As Bjørnson himself said, he had no respect for the Norwegian (or rather Danish) of the grammar-book—what he wrote was *Bryst-Norsk* (Breast-Norwegian). At the same time he wrote a number of plays based on themes from the medieval history of Norway which, except for the trilogy *Sigurd Slembe* (1862), are less noteworthy as literature, but were intended, together with the stories of peasant life, to reveal the Norwegians to themselves both as they were in the present and as they were in the past. In this way Bjørnson hoped to induce pride in themselves among Norwegians, but also to point the lesson that self-discipline was their most pressing need, especially for the gifted among them if they were to realize their human potential to the full. Like Wergeland before him, Bjørnson wanted to 'bring up the Norwegian people'. Bjørnson's early work was, of course, also written very much under the aegis of the National Romantic movement, but it had a much harder edge to it than many of the products of that movement. Today Bjørnson's peasant stories may seem idyllic, 'peasants in their Sunday-best' as has been said, but in their day they were criticized for being crassly realistic and crude.

The next important milestone in Bjørnson's writing career came with the short play *De Nygifte* (*The Newly-Married Couple*; 1865) which, though in itself a slight work, inaugurated the domestic-problem play in the North. Later in *En Fallit* (*A Bankruptcy*; 1875), *Redaktøren* (*The Editor*; 1875), and *Kongen* (*The King*; 1877) he carried further his pioneer work in the modern drama, using current themes to urge greater truths in the business world, in the press, and in the monarchy.

During these years Bjørnson had also been actively engaged in the theatre and in journalism, including the directorship of the theatre in Bergen and the Christiania Theater. In 1870 his first volume of poems and the epic poem *Arnljot Gelline* had appeared, and he had also published a new series of peasant stories and further plays on historical themes. At the same time he had been actively and controversially engaged in politics and in public debate on practically all the important issues of the day. He had also identified himself with the Grundtvigian Folk High School movement and had, in 1874, moved to Aulestad in Gausdal in eastern Norway to live near Christopher Bruun's Folk High School, Vonheim. However, his contact with modern ideas, especially with Darwin's, gradually took him away both from the Folk High School movement (which he began to feel was intolerably narrow in its outlook) and from orthodox Christian faith itself.

Bjørnson's later work tended to be less universal in the nature of the lesson it pointed and more geared in its didactic tendencies and criticisms to his own particular ideological position at the time. On the one hand, for example, in the short story *Støv* (*Dust*; 1882) he demonstrated the inhibiting effect of inherited beliefs, while in the play *En Hanske* (*A Gauntlet*)—at least in the 1886 version—he makes a sharp attack on the sexual morals of the time, something which stemmed from his antipathy towards the so-called 'Bohemian' movement. In his play *Over Ævne* (*Beyond our Power*; 1883), regarded by many as his best work in this form, he was implicitly critical of all he believed to be overwrought in the Norwegian psyche and also of the contemporary interest in hypnosis. Elsewhere in his novels of the period he pleads, under the influence of Herbert Spencer, the cause of a more modern education for girls—*Det flager i Byen og paa Havnen* (*The Flags are Flying in the Town and at the Harbour*; 1884); greater religious tolerance—*På Guds Veje* (*On God's Paths*; 1889); and in the play *Paul Lange og Tora Parsberg* (1898), which was based on an actual incident, for greater tolerance in political life.

When he died in Paris in 1910 the Norwegian government sent a warship to bring home his remains. Apart from his enormous contributions to the life of his own country in all sorts of areas, Bjørnson was also the first 'international' Norwegian, in the sense that what he wrote in the world's press was listened to. In the 1890s he was active in the International Peace Movement and he took up the cudgels on behalf of oppressed minorities like the Slovaks and individuals like Alfred Dreyfus. As a writer his work is naturally, in many respects, dated. His novels are Victorian and in his plays he had a weakness for melodrama, but at its best his work is suffused by his own warm, ebullient personality and carried along by his sheer joy in writing. His poems on national themes or those inspired by Norwegian nature often show true greatness in their capacity to transfigure a scene, an incident, or an emotion.

## Jonas Lie

It is customary for Norwegian literary historians to include under the heading *De fire store* (The Big Four) the names of Jonas Lie (1833–1908) and Alexander Kielland (1849–1906) along with those of Ibsen and Bjørnson. It is obvious why this should be so. Together the four writers form the backbone of Norwegian literature in the second half of the nineteenth century although, outside Scandinavia, Lie and Kielland never made the same impact as their two contemporaries; indeed, in English-speaking countries Lie and Kielland are relatively unknown, though some of their work has been translated. Yet they both made indispensable contributions to the development of the novel in Norway.

Of the two Lie is the more interesting, though Kielland is the better writer. Lie, who took to writing to pay off his debts after speculation in timber had led to bankruptcy, ranges widely in his work both geographically and in milieu. He was particularly good in depicting the domestic life of the middle classes and because of this he became known in Norway as *Hjemmenes dikter* (The Writer of the Home), a description which does less than justice to his talents. He had an acute eye for significant detail and used it to create authentic atmosphere and milieu. He was, in general, content to let this detail speak for itself, though there was, nevertheless, often a hidden *Tendens* in his work–for example, in his best-known novel *Familjen paa Gilje* (*The Family at Gilje*; 1883) which, though a first-rate description of the life of an official family, is also implicitly a criticism of the position of women in Norwegian society at the time. In a letter to Bjørnson, Lie said that his principal objective as a writer was 'to reflect the Fatherland, society and the character of the people', and like Bjørnson himself Lie does reveal the Norwegian people to themselves in his work and contributes to that literature of documentation which was so characteristic of the period. In his first novel, *Den Fremsynte* (*The Visionary*; 1870), he brought north Norway into Norwegian literature; in *Lodsen og hans Hustru* (*The Pilot and his Wife*; 1874) he wrote a novel both of the sea and marriage; in *En Malstrøm* (*A Maelstrom*; 1884) he depicted a commercial bankruptcy similar to his own; and in *Kommandørens Døtre* (*The Commander's Daughters*; 1886), set in a naval milieu, the position of women in contemporary society is again the underlying theme. However, Lie was no mere chronicler of Norwegian life. He had a deep interest in the psychology of the individual and an intuitive understanding of the vagaries of human nature. He had already shown this in *The Visionary* and in his later work, especially the novels from the 1880s onwards, he became more and more interested in the destructive trolls of the mind and character, and in the evil forces inherent in people which were ever ready to break out. The psychological novel *Onde Magter* (*Evil Powers*; 1890) is a particularly powerful portrayal of the havoc wrought by these subconscious forces. In his collections of fairy-tales, *Trold* (1891–92), set in north Norway, he again portrays the workings of the hidden forces of the mind. In this Lie was, of course, writing very much in the spirit of the literature of the late 1880s and the 1890s. Lie had always been an innovator both in his choice of subject and in his writing technique. He also developed a highly effective impressionistic style, and towards the end of his life he made some bold experiments with the form of the novel, especially in *Naar Jernteppet falder* (*When the Iron Curtain Falls*; 1901). Lie's originality has been more and more recognized in recent years. Regrettably, it is sometimes marred by compositional deficiencies which the watchful eye of his wife Thomasine, his lifelong literary helpmate, did not always eradicate.

### Alexander Kielland

Kielland, by contrast to Lie, had from the start a sure feeling for literary form and an innate elegance of style which stayed with him throughout his writing career and earned him a reputation as the greatest stylist of Norwegian letters of his period.

He belonged to a rich Stavanger merchant family – his grandfather was reputed to be the richest man in Norway – and followed a conventional career until he was nearly thirty. In 1879 he published a collection of elegantly written and highly attractive short stories, *Novelletter*, with which he at once established a reputation as a writer. The next year he followed up this success with the novel *Garman og Worse*, set in his native Stavanger a generation or so back in time and largely based on his own family. In it he depicts the clash of the generations in a richly articulated, well-characterized picture of the times, conveyed with irony, grace, and a distinct edge to its social criticism. In fact Kielland soon made it clear that he was only interested in literature in so far as it served some social purpose, and in his next novel *Arbeidsfolk* (*Working People*; 1881) he delivered a scathing attack on the official classes, especially those concerned with the administration of justice. In later works he attacked social and religious hypocrisy, the state Church, the educational system, and business morality. Like Bjørnson, the demand for truth is ever present in his work, and he had a keen sense of the social injustices of his times. His work was inspired by social indignation and that is its strength and also its weakness. At times *Tendens* gets the upper hand and he never really repeated the success of *Garman og Worse*. However, the trilogy *Gift* (*Poison*; 1883), *Fortuna* (1884), and *Sankt Hans Fest* (*The Midsummer Festival*; 1887) is noteworthy both for the range and effectiveness of its social critique and, especially, for the subtlety of the portraiture of its central character, Abraham Løvdal. In the novel *Sne* (*Snow*; 1886), Kielland uses snow as an equivalent of the dust in Bjørnson's short story *Dust* and the ghosts in Ibsen's *Ghosts*, as a symbol of all the old worn-out, cluttering conventions and beliefs which inhibit the free development of the individual.

Kielland's writing career was comparatively short. His last novel *Jacob* (1891), dealing with the career of an unpleasant parvenu, suggests that he had suffered disillusionment in his campaign for reform.

### Kristian Elster and Amalie Skram

Two lesser writers of this generation, the novelists Kristian Elster (1841–81) and Amalie Skram (1846–1905), have their own niches in the annals of Norwegian literature. Elster's reputation rests chiefly on the novels *Tora Trondal* (1879) and *Farlige Folk* (*Dangerous People*; 1881). In *Tora Trondal* he combines a broad social background, from which many implications for contemporary Norwegian culture emerge, with psychological insight into the principal characters, where the contrast between the 'ethic' and the 'esthetic' modes of experience also parallels differences between western and eastern Norway. Elster had written on this topic in an article of 1872, *Om Modsætningen mellem det vestlige og østlige Norge* (*Concerning the Difference between Western and Eastern Norway*). *Dangerous People* is much more of a *Tendens* novel and, on that account, given the literary fashion of the day, the only one of his works to be successful at the time of its publication. However, Elster's critique of the injustices of society is much more oblique than Kielland's and nothing like as virulent.

Amalie Skram's novels are immediately noteworthy; firstly, for their frank *exposé* of the inner life of their female characters, especially in its sexual aspects; and secondly, for the profound determinism which informs them. Amalie Skram's own unfortunate experiences in her first marriage provided the basic pattern for the depiction of a series of disastrous marriages in novels like *Constance Ring* (1885) and *Forraadt* (*Betrayed*; 1892), which shocked her contemporaries. To some extent they reflect the debates on sexual morality which the so-called Bohemian movement of the period had provoked. In her monumental tetralogy *Hellemyrsfolket* (*The People of Hellemyr*; 1887–98) the deterministic aspect of her work receives its most wide-ranging expression in the story of a family, doomed through several generations to go under. Poverty, drink, and a poor inheritance are the roots of the evil, but the tetralogy also includes a brisk story of life at sea and a well-considered portrait of life in Bergen. Amalie Skram puts across her often drab material with persuasive narrative skill. Her work often seems to have the nature of protest, but she believed herself to be objective and often was–it is then that her work makes its greatest impact.

*Arne Garborg*

Since the death of Vinje in 1870, *Landsmaal* literature had had no outstanding representative. Although, as has already been noted, Bjørnson did much to promote the Norwegianizing of the current Dano-Norwegian, Lie, Kielland, and Amalie Skram wrote in a language form which differed little from Danish. It was Arne Garborg (1851–1924), a farmer's son from south-western Norway, who took the next big step forward for *Landsmaal*.

Garborg was one of the brightest intelligences in Norway, who, in his life and work, epitomized the sweeping cultural changes which, affected Norwegian rural society in particular during the second half of the nineteenth century. He wrote in his own form of *Landsmaal*, making his breakthrough with the novel *Bondestudentar* (*Peasant Students*; 1883), the story of the vicissitudes of peasant students in Christiania, which reflected Garborg's own experiences as a penurious student and at the same time vividly documented characteristic features of the cultural background. The book implicitly questions the assumptions which brought the peasant students to the capital, showing how they came to despise their home background and culture, including their own dialect, and ended both socially and culturally as rootless individuals. Garborg also subjected the young people of Christiania, especially the intellectually- and artistically-inclined sector, to similar scrutiny in the novels *Mannfolk* (*Menfolk*; 1886), *Hjaa ho Mor* (*With Mother*; 1890), and *Trætte Mænd* (*Tired Men*; 1891; written in Dano-Norwegian) all of which, though less satisfactory than *Peasant Students*, give very good insights into the times and milieu they describe. After these analyses of life in the capital, Garborg returned in *Fred* (*Peace*; 1892) to the country. In this novel the chief character is based on his own father (who had committed suicide in a fit of religious mania when Garborg was a young man), and he depicts the consequences for Norwegian peasant society of the conjunction of gloomy hell-fire Pietism, financial difficulties, and the decay of social stability, all of which were closely connected with the change from a natural self-supplying rural economy to one based on money. Three years later, in the verse cycle *Haugtussa* (1895), he depicted peasant society as it had been in the old days, with its beliefs and superstitions going back to the Middle Ages, and before it was ravaged by Pietism and economic troubles. In the central character, the young girl called Veslemøy, he shows how the power of the trolls can be overcome by goodness and love, a message which was to become more and more insistent in his later works, of which the play *Læraren* (*The Teacher*; 1896) and *Den burtkomne Faderen* (*The Lost Father*; 1899) are notable, and which develop into a plea for an undogmatic, practical, humanistic type of Christianity.

Garborg also contributed many articles on the questions of the day to newspapers and journals, and was a prolific essayist. The position *Landsmaal* subsequently gained as a literary language owed much to his work and in particular to his stylistic gifts. He was more of a thinker than an imaginative writer, but in works like *Peace, Haugtussa*, and *The Lost Father* his literary artistry is of a very high order and demonstrates perfectly the literary possibilities of *Landsmaal*, particularly its evocative qualities.

## Hans Jæger

A minor writer whose work and activities exercised in one way or another an influence on most of the writers of the period was Hans Jæger (1854–1910). He became the leader of a group of radicals known as the Christiania 'Bohemians' (*Kristiania–Bohêmen*) whose opposition to the society in which they lived was absolute. They rejected its religion, its morality, and in particular its sexual morality. Jæger first gave expression to his views in public debates held in the Workers' Union and the Students' Union in Christiania; then in two plays; but principally in the largely autobiographical two-volume novel *Fra Kristiania–Bohêmen* (*From the Christiania Bohemia*; 1885). In this book Jæger places, often with tedious documentation, the blame for the misery of his characters squarely on society. Its sexual frankness led to immediate confiscation, the dismissal of the author from his position as a stenographer in the *Storting*, and a prison sentence. Bitter exchanges on the rights and wrongs of the case between the radical and conservative factions followed, and when, in 1886, the short story *Albertine* by the painter Christian Krohg was also confiscated, controversy rose to fever pitch. Jæger later went to live in France where he published three quasi-novels of a confessional kind: *Syk Kjælihet* (*Sick Love*; 1893), *Bekjendelser* (*Confessions*; 1902), and *Fængsel og Fortvilelse* (*Prison and Despair*; 1903), all intensely absorbing products of his neurotic, anarchistically-inclined mind. In a book called *Anarkiets Bibel* (*The Bible of Anarchy*; 1906) he attempted to give his social and anarchist ideas some shape, often showing much insight into the problems involved. It was Bjørnson who took strongest exception to the ideas of the Bohemians. His play *A Gauntlet* was a direct answer to them. He carried his campaign further by touring the country with a lecture entitled *Engifte og Mangegifte* (*Monogamy and Polygamy*), and his novel *The Flags are Flying in the Town and on the Harbour* and the play *Geografi og Kjærlighed* (*Geography and Love*; 1885) both bear traces of his anti-Bohemian views.

# Chapter 12

# The 1890s and Beyond

---

THE 1890S IN NORWAY are categorized by Norwegian literary historians as the period of New Romanticism (*Nyromantikken*). It was a period of reaction against the social preoccupations of the writers of the 1870s and 1880s, and one which saw the advent of a new literature concerned with the individual, not in his social context but in relation to his inner life and psychology. New Romanticism was a movement which had originally been generated by impulses from abroad, especially those deriving from the work of the French symbolists, the novels of Dostoevsky, and the philosophy of Nietzsche. It also manifested itself in the other Scandinavian countries. In Norway the literary 1890s are generally accounted as having been inaugurated by Knut Hamsun's article *Fra det ubevidste Sjæleliv* (*From the Unconscious Life of the Mind*) and by Vilhelm Krag's poem *Fandango*, both of which appeared in 1890 in the first volume of the newly-founded literary periodical *Samtiden*.

The change did not, of course, come about as abruptly as all that. We have seen how Ibsen, in plays like *Rosmersholm* and *The Lady from the Sea*, had probed into the deeper recesses of the psyche; how Jonas Lie had been concerned with the trolls of the mind; and how faith and faith-healing had been at the heart of Bjørnson's play *Beyond our Power*. Nevertheless, there was something different about the '90s, even if few of the writers of the new generation differed radically from their predecessors.

### Gunnar Heiberg

A writer who was very much a transitional figure was Gunnar Heiberg (1857–1929), the leading Norwegian dramatist of his generation. His first play, *Tante Ulrikke* (*Aunt Ulrikke*; 1883), was in the tradition of the 1880s with its passionate appeal for social justice. However, in the play *Kong Midas* (*King Midas*; 1890) there is a distinct change of emphasis. Indeed, in its insistence on what one of the principal characters calls 'holy relativity' the piece is in many ways implicitly critical of the demands which were characteristic of the work of the writers of the 1880s and in particular of Bjørnson's demands for truth and morality in all things. In dramatic technique, too, *King Midas* is a step towards the typically Heibergian technique in the two plays *Kunstnere* (*Artists*; 1893) and *Gerts Have* (*Gert's Garden*; 1894) where, within a well-defined milieu, dramatic interest is maintained by light inconsequential conversation, verbal effect, and atmosphere rather than by action. In the plays *Balkonen* (*The Balcony*; 1894) and *Kjærlighedens Tragedie* (*Love's Tragedy*; 1904), two dramas of erotic passion, Heiberg wrote both in the spirit of the 1890s and also, in a sense, continued the literature of woman's liberation, in that in both plays female emancipation, as instanced by their principal female characters, now extends to the erotic sphere. However, in his presentation which is to a degree stylized, even expressionistic, Heiberg maintains, in general, an underlying balance between the claims of sexual drive and those of work and everyday existence. Heiberg's other plays of the 1890s and those written in the first years of the twentieth century were mainly satires of Norwegian social and political life, including such topics as the press, slogan-mouthing politicians, and the union with Sweden. One of them—*Folkeraadet* (*The Popular Assembly*; 1897), with incidental music by Delius—caused a riot when it was first performed.[1] Heiberg was also an accomplished essayist.

### Sigbjørn Obstfelder and Others

We have already noted Vilhelm Krag's poem *Fandango* as one of the inaugural documents of the 1890s, and, in general, poetry began to flourish again in Norway after having been pushed very much into the background by the drama and the novel during the 1880s. Vilhelm Krag (1871–1933) certainly typified certain aspects of the 1890s in his collections of poems, more so than his more serious contemporary Nils Collett Vogt (1864–1937), but the most typical representative of the 1890s in Norway, as reflected in his life and work, was Sigbjørn Obstfelder (1866–1900).

Obstfelder died young and—typical of the period—of tuberculosis. He led a wandering, restless existence and, like the character in one of his best-known poems, *Jeg ser . . .* (*I see . . .*), seems to have felt a stranger to existence, as someone who had 'arrived on the wrong planet'. His first poems, called *Rhytmiske stemninger* (*Rhythmical Moods*), published in *Samtiden* in 1892, and a collection of *Digte* (*Poems*; 1893) were clearly highly individual contributions to Norwegian literature, with their evocative symbolism, rhythmic persuasiveness, and ethereal remoteness. Obstfelder was poet of *Angst*, of loneliness, and of the

---

[1] In his book on Delius, Philip Heseltine (Peter Warlock) states that a member of the audience actually fired revolver shots at the composer, because of the satirical use he had made of the Norwegian national anthem in his score.

searching but erotically-aware soul. Apart from his poems, his literary production included a play, some short stories, and an unfinished confessional journal, *En Præsts Dagbog* (*A Cleric's Journal*; 1900), in which his outsider cleric seeks for the security of the faith he has lost and community with others, a search which is implicit in much of Obstfelder's other work.

Three lesser writers, Thomas Krag (1868–1913)–a brother of Vilhelm–Tryggve Andersen (1866–1920), and Nils Kjær (1870–1924), typify to some extent the spirit of the period–Krag with his evocative short stories and novels dealing with lonely existences; Andersen with his 'Outsider' novel *Mod kvæld* (*Towards Evening*; 1900); and Kjær with his play *Regnskabets dag* (*The Day of Reckoning*; 1902). However, of these, Andersen is best known for his documentary novel *I Cancelliraadens dage* (*In The Days of the Chancery Councillor*; 1897), a depiction of life in eastern Norway in the first years of the nineteenth century, and for his stories of folk-life–he was one of the best short-story writers Norway has produced; Kjær for his witty comedy *Det lykkelige valg* (*The Happy Election*; 1913), with its barbs directed at various current 'causes' in Norway–female emancipation, temperance, the language question, and political life in general. Kjær is also noteworthy for his well-written essays.

### Knut Hamsun

Though Knut Hamsun (1859–1952) was the outstanding figure in Norwegian literature of the 1890s, it would be wrong to think of his work purely in the context of that period. His most famous book, *Markens Grøde* (*The Growth of the Soil*), which led to his being awarded the Nobel Prize for literature in 1920, appeared in 1917, and his last book in 1949. Nevertheless, his novels of the 1890s, especially *Sult* (*Hunger*; 1890), *Mysterier* (*Mysteries*; 1892), and *Pan* (1894), were remarkable examples of the new literature which Hamsun himself had called for in his article in *Samtiden* (see above, p. 248), and for which he continued to agitate in a series of lectures he held in a number of Norwegian towns in 1891. In them he not only amplified his own literary programme but was also highly critical of leading Norwegian writers, especially Ibsen, who heard him lecture, an experience which is reflected in *The Master Builder*.

Hamsun called for a literature which should deal, as he said, with 'The whisper of the blood, the entreaty of the bone, all the unconscious life of the mind', and in the acute psychology of his depiction of the starving littérateur in *Hunger*, in the antic disposition of Nagel, the hero of *Mysteries*, and in the combination of sheer lyricism and psychological insight in *Pan*, he not only implemented his own literary programme, but did so with a writing talent that effected little short of a revolution in the current Norwegian literary language, and established himself as one of the leading writers of Scandinavia and Europe.

Hamsun was born in humble circumstances, spent his childhood and early youth in north Norway, and later led a Jack-of-all-trades existence, including two periods in the United States, before he made his breakthrough as a writer in 1888 when he published a fragment of the novel *Hunger*. Eventually he settled down as a farmer, first in north Norway and then at Nørholm, near Grimstad in southern Norway. Much of his work does, in fact, have an autobiographical aspect and in his later and much more broadly based novels the wanderer-outsider is frequently juxtaposed with the settled dweller and the tiller of the soil. This is one aspect of the trilogy of novels *Under Høststjærnen* (*Under the Autumn Star*; 1906); *En Vandrer spiller med Sordin* (*On Muted Strings*; 1909); *Den sidste Glæde* (*The Last Happiness*; 1912); while in, especially, *The Growth of the Soil*; *Siste Kapitel* (*Chapter the Last*; 1923); and in the *August* trilogy (1927–33), the work of the soil is thrown into flattering relief by comparison with the degeneracy of life as lived in the towns and by (especially) the official classes. Elsewhere Hamsun depicted the growth of industry and the rise of a consumer society in an unfavourable light, especially in *Børn av Tiden* (*Children of the Age*; 1913) and *Segelfoss By* (*Segelfoss Town*; 1915).

In articles in the press, too, Hamsun often showed himself to be critical of modern trends and reactionary in his political views; but in his imaginative work things are invariably made to tremble in the balance by the expert use of point-of-view, narrative technique, and mixture of characters. Intellectually, there is no doubt an underlying pessimism in his work about man's existential situation, though combined with a belief in the 'life force', sometimes manifesting itself in a grotesque way (as in the character of Oliver in the novel *Konerne ved Vandposten*; *Women at the Pump*; 1920); in fact, Hamsun often depicts life as if it were a great comedy. His belief that the Germans were a vital people by contrast to the 'decadent Anglo-Saxons' led him to support Germany in both World Wars. As a consequence of this his support of the Quisling regime during World War II led to his alienation from the Norwegian people, a misfortune which he transmuted into literature in *Paa gjengrodde Stier* (*On Overgrown Paths*; 1949), an amalgam of apologia, autobiography, and literary fantasy. It is a book which bears striking testimony to the durability of his great literary gifts. Next to Ibsen, Hamsun is the greatest Norwegian writer of modern times and one of the important European writers of the period.

*Hans E. Kinck*

Hamsun's contemporary Hans E. Kinck (1865–1926), though highly esteemed by critical circles in Norway, never had the same appeal at home nor acquired the reputation abroad that Hamsun did. The son of a doctor, he ranged wide in his enormous literary production, writing short stories, novels, plays, and many essays. His short stories, *Flaggermusvinger* (*Bat-Wings*; 1895) were completely in the spirit of the New Romanticism of the 1890s, and he continued to write short stories with a wide variety of settings, including amusing and satirical stories of peasant life, and others where erotic initiation and experience are the principal themes. However, Kinck's main interest was in the depiction of the clash of cultures in Norway, between the peasant culture and culture of the official classes, as he had first experienced them when his father was moved from Setesdal in southern Norway to outer Hardanger on the west coast. His first novels, *Huldren* (*The Fairy*; 1892) and *Ungt Folk* (*Young People*; 1893), showed how deeply he had penetrated into the ethos of the west-country dwellers, and in the novel which eventually became *Herman Ek* (published 1923) he stated that he had sought out the fountainhead of nationality and the 'mystery of the people' (*Folkets Mystik*) in the psyche of the Norwegian people. He pursued this theme and that of the clash of cultures in a number of other novels, notably in the monumental three-volume *Sneskavlen brast* (*The Avalanche Broke*; 1918–19), one of the most impressive projections of Norwegian rural life in the whole corpus of Norwegian literature. Also in his most important dramatic work, the verse play *Driftekaren* (*The Horse-Coper*; 1908), he plunged deeply into the temperament, character, and hidden potential of the Norwegian peasant, creating in the central character, the poet-horsedealer Vraal, a figure which in many respects was quintessentially Norwegian. Kinck was also deeply interested in Italy and in Italian history and culture, especially at their periods of violent change. He wrote a play on Machiavelli and a number of essays on Italian social and political life, and on Italian writers.

Kinck was basically a literary sociologist. His deep delvings into folk-psychology were motivated by a desire to explain social and artistic phenomena on the basis of *rase* (race), though with no political overtones. His writing always had the object of pointing a lesson for his own contemporaries and he was often deeply critical of certain current social trends and abuses. He is not usually immediately appealing as a writer, but at his best he succeeds in depicting character, milieu, and nature, and their interplay, in terms which in their deeper resonances echo back through time and race.

### REGIONAL AND HISTORICAL NOVELISTS

The literature of the 1890s, by concerning itself with the individual and his inner life, had in effect been taking a closer look at things than had been the case with the more generalized social realism of the 1880s. This tendency to look more closely had also manifested itself in a renewed interest in the peasant and his culture, and in regional life. Moltke Moe (1859–1913), a son of Jørgen Moe, had in his many studies of Norwegian folk-life also concerned himself with what he called *Det mytiske Tænkesætt* (*Mythical Concepts*) in Norwegian folk-literature. The history and traditions of individual districts of Norway were also investigated, e.g. the work of Ivar Kleiven (1854–1934) in the Vågå area of Gudbrandsdalen, and folk-museums, like the ones at Bygdø near Oslo and at Maihaugen in Lillehammer, began to be established. At the same time, a whole host of mainly minor writers, many of them writing in *Landsmaal*, began to document life as it was lived in the mountains and valleys of Norway – so-called *Bygdediktning*. Most of these writers are very minor indeed, but some of them are worth mentioning, like Per Sivle (1857–1904) and Jens Tvedt (1857–1935), both of whom wrote in *Landsmaal*, while Hans Aanrud (1863–1953), who wrote in Dano-Norwegian, was one of the best and most stylish writers of short stories of folk-life Norway has produced.

What one had been seeing in this movement was, of course, the beginnings of a new realism. But in contrast to the earlier realism of the 1880s (though this had never totally lapsed), it did not have any particular *Tendens* or political aim. It was principally concerned with the depiction of life as it was lived in some particular, usually limited, area of Norway at a given time. After the turn of the century this kind of writing got a number of notable representatives whose work is often referred to as *Hjemstavnsdiktning* (regional literature). Most prominent among these writers were Peter Egge (1869–1959), Johan Bojer (1872–1959), and Gabriel Scott (1874–1958).

### Egge, Bojer, and Scott

Egge, who was born in the province of Trøndelag, set his best work there, especially his novel *Inde i fjordene* (*Along the Fjords*; 1920), the saga of a family covering the last decades of the nineteenth century and part of the twentieth. Bojer, who was also from Trøndelag, achieved his greatest success with the novel *Den siste viking* (*The Last Viking*; 1921), telling the saga of the Trøndelag fishermen's journeys to the fishing grounds of Lofoten in the far north, as Bojer had experienced them himself in his younger days. Scott was from southern Norway (the neighbourhood of Lillesand) and he used this

area as settings for his work, especially in the double novel *Jernbyrden*
(*The Ordeal*; 1915) and *Enok Rubens levnedsløb* (*The Life of Enok Ruben*;
1917), set during the period 1770–1814. In the context of literary
history a noteworthy feature of these novels is their quasi-historical
nature. Norwegian literature in the first three decades of the
twentieth century was to be very rich both in the historical novel and
in the novel depicting several generations of the same family, notably
in the work of Sigrid Undset, Johan Falkberget, and Olav Duun.

### Sigrid Undset

Together with Knut Hamsun, Sigrid Undset (1882–1949) was the
Norwegian writer of the twentieth century who gained the greatest
name outside Norway; she was awarded the Nobel Prize for literature
in 1928. She combines in her work the close scrutiny of a particular
section of the community, which, as we have noted, is a leading
characteristic of the school of regional writers, with a deep interest
in history; indeed, she is best known for her historical novels,
especially the trilogy *Kristin Lavransdatter* (1920–22).

Sigrid Undset was the daughter of a well-known Norwegian
archaeologist whose early death so reduced the family fortunes that
Sigrid was obliged to take a job in a Christiania office where she
remained for ten years. It was among the young middle-class working girls of the Norwegian capital that she found the theme for her
breakthrough novel *Jenny* (1911), the story of the life and loves of an
artistically gifted girl, set partly in Christiania and partly in Rome,
and based in part on the authoress's own life. It was the first time
that this particular social sector had been brought into Norwegian
literature in this way. Like the regional writers in general, and unlike
her predecessors Camilla Collett and Amalie Skram, Sigrid Undset's
work was without social or political *Tendens*.

In general Undset's early novels and short stories were concerned
with the personal problems of women: in marriage and in conflicts
arising from the demands of domestic life set against their personal
ambitions (often of an artistic kind) and their dreams. She made it
clear, implicitly in her imaginative work, and explicitly in a collection of essays, *Et kvindesynspunkt* (*A Woman's Point of View*; 1919) that
while she was in favour of the emancipation of women in certain
areas, she regarded marriage and the care of children as the field in
which they would find greatest fulfilment.

Sigrid Undset had long been interested in the early literature of
Norway and Iceland, and in the European Middle Ages in general.
Thus she was well equipped when she embarked in the 1920s on her
long series of novels set in thirteenth-century Norway: *Kristin
Lavransdatter* and *Olav Audunssøn* (2 volumes; 1925–27). However,

though these novels have historical settings and bear witness to her comprehensive knowledge of the life and cultural background of the period, they do not deal with historical personages, and actual happenings are very much in the background. Basically, they are not very different from her earlier works with modern settings. *Kristin Lavransdatter* is the personal, domestic, and religious drama of the title character from her childhood to old age as it is revealed in her relations with her father, with her husband Erlend (in some respects the most interesting character in the book), and with God. Similarly in *Olav Audunssøn* we follow the chief character from childhood to death in his family relationships and in his relationship to the ethical and religious complex of his times. In 1925 Sigrid Undset had become a Roman Catholic, which, given her religious preoccupations – especially in her historical novels – did not come as a surprise. In her later novels with modern settings, especially in the double novel *Gymnadenia* (*The Wild Orchid*) and *Den brændende busk* (*The Burning Bush*; 1929–30), with their hero Paul Selmer, the influence of Catholic beliefs is also prominent, though in many respects the themes treated in these works are similar to those in the modern novels of her first period. Undset's work forms very much a whole in its emphasis on the problems of women (often in their sexual aspects, into which enter society, religion, and belief) and in its insistence on the home and children as woman's most fruitful sphere. As a result, though she created a rich and varied gallery of female characters, her novels are often marred by an overdose of domestic detail, frequently of a dreary or somewhat stifling kind. But her power as a writer and her ethical and religious seriousness are never in doubt.

## Olav Duun

Olav Duun (1876–1939) combined in his work many different strands in Norwegian literature. First, he carried the literature of *Landsmaal*, or New Norwegian, on to a new eminence, and became the greatest writer to use that medium since Garborg. Secondly, he gave the short story of folk-life (*Folkelivsskildringen*) new dimensions and depth; and in his most famous work, *Juvikfolke* (*The People of Juvik*; 1918–23), expanded that tradition into a whole cycle of novels, which also combined the regional and historical interests of the regional (*Hjemstavn*) writers and Sigrid Undset. Finally, in the ethical seriousness and humanistic concerns of his work he was in the central tradition of Norwegian literature.

Duun was born in the coastal region of Namdal in the province of North Trøndelag. In his boyhood and early years he followed the farming and fishing pursuits of his native community, at the same time developing an awareness of the individuality and idiosyncracies of the people of those parts, and absorbing their heritage of folk-wisdom, popular custom, and turn of phrase, all of which were to provide the locus and basic constituents of his later work. In 1904 he became a teacher, spending the major part of his career in southern Norway, a profession he combined until 1927 with his vocation as a writer. His first book, a collection of short stories, appeared in 1907 and he continued to publish a book a year up to the appearance of *The People of Juvik*. Even in these early novels and short stories the essential traits of his literary physiognomy had begun to appear: his capacity as a depicter of children; his ability to give the purely local scene wider temporal, psychological, and moral perspectives; and the emergence of two contrasting human types in his work, symbolizing destructive and fruitful forces, which were to recur in his later work. His striking narrative and stylistic gifts had also become apparent.

*The People of Juvik* has been called 'a psychological history of Norway'. It depicts the saga of the Juvik family through 400 years, but with the action concentrated in the period 1814–1918. Apart from its insights into Norwegian folk-psychology and the clear delineation of its central characters, it gives a remarkable imaginative interpretation of the development of Norwegian rural society from the first half of the nineteenth century, with its almost pagan concepts and clan loyalties, to the coming of a new humanism and a new collective, though less vital, society in the early twentieth century. The problem of evil, the battle with the 'powers', are also there, and give the work deep perspectives. Like other Norwegian writers at the time, Duun was influenced in the writing of this work by the background of World War I. *The People of Juvik* has, implicitly, a humanistic message, and, in the specifically Norwegian cultural situation of the day, it also contains a plea for the integration of the best of the old peasant culture of Norway with newer developments.

Duun's preoccupation with the problem of evil, the dilemma of the ethical man in dealing with it, and the psychological vagaries of human personality, increased in his later work, especially in the trilogy *Medmenneske (Fellow Humans*; 1929), *Ragnhild* (1931), and *Siste leveåre (Last Year*; 1933), which with their psychological penetration, subtle characterization, and masterly composition rank among his very best works. In his last work, *Menneske og maktene* (translated as *Floodtide of Fate*; 1938), he treated a similar theme though on a smaller but more quintessential scale.

## Johan Falkberget

In the work of Johan Falkberget (1879–1967), regionalism and history are combined with the depiction of a sector of Norwegian society, the industrial working class, which hitherto had never been prominent in Norwegian literature. In general, Norwegian writers had, up to this time, found settings for their works in the official classes, the bourgeoisie, and the peasantry. Now, with Norway's incipient industrialization and the emergence of writers from the ranks of the proletariat, the mine-worker, the itinerant navvy (*rallar*) working on the building of industrial installations and railways in different parts of the country, and the factory-worker began to enter Norwegian literature.

Falkberget was born in Røros, the copper-mining town in the province of South Trøndelag. His father was a miner and Falkberget himself began working in the mines at an early age. It is in this milieu that the majority of his work is set. He made his real début as a writer in 1907, and his early novels, especially *Brændoffer* (*Burnt Offering*; 1917) were very much in the tradition of the novel of social criticism; but with *Eli Sjursdotter* (1913) he had already inaugurated the long series of historical novels, set in the Røros of earlier periods, which were to form the most impressive part of his literary production. During this period Falkberget had been living in south Norway, principally in Christiania, but in 1922 he returned to his native Røros to live permanently. This homecoming stimulated him to a deep study of the history and traditions of these regions and led to his writing the series of historical novels set there: *Den fjerde nattevakt* (*The Fourth Night Watch*; 1923), set in the early nineteenth century; *Christianus Sextus* (6 volumes; 1927–35), from the 1720s; and the tetralogy *Nattens brød* (*The Bread of Night*; 1940–59), set in the first half of the seventeenth century. In all these works the focus is on individual human fates which stand out, often with archetypal force, against a carefully composed background of society, historical events, and nature. At the same time Falkberget contrives to give this background a relevance to contemporary life, so that past and present seem to become as one. Suffusing the whole is his own brand of romanticism, humanism, and compassion for the toiling poor.

## Kristofer Uppdal and Oskar Braaten

In the work of Kristofer Uppdal (1878–1961) and Oskar Braaten (1881–1939), the saga of the working classes is given a contemporary setting. Uppdal, who as a young man had been a navvy (*rallar*), and had worked on hydro-electric and other installations in Norway, depicted in his ten-volume cycle of novels, *Dansen gjenom skuggeheimen* (*The Dance through the Land of Shadows*; 1911–24), the emergence of this particular class of worker from the peasantry, showing class interrelationships, the development of class solidarity, and trade union organization. His work gives important insights into the development of Norwegian society at a crucial period of industrialization and vivid pictures of some of its social manifestations from the 1890s to the 1920s. But his cycle of novels is no mere chronicle. It often rises to epic proportions. Events are focused on individual characters, often stubborn individualists, who lead their own lives, resist collective pressures, and pursue their own ideals. Indeed, the *rallar* himself often takes on a wider validity, as a symbol of man himself emerging, becoming, and creating himself. In a three-volume cycle of poems, *Kulten* (*The Cult*; 1947), the *rallar* reappears in the guise of a prophet of a new religion.

Oskar Braaten's work, of which the novels *Ulvehiet* (*The Wolf Lair*; 1919) and *Mathilde* (1920) are the most notable, is of a more intimate kind and mainly set in the grey everyday of the factory-workers of the East End of Christiania. It lacks the epic quality and colour of Falkberget's and Uppdal's work, but its merits lie in the authenticity of its descriptions of a milieu Braaten himself knew intimately. His work also contains a much more explicit *Tendens*, but it is always bisected by a deep sympathetic understanding of the worker and the less privileged in society, and is invested with much of the warmth and good humour characteristic of the story of folk-life.

### THE TWENTIETH CENTURY

The first decade of the twentieth century was remarkable in Norwegian literature for the number of prominent writers who made their débuts. In fact, the year 1907, when Olav Duun, Sigrid Undset, Johan Falkberget, and the poet Herman Wildenvey (1886–1959) published their first works, would be a convenient starting-date for any history of twentieth-century Norwegian literature.

A noteworthy feature of this particular blossoming was the number of poets whose names appeared for the first time. The New Romanticism of the 1890s had given a new impetus to poetry which, as one can see from Knut Hamsun's collection of poems *Det vilde Kor* (*The Wild Choir*; 1904), had continued after the turn of the century. However, the lyric poetry of the new writers was, generally speaking, very much tinged by the New Realism which characterized the prosewriting of the period.

### New Names in Poetry

Herman Wildenvey's collection of poems, *Nyinger* (*Bonfires*; 1907), was immediately successful with its freshness, casual but expert craftsmanship, irony and humour combined with a deeper seriousness, and its charm, all of which brought something new into Norwegian literature. In fact Wildenvey's style was so inimitable, his sunny charm so infectious, his power of versification so masterly, and his satire so devastating that he was destined, with his collections of poems which continued to flow (often with deep and sometimes melancholy undercurrents) from his pen for the next fifty years, to become something of an institution in Norway.

Olaf Bull (1883–1933) also made a successful début: with his collection of poems, *Digte* (1909), but it was clear that he was a poet with a more sombre view of life and a weightier approach to his craft than Wildenvey. Though spring is among his themes, death and the transience of life are never far away. In later collections his questionings as to the meaning of life, often characterized by loneliness and despair, became intensified, though he never lost his grip on reality and always found a firm anchor in the permanence of art and the healing power of nature. His collection of poems *Metope* (1927) provides the best conspectus of the different sides of his poetic imagination which was one of the most powerful in modern Norwegian literature.

Arnulf Øverland's (1889–1968) first collections of poems *Den ensomme fest* (*The Lonely Feast*) and *De hundrede violiner* (*The Hundred Violins*), published in 1911 and 1912, are both personal and also have affinities with other poetry of the period. In his later poems he developed into an often bitter critic of society and in the literary historical context his work belongs very much to the generation of Norwegian writers who became prominent in the 1920s and '30s (see below, p. 261).

New Norwegian (*Nynorsk*) also got two noteworthy representatives in Tore Ørjasæter (1886–1968) and Olav Aukrust (1883–1929). Ørjasæter made his début in 1908 with a collection of poems which in their themes and form were very much in the *Landsmaal* tradition going back to Aasen and Vinje. His principal work, the long epic poem *Gudbrand Langleite* (3 volumes; 1913–1927; revised 1941), is also very much concerned with the specific problems arising from the impact of the outside world on Norwegian peasant society. But through the artistically-gifted title figure of the poem, Ørjasæter gives these problems a personal and even universal focus in the conflicts between Gudbrand's own ambitions, which will carry him into the outside world, and all those forces which will keep him in his native milieu; a conflict which leads implicitly to self-realization and harmony. Ørjasæter took up similar themes in his later work, which also included some plays, of which the expressionistic *Christophoros* (1948) is a noteworthy example.

Olav Aukrust and Ørjasæter were from adjoining parishes in Gudbrandsdalen; Aukrust from Lom and Ørjasæter from Skjåk, an area which was particularly rich in Norwegian peasant culture. However, Aukrust's poetry, which is said to have derived initially

from a visionary experience he had in 1915, is very different from
Ørjasæter's. The verse cycles which followed this traumatic experience were all marked by a visionary intensity of language and a
cultic tone. In *Himmelvarden* (*The Cairn of Heaven*; 1916), the struggle
between good and evil forces in the soul is prominent, and in *Hamar i
Hellom* (1926) the specifically peasant-Norwegian (*det bygdenorske*) is
raised to a higher power of national, indeed of universal, importance.
Aukrust could be earthy and even humorous, and in the poem *Emne*
he gave striking and manly expression to the ideals of Norwegian
peasant culture. But although he could be sublime, his work is often
difficult, tortuous, and wordy.

### The Inter-war Years and Beyond

As we have seen, many of the leading Norwegian writers of the
older generation wrote their most important works either during
World War I or in the years immediately following. Some of these
works were coloured by the background of the war, like Hamsun's
*The Growth of the Soil*, or Gabriel Scott's *Kilden* (*Marcus the Fisherman*;
1918) in that they extolled the virtues and fruitfulness of the simple
life or of life lived close to the soil. Other leading writers of the
period were also inward- or backward-looking. It was the period of
Sigrid Undset's and Johan Falkberget's historical novels, Kristofer
Uppdal's saga of the industrialization of Norway, Olav Duun's
*People of Juvik*, and one in which a minor writer, Nini Roll Anker
(1873–1942), published between 1923 and 1927 a three-volume
series of novels covering the saga of a single family from 1848 to
World War I. The writers of this generation continued to enjoy
enormous prestige in Norway and they had great influence on
younger writers. The experiments in new literary forms which were
taking place in England, Germany, France, and even in the other
Scandinavian countries made little impact on Norwegian literature.

Nevertheless, a new generation of writers was in the making and
the impact of events and new trends in Europe gradually made itself
felt in Norway. As we have seen, the aftermath of the Russian revolution soon had consequences for Norwegian political life, and in
literature revolutionary ideals received expression in the poetry of
Rudolf Nilsen (1901–29). Interest in the psychology of Freud and
Jung also had literary repercussions, especially in the interest it
provoked in child psychology. Norwegian culture and literature
were becoming more outward-looking, and the appearance of the
so-called Yellow Series (Gyldendal's *Gule serie*), edited by Sigurd
Hoel, a series of translations from modern European literature, was
symptomatic. As the 1930s progressed, the course of events in Europe
also began to be reflected in Norwegian literature, notably in the

work of Olav Duun. However, Norwegian literature in the 1930s is characterized above all by three writers: Arnulf Øverland, Helge Krog, and Sigurd Hoel.

The linking of Øverland, Krog, and Hoel as the three writers who represented all that was quintessential in the Norway of the 1930s derives principally from the fact that they were all political radicals, as well as close friends and often associated in the same causes. They also had much in common both temperamentally and intellectually.

After his first collections of poems, Øverland was fired with indignation over the provisions of the Treaty of Versailles, which also led him into the socialist camp. This is reflected in an enlarged edition of the collection of poems *Brød og vin* (*Bread and Wine*; first published in 1919) which appeared in 1924. Øverland also began to engage actively in politics, and his political ideals and objectives are reflected and forcibly expressed in many poems in his later collections. In other areas of public life, too, he gained a reputation as a doughty polemicist and essayist on both national and international issues. However, it would be a mistake to think of him exclusively as a politicizing poet. As we see in the collection called *Hustavler* (*Decalogues*; 1929) and in the cycle of love poems *Jeg besverger dig* (*I Beseech Thee*; 1934), his individualism and many-sided personality ranged over many themes, and his poetic gifts commanded a wide and expressive register. His poems published clandestinely during the German occupation of World War II focused many of his best qualities and stiffened his compatriots' will to resist. Øverland was himself arrested early in the war and incarcerated in the concentration camp at Sachsenhausen. After the war his poems took on a more personal and harmonious character, though events in Hungary in 1956 brought out, in the collection *Den rykende tande* (*The Smoking Candle-wick*; 1960), all the old power of cutting denunciation. As has already been noted (see above, p. 204), Øverland was also actively engaged during the post-war years in the battles over the language question, an activity which gave full scope to the controversial side of his nature. He also tried his hand as a dramatist and as a short-story writer, but it is on his poems, with their direct, simple, yet pregnant language and their personal approach to fundamental themes, that his reputation as one of the leading poets of modern Norway rests.

Helge Krog (1889–1962) also became a convert to socialism in the early 1920s and developed into a polemicist *par excellence* with an even more finely pointed pen than Øverland's. However, his belletristic work was done exclusively in the field of drama where, in a sense, he continued in the tradition of Ibsen and Heiberg, though with a distinct and individual voice of his own. In a series of plays published in the late 1920s and '30s (of which *Konkylien* (*The Sounding Shell*; 1929) is a noteworthy example) and conducted mainly on the level of elegant comedy, though with consistently deeper undertones, he explored relationships between men and women, and especially the erotic life of women as an aspect of their personal and public emancipation, and as a means of exposing the shams of their menfolk. Artistically, Krog's work is marked by a sure sense for effective dialogue and convincing atmosphere. He worked within somewhat narrow limits but, as his volumes of critical and polemical essays also show, he knew how to make every point tell.

Sigurd Hoel (1890–1960) was the least politically and polemically active of the three. His interests were more psychological; in fact he was the first Norwegian author to show traces of the influence of Freud. Such social criticism as there is in his work emerges obliquely through the exposure of individual characters rather than through a critique of society as such. In a long series of novels Hoel ranged over a wide variety of themes, from his breakthrough novel *Syndere i sommersol* (*Sinners in the Summertime*; 1927), with its gay satire of socially and sexually liberated youth, to such peaks as *En dag i oktober* (*A Day in October*; 1931), with its 'collective' technique; *Veien til verdens ende* (*The Way to the End of the World*; 1933), a story of developing childhood; and the immediate post-war novel *Møte ved milepelen* (*Meeting at the Milestone*; 1947), one of the most striking of Hoel's works with its scrutiny of the genesis of a traitor, conducted on different time-levels and noteworthy for its richly varied material and subtle psychology. A notable post-war novel was *Trollringen* (*The Magic Ring*; 1958), set in a nineteenth-century peasant community and depicting, on the surface, the progressive individual against the rest, but becoming more deeply an exploration of the inner reasons for the hero's failure in the public sphere. Hoel's work, like that of Øverland and Krog, shows an implicit belief in the liberating effects of knowledge and truth in its insistence on bringing light to all that is hidden. Hoel was a writer in the great Norwegian radical tradition.

Of the other important Norwegian writers who were born in the years around the turn of the century, Nordahl Grieg (1902–43) was closest to the Øverland-Krog-Hoel group. His social interests were evident from the first in his novel *Skibet gaar videre* (*The Ship Sails On*; 1924), based on his own experiences as a seaman, and in the plays published in the 1930s where he criticized current social phenomena and attacked exploitation. He spent two years in the Soviet Union and became a convinced Marxist, and from 1936–37 he published the periodical *Veien frem* (*The Way Forward*), in which he gave full rein to his critique of current political, social, and cultural issues. However, his struggle for greater social justice and truth is always haunted by the problem of how far it is justified to use force to combat evil, a problem which is at the heart of his plays *Barrabas* (1927) and *Nederlaget* (*The Defeat*; 1937). At the same time as he wrote works in prose, the internationalist Grieg had shown himself a patriotic poet of rare quality in his collection of poems *Norge i våre hjerter* (*Norway in Our Hearts*; 1929), and while studying at Oxford in the 1920s he had written a dissertation entitled *Rudyard Kipling and the British Empire*. When Norway was invaded by the Germans in 1940 the man of action and the poet in him coalesced and all doubts as to where his duty lay were resolved. Before he met his death in a bombing raid over Berlin he had composed the collection of war poems, *Friheten* (*Freedom*; 1943), which set a seal on his life and work, as one of the immortals of the Norwegian Parnassus.

Two other writers of the period, both predominantly novelists, Ronald Fangen (1895–1946) and Sigurd Christiansen (1891–1947), represented somewhat different trends, especially the former. Though Fangen's work contains an implicit critique of the superficial aspects of contemporary life, he was principally concerned with the inner life of his characters in its psychological, idealistic, and especially its religious aspects; in fact the religious solution becomes more and more prominent in his work. Among his best books are the novel *Duel* (1932), a penetrating analysis of the duel-like relationship between two friends, and *En lysets engel* (*An Angel of Light*; 1945), an analysis (like Hoel's *Meeting at the Milestone*) of the making of a traitor, but treating the problem from the point of view of inner compulsion and ideals rather than from that of psychoanalysis. Christiansen was also a deeply serious writer whose themes almost invariably involve guilt, atonement, and the duty of the individual to face both, in an effort to find freedom coupled with responsibility. His work implicitly poses absolute ethical demands and much of it is heavy-going in the intensity of his probings into the inner lives of his characters and the inexorableness with which he pursues his central themes. In the remarkable and no doubt partly autobiographical *Jørgen Wendt* trilogy (1935–45) he traces, in his own special terms, the making of a creative artist in all its splendours and miseries. His work is more accessible in the shorter novels *To levende og en død* (*Two Living and One Dead*; 1931) and *Mannen fra bensinstasjonen* (*The Man from the Petrol Station*; 1941).

Cora Sandel (Sara Fabricius; 1880–) stood even more on the sidelines of current events than Sigurd Christiansen. She made her début somewhat late in life, in 1926, with the first of the so-called *Alberte* trilogy of novels; the other volumes appeared in 1931 and 1939. In them she traces with deep psychological insight the personal and artistic development of her artistic heroine Alberte, combining superb technical writing skill with a keen and discriminating eye for milieu and situation. In *Kranes konditori* (*Krane's Café*; 1945), her most successful work, she treated a basically similar theme with masterly compression and brilliant narrative skill. Her work, with its concern with the special problem of women in a male-dominated society, is in the line of Camilla Collett and Sigrid Undset, but its lasting merit lies in its sheer literary qualities, and she must rank as one of the most important Norwegian writers of her period.

The greatest experimenter in the Norwegian novel during this period was the Danish-born Aksel Sandemose (1899–1965). His mother was Norwegian and, after a series of novels written in Danish, he settled in Norway in 1930 and subsequently wrote in Norwegian. His early novels reflected his experiences at sea and of life in Canada. Although they revealed writing ability, they showed no great originality. It was in his first Norwegian novel, *En sjømann går i land* (*A Seaman Goes Ashore*; 1931), that Sandemose began to reveal his true literary physiognomy with his probings into the genesis of murder, a theme which was to recur in his later work. His next book, *En flyktning krysser sitt spor* (*A Fugitive Crosses his Tracks*; 1933), dealing with the childhood of the murderer, and written on different time-levels and with a disregard for chronology and logical sequence, reveals the true Sandemose style in all its chaotic but richly perceptive and poetic complexity. He always retained, however, the capacity he had shown in his first novels for brisk realistic description and in *Vi pynter oss med horn* (*Horns for Our Adornment*; 1936), he continues this, combining it with rich fantasy and experimentation. In his most successful novel, *Det svundne er en drøm* (*The Past is a Dream*; 1946), he provides a compendium of his own highly individual style and manner, treating, in the form of a fictive journal, the themes of love and murder which had continued to recur in his work. Here again outer description is presented in an apparently random manner, but within which deep soundings into the inner recesses of the psyche are compounded with richness of insight and carefully controlled atmosphere and mood. Among his post-war books *Varulven* (*The Werewolf*; 1958) provides a good example of Sandemose's ability to provide fresh variations on his central themes.

With the death of Tarjei Vesaas (see below, p. 265), Johan Borgen (1902–) must be accounted Norway's leading living writer, though he is by no means an avant-garde one. As a journalist and essayist he has his roots in the 1930s, but in this respect his virtues are stylistic rather than polemical. His talent for composing topical anecdotes with a concealed point was much appreciated in the pre-war years and he turned his talent to excellent account during the occupation. In his many short stories and novels he has much con-

cerned himself with the pressures of society on the individual—
especially the upper-class society of Oslo from which he himself
came—and with the problems of personal identity. The most sustained example of his capacity for depicting his chosen milieu and for
relating it to an individual fate is the so-called *lillelord* (*Little Lord*)
trilogy of novels (1955–57) in which the action stretches over the
period 1912–45 and where the gropings of the central character to
find his own identity are depicted with masterly psychological insight
and stylistic *bravura*. However, perhaps the most significant of
Borgen's merits as a writer is his capacity for finding the *mot juste* to
render the slightest inner vibration and change of mood or response
in his characters, a capacity which invests his work with a lyric
quality often outweighing its psychological and social aspects.

During this period the ranks of the New Norwegian (*Nynorsk*)
writers received recruits, like Inge Krokann (1893–1962) and Hans
Henrik Holm (1896–), who spanned both the generation of Olav
Duun and Olav Aukrust and the post-war generation, and who found
their inspiration in the folk-culture, history, and traditions of rural
Norway.

However, the most outstanding of them, Tarjei Vesaas (1897–
1970), though very much in this tradition, also transcends it, even
more than Olav Duun had done. In his first outstanding achievement as a novelist, the so-called *Klas Dyregodt* (1930–32) series, he
combines, as part of the *Bildung* of his principal character, intensity of
experience of a life lived close to the soil and to nature with a clear
recognition of the destructive potentialities of human nature, and it
is between these two points that Vesaas's work is always balanced. In
the novels *Det store spelet* (*The Great Cycle*) and its sequel *Kvinnor topar
heim* (*Women call Home*; 1934–35) the pendulum is swung towards the
blessings and fruitfulness of the life of the tiller of the soil. But in the
play *Ultimatum* (1934) and the novel *Kimen* (*The Seed*; 1940) it is the
destructive forces which dominate—the latter work was also a considerable step forward towards the highly concentrated, even symbolic, style which Vesaas was to use so effectively in the allegorical
novel of Norway during the occupation, *Huset i mørkret* (*The House
in the Darkness*; 1945). In later work, of which *Fuglane* (*The Birds*;
1957) and *Is-slottet* (*The Ice Castle*; 1963) are notable, Vesaas perfected
his peculiarly individual style with its short chiselled sentences,
pregnant symbolism, and studied stylization. His themes, too, continued to oscillate between an *exposé* of the lifegiving positive human
qualities and the negative destructive ones. Vesaas was a master
of the art of the implied, of the language of silence, but he always
managed to combine them with lyricism and drama. He was the
most considerable Norwegian writer of the mid-twentieth century

and contributed enormously to the prestige of New Norwegian.

## The Post-War Generation

The liberation of Norway in 1945 opened the literary floodgates after five years of censorship and a period during much of which leading writers had refused to have their work published. The immediate post-war years in Norway were ones of intense documentation, questioning, and self-scrutiny on every aspect of the war and the occupation. As we have already seen the genesis and the psychology of the traitor were a theme which had engaged the attention of a number of writers who had already established reputations before the war began. Some of the newer writers who became prominent in the immediate post-war years, like the novelists Sigurd Evensmo (1912–), Finn Havrevold (1905–), Kåre Holt (1917–), and Jens Bjørneboe (1920–), also wrote against the background of World War II, finding their themes in a scrutiny of the social and psychological causes of war and its manifestations in individual conduct. In a sense these writers were continuing the psychological interests which many Norwegian writers had shown in the 1930s, but often with a distinct 'anti-heroic' bias. The continuance of pre-war traditions can also be seen in the number of novels of development (*Utviklingsromaner*) which appeared in these years, for example in the *Little Lord* trilogy of Johan Borgen (see above, p. 265), Sigurd Evensmo's *Grenseland* (*Borderland*) trilogy (1947–51), and Agnar Mykle's (1915–) two novels on Ask Burlefot, *Lasso rundt fru Luna* (*Lasso Round the Moon*; 1954) and *Sangen om den røde rubin* (*The Song of the Red Ruby*; 1956). The multi-volume historical novel also continues to be written and is exemplified by Kåre Holt's novels on the Norwegian Labour movement and his series *Kongen* (*The King*; 1965–69), set in the time of King Sverre, and Alfred Hauge's (1915–) trilogy on Cleng Peerson–*Hundevakt* (*Middle-Watch*), *Landkjenning* (*Landfall*), and *Ankerfeste* (*Anchorage*)–(1961–65) which deals with Norwegian emigration to the United States. Post-war Norwegian literature has, in fact, been exceptionally rich in the novel.

In poetry Arnulf Øverland, who was critical of modernistic tendencies in verse, continued to dominate the scene, and Herman Wildenvey was still active. Nevertheless, even before the war there had been signs of new trends, especially in the work of Rolf Jacobsen (1907–), and after the war a modest school of poetic modernists began to emerge under the influence of new directions in Denmark and Sweden. It included the poet Gunnar Reiss-Andersen (1896–1964), who had made his début as far back as 1921, apart from new names like Paal Brekke (1923–) and Stein Mehren (1935–) who began to experiment in new forms in poetry. However, their experimentations have not been dramatically revolutionary and poets following more traditional lines, like André Bjerke (1918–), have been much esteemed. In New Norwegian, the poets Jan-Magnus Bruheim (1914–) and Tor Jonsson (1916–51) have carried that particular tradition forward. In general, post-war Norway has produced many very respectable poets, but it is still too early to say whether any really big name will emerge.

Much of the drama that has been written in post-war Norway has reflected the same preoccupations we found in the novel, but there has also been a continuation of the experimentation started by writers like Nordahl Grieg, Tarjei Vesaas, and Tore Ørjasæter in the 1930s. Principally it has been a move away from the conventions of the realist drama towards an often high degree of stylization, though the new forms have been frequently used in the service of the traditional concerns of the Norwegian theatre: the discussion of ideas and the debate of problems. Stein Mehren's stylized and symbolic play *Narren og hans hertug* (*The Fool and his Duke*; 1968) was a notable attempt to explore new directions technically, thematically, and in theatrical presentation, while at the same time giving the piece social and individual relevance.

In 1941 the Norwegian professor of literature and the history of ideas, A. H. Winsnes, asked in an article in *Samtiden*:[1] 'Is there a Norwegian line in literature?' Inevitably, the answer was yes. Winsnes characterized this Norwegianness, and gave reasons for it, as follows:

The special criterion, the distinguishing characteristic of our literature, is this: a call to the individual, to each individual person, a protest against the effacement of people as personal beings. This is no doubt heard in all literatures, this call and protest. But I wonder if it does not sound with particular strength from the North, and perhaps most of all from Norwegian literature, from the motherland of Henrik Ibsen? It is of course engendered by our struggle for existence. It is as if our country itself demands of our literature: nurture [*opdra*] individuals. As a nation of individuals Norway can survive as a living organic whole, as a mass it will inevitably go under.

Even when allowance is made for the background of the wartime occupation, against which this was written, it is easy to see that it

---

[1] In *Norsk ånd* (*Den norske linje i litteraturen*), quoted Sigurd Aa. Aarnes, *Norsk litteraturkritikk*, Oslo, 1970, p. 287.

represents an accurate assessment of the nature of Norwegian literature up to this point. As we have seen, Norwegian literature has
always been intimately associated with the life and history of the
country, and the writer, as well as being a chronicler, has often been
a leader and a spokesman. In these activities the writer has found an
active helpmate in the literary critic. Until comparatively recently
the biographical-historical method of criticism reigned supreme, the
examination of the facts of an author's life and the minutiae surrounding the literary work being regarded as more important than
the close study of the literary text itself. In 1969 Professor Francis
Bull, the principal exponent of the biographical-historical method,
wrote, echoing Winsnes:[1]

> The geography of Norway has shaped the temperament of our
> people and in it there is nothing 'satisfying', but there is yearning
> in it, a longing forwards, upwards, outwards—and inwards into
> the depths of the mind, but nothing satisfying. Our literature has
> been coloured by the temperament of the people. Just think of
> titles like *Brand, Over Ævne* [*Beyond our Power*], *Gå På!* [*Go Ahead!*],
> *Himmelvarden* [*The Cairn of Heaven*], *Blåtind* [*Blue Peak*].[2] They are
> words with a call in them, they are words which suit the Nor-
> wegian temperament, and Norwegian national literature.

In the inter-war years some literary criticism of an aesthetic-
philosophical kind was written in Norway, especially that associated
with the name of Peter Rokseth. Marxism and psychoanalysis also
made some impact on criticism, but in general such trends were
either given short shrift or were disregarded. In the post-war years
the range of literary methodology increased vastly in Norway, as
elsewhere, but without arousing the intensity of debate that it did in
the other Scandinavian countries. In the treatment of Norwegian
literature, biographical-historical interests remain strong and in
these Norwegian criticism parallels the realist interests which continue to dominate in Norwegian literature. As the Norwegian literary
critic, Willy Dahl, says in a survey of post-war Norwegian prose
literature:[3] 'Much more time-honoured, traditional prose is written
and printed than experimental prose, and it is not particularly risky
to prophesy that the realistic novel and short story will continue to
exist and flourish for many, many years to come.'

In an article entitled *Den moderne norske Literatur* (*Modern Norwegian
Literature*),[4] published in the mid-1890s, Bjørnstjerne Bjørnson

---

[1] In *Land og lynne*, Oslo, 1969, p. 8.
[2] Titles of works by Ibsen, Bjørnson, Lie, Aukrust, and Borgen.
[3] *Fra 40-tall til 60-tall*, Oslo, 1969, p. 147.
[4] Published in a number of periodicals, including *Kringsjaa*, Christiania, 1896

likened Norwegian writers somewhat unfairly to a fleet of ships moving sombrely forward: 'Not a pleasure craft in the whole fleet. No deviation from course. With one exception nothing elegant about the seamanship or the hull; but safe and reliable. Each vessel seemed to be a separate kingdom. They came together because they had to, but each in its own way.' Later, in 1896, the satirical periodical *Vikingen* published a cartoon of the Norwegian literary fleet (*Den norske dikterflåte*), showing an assemblage of craft of different sizes with the face of a leading writer staring out of the prow of each, all moving steadily forward in close formation.

In 1971 the Norwegian literary fleet looks less impressive than it did in 1890, indeed probably less impressive than it would have done had it been assembled at the beginning of any decade since 1890. No sturdy steamers bearing the bewhiskered faces of Ibsen and Bjørnson form the spearhead of the advance, but the flagship of the fleet (the *Johan Borgen*), going back to 1902, still has no difficulty in outstripping the rest.

# PART FOUR

# Norwegian Life and Culture
# in the Twentieth Century

# Chapter 13

# Aspects of Life

*Industry and Communications*

LIKE OTHER COUNTRIES OF WESTERN EUROPE, Norway progressed more rapidly than ever before during the first fifty years of the twentieth century. Economically, a prime reason for this was the ever-increasing harnessing of hydro-electric potential in which, per head of population, Norway is richer than any other country. Cheap electric power provided the basis for the development of electro-chemical and electro-metallurgical industries and, in general, the easy availability of electrical power has benefited Norwegian industry as a whole, including the important timber products industry.

The more traditional industries have also made their contribution to increased prosperity. The merchant fleet, in spite of setbacks during the two World Wars, has maintained its position among the front-runners in world tonnage and in 1971 had a gross tonnage of over 21 million; its earnings in foreign currency have covered roughly one-third of the cost of Norwegian imports. The fisheries, too, though they have been subjected to ups and downs, have continued to be one of the most important factors in the national budget, both in terms of fish exports and as providing the basis of industries based on fish products, especially the canning industry. One casualty, however, has been the Norwegian whaling industry in the Antarctic, which came to an end in 1968. The production of iron and steel has also increased rapidly, especially since the establishment of the state iron-works at Mo i Rana in north Norway which began production in 1955, and there has been a corresponding increase in shipbuilding and in the engineering industries in general. However, the most remarkable developments during the steady growth of the Norwegian economy during the post-World War II period have been in the production of aluminium, which doubled between 1963 and 1969, making Norway the third largest producer in the Western world, and in the electronics industry where the name of Tandberg has become almost an international household word.

The discovery in 1970 of the so-called Ekofisk oilfield in the Norwegian area of the North Sea, said to be among the twenty biggest in the world, promises an important boost to the country's natural

273

resources. It may be taken as a sign of the present strength of the Norwegian economy, which since 1950 has had an average growth-rate of about 4 per cent, that while Norway followed the United Kingdom devaluation of the pound in 1949 by devaluing the *krone*, she did not find it necessary to follow suit after the pound was devalued in 1967.

This increased prosperity, which in general has been fairly evenly spread throughout the population, has made an impact on all areas of national life. One aspect of it has been the rapid increase in population from 2,240,000 at the turn of the century to 3,860,000 today.

With the development of railways, roads, and public transport people have become more mobile than ever before, and this has been an important factor in the continuing break-up of the traditional ways of rural life, which had got underway in the second half of the nineteenth century, with all its consequences for Norwegian life and culture.

The first decades of the twentieth century were the big period in Norwegian railway-building: in 1902 the Ofoten line connecting Narvik in north Norway with Sweden was opened; in 1906 the Valdres line serving central Norway; in 1909 the Christiania–Bergen line was completed; in 1921 the Dovre line to Trondhjem; in 1944 the Oslo–Stavanger line; and the Nordland line from Trondheim has now been extended to Bodø; in addition, a number of other lines were brought into service. The coming of the motor-car and institution of public bus and coach services had the consequence of practically doubling the total length of roads in Norway and of improving their quality. This increase in the transport and road systems opened the way for a vast extension of the tourist industry.

Similar developments have occurred in other fields of communication. The number of telephones has increased astronomically and the usage made of the postal services has rocketed since the turn of the century. In July 1914 the Norwegian airman Tryggve Gran made the first crossing by air of the North Sea, a feat which led to attempts, for a while abortive, to start an air transport service in Norway. It was not until the 1930s that civil air transport really got going. This service was re-established with government aid after World War II, and in February 1951 was combined with leading Danish and Swedish airlines to form the Scandinavian Airlines System.

*Changing Patterns in Social Life*

Changes in the pattern of social life have been equally dramatic. In particular there has been a radical change in the position and status of women. Norwegian women had been given some enfranchisement in local elections as early as 1901 and in national elections in 1907; but in 1910 women received ordinary voting rights in local elections and in 1913 similar rights in the *Storting* elections, including the right to stand as candidates. In this respect Norway led the world. However, women were less rapid in coming into political prominence. Although a woman had acted as a deputy member of the *Storting* as early as 1911, it was not until 1922 that a woman became a full member, and during the 1920s and '30s the number of seats held by women was never more than three. The first woman minister of state (*Konsultativ statsråd*) took office in 1945 and the first departmental minister in 1948. In 1957 there were ten women members of the *Storting*; in 1969 fourteen women were elected.

In other areas the eligibility of women to hold official government appointments (*embeter*) was extended in 1912 to include all appointments except those in the military, diplomatic, and ecclesiastical spheres, and in the cabinet. These disabilities were removed for cabinet posts in 1922 and the others in 1938, though the ordination of female ministers in the state Church was still subject to the consent of local church councils. In 1952 all restrictions were swept away. However, the succession to the throne is still limited to the male line.

These developments have also been paralleled in other legislation. The marriage law of 1927 gave women equal rights and duties with men within marriage, and in government employment the principle of equal pay with men for equal work has been established, though there are still anomalies in the private sector.

As in other countries, improved standards of medical care, hygiene, nutrition, and housing have made major contributions to the transformation of Norwegian society in the twentieth century. In medical care, the reduction of infant mortality and of the incidence of tuberculosis (once the country's scourge) have been principal factors in reducing the mortality rate and increasing the expectation of life, now seventy-five for women and seventy-one for men. A state medical service provides benefits similar to those of the British National Health Service and, in other respects, Norway has become very much a welfare state.

The need to improve housing standards in Norway posed serious problems, especially in the towns, partly because of the great influx from the country districts in the later nineteenth century and partly because of the devastations caused during the fighting and bombing of towns in World War II, and the almost complete building stoppage during that period. Conditions were particularly bad in the capital during the 1920s when overcrowding was common and modern amenities slow to be introduced. In the immediate post-World War II years the shortage of living accommodation was Norway's most urgent social problem. In fact the state was obliged to take a hand in the financing of new building by establishing a so-called House Bank (*Husbanken*) which provided the major part of the capital required.

Twentieth-century developments in sport and popular culture, like the cinema, radio, and television, have by and large followed the common western European pattern. In winter sports and outdoor life Norway has developed her own special potential, especially since leisure-time and holidays have increased. In particular, the special Norwegian phenomenon, which got underway during the decade 1910–20, of a mass exodus from the towns during the Easter period has now grown to mammoth proportions so that many towns are practically deserted at this season.

## The Mass Media

The first cinema in Norway was opened in Christiania in 1904 and from 1915 onwards the ownership and operation of cinemas was gradually taken over by local authorities, and a rural travelling cinema service (*Bygdekino*) was introduced to cover remoter areas. The cinema in Norway has had to rely principally on foreign films, though Norwegian films have been made right from the early days of the cinema. However, unlike the Swedes, the Norwegians have not succeeded in developing a film industry of international class, though some good films have been made; one of the most successful Norwegian directors being Tancred Ibsen, grandson of Henrik Ibsen.

Regular broadcasting began in Norway in 1925 and in 1933 the present State Broadcasting Corporation (*Norsk rikskringkasting*) was formed. The Corporation enjoys a monopoly of broadcasting and provides a one-channel national service, with local transmitters broadcasting local items. Its policy and management have been very similar to that of the B.B.C. and links have, in fact, been close between the two organizations. During World War II the B.B.C. was the mouthpiece of free Norway, and for a number of years after the war the B.B.C.'s Norwegian service, largely manned by young Norwegians, many of whom have since become prominent in Norwegian broadcasting, was listened to with interest in Norway. One consequence of broadcasting in Norway has been the development, almost as a separate genre, of the radio play (*Hørespill*), to which many of the leading Norwegian writers have made contributions. In 1960 regular television transmissions began.

Though the cinema and broadcasting, especially the latter, have brought many purely Norwegian cultural benefits, they have also exposed the country more and more to cultural influences from abroad. The same can be said of the expansion of the book trade in Norway and changes in the character of the press.

In one important sense the book trade has become more Norwegian. While in the nineteenth century Norwegian authors had to rely principally on Danish publishers, and Norwegian publishers were few and unimportant, after the turn of the century purely Norwegian publishing houses began to emerge on a scale which enabled them to compete with the powerful Danish firms. Notable among them was the publishing house of Aschehoug, founded by William Nygaard, and that founded by Olaf Norli. But the most important event in Norwegian publishing occurred in 1925 when the Norwegian branch of the Danish house of Gyldendal, publishers of most of the great Norwegian writers, was bought out by the Norwegians and became an independent Norwegian concern. However, at the same time as this was happening, and as part of a general increase in book-sales, the number of books translated from foreign languages into Norwegian increased enormously. It meant that Norwegian readers were kept better informed of developments in foreign literature than ever before. Sigurd Hoel's 'Yellow Series' of translations of foreign avant-garde literature, which he started in 1929, was a notable feature of this trend, but when to this translated literature are added the books in foreign languages, especially English, which have been imported into Norway in increasing numbers, especially since World War II, it is clear that purely Norwegian literature has been in danger of being swamped.

The Norwegian press, like the press in other countries, had already begun to shed its sober guise by the turn of the century and this had been especially exemplified in the newspapers *Verdens Gang* and *Aftenposten*. News and matters of current interest, formerly presented in a discursive style, were now given a popular, polemical, and sensational form. A strong influence in this respect came from Denmark in the reporting style of the newspaper *Politiken*. Improved communications and new methods of transmitting news rapidly made many new areas of life newsworthy and immediately available, and especially the events of World War I speeded on this development. The circulation of the major newspapers rose, but so did their costs in collecting news. Many provincial newspapers could not compete with the national press and had to close down. To counteract this the *Storting* in 1969 voted 8·3 million *kroner* to subsidize the newspaper industry, mostly to subsidize the cost of newsprint. Provision is also made for reduced telecommunication charges, increased official advertising, and funds for training journalists. Like the trends we have already noted in book-publishing, the new-style newspapers made their contribution to opening up Norway to the outside world and its influences.

As already noted, the most persistent matter of public debate during these years was the language question. There were also, of course, the debates occasioned by the dissolution of the union with

Sweden in 1905 (see above, p. 140), but two questions which provoked great short-term public interest were prohibition and church
affairs.

## The Teetotal Issue

Teetotalism had been in lively issue in Norway even before World
War I and in many areas the sale of alcohol was restricted or entirely
forbidden. However, only a minority of teetotallers had advocated
the introduction of nationwide prohibition. The outbreak of hostilities in Europe in August 1914 gave this minority an unexpected
opportunity to gain wider support for their views. As soon as the war
started, the government of the day forbade the sale and distilling of
spirits and the brewing of beer, principally in order to conserve
supplies of the raw materials used in their manufacture, but also with
an eye to the influence on public order which the special conditions
created by the war might have. These measures continued in operation during the war and were for a time extended to include fortified
wines, heavy ales, and even table wines. The majority of the population accepted these restrictions as necessary, but the extreme teetotallers saw in them a chance to press for total prohibition, and their
views began to command more and more support, in the *Storting* as
well. In 1918 *Venstre* included the prohibition of all alcohol over a
certain volume percentage in their programme and were supported
by the Social Democrats and the Labour Party. In 1919 the government decided to hold a referendum on the sale, import, and manufacture of spirits and fortified wines, with the result that in October
1919, 489,017 people voted for prohibition and 304,673 against.
However, there was a great stumbling-block to the easy implementation of this decision. The wine-producing countries, France, Spain,
and Portugal, were among the best customers for Norwegian fish, and
efforts to negotiate new trade agreements with them, made necessary
by the introduction of prohibition, met with great difficulty.
Eventually an agreement was concluded with France, but not before
the Norwegians had had to agree to raise the permitted maximum
percentage volume of alcohol in wines and also to bind themselves
not only to import 400,000 litres of spirits, in practice brandy, but
also not to re-export them. It soon became clear that the negotiation
of new trade agreements with Spain and Portugal would be even
tougher, but the Norwegian government, fearing that these countries
wanted to influence its attitude to prohibition, determined to emphasize its adherence to this policy. In 1921 it passed a bill, though by
only a small majority, making prohibition permanent. (It is interesting to note that during the first two decades of the century Iceland,
the United States, and Finland all passed bills providing for per-

manent prohibition, all of which were repealed in the 1930s.)

Negotiations with Spain and Portugal continued to drag on and eventually a provisional agreement was reached with Spain, under which Norway was to import 500,000 litres of fortified wine, which of course could not be sold in Norway, a condition which even the prohibitionist majority in the *Storting* found difficult to swallow. With Portugal the Norwegian negotiators fared even worse. In 1923 a provisional trade agreement was put to the *Storting* for ratification, under which Norway was to import 850,000 litres of fortified wine a year. This was too much for the *Storting*. It rejected the proposals by a crushing majority. The government resigned and a new ministry at once set about getting the prohibition of fortified wines repealed, a measure which, in spite of demands that a referendum should first be held, was rapidly carried. This of course meant that the quota provisions of the treaties with Spain and Portugal were made superfluous, and it also meant that the whole of the policy of prohibition was in ruins.

Prohibition in Norway had in fact become steadily more unpopular, both because of its economic consequences for the Norwegian fisheries and also because of the many abuses it had led to. Doctors were permitted to prescribe alcohol for medicinal purposes and in the course of time this had taken on enormous proportions and had led to a number of scandals – one doctor had managed to write out over 48,000 prescriptions in one year. A lively and at times violent trade in the smuggling of liquor had also grown up and the illegal distilling of spirits eventually became widespread. All this, because of the lack of sympathy many otherwise law-abiding people had with prohibition, led to a lack of respect for the law itself.

In 1924, the government of Abraham Berge attempted to repeal the prohibition of spirits, largely on financial grounds, but was defeated. On 18 October 1926, however, a new referendum was held. 531,084 people voted against the prohibition of spirits and 423,031 for its continuance. Thus prohibition in Norway was now at an end after it had led to the fall of three governments and had been the most lively political and public issue of the day. In April 1927 the prohibition laws were repealed and spirits were once again legally on sale, though not through the same channels as formerly. On 16 September 1922 the import and sale of wines and spirits had been made the monopoly of *Vinmonopolet*, a quasi-official organization, which began operations in 1923, though of a necessarily limited kind.

## Church Affairs

Right back to the time of Hans Nielsen Hauge (see above, p. 115), around the turn of the nineteenth century, religious belief and the organization of the faithful had often been matters of momentous national concern. In general this concern had derived from conflicts between orthodoxy, as represented by the state Church,[1] and lay movements within the Church which, while they lacked nothing in dogmatism, seemed to accord better with the religious aspirations and tastes of the common man. Thus the devotionalism of Hauge's movement was a counter to the rationalistic tendencies of the state Church of the day, and, later in the nineteenth century, the 'Happy Christianity' of the Grundtvigian movement was in direct opposition to the Pietism which was especially associated with the name of Gisle Johnson (1822–94), a leading professor of theology at the University of Christiania.

In the 1870s and '80s the new realist currents in literature, coupled with the influence of the advances in the natural sciences, especially the influence of Darwinism, led to wide-ranging and at times bitter debates. Some leading writers, like Bjørnstjerne Bjørnson, publicly declared their defection from the Christian faith, and in general the leading Norwegian authors of the period tended to depict the Church and her ministers in an unfavourable light. The prime example of this was Alexander Kielland who, as we have seen, was refused a state pension by the *Storting* because of his attacks on the Church. At the same time the writer Arne Garborg, in his later works, advocated the practice of a more personal, Tolstoyan kind of religion.

The importance of the Church in the consciousness of the people in nineteenth-century Norway no doubt derived from the predominantly rural nature of the country. We see from Bjørnson's early stories of peasant life, and indeed from Garborg's novel *Peasant Students*, how the church occupied a central position in the life of the rural communities, both as a centre where people met and as a place of mystery and wonder. Thus debates on belief and dogma, on

[1] The 1814 constitution had provided that the Evangelical-Lutheran religion should be the official religion of the state and, in practice, all Norwegians were expected to belong to the state Church and to bring up their children in it. It was not until 1845, with the passing of the so-called *Dissenterloven* (The Law relating to Dissenters), that Norwegians could leave the state Church and other religious communities were officially tolerated. Subsequently, a number of free church movements sprang up in Norway, and many religious movements from abroad began to form congregations, among them the Methodists, the Baptists, and the Mormons. The Roman Catholic Church had been banned in Norway since the Reformation. Indeed the constitution had specifically prohibited monastic orders and Jesuits, provisions which were repealed in 1897 and 1951 respectively. In 1843 a group of Catholics in Christiania had been given a special dispensation to practise their religion, but it was not until 1845 that the first congregation was permitted. An interesting aspect of Roman Catholicism in Norway in the twentieth century has been the number of converts it has made among people prominent in intellectual and literary life, for example the authoress Sigrid Undset (see above, pp. 254–5). However, some 96 per cent of the population belong to the state Church, though their membership may be very nominal; all other congregations put together have a membership of about 150,000.

ecclesiastical appointments, on differences between high and low church, and on lay movements were frequently conducted with an intensity that carried them beyond the immediate religious sphere.

In the twentieth century these debates have raged more within the Church than on the national level, though there have been some notable exceptions. In the early 1920s the Marxist orientation of the Norwegian Labour Party made it openly hostile to the state Church and to religion in general, and though, later in the 1930s, the radicals tended merely to shrug off religion, there were two episodes in 1933 which showed the nature and depth of the underlying feelings. The first of these episodes concerned a proposed performance at the National Theatre in Oslo of the American playwright Marc Connelly's *The Green Pastures*, which, principally because it portrayed God on the stage in the shape of an American Negro pastor, led to a storm of protest, questions in the *Storting*, and the withdrawal of the piece and the resignation of the director of the theatre. The second episode arose from a lecture given by the poet Arnulf Øverland under the title *Kristendommen – den tiende landeplage (Christianity the Tenth Plague)*, the nature of which led to his being prosecuted for blasphemy and, although he was acquitted, the law relating to offences of this kind was strengthened in 1934.

Within the Church the debates of the 1870s and '80s had, on the one hand, led to the emergence of a more liberal school of theologians, especially within the university, who were prepared to take account of the advances in knowledge in the natural sciences, and, on the other, to the consolidation of the conservative factions within the Church into one defensive group where lay elements played a prominent part. An expression of the power of these groups was the expansion in the 1890s of the so-called *Indremisjon* (The Home Mission) and the China Mission Societies, all of which were in varying degrees hostile to the state Church.

These tensions came to a head in 1904 over an election to a vacant chair of divinity at the University of Christiania. The theological faculty of the university had recommended the appointment of the liberal theologian Johannes Ording, but because of protests from conservative church elements and from the missionary societies the government refused to accept the recommendation. The chair was advertised again and Ording, who reapplied, was again declared to be the best candidate. This time the Norwegian government agreed to his appointment, a decision which immediately led not only to protest and resignations in the conservative camp but also to the collecting of funds to set up a rival theological faculty for the training of the clergy. This new faculty, called *Menighetsfakultetet (The Congregational Faculty)*, was constituted in 1907 and in the following year opened its doors to students. In 1913 it was given official recognition by the *Storting* and has remained ever since the powerful centre of ecclesiastical conservatism in Norway and the doctrinal focus of the lay movements. Lay influence in the state Church was also increased in 1920 when congregational councils were established.

Conflict between the conservative-pietistical and the liberal wings of the Church was a recurring phenomenon, especially in the 1920s. Led by the fanatical Ole Hallesby (1879–1961), the conservatives lost no opportunity to attack what they regarded as liberal heresies and the appointment of liberal theologians to ecclesiastical office. The appointment of Eivind Berggrav (1884–1959), one of the most outstanding Norwegian public personalities of recent times, as bishop of Oslo in 1937 had a unifying effect on the Church, which proved to be especially beneficial during the German occupation, when Berggrav emerged as leader of Norwegian church resistance. However, even as late as the 1950s, the old antagonisms flared up when Kristian Schjelderup, bishop of Hamar, protested against the somewhat crude references to eternal damnation which Hallesby had made in a sermon. This protest sparked off a battle during which Schjelderup was charged with having denied the Church's doctrine. The dispute reached both the *Storting* and the cabinet, and was eventually resolved by a solemn declaration from the ministry for church affairs, supported by the theological faculty of the university, that Schjelderup had not been guilty of dereliction of duty.

### The Monarchy

The accession of Haakon VII, in November 1905, marked both a major turning-point and a new relationship between the Norwegians and their sovereign. Many of the disputes between the Norwegians and the Swedes during the nineteenth century derived from differing conceptions of the precise nature of the king's suspensive veto. Carl Johan had tried continually to get this veto made absolute and in other respects to increase the power of the sovereign *vis-à-vis* the *Storting*. Oscar II's reign, which culminated in the breakdown of the union with Sweden, consisted largely of a series of crises which arose from the king's inability to grasp the changed political situation in Norway, and his determination to maintain his royal prerogatives. In 1895 he seriously considered using armed force against the Norwegians. By contrast, Haakon VII was determined from the outset to be in every respect a constitutional monarch: throughout his reign he never came into constitutional conflict with his ministers or with the *Storting*.

In spite of the 69,264 Norwegians who voted in 1905 against monarchy, the monarchic principle was deeply embedded in Norway.

During the union with Denmark the medieval Norwegian kings had never been lost sight of, and they often figured in the patriotic verse which the events of 1814 generated. When Christian Frederik was elected king on 17 May 1814, he was, though a Danish prince, seen as the direct successor of the medieval kings. The universal jubilation which his accession let loose was as much a measure of enthusiasm for the idea of monarchy as for Christian Frederik as a person; in fact it may be doubted whether the Norwegian bid for independence would have achieved the degree of success it did without Christian Frederik's prestige. Even during the union with Sweden Norwegian poets could become panegyrical about their king. Henrik Herman Foss (1790–1853) praised Carl Johan as 'konge-helten' ('the hero king'), while the somewhat lightweight Carl XV is said to have been the model for the very modern monarch in Bjørnson's play *Kongen* and to have inspired Ibsen's poem *Uden navn (Nameless)*, in which Carl is praised for the great work he did not accomplish, the reason being that he was too much of a poet ('Skalden i ham var for stærk').

Haakon VII knew that he could count on massive support. His choice, on his accession, of the motto *Alt for Norge* (All for Norway) showed that he on his side intended to identify himself completely with his new country, and he soon put this into practice. He travelled widely, made a point of meeting people from all sectors of Norwegian society, and worked hard to inform himself on all aspects of Norwegian life and culture. At the same time he maintained complete impartiality in political matters. This, together with an open and unassuming manner, a sense of humour, and a modest and democratic life-style soon endeared him to Norwegians. Even the republican element could find nothing to complain of, and although the Labour Party, especially in the 1920s, was in principle republican and made efforts to reduce the king's Civil List, it had no grudge against the king personally. However, Haakon could, when occasion demanded, take action on his own initiative, though within the framework of the constitution. In 1928, after Labour had become the largest party in the *Storting*, but without an absolute majority, the king called its leader, Christopher Hornsrud, to form a ministry, adjudging this the correct procedure when the other parties were unable to agree on the formation of a government. This was regarded as a bold step, both because Labour had not yet shed the stigma of revolutionary extremism acquired in the early 1920s and also because it was believed that Labour would not take office until it had an absolute majority.

Royal initiative had its finest hour in April 1940 when the king's firmness in rejecting any compromise with the Nazis did much to strengthen the will of his ministers and the *Storting* to resist. His rejection, too, after he had arrived in England, of the demand that he should abdicate made him the rallying-point and the symbol of Norwegian resistance. During his five years in the United Kingdom Haakon was continually active, visiting units of the Norwegian armed forces and ships of the merchant marine, and taking every chance to make personal contact with his many subjects in exile. His seventieth birthday on 3 August 1942 was marked in London by a parade in Hyde Park and a rally in the Albert Hall at which Nygaardsvold, in a tribute to the king, said that there were few republicans left among Norwegians at that time. *The Times* gave a full report of the occasion and a special number of *Norsk Tidend*, the Norwegian newspaper published in London during the war, contained tributes from many heads of state and representatives of the Norwegian community in exile. The B.B.C. marked the occasion by an hour's programme on the Home Service.

No monarch was more closely identified with his people at this time than Haakon. As was often said, he was the people's king (*folkekongen*) and the father of his people. Poets paid tribute to him, especially Nordahl Grieg in his moving poem *Kongen* and Arnulf Øverland in his *Når kongen kommer hjem* (*When the King Comes Home*). After the jubilations on his return to Norway in 1945 the lustre which his name and person had acquired during the war years continued to glow around him, and when he died in 1957 at the age of eighty-five after a reign of fifty-two years, the Norwegians felt his passing not only as a national but as a personal loss. Again it was Arnulf Øverland, in his poem *Vår gamle konge* (*Our Aged King*), who found the right words to echo the feelings of the people—Haakon had been the best king Norway had had, he was Haakon the Good.

Haakon's son Olav (Olav V) was fifty-four when he succeeded. Though he had often acted as regent and had during the war been very active in furthering the Norwegian and Allied cause, he had inevitably been seen principally as his father's aide; in fact the two were often photographed together. His advantage, however, was of being completely Norwegian in upbringing and education. From an early age he had mixed in a normal way with his contemporaries. In particular he has identified himself with the Norwegian national pastimes of skiing and sailing. His informality and expansive manner have made him a popular monarch.

However, the Norwegian royal house has been very thin on the ground. Olav was Haakon's and Queen Maud's only child. Maud herself, who died in 1938 at the age of sixty-nine, had never enjoyed robust health. She was shy and retiring, spent a good part of each year in England, and was never prominent in public life. Her death and that of Olav's wife, Crown Princess Märtha, in 1954 meant that Norway has been without a queen for over thirty years. Olav's daughters, Ragnhild and Astrid, have married commoners, and when the heir to the throne, Crown Prince Harald (1937–), also married a commoner, Sonja Haraldsen (1937–), there were many Norwegians who felt that the days of the monarchy were numbered. However, the birth to the couple in 1971 of a daughter, Märtha Louise, has aroused discussion about the possibility of amending the Norwegian constitution to provide for succession in the female line. An opinion poll in December 1971 showed that 71 per cent of those asked were in favour of the constitution being changed.

The success of the monarchy in Norway since 1905 has depended very much on the personal qualities of the monarch. The mystique of monarchy seems to have counted for little. As prime minister Nygaardsvold put it in his speech mentioned above, the monarchy gave all the advantages of the republican system without its defects and drawbacks. When Olav succeeded, a coronation was dispensed with; instead he was blessed at a special ceremony in the Cathedral of Nidaros in 1958. Yet it would be difficult to envisage the key festival of Norwegian national life, the celebration of Constitution Day on 17 May, taking place in a republic. As long as processions form and march along Karl Johans gate up to the royal palace on that day, it will be necessary to have a monarch there to receive them.

*Education and the Universities*

The Norwegians, like the Scots, have always given high priority to education. As we have seen, compulsory schooling was introduced into Norway during the eighteenth century to provide the modicum of reading ability needed to cope with the requirements for confirmation. Nineteenth-century Norwegian literature gives many examples of the bright young peasant lad with a capacity for learning who makes his way into the higher reaches of society. Both in literature and in life academics and academic learning have been held in high esteem, though, in literature at any rate, the process of learning has often been depicted as if it were a singularly joyless thing–the term *lesehest* (lit. reading horse), used to denote a diligent student, has a somewhat ambivalent ring about it.

During the twentieth century there has been an expansion in all sectors of the Norwegian educational system. Private schools hardly exist and the vast majority of the population begin their school careers in one of the state primary schools (*Barneskolen*) at the age of seven. In 1959 a new Education Act provided for the extension, on the basis of local option, of primary education from a total of seven years to nine. This was made obligatory by the Act of 1969, to take effect from July 1971. It provides for a six-year course in the *Barneskole*, followed by three years in the *Ungdomsskole* (Young People's

School), a new type of school replacing the older *Framhaldsskole* (Continuation School) and *Realskole*. It is intended that the new arrangements should be fully operative by 1975. Beyond the *Ungdomsskole* is the *Gymnas* (High or Grammar School), leading to study at a university or at some other institution of higher education.

The Folk High School, which had a distinctly folk-nationalist, even religious, character, still continues, and provides a six-month course during the winter months with board and accommodation for young people over the age of seventeen, though its courses have become much more geared to the modern world. In 1969 the government agreed to set up a number of so-called *Distriktshøyskoler* (District Colleges) in various provincial areas, as part of a general programme of regional development, to provide two-year courses for young people in business, managerial, and related subjects.

There has also been a marked increase in the number of institutions of higher education. Among those founded in the present century are *Norges tekniske Høgskole* (Norwegian Technical University; 1910), which together with *Norges lærerhøgskole* (State College for Teachers; 1922), now make up the University of Trondheim; *Norges Handelshøyskole* (State College of Business Administration) in Bergen (1936); and the University of Bergen (1946). A university in Tromsø in north Norway is also being developed.

Norwegian scholarship and research have a very respectable record of recent achievement. Eminent work has been done in the scientific field by the meteorologist Vilhelm Bjerknes (1862–1951); the physicist Kristian Birkeland (1867–1917); the chemists Odd Hassel (1897–), who in 1969 shared the Nobel Prize for Chemistry, and the Norwegian-born Lars Onsager (1903–) who received the prize in 1968. The economist Ragnar Frisch (1895–), a pioneer of econometrics, shared the first Nobel Prize for Economic Science in 1969. Since World War II there has been a great upsurge in scholarship and research in Norway thanks largely to the establishment of research councils financed from the profits of the state-run football pools.

*Exploration and the Work of Fridtjof Nansen*

In exploration the great feats of the period were the polar explorations of Roald Amundsen (1872–1928). During the years 1903–06, in the *Gjøa*, he navigated the North-West Passage in its entirety, being the first to do so. Later he planned to repeat and improve on Nansen's feat with the *Fram*, but, in the event, turned south to the Antarctic and reached the South Pole on 14 December 1911, a month before the expedition led by Scott. Subsequently, in an expedition lasting a number of years, which included an unsuccessful attempt to fly over the North Pole, he attempted to drift over the Arctic Ocean from the coast of Siberia in the specially built *Maud*. On 12 May 1926, as one of the leaders of an expedition which included the Italian Umberto Nobile and the American Lincoln Ellsworth, he passed over the North Pole in the Italian airship *Norge*. He perished in 1928, in an attempt to rescue Nobile and his expedition in the airship *Italia*. Amundsen was one of the most intrepid polar explorers of all times, and his expeditions added greatly to scientific knowledge. More recently, in 1947, Thor Heyerdahl, with his voyage across the Pacific on a balsa-wood raft, *Kontiki*, has continued the Norwegian tradition of exploration set by Nansen and Amundsen.

Nansen's name retained international fame because of his many services to humanitarian causes. In 1920 he was appointed High Commissioner by the Council of the League of Nations to arrange for the repatriation of prisoners-of-war from many countries who were still living wretchedly in totally inadequate prison camps all over Europe. Before this task was completed, Nansen was asked to make arrangements for the rehabilitation of the millions of refugees and displaced persons, especially White Russians, who had been dispersed over Europe and Asia after World War I. Among other things, he instituted the so-called Nansen passport for stateless persons, which was recognized by fifty governments. At the same time, he organized large-scale relief in the Soviet Union, especially in the Ukraine and in the Volga region, where famine and epidemics had decimated the population and threatened even wider areas. Among his assistants was the later notorious Vidkun Quisling. Finally, in 1922, after the defeat of the Greeks in their war with the Turks, Nansen organized relief for Greek refugees who had been living in Turkey and arranged a large-scale exchange of minority populations between Greece and Turkey, a work that went on for many years. Nansen was awarded the Nobel Peace Prize in 1922.

*Chapter 14*

# The Theatre and the Arts

*The Theatre*

THE OPENING OF THE NATIONAL THEATRE in Christiania in 1899 proved a tremendous stimulus to the art in Norway. This foundation owed much to its first director, Bjørn Bjørnson, who gathered about him an outstanding galaxy of theatrical talent, including such famous names in Norwegian stage history as Johanne Dybwad (1867–1950), Ragna Wettergreen (1866–1958), Halfdan Christensen (1873–1950), and Hauk Aabel (1869–1961). He laid the foundations of what has been called the Golden Age of the National Theatre – the period from 1910 into the 1930s. Later generations have also produced their distinguished names, but few Norwegians would claim that in recent years the National Theatre has been in the van of theatrical innovation in Norway.

From 1903 to 1911, the private *Fahlstrøms Theater* enriched the theatrical life of the capital by the boldness of its repertoire, as did the *Centralteatret* for a much longer period, until 1959, with its wide-ranging programmes, including lighter entertainments of high quality. In 1929 *Det Nye Teater* (New Theatre) was founded, initially with the idea of providing better opportunities for Norwegian playwrights to get their plays staged than they had at the National Theatre. This aim succeeded, within the limits imposed on it by the lack of new work of real quality.

A lively theatre in recent decades has been *Det Norske Teatret*, founded in Christiania in 1913 to promote the performance of plays in *Nynorsk* and, especially, to further the cause of New Norwegian drama. In spite of early difficulties, especially those of recruiting players capable and willing to perform in New Norwegian, and the general hostility in the predominantly *Bokmål* capital to the whole undertaking, the theatre gradually earned the respect of the theatre-going public by its imaginative repertoire, especially its New Norwegian translations of modern foreign drama, and the distinction of its directors and players, especially Lars Tvinde (1886–1971).

The immediate post-World War II years in Oslo saw the emergence of two experiments in theatrical presentation. The first was *Studioteatret* (Studio Theatre), in existence during 1945–50 and experimental in the sense that, influenced by Stanislavsky's ideas, it attempted to explore new paths in theatrical production. The other experiment was *Folketeatret* (The People's Theatre) which opened its doors in 1952 and continued to 1958. (It has since become the home of the Norwegian Opera.) It attempted to bring serious drama to the people by means of subsidized prices, but although it had some artistic successes and much public financial support, the public it was supposed to be aiming at either stayed away or was in fact non-existent, at least as far as the Oslo East End was concerned.

The theatre in Bergen, *Den Nationale Scene* (see above, p. 25), has continued its, at times, difficult existence, but has succeeded in making a name for its adventurous productions of modern plays. The cities of Trondheim and Stavanger have also managed to keep permanent theatres going since World War I, though often under great difficulties. A post-war innovation has been the establishment of *Riksteatret*, a travelling theatre supported by the state, which gives theatrical performances all over Norway.

## Painting

Norwegian painting in the twentieth century has been dominated by the figure of Edvard Munch (see above, p. 55). Indeed, to the outside world Munch is the only Norwegian painter of any period to be considered of international importance, and his reputation has grown steadily.

At the turn of the century the naturalism, impressionism, and symbolism which we have noted in the 1880s and '90s were still evident in Norwegian art. However, a new movement, usually called New Impressionism, was also underway. Unlike the movements of the preceding decades the aim of New Impressionism was to paint 'objectively'. Its representatives, among whom Thorvald Erichsen (1868–1939) was the most prominent, formed a school of so-called 'pure' painting. They planned to reproduce an immediate visual impression in their pictures, with special reference to light and colour effects combined with scrupulous attention to composition. In a sense their aims can be compared with those of the New Realism movement in literature after 1900 (see above, p. 253), in that they were not interested in realism, impressionism, or symbolism for their own sake.

Though Norway could produce at this period a painter like Nikolai Astrup (1880–1928), whose paintings from Jølster in western Norway carried forward in a personal and modern idiom the tradition from J. C. Dahl and his contemporaries, the influence of French painters was strong in the early twentieth century, especially that of Henri Matisse, among whose pupils were the Norwegian artists Henrik Sørensen, Axel Revold, and Per Krohg, all of whom were later to become famous. Though each had a different outlook, they all shared a common artistic attitude in their reaction against impressionism and in their adherence to a greater discipline in composition and in the use of colour. They cultivated a style of painting which had a decorative aspect and it is not surprising that from it developed a school of mural painting which is a marked feature of Norwegian art in the 1920s and '30s.

Perhaps the most notable of these muralists was Per Krohg (1889–1965), whose work is to be seen in many public buildings in Oslo, including the University Library, the university buildings at Blindern, and the Oslo Town Hall. Though Edvard Munch had painted his set of murals for the *Aula* (Assembly Hall) of the university during the years 1910–16, the 'mural period' in Norway really got going in 1918 when Axel Revold (1887–1962) won the competition for murals to adorn the Stock Exchange in Bergen; his work is also to be seen in the University Library in Oslo and in the Town Hall. Together with Alf Rolfsen (1895–), Krohg and Revold have been responsible for most of the major murals in Norway. In fact the three often worked together as a team and had a marked technical and artistic influence on each other. Henrik Sørensen (1882–1962), too, though he was in many respects a very different painter from the Krohg–Revold–Rolfsen trio and others of his contemporaries and whose most striking contributions to Norwegian painting were his three so-called *Golgata* (Calvary) pictures (1920–23) and his *Inferno*, also painted murals, examples of which can also be seen in the Oslo Town Hall. In fact, such has been the cult of the mural in Norway that it seems to have brought with it a *horror vacui*, for no wall or ceiling in a public place has been safe from the attentions of the muralists. As the movement progressed, it also moved away from the purely artistic ideals of its origins. Because they were painting for the public at large, the muralists felt, no doubt, that their work should have a popular appeal. Thus it became necessary for the mural to tell a story or communicate a message, a development in which social considerations and the onward march of democracy also played a part. Thus their work had an increasingly realistic aspect and many may feel that in some of the Oslo Town Hall murals, especially those depicting events during the occupation, this realism approaches crassness.

The first years of the century were also to mark something of a turning-point in the work of Edvard Munch, though critics have insisted on the unbroken nature of his artistic development. In 1909, after a period of nervous collapse and treatment in a Copenhagen clinic, he returned after a long period abroad, mainly in Germany, to settle in Norway. His work, though it retained its highly personal and deeply emotive qualities, became less introspective, symbolic, and literary, and turned more and more to external reality, to lighter colours, landscapes and themes taken from everyday life and work. Like the work of his contemporaries, it also moved more towards the monumental, and during 1910–16 he painted his set of murals for the Assembly Hall of the University of Oslo, one of the most important examples of Norwegian mural painting. Later, after he had settled at Ekely near Oslo, where he lived virtually as a recluse, Munch began to devote himself to lithographs and woodcuts, which, during the 1920s and '30s, he produced in great numbers. At the same time, he continued to paint many important works: landscapes from the area around Ekely; female nudes, including *Modellen ved Armstolen* (*Nude by the Wicker Chair*; 1929); and self-portraits, among them the striking *Mellom klokken og sengen* (*Between Clock and Bed*; 1940).

The 'popular' nature which the muralists' art had taken on meant that one must look for newer trends in the work of other artists, though in a short survey it is difficult to distinguish adequately between all the many complex tendencies, variations, and contradictions which occurred. Among them Aage Storstein's frankly cubist painting *Storrengjøringen* (*Spring Cleaning*; 1931–32) was regarded at the time as being the ultimate of its kind, though he too, in the semicubist style of his murals in Oslo Town Hall, followed in the literary footsteps of the other muralists.

The 1930s, with their background of violence in Europe and economic and social crises at home, brought protest back into Norwegian painting. A thoroughgoing representative of this particular trend was Reidar Aulie (1904–), whose tendentious paintings of working-class life and protest were intended to be pictorially direct and easy to understand. In the work of Arne Ekeland (1908–), on the other hand, protest is elevated to a higher, even visionary, plane, and projected with such violence that it sometimes breaks the bounds of realism to become starkly symbolic. Kai Fjell (1907–) is also a symbolist, but his work is less violent, more romantic, and strongly compounded with lyricism. His roving imagination is kept in check by architectural principles and conscious composition.

Since World War II Norwegian painting has in general tended to become more abstract, and non-figurative painters have also made their appearance, among them Knut Rumohr (1916–) and Jacob Weidemann (1923–), in whose work one can nevertheless detect the Norwegian tradition. Rumohr's work developed almost imperceptibly from a decorative-style figurative art to an abstract art using forms and colours which were clearly derived from the decorative style of Norwegian folk-art. Weidemann's work has been more varied but he, too, in his abstract work has often been inspired by nature, painting in close-up the undergrowth of the forest with its mosses and autumn leaves in such paintings as *Brunt løv og mose* (*Brown Leaves and Moss*), *Rød jord og lyng* (*Red Earth and Heather*), and *Svart sten og rød kvist* (*Black Stone and Red Branches*). Finally, the German-born Rolf Nesch (1893–) has been an influence on the graphic arts in Norway with his *montages* and his experiments in reproduction processes. His frieze in the hall of Indeks-Huset in Oslo is generally regarded as his masterpiece.

*Sculpture*

As with painting, the art of sculpture in Norway at the turn of the century is associated especially with one name, that of Gustav Vigeland (1869–1943). Like Edvard Munch, whose bust he modelled in 1894, Vigeland had already made a name for himself in the 1890s. Also like Munch, his early work had very much reflected the expressionistic, neo-Romantic, symbolic, and literary trends of the 1890s. He had also begun on the series of busts and statues of celebrated Norwegians, especially Norwegian writers, which constitute the most remarkable aspect of his work around the turn of the century. The most striking of these works is perhaps the statue-monument to the early nineteenth-century Norwegian mathematician Niels Henrik Abel, now standing on an eminence near the Royal Palace in Oslo; but his other works, notably the busts of Ibsen and Bjørnson, and the statues of Henrik Wergeland in Kristiansand and Camilla Collett in the Royal Park in Oslo, reveal his great capacity for individual and varied portraiture, and his ability to combine in a satisfactory artistic unity realist presentation with symbolical significance.

Before the turn of the century Vigeland had also conceived the idea of *The Fountain*, the work which was eventually to become one of the central features of his great assemblage of sculptures in the Vigeland Park in Oslo. In 1906 a model of *The Fountain* was exhibited in Christiania, arousing enormous interest and controversy. It was then envisaged that it should be placed in front of the *Storting* building. It consisted of an enormous bowl supported by giant-size figures of naked men of different ages and temperaments, on whom the water from the bowl was to cascade down. Surrounding it were a number of bronze trees containing figures representing different stages in life. Public subscription and support from the municipality of Christiania enabled Vigeland to complete the work, but as time went on his plans and ambitions became even more grandiose. *The Fountain* was now to be the central feature of a grand sculptural park which was to depict nothing less than the whole saga of human life from birth to death in all its joys, sorrows, and activities.

In 1908 the municipality of Christiania had rebuilt Vigeland's studio for him, but with the putting into effect of his plans it had become far too small. He then had the idea of making over all his works to the state on condition that the authorities should provide him with a studio large enough to carry his project through. This proposal eventually came before the Christiania city authorities and in 1921 a remarkable contract was concluded between them and the sculptor, which in fact was based on the suggestions Vigeland had made. This provided him both with ideal working and living conditions and absolute artistic freedom. In 1924 the city corporation approved the plan Vigeland had put forward for a sculpture complex to be sited in the Frogner Park in Oslo, the dominating feature of which was to be an enormous pillar, *The Monolith*, encrusted with writhing and interlaced human figures struggling towards its summit, and clearly phallic in intent. Work on it began in 1927, but it was not until 1943 that the public got a view of the completed work. In the meantime Vigeland had been at work on the fifty-eight bronze figures which line the bridge in the park, again representing life in all its phases, and the four dragon-groups at either end. Numerous other sculptures, including *The Wheel of Life*, were placed in position after Vigeland's death in 1943.

Perhaps the most impressive things about the Vigeland Park are its very immensity and the tremendous expression of energy and will that it represents. There seems little doubt that quality did not always go hand in hand with quantity, and that among sculptures of high artistic merit there are others which have an air of mass production and lifelessness. Doubts have also been cast on the planning of the site as a whole, especially in relation to the natural features of the terrain. The overall impression is undoubtedly one of angularity and harshness, but the acceptance or otherwise of this may well go together with an acceptance or rejection of the predominantly deterministic, even pessimistic, character of the whole project. Those who like to find nymphs and fairies in a public park had better go elsewhere!

Vigeland's dominating position naturally put other sculptors of the period very much into the shade, especially in a country where sculpture was not a well-established art form. In the early years of the century this created a situation which was rather less than fair to talented artists like Gunnar Utsond (1864–1950) and Ingebrigt Vik (1867–1927). Work on statuary for the west front of the restored Nidaros Cathedral in Trondheim (on which Vigeland also worked) provided chances for a number of younger sculptors. Together, under the guidance of Wilhelm Rasmussen (1879–1965), professor at the Academy of Art (*Statens kunstakademi*) from 1921 to 1945, they helped create something of a Norwegian school of sculpture in the 1920s.

Another of Rasmussen's pupils, Rolf Lunde (1891–1928), showed distinct individuality as the most promising young sculptor of his generation. His powerful statue of Ludvig Wiese in Lillehammer is a landmark of Norwegian sculpture. Somewhat later, the new Oslo Town Hall added to the opportunities which Nidaros Cathedral had provided, but given the ecclesiastical and civic nature of these tasks, and especially, in the case of Oslo Town Hall, the national and social romanticism implicit in the whole concept of the building with its wealth of artistic embellishment of many kinds, it was no doubt inevitable that no revolutionary advances should have been made. However, the sculpture of Oslo Town Hall does include such highlights as the carved and painted wooden reliefs, depicting scenes from Old Norse mythology and legend, by Dagfin Werenskiold (1892–), which line the entrance porticos; the statue of Harald Hardråde surmounting a relief, showing timber floaters, and a fountain with animal decoration by Anne Grimdalen (1899–) on the west side; the bronze of Saint Hallvard (patron saint of Oslo) by Nic. Schiøll (1901–) on the south wall; *Oslopiken* (*The Oslo Girl*) by Joseph Grimeland (1916–); and the groups of women with children in the open space on the south side by Per Hurum (1910–). In Stavanger a statue of Arne Garborg by Gunnar Janson (1901–) is not only the sculptor's best work, but also a good example of the tendencies of the time, and is often singled out for special mention.

Inevitably the most recent period in Norwegian sculpture has produced its share of abstract and non-figurative work. A start was made in 1950 by the fifty-five-year-old Arthur Gustavson, but it was with Arnold Haukeland (1920–) that this type of sculptural modernity had its breakthrough in Norway in the 1960s. He had made a name for himself in the 1950s with his massive *Frihetsmonumentet* (*Freedom Monument*) outside the Town Hall in Sandvika, but in the years that followed his work took on a more abstract, even geometric character. At the same time he forsook modelling in clay for the welding bench. One of his best-known works is the composition in stainless steel called *Air* on the University of Oslo campus at Blindern; another is *Dynamikk* (Dynamism) on Strandpromenaden in Oslo, both expressions of a technological age, though with very different characters. Another of his works, situated in a park for the physically handicapped at Skjeberg in Østfold, is a composition called *Fra mørke til lys* (*From Dark to Light*; 1968), a kind of technological *Gesamtkunstwerk*, which includes electronic music (programmed by the composer Arne Nordheim), the 'play-out' being controlled by the changing light of the sun. Other sculptors of the Norwegian avant-garde include: Aase Texmon Rygh (1925–), whose strongly abstract work includes experiments in many types of material – noteworthy are her *Morphosis I* and *II* (1966–68); and the versatile Arne Vinje Gunnerud (1930–) whose *Bryggepelfantasi* (*A Fantasy on Jetty Piles*) turns homely materials and associations to abstract account.

## Music

In the early twentieth century Norwegian musical life continued to be dominated by composers who either remained in the National Romantic tradition of Grieg or who were particularly influenced by late nineteenth-century German music, especially Wagner. Sometimes these influences went hand in hand, as, for example, in the work of Christian Sinding (1856–1941), now remembered for his piano piece *Rustle of Spring*, but who was much admired in the earlier part of his career for his chamber music, piano concerto, and symphonic works, and whose influence carried over into the new century. Johan Halvorsen (1864–1935) was also an influential figure spanning both centuries whose output as a composer included symphonies, a violin concerto, and chamber music. His work also reflected his keen interest in Norwegian folk-music. He wrote three *Norwegian Rhapsodies* and it was also he who noted down the *Slåtter* which Grieg used for his piano pieces of that name; Halvorsen also arranged them for violin. In his incidental music to Sigurd Eldegard's play *Fossegrimen*, he made use of the Hardanger fiddle in his score. On the other hand, Sinding's and Halvorsen's contemporary, Gerhard Schjelderup (1859–1933), the composer of eight operas and other symphonic works, was a pronounced Wagnerian.

Two leading composers of a younger generation, Arne Eggen (1881–1955) and David Monrad Johansen (1888–), were both very much in the 'national' school. All Eggen's works, even those on a large scale, contain folk-music motifs and are otherwise strongly Norwegian in character. His choice of musical subjects is also indicative of this interest. Among other things, he composed a setting of the poem *Mjøsen* by Hulda Garborg (a well-known folklorist and wife of Arne Garborg) for chorus and orchestra, and an opera *Olav Liljekrans*, based on one of Ibsen's early plays. Monrad Johansen was the most pronounced Griegian of all the post-Grieg 'nationalist' composers of Norway; he also wrote the standard biography of Grieg. His oratorio *Voluspå* (1927), based on one of the lays of the *Elder Edda*, and his symphonic poem *Pan*, written to mark the eightieth birthday of Knut Hamsun in 1939, and inspired by Hamsun's novel of that name, are among his most noteworthy compositions. The use of folk-melody motifs in Norwegian art-music owed a very great deal to the scholarly researches and recordings of folk-melodies made by Catharinus Elling (1858–1942), the immediate successor of Lindeman, and later to the collections of O. M. Sandvik (1875–). The composers Sparre Olsen and Geirr Tveitt were also active as collectors of folk-melodies.

Thus, given the weight of these traditions, the appearance of Fartein Valen (1887–1952), who fitted into neither of these categories, but became the lone representative of atonalism in Norway, was surprising. Valen developed slowly; in fact between 1909, the date of his first composition, and 1921 he published only four works, but he had the whole time been trying to break away from the late Romantic style he had inherited from, among others, Max Bruch, with whom he had studied in Berlin. However, in the 1920s, with his Trio for violin, piano, and cello, he showed that he had mastered the new idiom – a highly individual and markedly polyphonic type of atonalism – towards which he had been working. Over the next thirty years Valen published a limited number of compositions, among them works for voice, string quartet, choir, and orchestra (including a violin concerto), which placed him with the avant-garde composers of the day. Valen left four symphonies and sketches for a fifth. Apart from its technical merits, Valen's work is characterized by its intimate expressiveness and often a deeply religious quality. At home in Norway Valen was practically disregarded until after World War II when his work began to attract some attention abroad – in 1949 a Valen society was founded in London. However, for all its merits, his work is likely to remain within the province of the connoisseur. Internationally Valen was, of course, overshadowed by Schönberg, Alban Berg, and Webern. In Norway, where he remained an isolated phenomenon, he was unfortunate enough to be composing during the period when nationalism in music was the fashion.

This 'nationalistic' trend had its most important representative in Harald Sæverud (1897–) who is probably regarded by the Norwegian musical public as the most important and distinctively Norwegian composer of the twentieth century. His first compositions, like Valen's, were in fulsome late Romantic style. In the 1920s he flirted with atonalism, but in the 1930s reverted to a more tonal, if dissonant, style of composition. A purely Norwegian element had been latent in his work, but it was not until the occupation of Norway that this native element came into its own. He wrote a number of Slåtter, of which the most celebrated, Kjempeviseslåtten, is dedicated to the Norwegian Home Front. During the war, too, he wrote a trilogy of symphonies, also inspired by events during the occupation. Sæverud created a great stir with his incidental music to Ibsen's play Peer Gynt (1948). Like the production for which it was written, the music represented a determined effort to de-romanticize the piece and, in particular, to dispel the idealizing tendency of Grieg's incidental music. Sæverud's score contains much that is lively, witty, and clever, but its acceptance as incidental music will depend very much on individual taste and on the sort of interpretation of Ibsen's play one finds acceptable.

Klaus Egge (1906–) is also one of the 'nationalist' group of composers whose sources of inspiration are often revealed in the titles he gave to his works, like the *Draumkvede* sonata for piano of 1934, called after the Norwegian visionary ballad (see above, p. 227). Egge's first symphony, written in 1940–42, was dedicated to Norwegian seamen and his second piano concerto uses a Norwegian folk-tune as the theme for a set of variations and a fugue. However, the most thoroughgoing of the group was Eivind Groven (1901–) whose compositions, which include symphonies, a piano concerto, and other large-scale works, have been largely influenced by the folk-music of his native Telemark and, at times, clearly inspired by the special melodic and harmonic characteristics of the Hardanger fiddle. Two other composers with very different characteristics who have made conscious use of folk-music in their compositions are Sparre Olsen (1903–) and Geirr Tveitt (1908–). In Sparre Olsen's work, which is mainly on a small scale, folk-elements have been completely absorbed and turned to original melodic and harmonic account in the carefully composed musical fabric which usually has a strongly lyrical character. Geirr Tveitt, on the other hand, has been much more prolific and ambitious, both in the scale of his compositions and in his theoretical pretentions. These he set out in 1937 in a dissertation explaining both the theoretical basis of his own compositions and claiming a special modal basis for Norwegian folk-music.

When one moves away from the composers who consciously made use of, or showed a definite orientation towards, Norwegian folk-music, it is difficult to make any clear grouping. Moreover, in the work of composers with a more European orientation like Ludvig Irgens Jensen (1894–1969), Bjarne Brustad (1895–), and Knut Nystedt (1915–), one finds that elements from folk-music have to a greater or lesser extent been brought into use. The reaction against the folk preoccupations of Norwegian composers did not really come until the 1950s when a new generation turned to serialism, dodecaphony, and other modern techniques. Among them are Finn Mortensen (1922–), Egil Hovland (1924–), and Arne Nordheim (1931–) – the boldest of the three who has made extensive use of electronic aids in his compositions.

There are many names in twentieth-century Norwegian music but, with the distinguished exception of the operatic soprano Kirsten Flagstad (1895–1962), none of any great international stature. However, at home music has achieved a much more secure position than it had in the nineteenth century. There are now permanent symphony orchestras in Oslo, Bergen, Stavanger, and Trondheim; a permanent Norwegian Opera was founded in Oslo in 1959; and concertgoing in general is organized on a national scale by groups like *Musikkens venner* (The Friends of Music). In the schools music has a much more important place in the curriculum and many local authorities have established schools of music in their areas, though no state academy of music as yet exists. Finally, the Bergen Festival, inaugurated in 1953, has given Norway a respectable position in international musical life.

# Postscript

IN THE PREAMBLE TO THE FIRST CHAPTER it was observed that it would be unrealistic to overlook the dictates of geography in any description of Norway and the Norwegians. Perhaps the greatest consequence of Norway's geographical situation for her life and culture has been the individualism which it has engendered, and which is still a marked feature of Norwegian ways of thinking and behaving. It would not be too much to speak of a 'cult of the individual'.

It is, of course, easy to see how this individualism developed out of the barriers which mountain, forest, and moorland placed between man and man in a sparsely populated country where, with its isolated farmsteads and small fishing communities, men and women were dependent on their own individual efforts for survival. Even the free and independent position of the peasant proprietors (*Odelsbønder*) was an aspect of a geographical situation which hindered the formation of large estates and engendered the attitude of stalwart independence admired by so many nineteenth-century travellers to Norway.

One concomitant of this individualism is the self-esteem which has long been an observed feature of Norwegian behaviour, and often the subject of ironic comment, not least by the Norwegians themselves. As far back as the thirteenth century Snorri Sturluson, in his account of the battle of Svold, reports King Olav Tryggvason as saying that he is not afraid of the 'miserable' Danes and that the Swedes would 'do better to stay at home and lick their sacrificial bowls'; but from the Norwegians under Earl Erik 'we can expect a sharp battle, for they are Norwegians like ourselves.' Both Saxo Grammaticus and Ludvig Holberg comment on the Norwegians' high opinion of themselves, but self-praise seems to have reached its acme around 1814 in the bombastic nationalist poetry of the period, of which Frede Castberg cites Simon Olaus Wolff's poem *Nordmandssang* (*The Norwegian's Song*; 1822) as the prime example. Hans Andersen, in his story *Laserne* (*The Rags*; 1869), put it in this way:

'I'm Norwegian', said the Norwegian. 'And when I say I'm Norwegian, I think I've said enough. I'm as firm in my foundations as the ancient mountains of old Norway. The country has a

Constitution, like Free America. It thrills me to the marrow to think what I am, and let my thoughts ring out in words of granite.'

More recently, in 1958, in a Gallup poll held concurrently in twelve countries, including Norway, 200 persons in each, mainly in the large towns, were asked which country they thought ranked highest in culture, food, living standards, natural beauty, female beauty, *joie de vivre*, and national pride. In their replies the 200 Norwegians (from Oslo) put Norway first in culture, food, natural beauty, and female beauty, a score which, with the exception of the U.S.A., was higher for the home side than from any other country. In the Norwegian version of the story about subjects chosen by different nationalities when asked to speak on the elephant in relation to a topic of their choice, the Norwegian elects to speak on 'Norway and the Norwegians.'

In the Norwegian ideal of personality as it emerges from literature and life, reference to qualities characteristic of the individual who is untarnished and uncompromised by society is pretty persistent. Bjørnson's motto 'At være i Sandhed' (To be in truth) was both an exhortation and an ideal, and its influence has been pervasive and continuing. In everyday speech the frequent use of words like *likefrem* (straightforward), *naturlig* (natural), *kjekk* (courageous and other good qualities) as descriptive adjectives of people suggests both an ideal and a personality unsullied by the deviousness which, implicitly, society might have imposed on it. In the sphere of legislation the freedom of the individual has been of paramount concern, as within relationships like sex and marriage. Thus a recent law permits a wife to retain her maiden name after marriage and children to choose either the father's or the mother's surname. In international affairs it is almost axiomatic that Norway would be on the side of the smaller party in any dispute. There is also a deep distrust of armed forces, imperialism (some Norwegian friends of the author cannot bear to listen to the music of Edward Elgar because of its imperialistic connections), international corporations, and in fact of any institution which would seem to obscure individualism. There is even a reluctance to believe that the individual can be blameworthy. Conduct which, elsewhere, would be regarded as culpable negligence is likely in Norway to be regarded as 'human failure'.

There is, of course, a reverse side to this medal. Other concomitants of the cult of the individual – excessive introspection, narrowness of view, even fanaticism – are often reflected in Norwegian life and literature. The debates on the language question, religious matters, teetotalism were often marked by such characteristics, while in literature Ibsen's Brand, with his uncompromising demand of 'All or

Nothing', has often been seen as specifically Norwegian. At the same time, failure to live up to the ideals of personal integrity implicit in the cult of the individual has continually been castigated by Norwegian writers, including such shortcomings as a lack of commitment (*halvhet*), a capacity for words rather than deeds (the phrasemonger is a familiar figure in Norwegian literature), and a lack of self-discipline. Ibsen's plays *Brand* and *Peer Gynt* were scathing attacks on alleged Norwegian *halvhet* and wordy pretensions; much of Bjørnson's work was an exhortation to self-discipline–in fact, like Wergeland, Bjørnson saw his task as that of bringing up the Norwegian people; and, in general, Norwegian literature has hardly ever lacked a 'message' with a distinctly Norwegian address. Nevertheless, Norwegians seem to have liked this crack of the whip, for there can be few countries where writers are so esteemed as they are in Norway. It has been said that in the nineteenth century she was a poetocracy, with Wergeland and Bjørnson as the uncrowned poet-kings. Writers could expect to receive front-page treatment from the newspapers on their fiftieth, sixtieth, seventieth, and subsequent birthdays, and after that national obsequies on an appropriate scale. There can also be few countries where the hunt for a philosophy of life (*livssyn*) is so persistent or argued about so intensely. All of which suggests that when the demands of the cult of the individual are not honoured in the observance they have caused much agonizing in the breach.

But to return to the dictates of geography. Short summers and long winters have meant that traditionally the work of the Norwegian farmer was concentrated in a few months of hectic activity while for the rest of the year there was comparatively little to do. The uncertainties of fishing, especially the capriciousness of the herring, called for spasmodic rather than continuing effort; in fact, Norwegian has a special word (*skippertak*) to denote a short all-out effort. The contrast between the high mountain wall and the deep valley below, which is often reflected in Norwegian literature, made for the elevation of the spirit, but also for its bemusing and imprisonment. Ludvig Holberg wrote that Norwegians are 'inclined to go to extremes' ('falde udi Ekstremiteter'). Gunnar Heggen in Sigrid Undset's novel *Jenny*, and clearly the spokesman of the authoress, laments the lack of a classical tradition in Norway, declaring that the most praiseworthy thing one can say of an artist or an individual in his country is that he has broken with something–a school, a tradition, or with accepted conventions. Whether geographically determined or not, there seems to be a clear predisposition on the part of the Norwegians to a pattern of thesis and antithesis rather than synthesis. (It is tempting in this context to see the concept of the Third Empire (*Det tredje Rige*), the desired but unobtainable synthesis, which permeates Ibsen's work as deriving from this rather than from the influence of Hegel.)

Bearing in mind the cult of the individual and the dichotomy of thesis and antithesis, we come to a related question: the Will and its role in Norwegian literature and life. In literature the importance of the will is epitomized in Ibsen's *Brand* ('Our nation has become a race effete,/Which has forgotten that the call to will/Is not revoked by any lack of power'), and in *Rosmersholm* ('The nobility of the future will be a nobility of the mind and the will'). In life there is no doubt that in ideal Norwegian thinking, deeds are prized above words. The Norwegian peasant is traditionally a man of few words; in the academic world abstract thinking and philosophy have never ranked high; and it is no wonder that the man of action *par excellence*, Fridtjof Nansen, should have become a national hero. To some observers this tendency shows itself in what has been called the 'willed' nature of Norwegian institutions. Given the vast geographical spread of the country, its historical background, and the nature of its society, it seems obvious that institutions in Norway and indeed the idea of nationhood itself could not grow organically as they could in more populous and in geographically and historically more favoured countries. We have seen how Harald Fairhair and Håkon Håkonsson tried to make the Norwegians one. In more recent times the fervent celebration of 17 May (Constitution Day) is an expression of the same will. Even today Norwegianness is not simply allowed to be in the air everyone breathes. It has to be brought out and emphasized. Travellers to Norway will be familiar with the ubiquity of the Norwegian flag (used as much in social as national contexts); the emphasis on the folksy; and the pervasiveness of the word *norsk* (Norwegian). One could speak of a 'cult of the national'.

Norwegians have also been adept at meeting the demands of political and social organization, and their stubborn respect for the law is an ancient heritage—*Með lögum skal land byggja en eigi með ólögum eyða* (With law shall the land be built and not by lawlessness destroyed). In more recent times co-operatives, especially farmers' co-operatives, are a feature of the rural scene; and in many other social, political, and cultural spheres there has been no lack of will in a nation of individualists to organize themselves and carry through corporate enterprises. It would seem that in such enterprises the cult of the individual can be accommodated, but this higher unity is often bisected by the 'cult of the national' we have just noted. It is remarkable how many names of organizations and associations in Norway are prefixed either by *Norges* (Norway's) or by *norsk* (Norwegian). Moreover, Norwegian pride in the country's culture often strikes one as being, in many ways, pride in its *national* qualities and aspects rather than in its intrinsic merits. As anyone who has professed Norwegian language and literature outside Norway knows, the fact that foreigners should wish to study these subjects seems incredible (or at best an interesting curiosity) to most Norwegians who invariably ask the questions: 'Why do they do it?', 'What use are they going to make of it?'

If the theory of the 'willed' nature of Norwegian institutions be correct, then it may account for the rigidity of many of these institutions. Things do not change easily in Norway. The Labour Party held power for twenty-five years and both the political and cultural establishments of the country must be even more closely knit than their counterparts in London. Will and flexibility do not go easily together and in this rigidity one may see the workings of the cult of the individual in the collective context.

Finally, there is one other dichotomy in the culture of Norway which it may not be so easy to overcome by will: the dichotomy between native life and culture and that of the outside world. We have earlier noted the debates and quarrels between the Wergeland and Welhaven factions in the early nineteenth century: the one noisy in its demands for Norwegianism, the other urging a continuance of cultural ties with Denmark. During the nineteenth century, too, Norwegians often spoke of their country as one with two cultures: the culture of the official classes with its more cosmopolitan, especially Danish-oriented, outlook; and the more purely Norwegian culture of which the literature of *landsmål* and folk-art were the prime expressions. Geography, too, played a part: on the one hand it induced a stay-at-home mentality, on the other it presented a challenge to see what was beyond the mountain wall. The hero of Bjørnson's short story *Arne* provides a good example of the *utlengsel* (longing-out) which the high mountain generated:

> Ut, vil jeg! ut!–å, så langt, langt, langt
>     over de høje fjælle!
> Her er så knugende, tærende trangt,
> og mit mot er så ungt og rankt,–
> lad det få stigningen friste,
> ikke mot murkanten briste!

> Out! I will out! so far, far from here
>     over the mountains so high!
> Below 'tis so crushingly, consumingly near,
> and my spirit's so young without fear,–
> let it to the heights aspire,
> not crushed on the crags to expire!

The enormous emigration to the United States in the nineteenth and early twentieth centuries was, at least in part, an expression of this *utlengsel* which also carried with it a certain ambivalence towards habitat and homeland.

For any small country the relationship of its culture to that of bigger countries must necessarily be of special importance and consequence to it. It would not be unfair to say that much of Norwegian literature and art has followed trends which were set abroad. However, one must make distinctions. Great creative artists like Ibsen, Hamsun, Munch, and Grieg carried these trends further, stamped them with their own genius, and at the same time gave their work an important Norwegian dimension; thus they belong both to Norway and the world. Lesser artists, though they are clearly epigonous, may have an importance within a purely Norwegian context, but their position and the aspect of Norwegian culture they represent are less secure because they depend on the continuance of the close connection between the work of the creative artist and national life. Finally there is folk-art, literature, and culture which exist both in their own right and as an underlay to much Norwegian high art and literature, the latter being reflected both in the actual use that is made of folk-material and in an artistic method reminiscent of the limited objectives of folk-art – the embellishment of something of limited scope and which is basically useful. We have noted the didactic nature of much Norwegian literature. It is also noteworthy that, in general, Norwegian writers are most successful in the shorter forms; even in the structure of many Norwegian novels the short story and the anecdote are not far away. Both in this and in the careful writing craftsmanship of most Norwegian writers, the traditions of folk-art seem to be apparent. It is not surprising that in recent times Norway has excelled in *brukskunst*: the production of furniture and other useful items of high and artistic quality. In fact artistic production in general seems to have been at its most secure when rooted in something specifically Norwegian, but in the world of today these specifically Norwegian things are in a terribly exposed position.

The question hanging over Norwegian culture seems to be how far Norwegianness (especially bearing in mind its 'willed' aspects) can withstand new forms of cultural and physical *utlengsel* which the increasing urbanization and prosperity of the country bring with it. Norwegians who are opposed to Norway's entry into the Common Market often base their opposition on the fear that the country would lose its *egenart*, or special individuality, if they joined. The danger to Norwegian literature of the influx of foreign literature either in translation or in the original has already been noted. In a newspaper interview in September 1969 the Norwegian writer Alfred Hauge said that the day might come when Norwegian writers would decide to write in English so as to reach a wider public. Nevertheless, the present writer would like to end on an optimistic note and express the belief that with increased prosperity, including an industrial growth-rate praised by the *Financial Times*[1], the Norwegians are likely to become more secure and less 'willed' in their culture. Already they seem no longer to have the old need for a 'poet-king' to tell them how to behave and what to do. Nor do there seem to be the same sharp divisions on issues like the language question. And the old obscurantism of the Norse–Norse faction, or of Hidden Norway (*Det skjulte Norge*), as the Dane Jørgen Bukdahl called it, seems to be evaporating. In short, one detects more flexibility on all sides. Even Norwegian language and literature have become items worthy of export. At one time, not so very long ago, mere titbits of tourist information were all the Norwegian cultural authorities thought the foreigner needed to know about Norway and the Norwegians.

[1] Special Supplement, 16 October 1969.

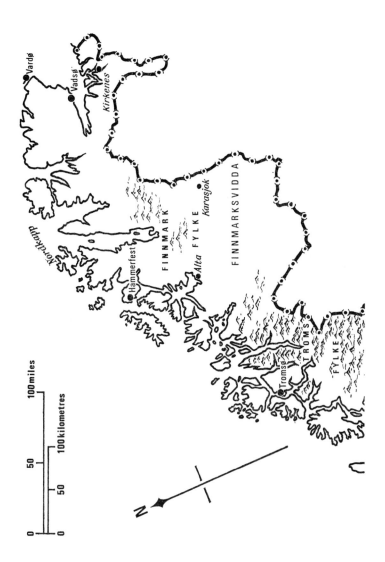

1 Norway: general map.

The inset shows regional divisions. Within the darkened areas 75 per cent of Norway's population is concentrated.

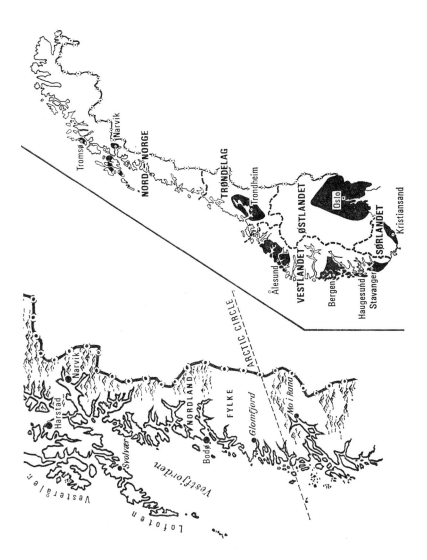

NORD-NORGE
TRØNDELAG
ØSTLANDET
VESTLANDET
SØRLANDET

Tromsø
Narvik
Trondheim
Ålesund
Bergen
Haugesund
Stavanger
Oslo
Kristiansand

ARCTIC CIRCLE
Narvik
Harstad
NORDLAND
FYLKE
Svolvær
Bodø
Glomfjord
Mo i Rana
Vestfjorden
Vesterålen
Lofoten

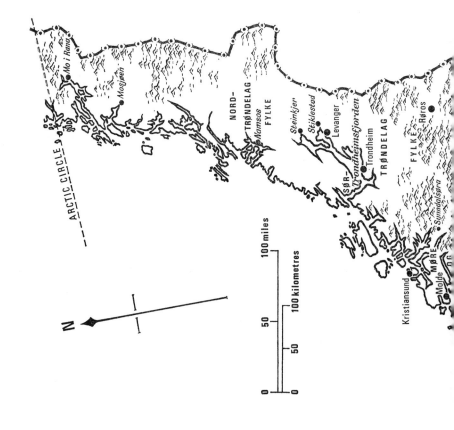

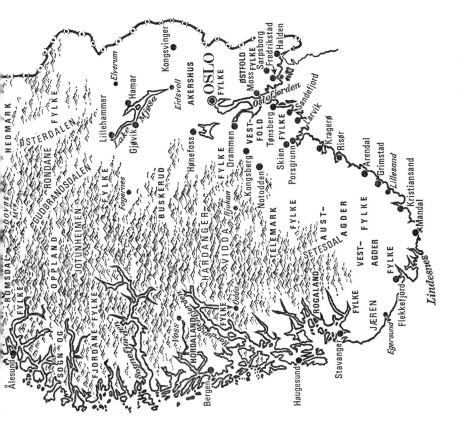

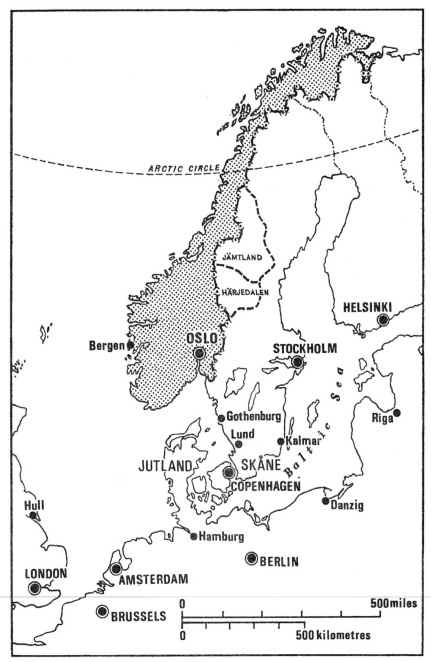

2 Norway in relation to northern Europe.

# Select Bibliography

THIS IS PRINCIPALLY a bibliography of works which have been found useful in the preparation of the present volume.

Aars, Harald, and others: *Norsk Kunsthistorie*, 2 vols., Oslo, 1925–27.

Alstad, Bjørn (ed.): *Norske meninger*, 3 vols., Oslo, 1969.

Andenæs, Johs, Riste, O., and Skodvin, M.: *Norway and the Second World War*, Oslo, 1966.

Andenæs, Tønnes (ed.): *The Constitution of Norway*, Oslo, 1951.

Andresen, A. F., and others: *Norway Today*, 9th ed. Oslo, 1970.

Anker, Øyvind: *Scenekunsten i Norge fra fortid til nutid*, Oslo, 1968.

Arbman, Holger: *The Vikings*, London, 1961.

Arstal, Aksel, and Just, Carl: *Oslo byleksikon*, Oslo, 1966.

Askeland, Jan: *A Survey of Norwegian Painting*, Oslo, 1963.

Baden, Conrad: 'Modern Norwegian Composers' in *American-Scandinavian Review*, vol. 53, 1970, 40–47.

Baedeker, Karl: *Norway, Sweden and Denmark*, 10th ed. Leipzig, 1912.

Benesch, Otto: *Edvard Munch*, London, 1960.

Benestad, Finn, and others: *Norsk musikk*, Oslo, 1968.

*Bergen its Attractions and Institutions*: [Published by the Tourist Club of the City and Province of Bergen], Bergen, 1907.

Bergsgård, Arne: *Frå 17, mai til 9 april*, Oslo, 1958.

Beyer, Harald: *A History of Norwegian Literature* (transl. and ed. Einar Haugen), New York, 1956.

Beyer, Harald and Edvard: *Norsk litteraturhistorie*, Oslo, 1970.
[This work contains a very large bibliography of Norwegian literature and of works of criticism].

Blanc, T.: *Christiania Theaters Historie 1827–1877*, Christiania, 1899.

Blom, Grethe Authén; Dahlback, Arne; Mykland, Knut; Danielsen, Rolf: *Trondheim bys historie*, Trondheim, 4 vols., 1955–58.

Bøstrup, Bjørn A.: *The Foreign Policy of Norway*, Oslo, 1968.

Brækstad, H. L.: *The Constitution of the Kingdom of Norway*, London, 1905.

Bredsdorff, Elias; Mortensen, Brita; and Popperwell, Ronald: *An Introduction to Scandinavian Literature*, Copenhagen/Cambridge, 1951; reprinted Westport, Conn., 1970.

Buch, Leopold von: *Travels through Norway and Lapland, during the years 1806–1808* (transl. J. Black), London, 1813.

Bugge, Anders, and Steen, Sverre: *Norsk kulturhistorie*, 5 vols., Oslo, 1938–42.

Bukdahl, Jørgen: *Det skjulte Norge*, Copenhagen, 1926.

Bull, Edv.; Hammer, S. C.; Sønstevold, Valborg: *Kristianias historie*, 5 vols., Oslo, 1922–28.

Bull, Edvard, and others: *Det norske folks liv og historie*, 12 vols., Oslo, 1929–38.

Bull, Edvard: *Arbeiderklassen i norsk historie*, Oslo, 1947.

Bull, Francis; Paasche, Fredrik; Winsnes, A. H.; Houm, Philip: *Norsk litteraturhistorie*, 6 vols., revised ed., 1957–64.

Castberg, Frede: *The Norwegian Way of Life*, London, 1954.

Christensen, Chra. A. R.: 'Norge i 1945' (and subsequent yearly surveys to 1965) in *Nordisk Tidskrift*, Stockholm, 1946–66.

Christensen, Hjalmar: *Det nittende Aarhundredes Kulturkamp i Norge*, Kristiania, 1905.

Clarke, Edward Daniel: *Travels*, 6 vols., London, 1810–23.

Collett, A.: *Gamle Christiania Billeder*, new ed., Christiania, 1909.

Cook, T. G.: 'Looking Ahead in Norwegian Education: Some Recent Reports on the Future Development of Norwegian Education', in *Durham Research Review*, 1970, 455–65.

Dahl, Thorleif, and others (ed.): *Vårt folks historie*, 9 vols., Oslo, 1961–64.

Davidson, H. R. Ellis: *Pagan Scandinavia*, London, 1967.

Derry, T. K.: *The Campaign in Norway*, London, 1952.

—: *A Short History of Norway*, 2nd ed. London, 1968.

—: *Introducing Oslo*, Oslo, 1969.

Downs, Brian W.: *Modern Norwegian Literature 1860–1918*, Cambridge, 1966.

Drake, Michael: *Population and Society in Norway 1735–1865*, Cambridge, 1969.

Eckstein, Harry: *Division and Cohesion in Democracy (A Study of Norway)*, Princeton, 1966.

Einarsson, Stefán: *A History of Icelandic Literature*, New York, 1957.

Ekeland, Sigurd: *Norway in Europe (An Economic Survey)*, Oslo, 1970.

Evensmo, Sigurd: *Det store tivoli (Film og kino i Norge gjennom 70 år)*, Oslo, 1967.

Foote, P., and Wilson, D. M.: *The Viking Achievement*, London, 1970.

*Framlegg til læreboknormal 1957* [Norsk språknemnd], Oslo, 1957.

Gathorne Hardy, G.: *Norway*, London, 1925.

Gauguin, Pola: *Edvard Munch*, 2nd ed. Oslo, 1946.

Gjerset, Knut: *History of the Norwegian People*, 2 vols., New York, 1915.

Gjesdahl, Paul: *Centralteatrets historie*, Oslo, 1964.

Gosse, Edmund: 'Norway Revisited' in *The North American Review*, vol. 167, 1898.

Gran, Gerhard (ed.): *Nordmænd i det 19de Aarhundrede*, 3 vols., Kristiania, 1914.

Greve, Tim: 'Norge i 1966' (and subsequent yearly surveys to 1970) in *Nordisk Tidskrift*, Stockholm, 1967–71.

—: *Norway and NATO*, Oslo, 1968.

Grinde, Nils: *Norsk musikkhistorie*, Oslo, 1971.

Haarr, Arne: *The Industrial Policy of Norway*, Oslo, 1970.

Hagen, Anders: *Norway*, London, 1967.

Halvorsen, Arne: *Et universitet i vekst*, Oslo, 1967. [On the University of Bergen].

Hanssen, Eskil (ed.): *Om norsk språkhistorie*, Oslo, 1970.

Haugen, Einar: *Language Conflict and Language Planning* (The Case of Modern Norwegian), Cambridge, Mass., 1966.

Haugen, Einar: *Riksspråk og folkemål: Norsk språkpolitikk i det 20 århundre*, Oslo, 1968.
[A revised ed. of *Language Conflict and Language Planning*].

Heseltine, Philip: *Frederick Delius*, London, 1923.

Holmsen, Andreas, and Jensen, Magnus: *Norges historie*, 4 vols., Oslo, 1960–68.

Holmsen, Andreas, and Simensen, Jarle: *Norske historikere i utvalg*, 4 vols., Oslo, 1967–69.

Hovde, B. J.: *The Scandinavian Countries, 1720–1865 (The Rise of the Middle Classes)*, 2 vols., Boston, 1943.

Hove, Olav: *The System of Education in Norway*, Oslo, 1968.

Huitfeldt, Carl: *Norge i andres øyne (Utdrag av utenlandske reisebeskrivelser gjenom 2000 år)*, Oslo, 1970.

James, Patricia (ed.): *The Travel Diaries of T. R. Malthus*, Cambridge, 1966.

Jensen, Bjørn: *Norway in the United Nations*, Oslo, 1967.

Jensson, Liv: *Teaterliv i Trondhjem 1800–1835*, Oslo, 1965.

Jerman, Gunnar, and Nyquist, Finn P. (eds.): *Det nye Norge (En introduksjon til Norges industri ved begynnelsen av 1970 årene)*, Oslo, 1970.

Johnsen, Oscar Albert: *Norges Bønder*, 2nd revised ed. Oslo, 1936.

Jones, Gwyn: *A History of the Vikings*, London, 1968.

Just, Carl: *Carl Johans gate*, Oslo, 1950.

Koht, Halvdan: *Norway Neutral and Invaded*, London, 1941.

Konow, Sten, and Fischer, Karl: *Norway (Official Publication for the Paris Exhibition 1900)*, Kristiania, 1900.

Langaard, Johan H., and Revold, Reidar: *Edvard Munch (Mesterverker i Munchmuseet Oslo)*, Oslo, 1963.

Lange, Kristian, and Østvedt, Arne: *Norwegian Music (A Brief Survey)*, London, 1958.

Lange, Kristian: *Norwegian Music*, Oslo, 1971.

Laing, Samuel: *Journal of a Residence in Norway*, London, 1836.

Larsen, Karen: *A History of Norway*, New York, 1948.

Lexow, Einar: *Norges Kunst*, 2nd revised ed. Oslo, 1942.

Lieberman, Sima: *The Industrialisation of Norway 1800–1920*, Oslo, 1970.

Lundeby, Einar, and Torvik, Ingvald: *Språket vårt gjennom tidene*, Oslo, 1967.

Lyche, Ingeborg: *Adult Education in Norway*, Oslo, 1964.

McFarlane, James Walter: *Ibsen and the Temper of Norwegian Literature*, London, 1960.

Midgaard, John: *A Brief History of Norway*, Oslo, 1969.

Millward, Roy: *Scandinavian Lands*, London, 1964.

Molland, Einar: *Fra Hans Nielsen Hauge til Eivind Berggrav (Hovedlinjer i Norges kirkehistorie i det 19. og 20. århundre)*, revised ed. Oslo, 1968.

Moulton, J. L.: *The Norwegian Campaign of 1940*, London, 1966.

[Munch, Edvard]: *Catalogue of the Exhibition held at the Solomon R. Guggenheim Museum, New York*, New York, 1965.

*Murrays Handbook, Norway*, 5th ed. London, 1874.

Myklebost, Hallstein, and others (eds.): *Norge*, 4 vols., Oslo, 1963.

Nansen, Fridtjof: *Framover Polhavet*, 2 vols., Kristiania, 1897.

Nielsen, Yngvar: *Reisehaandbog over Norge*, 7th ed. Christiania, 1893.

Normann, Harald: *De fem første dagene* (9. april i perspektiv), Oslo, 1970.

Nyquist, Finn P. (ed.): *Den gang det het Christiania*, Oslo, 1967.

Østvedt, Arne: *Music and Musicians in Norway Today*, Oslo, 1961.

Parmann, Øistein: *Norsk Skulptur*, Oslo, 1969.

Pontoppidan, Erik: *Det første Forsøg paa Norges Naturlige Historie*, Copenhagen, 1752.

Ramsøy, Natalie Rogoff (ed.): *Det norske samfunn*, Oslo, 1968.

Rolfsen, Nordahl, and Werenskiold, E. (eds): *Norge i det nittende Aarhundrede*, 2 vols., Kristiania, 1900.

Rom, Per (ed.): *The Decorations of the Oslo City Hall*, Oslo, 1952.

Rønneberg, Anton: *Nationaltheatret gjennom femti år*, Oslo, 1949.

Røsoch, Henry: *Trondheims historie*, Trondheim, 1939.

—: *På vandring i Christiania*, Oslo, 1953.

Ruud, Johan T., and others (eds): *Dette er Norge 1814–1964*, 3 vols., Oslo, 1963–64.

Semmingsen, Ingrid: *Veien mot vest*, 2 vols., Oslo, 1942–50.

Sjøvold, Thorleif: *Osebergfunnet*, Oslo, 1957.

Smith, Mortimer: *The Life of Ole Bull*, Princeton, 1943.

Stagg, Frank Noel: *North Norway*, London, 1952.

—: *The Heart of Norway*, London, 1953.

—: *West Norway and its Fjords*, London, 1954.

—: *East Norway and its Frontier*, London, 1956.

—: *South Norway*, London, 1958.

Stai, Arne: *Norsk Kultur- og moraldebatt i 1930-årene*, Oslo, 1954.

Stang, Ragna: *Gustav Vigeland: The Sculptor and his Works*, Oslo, 1968.

*Statistisk årbok*, Oslo.

Steen, Sverre: *Det frie Norge*, 5 vols., Oslo, 1951–62.

—: *Bergen byen mellom fjellene*, Bergen, 1970.

Stenersen, Rolf: *Edvard Munch*, revised ed. Oslo, 1946.

—: *Edvard Munch: Close-up of a Genius*, transl. and ed. R. Dittmann, Oslo, 1969.

Stenstadvold, Håkon (ed.): *Norwegian Paintings*, Oslo, 1951.

Støverud, Torbjørn: *Milestones of Norwegian Literature*, Oslo, 1967.

Tennant, P. F. D. (ed.): *The Scandinavian Book*, London, 1951.

Timm, Werner: *The Graphic Art of Edvard Munch*, New York, 1969.

Toynbee, Arnold J.: *A Study of History* (abridged D. C. Somervell), London, 1946.

Turville-Petre, E. O. G.: *Origins of Icelandic Literature*, Oxford, 1953.

—: *Myth and Religion of the North*, London, 1964.

Tveterås, Egil (ed.): *The Norway Year Book*, 7th ed., Oslo, 1966.

Valen, Henry, and Katz, Daniel: *Political Parties in Norway*, Oslo, 1964.

Werenskiold, Werner, and Eskeland, Arnold (eds.): *Norge vårt land*, 2 vols., Oslo, 1957.

*Translations from Norwegian into English*

Grønland, Erling: *Norway in English*, Oslo, 1961. See also: articles by Ronald G. Popperwell on Norwegian authors in *Cassell's Encyclopaedia of Literature*, ed. S. H. Steinberg, 2 vols., London, 1953, and in *The Penguin Companion to Literature (European)*, ed. A. K. Thorlby, London, 1969.

# Index

Aabel, Hauk, 288
Aall, Jacob, 226
Aanrud, Hans, 253
Aarnes, Sigurd Aa., 267*n*
Aasen, Ivar, 19, 195–6, 201, 202, 226, 259
Aastrup, Nikolai, 289
Abel, Niels Henrik, 47, 292
Absalon, of Lund, 86
Absalon Pederssøn Beyer, 48, 219
absolutism, *see* monarchy
actors, 49–50; Danish, 194, 196
administration, national: 10th c., 74;
  Harald Hardråde, 79; 12th c., 84;
  14th c., 93; at Black Death, 95; on
  Kalmar Union, 97; at Reformation,
  101; 17th c., 103–4, 106, 107; and
  Danish Civil Service, 111, 112;
  inter-Scandinavian standardization,
  184; *see also* government departments
  and agencies; *Stattholder*
administration, local: under
  occupation, 156
Administrative Council: under
  occupation, 155; investigated, 165
Agdanes, 73
agriculture: early, 65, 66, 67, 68;
  12th c. land clearance, 85; *and*
  Black Death, 95; 18th c., 113;
  Napoleonic War, 116; training, 134;
  *and* EEC, 187
*Ágrip*, 216
air force: *see* armed forces
Akerselva, 21, 23
Akershus, 21, 93; attacked, 100, 108;
  *Slottsloven*, 107–8
Albrecht of Mecklenburg, 96
Ålesund, 156
Alexander III, pope, 83
Alfred, k. of England, 72
Alta, 65
*Althing*, 71
*Altmark*, 152
aluminium, 167, 173, 273
amber, 66
America: Viking discovery, 69, 70
Amundsen, Roald, 286–7
Åndalsnes, 154
Andersen, Hans Christian, 299
Andersen, Tryggve, 250

Angell family, 26
Anglo-Saxon Chronicle: on Viking
  raids, 69
Angola, 176
Anker family, 21
Anker, Bernt, 23
Anker, Carsten, 120
Anker, Herman, 34
Anker, Nini Roll, 260
Antarctic: territory, 151; whaling, 273;
  Amundsen in, 286
anti-clericalism, 13th c., 91
anti-colonialism, 176
Arctic: seasonal variation, 19;
  exploration, 47; Amundsen, 287
Arendal, 37, 103, 114
Ari Þorgilsson, 71, 215
armed forces: 20th c. legislation, 145;
  mobilization (1939), 151–2; in exile,
  World War II, 159–60; army:
  17th c., 103, 104, 106; 18th c., 108;
  Napoleonic War, 116–17; 19th c.
  legislation, 135; leaders investigated,
  165; *see also* conscription; military
  organization
Armfeldt, Karl Gustav, 108
art: Viking, 70; galleries, 23; *see also*
  painting; sculpture
Art Society, 53–4, 55
artisans: 13th c. control of, 91
Arvesen, Ole, 34
Asbjørnsen, Peter Christen, 55, 57, 58,
  195, 197, 210, 226, 230
Aschehoug (publishers), 277
Åse, queen, 72
Astrid, princess, 285
Athelstan, k. of England: *and* Harald
  Fairhair, 73
Atlantic Pact, 179; *see also* NATO
atomic and nuclear weapons, 170–1,
  176, 180
Aukrust, Olav, 259–60; mentioned,
  268*n*
Aulie, Reidar, 291
Austria: war with Denmark, 129, 132,
  234; *and* EFTA, 185
authors, societies of, 206–7, 210; *and*
  language question, 205; *and* public,
  223, 301

317

*Printed in Great Britain
by W & J Mackay Limited, Chatham*